ROUTLEDGE LIBRARY EDITIONS: WW2

Volume 27

RESISTANCE AND REVOLUTION IN MEDITERRANEAN EUROPE 1939–1948

RESISTANCE AND REVOLUTION IN MEDITERRANEAN EUROPE 1939–1948

Edited by
TONY JUDT

LONDON AND NEW YORK

First published in 1989 by Routledge

This edition first published in 2022
by Routledge
2 Park Square, Milton Park, Abingdon, Oxon OX14 4RN

and by Routledge
605 Third Avenue, New York, NY 10158

Routledge is an imprint of the Taylor & Francis Group, an informa business

© 1989 Routledge
Individual contributions © 1989 Respective authors

All rights reserved. No part of this book may be reprinted or reproduced or utilised in any form or by any electronic, mechanical, or other means, now known or hereafter invented, including photocopying and recording, or in any information storage or retrieval system, without permission in writing from the publishers.

Trademark notice: Product or corporate names may be trademarks or registered trademarks, and are used only for identification and explanation without intent to infringe.

British Library Cataloguing in Publication Data
A catalogue record for this book is available from the British Library

ISBN: 978-1-03-201217-9 (Set)
ISBN: 978-1-00-319367-8 (Set) (ebk)
ISBN: 978-1-03-207456-6 (Volume 27) (hbk)
ISBN: 978-1-03-207457-3 (Volume 27) (pbk)
ISBN: 978-1-00-320701-6 (Volume 27) (ebk)

DOI: 10.4324/9781003207016

Publisher's Note
The publisher has gone to great lengths to ensure the quality of this reprint but points out that some imperfections in the original copies may be apparent.

Disclaimer
The publisher has made every effort to trace copyright holders and would welcome correspondence from those they have been unable to trace.

Resistance and Revolution in Mediterranean Europe 1939–1948

edited by
TONY JUDT

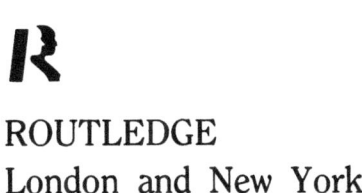

ROUTLEDGE
London and New York

First published in 1989
by Routledge
11 New Fetter Lane, London EC4P 4EE
29 West 35th Street, New York, NY 10001

Collection © Routledge, individual contributions © respective authors 1989

Typeset by Scarborough Typesetting Services
Printed in Great Britain
by T.J. Press (Padstow) Ltd, Padstow, Cornwall

All rights reserved. No part of this book may be reprinted or reproduced or utilized in any form or by any electronic, mechanical, or other means, now known or hereafter invented, including photocopying and recording, or in any information storage or retrieval system, without permission in writing from the publishers.

British Library Cataloguing in Publication Data
Resistance and revolution in Mediterranean
   Europe 1939–1948.
   1. Southern Europe. Resistance movements,
   & revolutionary movements, 1939–1945
   I. Judt, Tony
   940.53'37

Library of Congress Cataloging in Publication Data
   Includes index.
   1. World War, 1939–1945 — Underground movements — Europe, Southern. 2. Europe, Southern — Politics and government. 3. Communism — Europe, Southern — History.
   I. Judt, Tony.
   D802.E94R48   1989   940.53'4   88-26364

ISBN 0-415-01580-4

Contents

Introduction 1
Tony Judt

1 The Comintern and southern Europe, 1938–43 29
  Geoffrey Swain

2 The Parti Communiste Français and the French resistance in the Second World War 53
  Lynne Taylor

3 Communism and resistance in Italy, 1943–8 80
  David Travis

4 Pariahs to partisans to power: the Communist Party of Yugoslavia 110
  Mark Wheeler

5 The Greek Communist Party: in search of a revolution 157
  Haris Vlavianos

Appendix: chronologies 213

Notes on contributors 220

Index 222

Introduction
TONY JUDT

The division of contemporary Europe, prepared at Yalta and consecrated in the years that followed, is a lasting and ironic monument to the achievements of Hitler and his war. It so dominates the landscape of the continent that it takes a constant effort of the imagination to see recent history in terms other than those of 'east' and 'west'. And even when we manage to recast this history through the revival of such a category as 'central Europe', it is still the shadow of Yalta against which we are struggling, an iron curtain of the mind whose centrality we reassert through the very obsession with its removal.

Matters were not always thus. Nor do we need to go back to 1939 and beyond to rediscover a time when Europe and its problems seemed quite different. It was not until 1948 at the earliest that the terms in which historians, political scientists, and policy-makers saw Europe's prospects began to harden into a single vertical division. In the immediate post-war years, the future of south-eastern Europe (Yugoslavia, Bulgaria, Albania, and Greece) occupied people's minds no less than the problem of Poland, for example. Nor was attention confined to the eastern fringes of southern Europe. A generation of Fascist government in Italy, and the appalling débâcle with which the French Third Republic had ended in 1940, not to speak of continuing uncertainty about the future of Spain, had thrown into profound turmoil the political and institutional arrangements in the mediterranean region of western Europe itself. The organized strength and very real popular support enjoyed by the Communist parties of Italy and France opened up the disturbing scenario of post-war social revolution in these countries no less than in Greece or the Balkans.

We know now, of course, that the chance of a Communist seizure of power in France or Italy in 1944–5 was small. But such was not the perception at the time. Communist partisans in Italy (like their counterparts in Greece, for that matter) were not privy to the agreement at Yalta, nor to the thinking of Stalin in the months that followed. Nor was such ignorance confined to the lower echelons of these movements. Dimitrov, the Bulgarian Communist and former head of the Comintern, was still talking in February 1948 in terms that would be disavowed by Stalin, while the leadership of the Yugoslav and French parties were both, in different ways, pursuing tactics that would shortly be condemned by the Kremlin.[1] No one, in short, had a secure vision of the likely shape of a definitive post-war settlement (including Stalin himself, who wavered between a number of options during these years). And the presence of allied armies in France and Italy did not in itself constitute an insuperable barrier to eventual revolution – many assumed, by analogy with the situation after the First World War, that the foreign troops would in due course be withdrawn and that the Americans, at least, would seek to disentangle themselves from Europe as soon as possible.

Precisely because the Russian position on southern and south-eastern Europe remained undefined (in contrast to the Stalinist plans for Poland or the Soviet zone of Germany, where the presence of the Red Army left little room for ambiguity), it was on the future of the lands of Mediterranean Europe that much attention was directed in the post-war years. These were also, and not coincidentally, the countries which had seen the emergence of an autonomous resistance movement during the war, a resistance in which the Communists had played a central (and in the Yugoslav case, pivotal) role. In these countries it was far from unrealistic to imagine that the mass support generated through the resistance to Fascism could be converted, under the direction of a Leninist party, into a political takeover. This was all the more plausible given that these were not regions in which liberation had come at the hands of the Soviet troops (with the brief and cautionary exception of north-eastern Serbia).

Considerations such as these give the Communist experience in Mediterranean Europe between the outbreak of war in 1939 and the final division of Europe nine years later a unity since obscured by later developments. And it is this experience which constitutes the common theme of these essays. Within such a general frame of reference many differences emerge, and some of these will be noted later in this introduction. But much more striking is the unity provided by a number of issues and choices which faced the anti-Fascist Left everywhere in southern Europe at this time.

All the European Communist movements in the years after 1939 faced certain common dilemmas. How should they respond to the Molotov–Ribbentrop pact of that year, which undercut the anti-Fascist role of Communist parties in the popular front era? Should they treat the war that followed as a conflict between capitalists and stand aside, or should they from the outset adopt the policy of 'national defence'? Such questions were harder in France, where Communist resistance would also entail opposing the 'legitimate' government of Vichy (for this reason, the German attack on the USSR, releasing Communists everywhere from the mortgage of the 1939 pact, mattered more in France than in, say, Yugoslavia, where resistance against Italian and German invaders had not depended upon such international considerations to the same extent).

The international dimension itself changed radically for all Communists with the dissolution of the Comintern in May 1943. In the short run this freed domestic Communist movements in their respective national resistance groupings from the charge that they were little more than the foreign arm of Soviet policy. Hence the greater latitude available to men like Togliatti or Tito, able within limits to adapt their tactics to a strategic vision of their role in national politics. But taking a slightly longer view, we can see that the removal of a central direction was a distinct handicap. For it was not as though Stalin had lost all interest in the Communist movements of Europe. The dismantling of the Comintern enabled him to deal more flexibly with the western Allies, and it gave plausibility to the Kremlin's claim that it did not seek to turn the victory over Hitler into a springboard for revolutionary takeovers. But from Moscow's perspective such flexibility diminished in its appeal once the war was over and Soviet hegemony had been established in Poland and eastern Germany. At that point it became more urgent to ensure that the relative independence of the Communist movements in Mediterranean Europe especially did not encourage them to pursue goals *incompatible* with those of Moscow.

In the first place, the very fact of organizing a resistance movement had meant appealing to national sentiment, whether against the Germans or against their local collaborators. This reinforced the instinct among Communists to think in national rather than international terms, and by extension to emphasize their patriotic identity over their revolutionary affiliations. Secondly, the war had *de facto* undermined the authority of the Comintern long before it was abolished. Communications in wartime being what they were, local Communist tactics were decided by increasingly independent partisan leaders operating far away from any instructions from the international 'Centre'.[2] If we think of this process as an extension of the experience of the civil war in Spain, in which Italian, French, and Balkan Communists played an active role, we can see that by 1945 a generation of Communist leaders and militants was emerging in southern Europe who were (from Stalin's perspective) dangerously disinclined to look to the USSR for instructions or for a model of revolutionary strategy.

After 1945, therefore, the dominant common theme was the ensuing tension between the local actions of Communists in Greece or Yugoslavia, in France or Italy, and the Soviet Union's interest in reconstructing an international movement once again subservient to a common strategy. It may seem odd to argue thus, given that the various national parties were behaving very differently among themselves. The Greeks were seriously envisaging a revolutionary resolution of their conflict with the British-backed 'official' government, while the Italians, prompted by Togliatti's 'svolta', were working hard to integrate themselves into the still-fluid mould of post-Fascist politics in Italy. Simultaneously, Tito's Communist partisans were actively converting a successful national resistance into a genuinely Leninist revolution. But this, of course, is precisely the point. These various different 'roads to socialism' (to use the phrase of the time) were direct outcomes of a reading of the local situation. They might well be what Stalin would have wished (in the Italian case in particular), but it was not his wishes that had fathered the local thought. And such independence boded ill for the future.

By 1948 Soviet hegemony had been reasserted. In France and Italy, this was achieved by enforcing the return of the Communist parties to the political ghetto they had occupied before the popular front (a process abetted, though not as much as 'revisionist' historians sometimes suggest, by American pressure on non-Communist parties in these countries). In the Balkans matters were more complex, precisely because the local Communists had gone further along the road to power. The pivotal question concerned Yugoslavia, which was fast becoming an alternative 'centre' to Moscow, both as a model of revolutionary success and as the lynchpin of a projected 'Balkan Federation' in which it would have been the dominant power. The Soviet solution was to discredit the notion of any such Federation except in the most anodine form of an 'economic union', to withhold support for the Greek Communist insurgents (in accordance with the agreement with Churchill initialled in Moscow in 1944), and to seek the isolation of Tito and his revolution.

Hence the rapid moves in Hungary and Czechoslovakia, aimed at stopping any Titoist enthusiasms on the part of the local Communist parties, and hence the significance of the creation of the 'Cominform' in September 1947, whose only strategic purpose was to provide a formal device for the reassertion of the authority of the Soviet Union in matters of Communist revolution. The Russians' response was not, in its own terms, unreasonable. 'Titoism' was indeed emerging as a popular model for revolutionary action, for Yugoslavia was now the only country in Europe besides the USSR itself that could claim to have made an indigenous Communist revolution. Nor was this a revolution that could be dismissed as lacking in radicalism, for in its first few years the Communist regime under Tito was more Catholic than the Pope, pursuing democratic centralism *à la* Lenin in a way calculated to embarrass a Soviet government still (until 1947) seeking geopolitical compromise with its capitalist allies. And this Titoist 'heresy' appealed especially strongly in the other countries of southern Europe that had experienced comparably strong Communist partisan movements. Their leaders might know better, but many militant Communists in southern France or northern Italy looked to Yugoslavia and asked, 'Why not here?'. Even the Greeks, furious with Tito for closing the frontier at a vital moment in the Greek Civil War, still saw in Yugoslavia a possible model for their own revolution, based in the partisans of the mountains and seeking to convert anti-Fascist resistance into social revolution.

Thus far I have laid the emphasis on the specifically *Communist* dimension of the experience of the protagonists of this book. But the theme of *resistance* is just as important. Indeed, as David Travis argues in his essay, without a grasp of the experience of resistance in Italy we cannot properly appreciate the peculiarities of Italian Communist behaviour in the post-war world. And the same observation applies, *mutatis mutandis*, in the other countries treated here. Resisting the Nazis was a very, very difficult proposition. In central Europe (Poland, Czechoslovakia, later in Hungary, not to mention the occupied lands of the Soviet Union) resistance carried with it the very high likelihood of arrest and imprisonment or, more probably, death. The potential leadership of any such resistance, whether political, religious, or intellectual, had been effectively destroyed (in Poland as a result of deliberate policy). It is easier to understand the limited resistance offered by the east European Jews to their own extermination when we recall that resistance as a whole in this region was weak and vulnerable. With the prospects of liberation so very slim, how many Lidices[3] was it rational to provoke?

In western Europe the risks were lower, if only because of the absence of a Nazi predilection for treating the occupied peoples as sub-human. But even so, and even allowing for greater local support, the organized resistance in Denmark, Belgium, Norway, or the Netherlands never amounted to a serious *political* threat to the occupiers – at best, as in Denmark, it could aspire to save some Jews, for example, by facilitating their escape. In France, matters were more complex. There was little by way of organized resistance in the country before 1942. When the *maquis* began to grow, this was in large part because of the influx of men who would otherwise have been forced to go and work in German factories as part of Laval's 'deals' with the occupiers (something similar happened in Italy, where the conscription imposed by the post-1943 'Republic of Saló' and the German demand for workers drove many Italians into the mountains – and into *de facto* resistance). The disappearance of the Vichy 'zone' after November 1942 (when the Nazis occupied the whole of the country in response to the threat posed by the Allied landings in North Africa) also facilitated resistance, now that the fiction of an autonomous French government had been abandoned.

It was not that Vichy and Marshal Pétain provided an excuse for collaboration; rather, the existence of an administration which could claim to have been installed by the votes of the last parliament of the Third Republic made a genuinely patriotic resistance hard to organize. Pétain himself was wrapped in patriotic glory attendant upon his role as the 'Victor' of Verdun, and resisting the occupier in wartime France thus meant opposing an apparently legitimate and unquestionably popular regime, purporting to govern in some independence over one-third of the country. And a further complication arose from the general distaste for the parliamentary republic which Vichy had replaced – for their different reasons, very few parties or politicians had a good thing to say about the political system of the 1930s and its failures and disappointments.[4]

It followed that resistance in France could not appeal in the name of what had been destroyed, but only by promising something new. In effect, and in contrast to the resistance in the rest of north-west Europe, resistance in France was necessarily revolutionary. This was at least as true of Léon Blum, the socialist leader, writing of a moral regeneration of the nation, or the Gaullists planning radical post-war social change, as it was of the Communists themselves.[5] The prominence of the Communists in the resistance in its later stages was in part a function of this perception, in part a result of the refusal of the non-Communist movements to constitute themselves as political organizations (thus conceding political visibility to the PCF, the Parti Communiste Français), in part the consequence of excellent underground structures, something to which communists were necessarily better adapted than were their non-Communist allies within the resistance councils.

Seen in this light, the experience of resistance in France comes much closer to that of the Italians (and one might add that the topography of southern France resembled that of Italy or the Balkans in the advantages it could offer to a partisan movement). For resistance in Italy, before July 1943, was also complicated by the difficulty of opposing an established government in the name of the 'national interest'. 'Revolutionary' opposition to Mussolini was easier, and had been the official position of the Italian Communists in earlier years. But it had never generated mass opposition to the Fascist regime, and would probably not have been able to mobilize many people even after the Italian entry into the war, with its attendant costs. It was only with the Allied invasion of the south, Badoglio's replacement of Mussolini, and the latter's collaboration with the German occupiers in the 'Republic of Salò' that anti-Fascist resistance could adapt itself unambiguously into a mass patriotic movement, fighting Fascism and German Nazism at the same time.[6]

As in France, the resistance could not look to the past. By 1943 the memories of liberal Italy were fading (indeed, for anyone under 30, the case of many of the resistance partisans, liberal Italy was history, not part of their own experience). Moreover, the *manner* in which parliamentary liberalism had collapsed in Italy in the early 1920s, much like the collapse of the French Third Republic, offered little by way of positive reference for those looking ahead to post-war Italy. Resistance, it was supposed, was the prelude to a major recasting of the social and political structure of the country. Togliatti's vision consisted of preparing his party to play an active and *positive* role in that process (in contrast with the failure of the Left to pursue any coherent policy in the face of the rise of Fascism twenty years before).[7]

In the Balkans, the implicitly revolutionary character of the partisan resistance movement was quite unambiguous. This was less a result of any programmatic intentions on the part of the resistance movements themselves, more the outcome of the impact of the war. For here as in east-central Europe, the Second World War constituted in itself a major social upheaval. The Nazi occupation of these lands, and the destruction of the pre-war social and economic fabric, was to leave the region in a condition profoundly different from that which had prevailed on the eve of the conflict. With national minorities decimated, property (and property records) transferred or destroyed, old elites discredited, and the local population systematically victimized by occupation and civil war, a return to the *status quo ante* was unimaginable. As in Czechoslovakia, Poland, or Hungary, so in Yugoslavia (and to a lesser extent Greece): whatever was to emerge by way of a social system following the defeat of the Germans and their allies would at a minimum have to offer a degree of social and economic justice, as well as centralized control of national reconstruction. If the resistance movements in the countryside were to emerge victorious, they would be well positioned to take control and direct a *de facto* social revolution according to their own ideological vision.[8]

In this respect, it is perhaps not too fanciful to think of the events of this period as constituting a return to the unfinished business of the revolutionary 'moment' that followed the end of the First World War. From 1918 until 1923, central and southern Europe were in a tumultuously unstable condition. The new nation-states between Russia and Germany had, all of them, grounds for dissatisfaction with the post-war territorial settlements (as had the Italians, resentful at the cession of border territories to the new Yugoslav state). The established socialist parties were uncertain how to proceed in the new circumstances: should they try to exploit post-war institutional anarchy and social conflict to foment political revolution, or should they reaffirm their commitment to the parliamentary politics of the pre-war generation? The left-wing of most of Europe's socialist parties broke away between 1919 and 1921 to form Communist parties, modelled on that of Lenin and defined not by any ideological differences with their former colleagues but by their acknowledgement of the direction newly-imposed from Moscow by the Third International.

By the time the Communist parties of Europe had come into existence, however, and had begun to practise 'Leninism' as then understood, the revolutionary moment had passed, the Red Army was in retreat (having advanced as far as Warsaw in June 1920), and the initiative lay with the radical reactionary movements born out of the fear of the very revolution that the Left had failed to carry through. From 1922 onwards, the existence of at least two Marxist parties in most European countries divided the Left at the very moment when unity in the face of the Right was most needed. Where parliamentary politics survived, the socialists reintegrated, more or less successfully, into the system. The Communists, whether legally or clandestinely, retreated to the status of a revolutionary clique, were progressively purged of their independent elements, and were 'bolshevized' under the direction of Stalin's Comintern.[9]

But the Left was not handicapped by bad timing alone. Even if the revolutionary opportunity of 1919 had been open to them in the 1920s they would still have been handicapped by their failure to address the national question. For the upheavals of 1918–23 were as much nationalist as they were social. All over central and southern Europe (and in contrast to the effects of the Second World War) it was the destruction of national, not social, structures which set the agenda for the post-war conflicts. And both from ideological predilection and tactical optimism, the Communists were unable to respond sensitively to such matters. In the new multinational states of Czechoslovakia, Rumania, and Yugoslavia, the Communist parties persisted in treating the new regimes as a bourgeois creation, an impediment to the international revolution. In the quarrels between Czechs and Slovaks, in the Greek–Turkish wars of 1922–3, in the unceasing disputes among the nations, ethnic groups, and religious minorities of Yugoslavia, the Communists took a position consistent with Rosa Luxemburg rather than Lenin; they emphasized a proletarian unity across national and ethnic divisions, a unity whose absence was painfully clear. The socialists (in Czechoslovakia notably) did rather better on this subject – not least through the influence of an earlier central European socialist sensitivity to the national question in the writings of men like Otto Bauer – but at the price of preferring nation-building to social revolution.[10]

The marginality of the Communists and the divisions of the Left were further accentuated by the Comintern strategy of the so-called Third Period, beginning in 1928. This constituted a further hardening of the ideological line on the grounds of the imminent return to revolutionary conditions in Europe. It meant treating the socialists, rather than Fascists or local nationalists and Rightist movements, as the enemy, the better to claim for the Communists a unique role on the revolutionary Left. The outcome is well-known in the case of Germany, but had its counterparts everywhere. Only in 1935, with this strategy in ruins, and Nazis or Fascists or reactionary nationalists and populists in control almost everywhere, did the Comintern switch to a policy of accommodation with the rest of the Left and Centre in the name of anti-Fascism.

This switch, inaugurating the popular front era, had the advantage of freeing the domestic Communist movements to benefit from patriotic or democratic local sentiment. But it quite removed revolution from the political agenda, in regions of Europe where the profound social and economic inequities, the political restrictions, and civil inequality had altered little since 1920 (or, in many cases, since 1914). That the Marxist Left was beginning to re-establish its credentials (whether on the ground or in exile) in national political debates, but at the price of abandoning any foreseeable plans for social revolution, was a paradox that could not indefinitely endure. From 1935 until 1944 the virtually unbroken struggle against Fascism, domestic and foreign, postponed any resolution of the dilemma (in this sense the 'hiccup' of 1939–41 was an irrelevance). After the defeat of Fascism, and in conditions which not only invited revolution but had to some degree already initiated it, Communist movements in their national contexts could no longer avoid the choice. But whereas local conditions after 1918 dictated the very flexibility and *political* sensitivity of which the newly-formed Communist parties were incapable, after 1944 these parties showed just such a nuanced responsiveness to local conditions and possibilities. Hence their strength – and hence, too, the fears of the Russians.

It was not that the Soviet leadership did not seek to capitalize upon the revolutionary situation in Europe. As in 1918, so in 1945, the security of the regime in Moscow was seen to depend in some measure upon the stability of its western frontiers, a lesson conveyed with efficient clarity by the invasion of 1941. The revolutionary upheavals of the years immediately following the end of the First World War had offered a brief prospect of Communist regimes in Poland, Germany, and Hungary, and of socialist-led revolutionary attempts in Austria and Italy. Once these all crumbled, and with the rise to power of Hitler in particular, the Soviet Union was vulnerable. Hence the popular front strategy of reassuring the western democracies of their common interest in defeating Fascism, even if this meant suspending all talk of revolution. With the collapse of the popular fronts the Soviet interest reverted to territorial security. On the eve of war it secured eastern Poland and the Baltic states. During the war it negotiated and eventually claimed parts of eastern Czechoslovakia and northern Rumania.

Then came the post-war uncertainty. If revolution in the Balkans would secure the region for Soviet interests, then it was to be approved, but not at the risk of provoking Anglo-American hostility. The same was true in principle for Italy or France, except that there, given the greater interests and presence of the western Allies, revolution was *de facto* out of the question. Elsewhere, in Czechoslovakia and Hungary, for example, the Soviet Union initially encouraged a mixture of social revolution and political stability, seeking to ensure its indirect control of these lands without the need either to foment or suppress popular demands. Only in the face of the emergence of the Titoist alternative, revolutionary but independent, did the Russians move to impose by force their effective control of central Europe. In every case, political revolution might well be the preferred *form* in which Soviet security interests were protected, but it was always and everywhere subservient to the perceived demands of those interests.[11]

The connecting link in much of this story, the *grand absent* in the French sense, is of course the Spanish Civil War. Indeed, it might be supposed that a book dealing with resistance and revolution in Mediterranean Europe would contain at the very least a chapter on Spain itself. This would certainly be the case had this been a book whose subject was the 1930s, when Spain would have been not just one part of the story, but pretty much the whole story. After 1939, however, Spain dropped out of the picture. The refugees from the republican side straggled across into France (only to be interned and in some cases handed over to the Germans). The Communists abandoned the defeated republicans, while the leadership of the latter went off into a generation of exile. There was very little effective resistance against Franco after 1939, and the Spanish revolution(s) were defeated and destroyed well before then.[12]

The experience of the civil war, however, was central in forming the political imagination of the radical generation of the 1940s. There is no aspect of left-wing thought or action which was not coloured by the lessons of Spain. In the first place, it proved in retrospect to have been something of a rehearsal for the resistance movements of the 1940s, many of whose leaders learnt their soldiering in the Spanish battles. This was true for non-Communists (socialists and others) as much as for the communist partisans themselves. Indeed, for many non-Communists, a major lesson of the civil war had been that the Communists had an agenda of their own and were not to be trusted; hence the suspicions and divisions which marked the French and Italian Resistance movements.

For the Communists, the Spanish Civil War had provided invaluable political as well as military experience. Men like Togliatti, or some of the Czech, Hungarian, and Yugoslav participants who were to play prominent roles after the war, acquired a certain independence of perspective from their time in Spain. This served them well during the war and in the post-war conflicts – the Communists emerged in 1945, after nearly a decade of continuous fighting and political manoeuvring, as master political tacticians. And in combining their credentials as veterans of civil war and resistance alike, they could take the moral high ground in radical politics (boosted still further by their association with the victory of Stalingrad, a powerful emotional asset in countries that had suffered Nazi occupation).

But there were ambiguities in the Spanish 'inheritance'. The Communist role in Spain was not widely known, but it was not exactly a secret. In the writings of Malraux, Orwell, Koestler, and others the Communists, especially in their relations with other parties of the Left (the Anarchists, or the POUM), had been revealed as self-interested, calculating, cynical, and brutal. For every Togliatti, a brilliant intermediary between local needs and Comintern strategy, there was an André Marty, prominent in the post-war French Communist leadership but known to many as a brutal commissar in the in-fighting of the 'allied' Republican forces in Spain.[13]

Nor were the ambiguities of the legacy of Spain confined to relations between the Communists and others. If it had just been a matter of convincing their wartime allies of their good intentions and patriotic (or revolutionary) sincerity, the Communists would have been relatively untroubled by the memories of Spain. But an important aspect of the Communist role in Spain was the problems it posed, to the Comintern, concerning international control and discipline. For the men and women who fought in Spain were often the same ones who were to go on and join the Communist partisans in the Balkans, in France, and in Italy. Displaced or exiled Communists from all over Europe, finding themselves abandoned by Moscow in August 1939, had little choice but to enter the resistance, especially following the fall of France. The French resistance especially was full of Czechs, Hungarians, Spaniards, Italians, and others, many of whom had first made contact in Spain. In due course they returned to their own country and played prominent roles in the establishment of Communist regimes in central Europe. But these were not people to the taste of the Kremlin. They were too independent, with an independence they had often displayed by opposing the Molotov–Ribbentrop pact, by preparing post-war alliances and programmes without waiting for Soviet instructions (or else failing correctly to anticipate what these would be), and above all by achieving a political credibility and support which was not dependent upon the official imprimatur of Soviet approval.

The Spanish Civil War, in other words, had spawned a generation of potential Titoists. In France or Italy their independent views might amount to little more than a reputation for personal heroism in the resistance. But in countries like Greece or Hungary, where they nurtured hopes of ending up in political control, their instinctive reliance on their own judgement and popular backing boded ill for Soviet influence in these places. The Russians felt more comfortable with their own chosen instruments, men who had spent the 1930s and the war years in Moscow without showing the slightest inclination to question Stalin or his policies. They might lack charisma or any popular appeal, but for just that reason they would be all the more dependent on Russian support and thus the less likely to question Soviet desires.

It was thus no coincidence that so many of the people purged in the arrests and trials which accompanied the Soviet establishment of control in eastern Europe after 1948 were veterans of Spain. Indeed, one of the main charges against them was that, starting in Spain, they had established relations with westerners and begun a trajectory which led them into 'anti-Soviet' actions. But these purges could only operate in areas under direct Russian control – Rumania, Bulgaria, Poland, Hungary, and Czechoslovakia. In the Communist movements of Greece, Yugoslavia, Italy, and France, where the impact of the fighting in Spain and the local resistance had been greatest, such independent-minded Communists could not so readily be removed. In Italy they had the partial protection of Togliatti, in Yugoslavia they were in power. There were indeed a number of secret 'trials' in the French Communist Party during the early 1950s, in which prominent communist partisans like Charles Tillon or André Marty (!) were accused of precisely the same heresy and indiscipline which had characterized the indictments of Rajk in Hungary or Slánsky in Czechoslovakia. But the PCF could only imitate the Soviet model up to a certain point, and the victims of these 'trials' survived the experience, bearing witness in their memoirs to the Stalinist dislike of any Communist partisan who made a name for himself in Spain.[14]

The ambiguous legacy of the Spanish experience lay at the heart of the larger ambiguity of the popular front strategy. The latter, which lasted in fact if not in name from 1935 until 1947 and which gives a certain coherence to Communist behaviour in this period, hinged on the need to contain and defeat Fascism. It gave very little thought to the question of what comes next (the same dilemma confronted the Socialists in the popular front, both in the Spanish revolution and in France, where Léon Blum's party had no clear idea of what to do with the power it had won in the popular front elections of 1936). Purging the international Communist movement of those of its militants who had learned their politics in the era of popular front, civil war, and resistance was a way to re-establish the discipline that had existed before 1935, but it was not a solution to other difficulties. In essence, these boiled down to the following question – what does a Communist movement exist to achieve? The cynical reply, that it exists in order to advance the interests of the Soviet Union, rather misses the point, since that was never in doubt. What, after all, were the 'interests' of the Soviet Union? If they were not the fomenting of revolution, then the European Communists after 1945 were in an absurd condition, with no reason to exist. And if, in the longer run, the USSR *did* indeed wish to support Communist revolutions elsewhere, why did it so conspicuously fail to support the efforts of the Greek Communists? Why did it oppose any discussion of armed Communist insurrection in France or Italy? And why was it so ambivalent (and ultimately antagonistic) towards Tito's revolution? In the case of Yugoslavia the Soviet argument was rule-utilitarian: whatever the specific local advantages of independent Communist revolutions, they constituted a weakening of international Communist direction and discipline, and were thus undesirable in the wider interests of Soviet (revolutionary) strategy. Once the USSR had definitively, if briefly, re-established its complete control (a control lasting from 1948 until 1956), it had no need of such sophisms, of course, and could simply assert the primacy of Stalinist authority.

There is a risk inherent in this way of presenting the history of Communism and resistance in these years. The emphasis upon the international dimensions of the Communist movement, and the common or overlapping experiences of war and resistance in Europe, whether in Spain or in the rest of the continent, cannot help but imply a degree of uniformity in the history thus told. That some such uniformity existed is not in question – indeed it is one of the purposes of this collection of essays to bring out the various ways in which it is helpful to think of these years in Mediterranean Europe as a whole. But, and this will be clear to anyone reading the various contributions gathered here, there were important, sometimes startling, differences in the various national histories, differences that have had a marked impact on the contemporary development of these countries. It may thus be helpful to point to a few of them here.

Perhaps the most important concerns the special nature of the Balkans. This region, broadly encompassing what is now Rumania, Bulgaria, Yugoslavia, Albania, and Greece (together with European Turkey), was the heart of the Eastern Question which so absorbed nineteenth-century statesmen. Its difficulties were multifold. The decline of the Turkish Empire risked leaving a vacuum of power, one into which all the Great Powers aspired to insert themselves. The chief actors were Russia and Germany, for whom the lands of eastern and south-eastern Europe constituted an opportunity for economic as well as political control. The French also had an economic interest (notably in Serbia) while the British were above all concerned with keeping the Russians *out* of the area.

These conflicting interests were played out via the national aspirations and conflicts of the local populations. At various times between 1878 and 1914, the Great Powers gave their support to Greek, Serbian, Bulgarian, and Rumanian efforts at state-building or expansion, doing little to resolve the local disputes but a lot to inflame ethnic resentment. When the First World War brought about the collapse and disappearance of both the Turkish and Austro-Hungarian Empires, the Eastern Question was still as yet unanswered.[15]

The post-war settlement was inevitably a compromise. The Greeks sought unsuccessfully to take advantage of Turkish defeat to assert territorial claims to the east. Bulgaria (like Hungary) was disadvantaged by its wartime alliance with the central powers and lost territory to its neighbours, one of whom, Serbia, now saw itself expanded into a South Slav (Yugoslav) state incorporating national groups from both the defeated empires. These constituent elements of the new Yugoslavia varied enormously in their nature and expectations. The Slovenes and Croats of the north and north-west were culturally and economically a part of central Europe, and resented from the start the hegemony of a Serb nation different in its historical, religious, and social formation. Albanian, Montenegrin, and Macedonian minorities all protested against their inclusion in the new state, and the Macedonian region in particular proved volatile, with local resentment fuelled by Greek and Bulgarian encouragement.

From the outset, therefore, it was natural for the Balkans to play an important role in the history of Communism. In the first place the Russian strategic interest in the region was in no way diminished by the Soviet takeover – on the contrary, the Comintern in the years 1922–3 especially saw south-eastern Europe as the best medium-term hope for revolutionary expansion. The very fact that the post-war national settlements had *not* been accompanied by social revolution (in this region any more than in Germany or central Europe) made the new states and their ruling elites potentially vulnerable to widespread social protest. That the Communists failed to benefit from this situation owed much to the growing tactical rigidity of the Comintern under Stalin, wilfully ignoring and denying national sentiment and downplaying the importance of peasant protest in a part of Europe where the working class was still in a tiny minority.[16]

In the Balkans as in Italy, therefore, it was radical populism rather than Marxism which appealed successfully to peasant resentment, and despite continuing Comintern interest in the area the role of the Communists was negligible after 1925. By contrast, the Communist focus upon the region after the Second World War was tied to a much more realistic sense of local needs. The Communists still had little purchase on the mass of the rural population (and in the course of establishing Soviet control had to suppress by force the populist movements in Bulgaria or Poland, for example). But, following the example of the Yugoslavs, they no longer treated with disdain the national and ethnic considerations at the heart of the region's history.

This was, of course, peculiarly the case in Yugoslavia. From April 1940, Tito pursued a policy aimed at an eventual federal South Slav state which contrasted not only with the policies of his non-Communist rivals (all of them rooted in ethnic or regional interests), but also and more remarkably with the policies of his own party over the previous twenty years. The KPJ (Communist Party of Yugoslavia) could hardly avoid being dominated in practice by Serbs, but it was distinctly concerned, and was seen to be concerned, with the country as a whole. This gave it an advantage over the political movements of the Croats, for example, whose parochial perspective limited their appeal and tempted some of them into collaboration with the occupier (in a clear parallel with the Slovaks, whose anti-Czech sentiment led them to similar acts after 1940). The political legitimacy that the KJP acquired from its new stance on the national question was to last for over thirty years, and quite obliterate from memory its position in the years 1928–35, for example, when it had favoured secession from the Yugoslav state for all non-Serb peoples.

The Greek case was in some ways more complex still. Greece was the Balkans' Balkans. It had achieved independence from Turkey in the early part of the nineteenth century (1821–9), but with a very restricted territory, leaving many ethnic Greeks still ruled by foreigners. Even after the 1881 acquisition of Thessaly the national aspirations of the country remained unfulfilled and Greece was engaged in a series of wars with Turkey and Bulgaria right up to the eve of the First World War. The disputed territories, essentially Macedonia and the coastal fringe of Turkey-in-Asia, were still being fought over in the 1920s, and the Macedonian question especially ensured that Greece would be embroiled in the wider political disputes of the region, despite the relative ethnic, linguistic, and religious homogeneity of Greece itself.

Thus although the Greek Communists did not have to struggle with the national question *per se* (the legitimacy of a Greek state was not in question), and although the Greek resistance was an unambiguous matter of fighting the invader (first Italy, then the Germans), the post-war settlement could not help but depend upon events in the rest of the Balkan peninsula. Initially the Greek Communists were absorbed with the question of the allocation of power *within* the domestic resistance. The question of whether to work with the non-Communist resistance, and on what terms, resembled the dilemmas facing the French Communists at the same time. But once the Greek Communists made the decision to oppose the British-backed monarchy and its local supporters, they placed themselves in a difficult situation. Greece was a vital strategic region for the western Allies, given its maritime location, and the October 1944 understanding between Stalin and Churchill had confirmed the determination of the British to keep it out of the Soviet sphere, a position which Stalin seems to have accepted. But unlike Tito, the Greek Communist leadership was not in a position to impose its will on the ground. The partisans might hold the mountainous north, but any serious attempt to take Athens would bring them into conflict not just with the anti-Communist resistance but also with the British (and, later, the Americans).

The actions of the Greek Communists were thus from the outset in conflict with the preferences of Stalin, and the pursuit of the civil war depended heavily on the support of the Yugoslav Communists to the north. But the latter had no good reason to jeopardize unnecessarily their relations with the Soviet Union (or Bulgaria, with whom a Balkan Federation was still being discussed as late as January 1948). If the Greeks had succeeded in moving rapidly and successfully from partisan resistance to social revolution the Yugoslavs would have been willing to provide the necessary assistance, as they initially did. But the Greeks had no such realistic chance of success, and their eventual isolation was inevitable. The Greek Communists were thus the unique instance of a resistance movement flying in the face of local and geopolitical reality in the attempt to convert popular resistance into political revolution. It is significant that the Italian Communist leadership quoted the Greek example as a warning against those partisans who dreamt of similar efforts in Italy itself.

Both the Greeks and the Yugoslavs, then, were refractory in the face of international (and Russian) considerations, though with markedly different outcomes. It is noteworthy that the German invasion of Russia in June 1941, and the abolition of the Comintern in May 1943, played little part in developments in these countries. The contrast with France and Italy is notable. Much of the history of the role of the Communists in the French resistance turns on the significance of these international shifts. Indeed, as we shall see, the whole historiographical controversy surrounding the French Communists in these years is focused on the period August 1939–June 1941, when the PCF opposed official resistance against the Germans and treated the war as an imperialist conflict of no concern to French workers. It took a lot of dead Communist partisans, and some selective historiographical airbrushing, to erase the memory of this period of near-collaboration.

That such a situation should have arisen was not the result of some peculiar deficiency in the moral make-up of Communists in France. The problem lay elsewhere. By 1934, the PCF was the only major Communist party still operating freely in a political democracy. As such it had benefited from the full focus of Comintern attentions. More than any other party, the French Communists by 1939 were a disciplined local extension of Soviet policy. The party leadership (Maurice Thorez in Moscow during the war years, Jacques Duclos in Paris) followed Russian tactical shifts faithfully. Like Communist leaders everywhere, they knew quite well that their party would do better if it were more responsive to local needs and the exigencies of republican politics in France in particular. The successes of the popular front era, when the party membership rose from fewer than 35,000 to nearly 400,000 in just three years, were proof enough. But they were also willing to risk the loss of such a national prominence in order to keep faith with international Communist tactics – in 1939, but also in 1947 and again as recently as 1977.

Thus the German invasion of the USSR came as a great relief, since it allowed the PCF to throw itself into the resistance 100 per cent, in the name of the defence of all the democracies (socialist and capitalist alike) against the forces of evil. But there could never be any question of converting the successes of armed resistance into popular insurrection. When Stalin recognized de Gaulle as the legitimate leader of the French, and Thorez returned from Moscow after the war with instructions to work with de Gaulle and the rest of the resistance coalition in the reconstruction of French democracy, the party leadership readily obeyed. This meant instructing the well-organized and -equipped Communist partisans of the south and south-west to hand in their weapons and accept the authority of de Gaulle's representatives, and encouraging the organized industrial workers of the north to produce more coal. It was not even a question of calculating the chances of success in a struggle for power against the Gaullists and the Allied armies; the instructions from Moscow were clear and they were followed – indeed, getting the partisans to obey was one of the ways in which the PCF leadership could re-establish its authority over the rather too independent Communist militants of the local resistance networks.[17]

The Italian case both resembles the French and differs from it in vital respects. But it is the differences which are most striking. Because the Italian Communists had been in exile for nearly two decades, they had not been embroiled in the domestic politics of pre-war Italy, nor had they been the concentrated target of Comintern attention, since their capacity to influence Italian policy was negligible after 1926. In exile, whether in Paris or Moscow, they had had ample occasion to reflect upon the failure of their policies of the 1920s, and the ease with which liberal Italy had slipped under Fascist control. Their leaders were all educated and literate political thinkers (in contrast with most of the French leadership, for example), and by 1943 they had spent a lot of time analysing the Italian condition and its requirements and limitations. When Togliatti arrived at Salerno in 1944 and announced his policy of participation in the national liberation and renewal, effectively removing revolution from the Communist agenda, he was offering in a summary form the conclusions of a reflection upon Fascism, the fragility of Italian democracy, and the limited possibilities (and serious risks) for political revolution of the kind to which his party had been committed before Mussolini.

The new thinking of the Italian Communists owed little to immediate Soviet or geopolitical requirements. The presence of Allied troops in Italy certainly made it very unlikely that a social revolution would succeed, but Togliatti's point was that it was an untimely project in any event, Allies or no Allies. This point was important, because once the resistance took off in Italy it resembled the Yugoslav, and also the Greek, rather than the French model. With no anterior burden of collaboration or ambivalence, with a clear foreign enemy and mass backing of the kind which *never* materialized in France, the Italian resistance could reasonably imagine moving from popular Resistance to popular revolution on the Yugoslav model next door. And like the Greeks, it also had a well-grounded suspicion of the monarchy and its supporters, making it hard to ask partisans to risk their lives in the mountains, only for a liberated Italy to be turned over to the very people who, like their Greek counterparts, had conspicuously failed in the previous decade to oppose domestic Fascism.

Togliatti's achievement was thus really rather remarkable – the more so in that he managed to channel his party and its supporters away from a revolutionary perspective *without* undermining his or its left-wing credentials. If in the years 1945–8 the Italian situation came rather more to resemble the French, this was for different reasons. The Communists' role in rebuilding shattered democracies was a worthy one, but carried attendant risks. In the economic conditions of Europe at that time, an emphasis on infrastructural reconstruction inevitably meant economic hardship for the mass of the population. As participants in government (for the first time) Communists stood to lose contact with their social base, as they were identified with the policies of austerity. The very real social reforms of the period – nationalizations, welfare provisions, improved public services – were poor compensation for the suppression of revolutionary expectations, while the struggle to rebuild and sustain a parliamentary system lacked dramatic appeal.

The Communist parties of France and Italy (and Belgium) thus had no good answer to offer the Soviets when, in the autumn of 1947 at the founding conference of the Cominform, they were accused of having neglected their revolutionary tasks and lost the confidence of the workers by their 'collaboration' with the pro-American ruling class. The accusation was in bad faith, of course – the Communists in France especially had been doing just what they had been given to understand the Kremlin would have wished – but it stung. From 1948 until the 1970s, the Communist Parties of both countries took care to avoid any repetition of such errors – assisted by the refusal of most other political parties in the two countries to consider allowing the Communists back into government. There remained, however, vital differences between the two movements. The Italian *socialists* joined the PCI (Partito Communista Italiano) in the wilderness after 1948, thereby limiting the latter's isolation; the French socialists, by a narrow margin, voted to stay with the parties of the governing coalition. And the Italians under Togliatti never quite lost the sense that their trajectory since 1943 was at least in part of their own choosing, a function of their *own* understanding of what was possible and what was necessary in Italy. The French remained for nearly a generation under the direct tutelage of the Russians.

Modern political philosophers make occasional reference to a formal category of questions which they call 'essentially contested'. It seems to me that, more than many other controversial issues in history, the themes discussed in this book meet that description. Every one of the essays in this book (including this one) implicitly takes a stand on a number of acute historiographical disputes. This is unavoidable, and it would be uninteresting (and probably impossible) to write about these subjects without taking some controversial positions. Readers may see for themselves what is at issue by reading the essays and in particular the notes. But it may be helpful to conclude this introduction by providing a few signposts to the major areas of disagreement.

The first of these concerns the general question of Soviet influence and control over the behaviour of the various Communist parties of different countries. In 1935, for example, the seventh congress of the Comintern affirmed the move from a position of self-defeating isolation to that of common alliances with other parties in an anti-Fascist 'united front'. Attempts have been made to suggest that this switch, which led directly to the popular fronts of France, Spain, and elsewhere, merely rendered formal and official the practices of Communists in western or southern Europe. This seems unlikely. In the first place, the so-called 'united fronts from below' which did indeed operate before 1935 were nothing more than manoeuvres to attract away from the other parties of the Left their radical and proletarian support. They had been little appreciated by the non-Communist Left, and had themselves served further to weaken the already divided democratic forces. The linguistic shift to 'united fronts from above' may not seem much, but it signalled a willingness to work with, rather than against, the rest of the Left (and, now, the Centre as well).

And on the evidence of the Italian or French cases, at least, it was not until the volte-face of the Comintern that the new tactics fell securely into place.[18]

There is no doubt, of course, that the old tactics had been a disaster, and many inside the Communist parties as well as among their opponents were to welcome the change. But they could hardly have sought too actively to precipitate it. The 'bolshevization' of the European Communists had taken a decade to effect. Until the early 1930s the parties of Yugoslavia, France, and Germany, for example, were still given to outbursts of independent thinking by their local cadres, men and women whose political formation stretched back beyond 1917 and who were not always comfortable taking their instructions and organization from Moscow (even though it was the willingness to do so which in principle distinguished Communists from Marxist socialists in these years). Following the final installation of reliable leaders like Thorez in France, and the purging of the Polish, Yugoslav, and other parties during the 1930s, the Comintern leadership could count on solid disciplinary stability in the satellite parties, even at the price of their own local survival. The wholesale switch to popular front tactics in 1935 is evidence of this no less than the obedient departure into political suicide following the Molotov–Ribbentrop pact of August 1939.[19]

Matters are less clear for the wartime years, as all the contributions in this book illustrate, and there are separate and distinct disputes regarding each of the national cases. But following the war, Stalin's desire to reaffirm the centrality of Russian experience, interests, and authority seems clear. As we have seen, it was just *because* some of the wartime Communists appeared to have aspirations to independence of strategy and tactics that the Soviet hold was progressively reasserted, culminating in the creation of the Cominform, the crackdown in Hungary and the coup in Czechoslovakia, and the aggressive reassertion, to the point of caricature, of the status of Stalin and Stalinism in France and Italy. Hence the virtual war waged against Tito and 'Titoism' in the years 1948–54, and hence, too, the deadly measures taken against any Communist suspected of Titoist sentiments in these years.

The point is not that everything that happened in the years 1939–48 (or indeed 1935–56) can be explained simply in terms of Soviet interests and instructions. On the contrary, and for 1943–7 in particular, this was far from the case. But this autonomy of local practice could not last, since it made nonsense of the very characteristic of Communism – its Leninist affiliation and uniformity – which had been the distinguishing feature of Communism as a radical movement, and which was in the longer run its greatest strength *and* weakness. The period covered by this book is the one in which, for reasons of war and diplomatic and social uncertainty, the Communist movements in southern Europe especially had a certain latitude. How they used it, and with what results, and how they readapted to the return of Soviet authority, are thus questions of particular interest; the more so in that none of them, at any time, would openly have asserted that there was a contradiction between Soviet and local (Italian or Greek) interests.

Hence the importance of the Yugoslav instance, where these matters were at their most acute. There are many contentious issues surrounding Tito and his party, dating back to the 1930s and the shadowy acts of the difficult years in the Moscow of the purges. But of more direct relevance here is the wider question of Tito's motives in breaking with Stalin. What seems likely is that, despite the KPJ's decision to press for a federated post-war Yugoslav state, and despite Tito's later turn towards the west, the Yugoslav party had no particular objections to Stalinism, at least on the home front. The initial revolution there was as dictatorial, centralized, and antipluralist as the moves in Poland or Rumania (or in Russia a generation earlier, come to that).[20]

What seems to have provoked the Russians (and there is of course some argument as to whether it was Yugoslavs or Russians who were responsible for initiating the schism) was the imperial, or export-oriented nature of Tito's revolution. Not only was he helping the Greeks in their 'unauthorized' undertakings, and gaining a lot of admiration and praise from western fellow travellers, but his view of a Balkan Federation, a vision of the region under effective if unannounced Yugoslav tutelage, was very different from the sort of set-up Stalin was willing to envisage. He was making the Bulgarians nervous, of this there is no doubt. And one effect of his actions, at home and abroad, was to provoke British and American engagement and hostility (e.g. over the Greek insurgency) at a time when Stalin was still hoping for an advantageous outcome to the talks over the future of Germany.

It would seem, then, that Tito provoked the Russians.[21] But it could as well be argued that the split was unavoidable. The very success of the Communist resistance in Yugoslavia, the fact that Tito came to power without external assistance, created as I have already said a *de facto* alternative model and 'myth', and this was intolerable whatever the legitimacy (and orthodoxy) of the Titoist revolution itself. Tito's conciliatory moves towards the west – refusing aid to the Greek Communists, easing domestic restrictions, seeking US aid – were a boon to Soviet propaganda, but they were not the cause of his excommunication.

The historiography of the Greek Communists and the events leading up to the civil war in their country is indirectly related to the Yugoslav question. One argument revolves around the responsibility for starting the war itself. Historians of both sides (the Communists and the anti-Communist, British-backed monarchists and others) claim that their own party sought reconciliation and compromise and was pushed into a civil conflict. The two claims are not inherently incompatible, of course, resembling in this the disputes about the various groups within the Yugoslav resistance and the motives of their backers (Croats, Communists, the British, etc.). What is special in the Greek case is that there is a second, and overlapping dispute. Why did the Greek Communists go for a revolutionary outcome, given their weak position and the absence of Soviet encouragement?

Part of the answer lies in the divided nature of the Communist leadership in Greece. As Vlavianos notes, there was a prolonged moment during the war itself when there existed two Communist leadership networks, each aware of and denying legitimacy to the other, and with at least one of them deeply implicated in collaboration with the anti-Communist authorities! In these circumstances discipline and unity were necessarily lacking in the later Communist resistance. And the lack of Soviet enthusiasm for an uncompromising post-war stance was not enough to discourage the frustrated military wing of the Communist-dominated resistance from its initial attempt at a coup in Athens. The later conflicts were even more hopeless, and there the wilful ignoring of reality and Soviet requirements was even more marked. Given that Soviet support could never realistically have been expected, and that the British (later the Americans) were clearly not going to abandon their local clients, and given above all the lack of local support outside certain northern strongholds, Zachariadis must surely bear a heavy responsibility. In seeking to turn the 'bourgeois' revolution of the resistance into a proletarian uprising he led the Greek Left into a tragic dead end, contributing as he did so to the further deepening of bitter and violent divisions within Greek society.

For this débâcle it seems unreasonable and counter-intuitive to blame outside forces, whether the Russians and Yugoslavs for abandoning the Greeks, or the Anglo-Americans for supporting their own side. The behaviour of all these observers was predictable and in keeping with their earlier stance (with the possible exception of that of Tito, who may initially have misled the Greek partisans into anticipating his support). Revolution was not on the agenda in Greece, and the Communists squandered some of the support they had achieved in the wartime struggles by the manner in which they tried to bring it to their country.

The contrast with Italy could not be more marked. Not only did Togliatti resolutely turn aside all talk of social revolution or seizure of power, but in so doing he (paradoxically?) established his party as a major actor on the stage of parliamentary politics, a new model for post-war Communist practice. In this case there is not much argument about what happened, or who was responsible. The differences of interpretation concern, as it were, the 'meaning' of the Italian experience within the history of Communism. For some historians, the 'Italian road to socialism' is the practical incarnation of the thought of Antonio Gramsci, who died in 1937 after a decade in Fascist prisons but whose work was published after the war and has had a deep impact on the recent history of Marxist ideas. Gramsci's writings all deal in some way or another with the role of the party and its members in bringing about social and political change in a divided, semi-rural society like Italy. The lesson he drew from the failures of the 1920s is ambiguous and slightly obscure, but that he attributed the rise of Fascism in part to a lack of strategic imagination on the part of the Communists is certainly clear. Togliatti, it is suggested, was pursuing a Gramscian strategy (a 'war of position') in his post-war calculations.[22]

A second line of reasoning treats the behaviour of the Italian Communists as a reasonably direct outcome of Soviet preferences. Togliatti, after all, was one of the historic leaders of the Comintern; after Dimitrov, he was the most prominent survivor of the leadership of the 1930s. He knew what Stalin sought, and knew, too, that the Italian role could only be to create a stable democracy within which

Communists could manoeuvre to encourage support for Soviet diplomatic goals. The revival of Fascism was the most immediate post-war danger (as it seemed to many non-Communists as well), and the tasks of the Italian Communists were thus to contribute to its complete destruction in Italy, by working with all other anti-Fascists (foreign Allies included) to this end.[23]

This is a plausible reading of events, and is not incompatible with the distance that Togliatti kept from the more extreme manifestations of international Stalinism in later years. But there is a third account, the one proposed by David Travis in his essay. He argues that the PCI was effectively born again in the resistance, that its tactics, nationally and locally, were a direct response to the circumstances of this rebirth, and that the habit of thinking in Italian rather than international terms became ingrained in the Italian party, which practised Gramscian strategy only to the extent that Togliatti shared Gramsci's earlier desire to avoid a repeat of the calamity of 1922-6. I think that on this latter score in particular Travis is probably correct. The emphasis on Gramsci and the 'strategic' perspective not only takes no account of the circumstances of 1943-5 and the nature of the re-emergent partisan-based party; it also imposes order where none existed on the chaotic years up to 1948, when economic survival and institution-building dominated the agenda, and where the international uncertainties and the strength of domestic opposition precluded any serious consideration of revolution in all but the most formal, incantatory sense.

The overemphasis on Gramsci has been the besetting sin, the professional deformation of PCI-observers in recent years. But the international dimension, though it too has been overstated by Soviet-watchers in particular, should not perhaps be neglected completely. The Italian party might be dominated by men and women formed in the local anti-Fascist conflict (though even they were great admirers of the Victor of Stalingrad), but the leaders (men like Togliatti or Luigi Longo) were decades-long bolsheviks. They were probably incapable of acknowledging a clear distinction between the interests of the PCI and the international movement of which it was a part. In one sense they were lucky – had Soviet policy dictated a revolutionary insurrection in Italy in 1944-5, they would certainly have been unhappy, but not necessarily to the point of opposition. There were, as Travis notes, significant numbers of Communist partisans armed and enthusiastic for such an insurrection, and though it would certainly have failed, Togliatti would have been unlikely to divide his party by refusing to go along.

In fact, the Italians remained loyal, if uncomfortable, members of the international Communist community well into the 1970s, breaking only and definitively with the imposition of martial law in Poland in December 1981.[24] Party discipline remained strong and internal controls and organization did not change very much in the generation following the Liberation. Where the Italians *were* different, where Italian Communism acquired its special reputation, was in the high quality of its leadership, intellectual and tactical alike, and in the flexible role it played in the difficult world of Italian domestic politics.[25]

It is this, above all, that points up the difference between the Italians and the French Communists. The latter, always unfortunate in their leaders from the very outset, have also invited debate among analysts and historians over the nature and extent of their links to the Soviet Union (that the links are close and strong no one has ever denied; except, and disingenuously, the Communists themselves on certain select occasions). But the more controversial matter, itself part of the theme of 'linkage', concerns the crucial years 1939–41. Every Communist party in the world 'rolled' in August 1939. But only in France, and for the specific reasons already noted, did the switch to neutrality in the face of the Nazi aggression have such dramatic local effects. It now seems likely, on the basis of personal memories and the limited documentation available, that official representatives of the PCF sought to collaborate with the German occupiers to the extent of getting the party newspaper openly published (fortunately for their sake, they were rejected by the German authorities). What is absolutely certain is that French Communist leaders offered their services to the Vichy authorities as witnesses for the prosecution in the political trial of Léon Blum at Riom in 1941. On the other hand individual, isolated Communists undertook acts of resistance against the occupier during this period – in defiance of party instructions, it would seem. Later they would be offered in evidence for the party's commitment to resisting from the outset, but this seems implausible – all the more so in that a number of such people were also punished for acts of wartime indiscipline, a sure sign that their precocious courage made them untrustworthy within a Stalinist structure.[26]

The French Communists, then, had better cause than most to be grateful for Hitler's attack on the Soviet Union on 22 June 1941. From then until May 1947 the Communists' role in France was straightforward. Like the Greeks, they sought to negotiate a place for themselves in the official organizations of resistance and the provisional government; like Togliatti, Thorez returned promising full Communist co-operation in the rebuilding of the country; and like the Italians, again, the PCF left office in the spring of 1947. But there the similarities cease. The shadow of collaboration continued to hang over the PCF (as it hangs still over its present leader Georges Marchais), sitting uneasily alongside the party's claim to be the 'Parti des Fusillés' and the heart of the resistance. Thorez never had Togliatti's vision, and his party lurched from enthusiastic integration in the post-war political system into rigid and hyper-Stalinist opposition after 1947 (there is still some debate about how far the PCF's insertion of itself and its representatives into union and government agencies after 1945 was part of a long-term revolutionary strategy; but this seems to me far-fetched – Communists instinctively sought to maximize their role in political and economic organs, and would doubtless have claimed strategic intentions had there in fact been a revolutionary outcome. But no such outcome was in the offing, and they lost most of what they had gained soon after).

At this point, the historiography of the French Communists blends back into the last significant controversy, that concerning the origins of the Cold War. Were the Communists planning a coup (in France, or elsewhere)? Were the strike movements of 1948, together with the Czech coup, events in Poland and Hungary, etc., part of a strategic offensive that could only be contained by a resolute west, united in support of the anti-Communist forces in Greece, Italy, France, and so forth? This, and the entailed assumption regarding Stalin's wider post-war strategy, is the version of the history of these years traditionally offered in 'Cold War' historiography.[27] The predictable response was the revisionist history of the 1960s and 1970s, which laid the blame on the west, the British and Americans especially. Using Marshall Aid as a carrot, it is contended, the Americans pressed their clients in France, Belgium, and Italy to expel the Communists from government. They refused to compromise with Stalin over the German question, they backed reactionary forces in Greece and central Europe (and China) and forced the Russians to build a rigid international defence network for their own survival in the face of an impending anti-Communist crusade, exemplified in the 1949 creation of NATO on British and French initiative.

The revisionist thesis is excessively one-dimensional (it is notable that it was often the work of historians with little or no ability to read materials in the major and minor European languages, and thus with no access to much of the relevant European, especially East European, sources). It is culturally of interest as a product of New Left enthusiasm and naïvety, and historiographical evidence of the continuing capacity of actions in print as elsewhere to produce equal and opposite reactions. But the real interest, and problem, concerns the original Cold War thesis.

The lesser difficulty with the 'Cold War historiography' is that it takes altogether too seriously the Communists' own ideological and programmatic language. Ever since 1917, Communists would necessarily claim that their goal was to seize revolutionary power – this, after all, was their distinguishing characteristic within the political community of the Left. But it does not follow from this that at any given moment the Communists outside the USSR were actually *engaged* in preparing such a revolution. On the contrary, the French and Italians until 1948 were deeply involved in the daily manoeuvrings of democratic politics. Their accusers at Szklarska Poreba, the founding meeting of the Cominform, were absolutely correct to charge them with having neglected to prepare for conflict and confrontation with their erstwhile allies. And even the Czechs, at least until early 1947, were genuinely tempted by the prospect of a Communist success attained via open parliamentary elections.[28]

More seriously, the anti-Communist thesis imposes altogether too much coherence, too much strategic foresight, on the international Communist movement. It is an anachronistic reading of events, and one which flatters Stalin and his European followers. If there is anything that emerges in the last generation of research on this period, much of it summarized in these essays, it is that the years 1939–48 were ones of deep muddle. Stalin at Yalta knew what he wanted, but then and for some time to come had vaccillating ideas about how to achieve it. And the same was true for Communists in the various national resistance movements, with the added complication that anything *they* might seek to achieve was always contingent upon Stalin's own (far from clear) intentions. The division of Europe into spheres of influence after 1944 settled relatively little. It virtually guaranteed the loss of Poland to Soviet hegemony, and it left Rumania and Bulgaria firmly in Russian hands (not to mention the Baltic nations). But these were outcomes likely to have come about as a result of the fortunes of war in any case. Everywhere else matters were left unresolved, affected at the outset only by the relative presence or absence of Soviet or western military power.

One can go further. The whole period after 1935 and the creation of the popular front tactic was one of fluidity. The Communists in France in 1936 had no readymade notion of what to do with a potentially revolutionary strike movement (Thorez's only solution was to announce to the workers in occupied factories that a good communist 'knows how to end a strike'), and even in Spain the communists had a good organization, but no long-term vision. Only in the 'hard' periods, from 1928 to 1935 and again from 1948 to 1956, did Europe's Communists have a clear path mapped out for them, albeit led into the wilderness. In the conditions of compromise and co-operation obtaining for most of the period 1935–48, the Communists had not much better an idea of where they were going than did their opponents.

The Soviet Union was to some extent able to capitalize upon the hopes of the resistance even after 1948. In Czechoslovakia, for example, there was genuine initial enthusiasm in many people for a 'transition to Socialism' following on the initial post-war reforms of the Beneš government. In Poland there could be no return to the *status quo ante* following the utter destruction of the fabric of Polish society, and there as in Yugoslavia it seemed logical to look to the Communists to lead the necessary changes (an illusion which in the former case did not last long). And in Italy and (especially) France there were waves of strikes and demonstrations in 1948, led by the Communists but driven by real discontent, both with the economic hardships and the political compromises that had been made after 1945.

Thus when men like the French Socialist Minister of the Interior Jules Moch saw themselves in 1948 as facing a Communist insurrection, they exaggerated but they did not wholly invent what they described.[29] What was distinctly absent was any overall plan, any Soviet-led attempt to revise the post-war settlement. Indigenous revolution was a very unlikely prospect in any of the countries of western Europe after 1944. And with the famous exception of Yugoslavia it was almost as unthinkable in the east. What the USSR sought was stable western neighbours, economically servile and politically docile. The best way to achieve this end was, literally, to remake the lands of central and eastern Europe in the Soviet image. To the extent that this entailed restructuring their societies and destroying their political systems, this constituted revolution – revolution from abroad, as Jan Gross has aptly called it.[30] But revolution in the commonly understood sense, as anticipated and feared by the west, was neither strategically envisaged nor tactically attempted.

These and other contentious issues are variously addressed in the essays that follow. Overall, they thus present a complicated and fluid account of the decade

1939–48, and this seems to me as it should be – this *was* an uncertain period of enormous change, in which Communists and non-Communists alike had only the dimmest sense of what might emerge. Indeed, together with the stress upon the unity that is provided by seeing the experience of resistance and Communism in Mediterranean Europe as a whole, the theme of open-ended possibilities and rapid shifts in perspective is what gives this book its shape. This is not very strange or uncommon in a work of contemporary history, of course. It is often the case that history as a discipline finds itself asserting the claims of chaos and chance where others find order and purpose. And this is perhaps especially true for the history of such an ideologically solipsistic subject as the international Communist movement, which thrives on its own claim to foresight and control (and tempts those who study it to see it in that light). For this very reason, it is important for mournful historical Penelopes to unravel on every possible occasion the winding sheets of tidy explanation. The present book may thus serve as a contributor to the continuing Odyssey of Europe's recent past.

NOTES

1 See Lilly Marcou, *Le Kominform* (Paris, 1977), pp. 181–9.
2 See Ken Jowitt, 'Moscow "Centre"', *Eastern European Politics and Societies*, 1, iii, 1987, pp. 296–349.
3 Lidice was the Czech village slaughtered by the Nazis as retribution for the Czech partisans' assassination of Heydrich.
4 For France in these years, see especially Robert O. Paxton, *Vichy France. Old Guard and New Order 1940–1944* (New York, 1972), and H. R. Kedward, *Resistance in Vichy France* (Oxford, 1978).
5 See Léon Blum, *A l'Echelle Humaine* (Paris, 1945).
6 In addition to the works cited by Travis, see for example Antonio Bianchi, *Storia del Movimento Operaio di la Spezia e Lunigiana* (Rome, 1975), pp. 235–387.
7 For the collapse of liberal Italy, see Adrian Lyttleton, *The Seizure of Power* (London, 1973).
8 The case for treating the Second World War as a *de facto* social revolution in this part of Europe is elegantly presented by Jan T. Gross. See his paper, 'East-central Europe, 1938–1948. . . . Themes for interpretation', presented to the conference on 'The effects of Communism on social and economic change: Eastern Europe in comparative perspective' (Bologna, Italy, 23–8 June 1986).
9 There is still no good overall survey of the years 1917–23 in Europe. See, within its limits, A. S. Lindemann, *The Red Years: European Socialism versus Bolshevism, 1919–1921* (Berkeley, 1974). For the advance of the Red Army to Warsaw, and its subsequent defeat, see Norman Davies, *White Eagle–Red Star: The Soviet-Polish War 1919–1920* (London, 1972). Good case studies of the creation of Communist parties are Annie Kriegel, *Aux Origines du Communisme français, 1914–1920* (2 vols, Paris, 1964) and Helmut König, *Lenin und der Italienischer Sozialismus, 1915–1921* (Tübingen, 1967). The transformation of the Comintern under Stalin is well covered in F. Claudin, *La Crise du mouvement Communiste: du Komintern au Kominform* (2 vols, Paris, 1972).
10 For the classical analyses of the national question in Socialist thought, see Otto Bauer, *Die Nationalitätenfrage und die Sozialdemokratie* (Vienna, 1907); V. I. Lenin, 'The right of nations to self-determination', in Robert C. Tucker (ed.), *The Lenin Anthology*

(New York, 1975), pp. 153–81; Horace B. Davis (ed.), *The National Question: Selected Writings by Rosa Luxemburg* (New York, 1976).

There is a general survey of the various major and minor nations of Eastern Europe in Raymond Pearson, *National Minorities in Eastern Europe, 1848–1945* (London, 1983). For the problems of the new states after 1918, see Joseph Rothschild, *East-Central Europe between the Two World Wars* (Seattle, 1974). The special case of Yugoslavia is very well covered in Ivo Banac, *The National Question in Yugoslavia: Origins, History, Politics* (Ithaca, NY, 1984). For the Graeco-Turkish conflict, see M. L. Smith, *Ionian Vision: Greece in Asia Minor, 1919–1922* (London, 1973).

11 For Czechoslovakia in the years immediately preceding the Communist Coup, see V. S. Mamatey and R. Luža (eds), *A History of the Czechoslovak Republic 1918–1948* (Princeton, NJ, 1973), pp. 387–475; Jacques Rupnik, *Histoire du Parti Communiste Tchécoslovaque: des origines à la prise du pouvoir* (Paris, 1981); Karel Kaplan, 'Hospodárská demokracie v letech 1945–1948', *Československy časopis historický*, XIV, 1966, pp. 844–61.

For Hungary, see S. D. Kertesz, *Between Russia and the West: Hungary and the Illusions of Peacemaking, 1945–1947* (Notre Dame, Ind., 1984); Miklos Molnár, *De Béla Kun à János Kádár* (Paris, 1987), esp. chs 6, 7.

12 Among the best recent histories of the Spanish Civil War in English are Paul Preston (ed.), *Revolution and War in Spain, 1931–1939* (London, 1984); Paul Preston, *The Spanish Civil War* (New York, 1986); Stanley Payne, *The Franco Regime 1936–1975* (Madison, Wis. 1987) and his earlier work, *The Spanish Revolution* (New York, 1970). The conflicts within the Left during the war are well presented (from a perspective sympathetic to the Trotskyists) by Pierre Broué and Emile Témine, *La Révolution et la guerre d'Espagne* (Paris, 1961).

13 See André Malraux, *l'Espoir* (Paris, 1937); Arthur Koestler, *Spanish Testament* (London, 1938); George Orwell, *Homage to Catalonia* (London, 1938). I have discussed some aspects of the engagement in Spain of the intellectual Left in a recent article. See Tony Judt, 'Wojna sie skonczyla? – o wojnie hiszpanskiej po 50 latach', *Zeszyty Literackie*, 19, 1987, pp. 140–5.

14 For the east European show trials, see e.g. the following: Jiří Pelikán, *The Czechoslovak Political Trials 1950–1954* (Stanford, 1971); Karen Kaplan, *Procès Politiques à Prague* (Brussels, 1980); Karel Kaplan, 'Zamýslení nad politickymi procesy', *Nová Mysl*, 6–8, June–August 1968; Eugen Loebl, *My Mind on Trial* (New York, 1976); Artur London, *L'Aveu* (Paris, 1968); Béla Szász, *Volunteers for the Gallows* (London, 1971); Annie Kriegel, *Les Grands procès dans les systèmes communistes* (Paris, 1972). For a first-person account of a Parisian 'trial', see Charles Tillon, *Un 'procès de Moscou' à Paris* (Paris, 1971).

15 One of the best summaries of European diplomacy in this era is still A. J. P. Taylor, *The Struggle for Mastery in Europe 1848–1918* (Oxford, 1951). For Austria–Hungary see C. A. Macartney, *The Habsburg Empire 1790–1918* (London, 1969). For the Balkans, see M. S. Anderson, *The Eastern Question 1774–1923* (London, 1966).

16 Good starting places for a study of the attitude of the Comintern in its early years to the national question are Jane Degras (ed.), *The Communist International 1919–1943* (3 vols, London, 1956–65), and *Manifestes, thèses et résolutions des quatre premiers Congrès Mondiaux de l'internationale Communiste 1919–1923* (Paris, 1934, repr. 1969).

17 There is still no satisfactory history of the French Communist Party. But see Philippe Robrieux, *Histoire intérieure du parti communiste* (4 vols, Paris, 1980–4) esp. vol. 1; Edward Mortimer, *The Rise of the French Communist Party 1920–1947* (London, 1984); Ronald Tiersky, *French Communism 1920–1972* (New York, 1974). Still valuable, though not really a history, is Annie Kriegel, *Les Communistes français* (Paris, 1970).

18 See L. Allen, 'The French Left and Russia: origins of the popular front', *World Affairs Quarterly*, XXX, 2, 1959; Jane Degras, 'United Front tactics in the Comintern 1921–1928', in D. Footman (ed.), *International Communism* (London, 1960); Albert and Célie Vassart, 'The Moscow origins of the French "Popular Front"', in Milorad M. Drachkovitch and Branko Lazitch (eds), *The Comintern: Historical Highlights* (New York, 1966). For an official Communist account, see e.g. Georges Cogniot, 'Georges Dimitrov et le Parti communiste français', *Cahiers d'histoire de l'Institut Maurice Thorez*, 25–6, 1978.
19 Good studies of the process of bringing Communist parties into line under Moscow are Jedermann (pseud.), *La Bolchévisation du parti communiste français, 1923–1928* (Paris, 1971); Hermann Weber, *Die Wandlung des deutschen Kommunismus* (Frankfurt-am-Main, 1969); Ruth Fischer, *Stalin and German Communism* (Cambridge, Mass, 1948).
26 See e.g. Phyllis Auty, *Tito* (London, 1974); Adam B. Ulam, *Titoism and the Cominform* (Cambridge, Mass, 1952); Milovan Djilas, *The New Class* (London, 1957); A. Ross Johnson, *The Transformation of Communist Ideology: The Yugoslav Case, 1945–1953* (Cambridge, Mass, 1972).
21 In addition to works cited in note 19, see Marcou, *Le Kominform*; Thomas W. Wolfe, *Soviet Power and Europe, 1945–1970* (Baltimore, 1970) and Vladimir Dedijer, *Le Défi de Tito: Staline et la Yougoslavie* (Paris, 1970).
22 For Gramsci's writings, see *Selections from the Prison Notebooks* (London, 1971). On his thought as a whole, see Joseph Femia, *Gramsci's Political Thought* (Oxford, 1981). Among the more recent English-language accounts of Italian Communism in 'strategic' terms, see Grant Amyot, *The Italian Communist Party: The Crisis of the Popular Front Strategy* (London, 1981); Alastair Davidson, *The Theory and Practice of Italian Communism* (London, 1982); Donald Sassoon, *The Strategy of the Italian Communist Party* (London, 1981). I have reviewed these at some length in the *Historical Journal*, 28, iv, 1985, pp. 1011–1021.
23 The most thorough English-language account of the PCI in the 'international' perspective is Donald Blackmer, *Unity in Diversity: Italian Communism and the Communist World* (Cambridge, Mass., 1968).
24 See Enrico Berlinguer, *After Poland* (Nottingham, 1982).
25 On Togliatti, see Giorgio Bocca, *Palmiro Togliatti* (Bari, 1973) and Giulio Ceretti, *A l'ombre des deux T* (Paris, 1973). Also Paolo Spriano, *Le Passioni di un Decennio, 1946–1956* (Rome, 1986).
26 See Charles Tillon, *On Chantait Rouge* (Paris, 1977); Auguste Lecoeur, *Le Parti communiste français et la Résistance août 1939–juin 1941* (Paris, 1968); A. Rossi (ps. for A. Tasca), *Les Communistes français pendant la drôle de guerre* (Paris, 1951); Guy Rossi-Landi, *La drôle de guerre* (Paris, 1971); Claude Delattre, 'L'attitude communiste à travers l'Humanité clandestine pendant l'occupation allemande: juin 1940–juin 1941', *Mouvement Social*, 74, 1971. The official PCF account is well presented in R. Bourderon et al., *Le PCF: étapes et problèmes 1920–1972* (Paris, 1981). The most recent discussion, which adds little new, is J.-P. Azéma et al., *Le PCF des années sombres, 1938–1941* (Paris, 1986). On the Communists' enthusiastic efforts to contribute to the persecution of Léon Blum, see Annie Kriegel, 'Un phénomène de haine fratricide: Léon Blum vu par les communistes', in Annie Kriegel, *Le Pain et les roses* (Paris, 1968), pp. 235–55.
27 See, classically, Dean Acheson, *Present at the Creation* (New York, 1969). Also Adam B. Ulam, *Expansion and Coexistence: The history of Soviet Foreign Policy, 1917–1967* (London, 1968). For the revisionist accounts, see e.g. Walter Lafeber, *America, Russia and the Cold War* (New York, 1967), and Daniel Yergin, *Shattered Peace: The Origins of the Cold War and the National Security State* (Boston, 1977).
28 For the speeches and condemnations at the founding meeting of the Cominform, see Marcou, *op. cit.* ch. 2, and Eugenio Reale, *Avec Jacques Duclos au banc des accusés*

(Paris, 1958). For the Czech Communists, see sources cited in note 10, together with François Fejtö, *Le Coup de Prague* (Paris, 1976).
29 See Jules Moch, *Une si longue vie* (Paris, 1976).
30 See the important new book by Jan T. Gross, *Revolution from Abroad: The Soviet Conquest of Poland's Western Ukraine and Western Byelorussia* (Princeton, NJ, 1988).

1 The Comintern and southern Europe, 1938–43

GEOFFREY SWAIN

The subject of the Comintern during its final phase has found little favour among historians: the romance of the Comintern under Lenin had disappeared long before 1938. Those who have turned to the subject, in particular Fernando Claudin and Paolo Spriano, have in their different ways been caught up in the histories of two of southern Europe's leading Communist parties, the Spanish and the Italian. Their approaches reflect the histories of those parties. Spriano's account, while anti-Stalin, sees as Stalin's final betrayal the ending of the 'separate roads to Socialism' proclaimed during the years 1944–7, a stance which reflects the polycentrism of Togliatti. Claudin's account bristles with denunciations of Stalin's decision to sacrifice the Spanish, and later the Greek, revolutions to the foreign-policy needs of the Soviet Union, a stirring denunciation of the diplomacy of spheres of influence. As we shall see, these historians' accounts mirror the two tendencies which can be discerned within the ranks of the Comintern and indeed the Cominform.[1]

The international Communist movement under Stalin was not a monolith. Stalin's approach to all policy debates was to encourage two factions, intervening decisively only when he thought it crucial. Within the Comintern the perennial debate was about united action with social democrats and other radical groups. Georgi Dimitrov, chairman of the Comintern executive from 1934 until its dissolution in 1943, advanced the theory of an anti-Fascist popular front as a sophisticated strategy for combining united action 'above' – among party leaders – and 'below' – among the masses – in order to establish a new state power of transition between capitalism and socialism. The attraction of this theory to Stalin was that it helped to underpin the Franco-Soviet Alliance of May 1935. Stalin therefore supported the change of line at the Seventh Comintern Congress in July 1935, dropping his earlier support for those who called social-democrats 'social-fascists'.[2]

Stalin intervened again in Comintern affairs in spring 1938 at the time of the German occupation of Austria. His search for a collective security agreement with Britain and France was already in jeopardy from the steady drift towards the Right within the governing circles of those two countries; it was out of the question for him to support those Spanish Communists who were now arguing that the civil war could only be won if the transition towards socialism were begun and a workers' government established. Instead the popular front was broadened to the national front; unity 'from above' was all-important and Spain heard little more talk of socialism.[3]

Stalin's most dramatic intervention, his pact with Nazi Germany in August 1939, had an immediate impact on the Comintern. It made quite irrelevant unity 'from above': the previous year's policy of reducing the concept of the popular front to minority Communist participation in a coalition government was a concession designed to placate Britain and France. The failure of this policy in Spain and Stalin's designation of the Second World War as 'imperialist' combined to persuade the Comintern that socialist revolution was again on the agenda. In this context it made sense to revive the policy of unity 'from below', last used before Hitler's consolidation of power. This meant an offensive alliance between the Communists and rank-and-file socialists opposed to their reformist leaders, with the explicit aim of socialist revolution. If such a revolution were now imminent, bourgeois allies were unnecessary.

The Nazi invasion of Russia on 22 June 1941 meant a return within the Comintern to Dimitrov's original concept of the anti-Fascist popular front, though the 1938 term 'national front' was retained. The main purpose of the front was once more defensive rather than offensive: fascism had to be defeated, but the possibility of that defeat resulting in a new type of 'people's' rather than bourgeois democracy was not ruled out. Stalin's intervention came later when, to reassure his new western allies, he first insisted on a return to the 1938 national-front policy of coalition governments, in autumn 1942, and then dissolved the Comintern in June 1943.

Four years later, with the collapse of the wartime Grand Alliance and the start of the Cold War, Stalin changed tack again; the 'dollar imperialism' of Marshall Aid had to be resisted. The policy of different roads to socialism was abandoned and all Communist parties forced into a new straitjacket imposed by the Cominform. The new policy held that the people's democracies established after the Second World War were ready for Soviet-style socialist revolution, but equally it meant that such transformation was only on the agenda in those areas within the Soviet sphere of influence.

Little more need be said about Stalin and the Comintern, except perhaps to note how he retained control of the organization. D. Manuilsky, the representative of the Soviet Communist Party on the Comintern executive could ultimately overrule Dimitrov, while Manuilsky in turn had to report to Zhdanov, the member of the Politburo's Foreign Affairs Commission responsible for the Comintern. At the same time, the Comintern had its own quota of NKVD agents. Dimitrov once explained to Ernst Fischer, editor of *Communist International*, that he had no authority to intervene in the affairs of the NKVD. He could speed up enquiries, but that was the limit of his influence.[4]

Stalin never considered revolution in the west a serious proposition: the Comintern did. It took seriously Dimitrov's writings on the popular front and the transition to socialism. Those writings were immediately put to the test when the Spanish Communist Party joined the popular front government during that country's civil war. The experience of that war threw up two tendencies within the international Communist movement, two differing explanations of what went wrong in Spain. Those tendencies then competed throughout the period 1938–48. One tendency, the democratic, was always associated with Togliatti. The other, the revolutionary or 'sectarian', was first associated with the Spanish Communists and then later with Tito. Both tendencies found themselves on different occasions supported and opposed by Stalin.

Togliatti was the Comintern's special representative in Spain. The dominant theme of both his reports back to Moscow during the war and his contribution to the inquest after the war was that the Spanish Communist Party had not been securely enough based in the masses. Its trade-union work had been poor and it had tended to rely on positions secured in the government bureaucracy and the army. The party had organized far too few factory meetings and the popular-front committees had been used for backstairs deals between parties rather than serving as forums for popular pressure. Given this weak link with the masses, the talk of taking power often heard within the Spanish Party had according to Togliatti, been mere sectarian arrogance.[5]

This failing had been part and parcel of a greater failing, the party's refusal to push through with fresh elections to the Cortes and provincial assemblies. In autumn 1937 the Comintern had instructed the Spanish party to do just this. Party leader Pepe Diaz had stressed the point at the November plenum of the central committee. However, despite a further reminder in the form of a letter from Dimitrov, the party had decided to shelve the matter on the grounds that the other popular-front parties opposed such elections. Yet paradoxically, while so keen not to upset ministerial colleagues on this matter, the Communist ministers had made no serious attempt to win them over at a personal level and convince them through joint work that the Communists were not secretly planning to seize power. By keeping their distance they had never established a decent working relationship with the socialist Prime Minister Negrin.[6]

To overcome this gap between the party and the masses, Stalin's instruction of March 1938, that the popular front should be broadened into a national front, had made perfect sense to Togliatti. He had had no difficulty in adopting it as his own. As he noted in one of his reports: 'your instructions are opportune and appropriate to the situation'.[7] His experience of Spain, and his experience of the Soviet purges, had convinced him at this time that if 'Communists did not act as the most consistent of democrats history would pass them by'.[8] The governmental reshuffle in Spain in April 1938 had given Spanish Communists a chance to show themselves true democrats. Rather than seize power, they would reduce their influence in the government, signalling their absolute commitment to working with other parties.

Togliatti had put forward the same solution when in the dying weeks of the civil war General Casado had seized power in an attempt to negotiate a last-minute deal with Franco. Togliatti argued that Casado had been helped to power by the failure of the party to recognize that it no longer spoke for the masses. Its response to the loss of Catalonia had been to denounce the government, blame the cowardice of others, and see traitors and capitulators on every side, completely ignoring the spirit of the people, demoralized, desperate for peace and unsure why the struggle should go on if Franco were prepared to negotiate. Togliatti was convinced that if the Communists had been more conciliatory and not appeared to want sole power by waiting a week before re-establishing a coalition government in what remained of republican territory, the ground would have been cut from under Casado's feet.[9]

Even after the coup, Togliatti was convinced that negotiations with Casado were possible. Despite the brutal attack on the Communist Party, Togliatti argued that the party could still be legalized, for there were some Casadists unhappy at the attack on the Communists. He therefore dismissed out of hand suggestions that the party should respond to the coup with an armed uprising. He preferred to sound out any members of the new Casadist junta prepared to listen, offering to negotiate an end to the crisis whereby the communists would renounce all claims to a seat in any future government. He also pointed out that it was just possible that in the aftermath of Hitler's occupation of the whole of Czechoslovakia in violation of the Munich Agreement the western powers might reassess their attitude to Spain.[10]

The 'sectarian' experience of the Spanish Civil War was very different and articulated most clearly by Claudin, writing after the event: 'All the sacrifice and heroism of three years went down with a policy that, from the first day of the war had turned its back on the essential demands of Spanish revolutionary reality in order to adapt itself to the international strategy of Stalin'; 'The spirit which made possible the defence of Madrid was that of proletarian revolution . . . but that would have necessitated the setting up of a revolutionary proletarian government . . . together with . . . large scale guerrilla activity in areas dominated by the rebel generals'.[11]

Stalin's spring 1938 intervention, which Togliatti had taken so calmly, devastated the 'sectarians'. During the second half of 1937 the republican parties and the western powers had talked increasingly of capitulation, compromise, and a negotiated settlement: why, the 'sectarians' argued, make further concessions to keep such a coalition alive when there was still a chance of fighting a revolutionary war and establishing a socialist state? Stalin's decision seemed to them to run counter to the whole strategy of the party adopted in the autumn of 1937, which concentrated on exposing capitulationists among republicans and reformists and consolidating relations with the socialist party.[12]

At the November 1937 plenum General Secretary Diaz had stressed that the popular front should not degenerate into a simple coalition but remain committed to an action programme. This meant closer relations with the 'brother' parties, the socialists and anarchists. 'The hegemony of the proletariat in the popular front', he said, 'is the form of power which conveys firmness of direction, a policy without vacillation and which assures triumph'.[13] In February 1938, on the eve of the ministerial crisis, Diaz had reminded the party that this was a war for justice, liberty, and social progress. The war was both for national independence and a revolution. 'The people fighting the war are at the same time implementing a revolution'.[14] The clear policy of the party was to use the ministerial crisis of April 1938 to remove both the reformist socialist prime minister and the republican ministers and establish a proletarian government.[15]

All the evidence supports the view that the Politburo was completely taken by surprise when Togliatti explained Stalin's instruction.[16] Not surprisingly, the whole sectarian issue flared up again with the Casado coup. The party's response to the loss of Catalonia did not seem unreasonable to the 'sectarians'. There was no great enthusiasm among the party leadership for another government under former Prime Minister Negrin. Besides, as Togliatti himself made clear, one of the other Comintern emissaries in Spain, Stepanov, had sanctioned the party's militant stance. 'Sectarians' among the Spanish Communists had therefore been appalled when Togliatti had shown himself ready to negotiate with Casado. The idea of not resisting a military coup by force of arms and, if successful in overthrowing the dictator, going on to replace him with a communist government, seemed extraordinary to the 'sectarians'.[17]

The argument between Togliatti and the 'sectarians' continued in Moscow during the inquest into the civil war held from May to December 1939. Some of the proceedings of this commission of inquiry were bitter and stormy. The party's excessively defensive stance was certainly criticized, and Stepanov tried to make Togliatti the scapegoat for the Spanish party's failure.[18] The debates were complex and each of the Spanish members of the commission was asked to write his or her own account of the March 1939 events: Diaz concluded that the party had indeed committed grave errors in those last days in Spain.[19] His article 'on the lessons of the war of the Spanish people' was critical of Togliatti.[20]

Criticism of Togliatti was also evident in Diaz's treatment of the question of links between the party and the masses. Togliatti's concern with this had centred on reviving democracy in the Cortes and municipalities. Diaz recognized the problem, but his solution was to 'break the old state apparatus, which serves reaction, and replace it with a new apparatus which serves the working class'. And, to avoid the 'vacillations' inherent in dealing with allied parties, it was necessary to ensure the independent activity of the Communist Party. As the Yugoslav 'sectarians' would do later, the Spanish 'sectarians' recognized the need for democracy to serve as a link between party and masses, but saw the solution in new forms of popular democracy rather than in playing 'coalition politics'.[21]

The conclusion that Togliatti had in some way been responsible for the defeat of the Spanish republic was part and parcel of the new Comintern line resulting from the Hitler–Stalin pact of August 1939. Togliatti's defeat was a victory for the 'sectarians', and with the pact the Comintern line swung to the Left, an about-turn welcomed by the Spanish party. As even Togliatti had recognized, Britain and France, the Soviet Union's erstwhile allies, bore the greatest responsibility for the defeat of the Spanish republic. Their policy of non-intervention had resulted in blockade. By Stalin's masterful deal with Hitler, the Spanish and other 'sectarians' argued, the western powers had got their come-uppance.[22]

The full implications of the new line were not immediately apparent, particularly to Togliatti who did not wait in Moscow until the commission of inquiry into the Spanish Civil War had concluded its work. He had been sent to Paris to re-establish links with the Italian party in emigration and the French party. Called upon to inform the Italian and the French party leaders of the Hitler–Stalin pact at a meeting in Brussels on 19 August, Togliatti and the French Communist Party leader Thorez had assumed at first there would be no fundamental shift in Comintern policy. The pact, they argued, made Nazi criticisms of Communism and Soviet Russia look silly, gave the Soviet Union security, and was revenge for Munich; it left unaffected the necessity to struggle against Fascism. Operating on this assumption the French party voted for war credits on 2 September.[23]

When the Comintern Secretariat met to consider the pact on 9 September it decided that the war was between two capitalist and imperialist blocs. As such, both sides were to be condemned and the working class should oppose the war. Since the social democrats and petty bourgeois parties had rallied to their governments, the popular front tactic no longer suited the changed situation. Mass work should now concentrate on the 'formation from below of a popular front against war and reaction'. The coalition or 'united front from above' of Stalin's 1938 national front was being abandoned, Dimitrov's concept of a 'united front from above supported by a united front from below' was being abandoned, and the Comintern had returned to its pre-Seventh Congress policy of 'unity from below'.[24]

The Comintern resolution adopted on 9 September has never been published. The line changed again with the signing of the German–Soviet Boundary and Friendship Treaty on 29 September. This committed the two powers to a joint appeal for peace which, if rejected, would demonstrate that Britain and France were responsible for continuing the war. While the Comintern's first comment on the war in *Communist International* reflected the view that both sides bore equal responsibility – the article 'The war mongers' attacked the German imperialists first and referred to Nazi concentration camps before going on to criticize Britain and France[25] – subsequent comment singled out Britain and France for criticism. This was the tone of Dimitrov's 'The War and the working class of the capitalist countries' published in the November issue. Another article in that issue portrayed Germany as the underdog from whom Britain was trying to steal markets.[26]

This pro-German stance reached its zenith in an article by Wilhelm Pieck in the December issue of *Communist International*. He proposed that in voting for Hitler the German people had been motivated by opposition to capitalism; they had taken seriously the claim of the Nazis to be a socialist party.[27] In defence of the Comintern it could be pointed out that when, at the end of November 1939, the Secretariat debated the situation in Germany, Austria and Czechoslovakia, it did call for unity between the German workers' struggle against Fascism and the liberation struggles of the Czechs, Slovaks, Austrians, and Poles. But this resolution when published was lost in a preamble attacking Britain and France. During the spring of 1940 these attacks on Britain and France continued, spurred on by British and French plans to intervene in the Finno-Soviet War.[28]

In line with the dominant position of 'sectarians' in the Comintern, much space was devoted in the journal to an attack on former reformist allies in the popular front,[29] and to arguing the case for imminent transition to socialism. Socialist revolution would result, since this was an imperialist war, just as after the First World War. Although Dimitrov was cautious on this and careful not to mention the word socialism, Ernst Fischer spelt out clearly that a new era of war and revolution had come: 'Capitalism is shattered to the core. In many lands workers and labouring people are opposing imperialist robbers and oppressors with weapons in their hands', and later 'Lenin described imperialism as the eve of socialist revolution. This year finance capital, in shock, is itself painting in flaming letters the words "revolution and socialism" in the sky'.[30]

How this revolution was to come about was not very clear; but we know from Fischer's memoirs that the Nazi–Soviet pact led to talk within the Comintern of the possibility of spreading socialism by using the diplomacy of spheres of influence and the armed might of occupying armies, a concept of revolution far less worrying to Nazi Germany than the traditional Comintern policy of armed proletarian uprisings. The Spanish communist Castro Delgado recalled in his memoirs the tense atmosphere in the Comintern when the Finnish party proved incapable of preventing determined opposition to the Soviet Union when Finland was invaded by the Red Army in the winter of 1939–40.[31] Plans for a quick repetition of the Finnish scenario in Rumania had to be hastily abandoned.[32]

Certainly the slogan of incorporation into the Soviet Union was common enough during 1940 in parts of eastern Europe bordering on the Soviet Union or within its anticipated sphere of influence. The demand for a 'Soviet Bulgaria' was used until August 1941 and the demand for a 'Soviet Slovakia' was used until 1942. These two states had diplomatic relations with the Soviet Union, and the demands for a 'Soviet Slovenia' and 'Soviet Macedonia' were current during preparations for the Fifth Conference of the Yugoslav Communist Party (in October 1940), following the establishment of Soviet–Yugoslav relations in June 1940, by which time the Baltic States had indeed been absorbed into the Soviet Union.[33] The issue of revolution would remain at the forefront of the Comintern's concerns as it gradually began to reassess the nature of the Second World War.

In private the Comintern was far less subservient to Germany that it had to be on the pages of *Communist International*. With the occupation of Denmark, Fischer visited Dimitrov and urged him to state publicly that this new German aggression meant that the nature of the war had changed; if *realpolitik* meant it was impossible for the Comintern to appeal for united action against Germany, it should at least be possible to call on the workers to defend their independence. Dimitrov agreed, but told Fischer he could not decide this 'off his own bat'. However, two communications from Moscow to Denmark at this time suggest Fischer got his way. On 9 April the secretariat called on the Danish Communists to organize resistance to the occupier, while on the 10th Dimitrov urged them to build a broad and 'genuine' popular front to defend the interests of the Danish people.[34]

The new emphasis on defence became even clearer during and after the fall of France. While the German invasion of France was still under way an angry clash occurred in the Comintern as Manuilsky, Dimitrov, and Togliatti debated the current situation with German party leader Wilhelm Pieck. Breaking with the official line Manuilsky was reported as saying that France was fighting on behalf of the Soviet Union; in his view a German victory over France would be quickly followed by an attack on the Soviet Union. Togliatti supported this open heresy, adding that while the Nazi–Soviet pact was a fact at present, it would not be one for ever.[35]

On 6 June 1940, shortly before the armistice, the French Communist Party called on its government to change the nature of the war, turning it into a 'national war for freedom and independence'. This would be done by freeing the arrested Communist deputies and militants, arresting enemy agents, decreeing mass mobilization, arming the people, and turning Paris into an impregnable fortress. The Comintern secretariat supported these proposals, but stressed that 'only the working class, led by the communist party, is able to rally the nation into a mighty front able to defend its basic interests and struggle against foreign oppression and for independence and a genuinely free France'.[36]

This qualification was important. Clearly at this stage working-class leadership of any resistance activity was seen as essential. While the Comintern might be ready to admit that the nature of the war had changed and Communists were justified in defending their homelands, the sectarian policy of 'unity from below' had not been abandoned: nor, logically, had the belief that such a war would result in revolution. However, in July 1940 Togliatti sent an appeal to the Italian people which omitted the demand for proletarian hegemony, and on 20 July the Comintern urged the French party not to criticize de Gaulle. In August Dimitrov drafted some theses, which stressed that a popular front from below could only come about through joint collaboration between Communists and socal democrats. By January 1941 Comintern directives were stressing that de Gaulle's role was 'objectively positive'.[37]

This further softening of the line sprang from the review of Comintern activity in the Balkans undertaken in the autumn of 1940. As Manuilsky told students at the Frunze Military Academy in September, the Balkans were considered a Soviet sphere of influence. After the Nazi conquest of western Europe – between April and June Denmark, Norway, and France had all succumbed – Stalin had moved quickly to incorporate the Baltic states into the Soviet Union in July. Then, acting on Ribbentrop's assurance of June 1940 that Germany's interest in the Balkans was in trade rather than territory, he incorporated Bessarabia and northern Bukovina into the Soviet Union. Both territories had formerly been part of Rumania.

The German response to Soviet activity in Rumania was not encouraging for Stalin. Hitler, after allowing the Hungarians to take a share of Rumanian territory, guaranteed the security of the whole of the remaining state. Thus Germany staked a claim to an area in a region seen by Stalin as his sphere of influence. (The situation became even more alarming for Stalin when the Italians invaded Greece on 29 October). The Balkans naturally dominated discussion at the Ribbentrop–Molotov summit on 12–13 November 1940. Wanting to know if the Nazis really recognized the Balkans as a Soviet sphere, Stalin asked that he be allowed to guarantee the territorial integrity of Bulgaria.

Later in November the decision of the Slovak, Rumanian, and Hungarian governments to associate themselves openly with Germany by adhering to the Tripartite Pact further weakened the Soviet position. When Bulgaria first ignored the Soviet offer of a guarantee, then allowed German troops to cross its territory to reach Greece, and then finally joined the Tripartite Pact on 1 March 1941, it was clear that the Balkans could no longer be seriously considered as a Soviet sphere of influence. When the decision of the Yugoslav government to join the Tripartite Pact provoked a coup in that country later in March, the Germans saw the coup leaders' decision to open negotiations with the Russians as a reason for invasion. By the end of April 1941 the Balkans were not a Soviet sphere of influence, but part of the Nazi 'new order'.[38]

Perhaps because the Soviet government saw the Balkans as its sphere of influence, the Comintern had been allowed far more latitude in its operations there. It made no bones about its view that the wars in Greece and later in Yugoslavia were not imperialist wars, but just wars of national defence. Indeed, in February 1941, *Communist International* published an article on the disagreement between Lenin and Rosa Luxemburg during the First World War on the role played by small nations. In this obscure wrangle, Lenin had noted that in an imperialist context, the struggle of a small nation against a great power could be a force for progress if linked at the same time to proletarian revolution in advanced countries. Luxemburg had denied the progressive role of any small nation.

In the context of the second 'imperialist' war, the Comintern was clearly now prepared to argue that small nations could again play a progressive role. As a result all sections were called on to express their support for the Greek and Yugoslav people, and the last German-language edition of *Communist International* published a long resolution from the German Communist Party which did just that.[39] Axis activity in the Balkans convinced the Comintern that a war between Germany and the Soviet Union was inevitable.[40] Such an attack could change the nature of the war still further.

As the Comintern prepared itself ideologically for this new war, echoes of the dispute between Togliatti and the 'sectarians' could again be heard. The Comintern had already conceded that parts of the fighting in Europe involved just rather than imperial wars, and it had urged parties to form broad alliances when opposing Nazi invasion rather than insisting on the 'united front from below'. Was it now also the time to confront the issue of whether or not the war in Europe would culminate in socialist revolution, or whether that too was 'sectarian' jargon that could soon be jettisoned. Should the Comintern not make clear that bourgeois democracy might be as satisfactory an end to the present fighting as socialism, or had Lenin been right to link the progressive element of a small nation's struggle to the success of a proletarian uprising?

Details are understandably sketchy, but in November 1939 Comintern correspondence with the Yugoslav Communist Party stressed the 'great possibilities for the revolutionary mobilization of the working masses' which existed in that country, and linked this to the 'overthrow of capitalism'. In September 1940, however, the Comintern took a far more cautious line. It warned the Yugoslav party not to use any slogans which implied support for 'the dictatorship of the proletariat' and to concentrate its efforts on resisting capitulation by a quisling government; this meant preparing for armed resistance to preserve the country's independence. Work within the armed forces was essential for this, as was closer collaboration with other opposition groups; such collaboration, however, should be strictly limited in scope and temporary.

The same issue came up in March 1941 when the Comintern executive discussed the future of Italy. Two views were advanced. Was the way forward a government 'dependent on the masses' which would end Fascism and bring peace, or, as Togliatti proposed, the broadest possible anti-Fascist alliance? In the discussion which followed Dimitrov was reported as saying that it did not matter whether Mussolini was overthrown by a socialist revolution or any other kind of revolution as long as he was removed from power. Dimitrov did add, however, that he did not exclude the possibility of an anti-Fascist movement ending in a proletarian revolution.[41]

When in April 1941 the Comintern executive sent out a firm directive to the Italian party, it called for a stance to be adopted which would facilitate the formation of a bloc comprising all opposed to Fascism. An instruction to Tito and the Yugoslav Party issued at the end of March took a similar line. The overthrow of the pro-Axis government in Yugoslavia and the opening of negotiations with the Russians had been accompanied by mass street demonstrations. Dimitrov urged Tito to be cautious and not to mistake the growing anti-Axis movement with a revolution; that, he stressed, was still a long way off. Tito's decision to ignore this advice and organize his party on the assumption that resistance to the Nazis would result in the social transformation of Yugoslavia meant the Yugoslav party saw no reason for the Comintern to abandon its 'sectarian' policy.[42]

This decision of the Yugoslav party, which from now on replaced the Spanish party as the leading proponent of a 'sectarian' policy, was more important than it might seem at first sight. During the period 1939–41 the Yugoslav Communist Party played a crucial role in Comintern affairs. This was partly because that party had proved itself capable of operating successfully underground, in an era when all the major communist parties found great difficulty in adapting to the illegality imposed by war, and partly because as a neutral state Yugoslavia provided a relatively safe haven for Comintern activity in a strategically important part of the world. In January 1940 the Comintern established a radio transmitter in Zagreb from which to make contact with the Italian, Swiss, Austrian, Hungarian, Bulgarian, Greek, Slovak, and Yugoslav parties. This station was fully operational by the summer of that year.[43]

As with previous Comintern operations, such as co-ordinating support for republican Spain via the French Communist Party, the host Communist party was expected to provide back-up facilities and help implement Comintern decisions. Thus small groups of Yugoslav party members were put at the Comintern's disposal to act as couriers with the other parties. By far the most important of these undertakings was to provide facilities for implementing the Comintern's decision of July 1940 to relocate the foreign base of the Italian Communist Party in Yugoslavia rather than France. Providing the expected support in terms of printing presses and personnel severely stretched the Yugoslav party – and resulted in considerable tension between the two parties – but it gave the Yugoslav party a kudos in the international Communist movement it had never experienced before. When Nazi Germany invaded Russia on 22 June 1941, the Yugoslav Communist Party was first among equals.[44]

Yugoslav predominance in the affairs of the Comintern continued during the first year of the Great Patriotic War. In June 1941 Tito informed Dimitrov that he was planning a partisan war and asked for Dimitrov's comments. The latter was enthusiastic: 'The time has come', he wrote, 'when communists should arouse the people to open struggle against the occupier.'[45] Although the policy of an uprising seemed adventurist to some members of the Balkan section of the Comintern (the Bulgarian V. Kolarov remembered the disaster of the Bulgarian peasant uprising in 1923), Dimitrov was unequivocally in favour. He instructed the Bulgarian party to go over from acts of individual sabotage to the organization of partisan struggle, and settled the vexed question of Macedonia in favour of the Yugoslav Party.[46]

The journal *Communist International* took up the cause of the Yugoslav partisans enthusiastically. It argued from the start of the Nazi invasion that the people of occupied Europe would play a crucial role in winning the war; to report on such developments it started a regular feature entitled 'The United Anti-Hitler People's Front'. This gave its first coverage to the Yugoslav partisans in September 1941. They were credited with opening a 'new front', and in the same issue Thorez stressed that the moment was right for the French party to launch a similar uprising. This recognition given to the partisans steadily increased. By December 1941 Yugoslavia was described as no longer being an occupied country, but a country at war with the Germans.

By the spring of 1942 the Yugoslav partisans were being held up as a model and all other resistance movements urged to follow their lead. An article in *Communist International* stressed that the Yugoslavs had shown how armed resistance was possible and how guerrilla tactics, far from being a relic of nineteenth-century Spain, were quite possible in an age of mechanized warfare. The secret of success was to begin: once fighting had begun, plenty of volunteers would join. Of course, there would be high casualties, but, the journal argued, every day thousands who did not resist became victims of the Nazi 'new order'. The choice was to suffer casualties sitting doing nothing, or in active struggle for freedom; under Nazi occupation there would always be casualties.

This article went out of its way to stress that Yugoslavia was not a special case. The Yugoslav experience had not been dependent on mountainous terrain; partisans operated equally effectively in industrial areas. Nor had the Yugoslavs obtained very many arms before embarking on their campaign, as was sometimes suggested. While the collapse of the Royal Army in April 1941 had left many arms in the hands of soldiers, the Yugoslav partisans had had to obtain most of their arms from the enemy. The only thing different about the Yugoslavs was that they had begun to fight when the fate of Soviet Russia was unclear. Now that the Red Army was counterattacking and drawing more and more troops away from occupation duties, the task of armed resisters in Europe was that much easier.[47]

This pro-Yugoslav line dominated *Communist International* throughout the summer of 1942. The May Day slogan was 'Forward onto the attack!', and the May Day issue sang the praises of the Yugoslavs, Albanians, Bulgarians, Greeks, and Carpathian Slovaks who had indeed formed partisan groups. The July issue stressed that it had now been 'proved' that partisan war was not a question of terrain: 'the source of partisan strength is not nature, but the people'. The same issue proclaimed: 'The valiant sons of Yugoslavia again and again show all the peoples of occupied Europe an example of heroic, selfless struggle for the liberation of their homeland.'[48]

However, despite this public support for developments in Yugoslavia, the Comintern remained concerned at the continuing 'sectarian' attitude of the Yugoslav party. On the eve of the Nazi invasion of Soviet Russia, it will be recalled, the Comintern had been ambivalent about the possibility of anti-Fascist struggle leading to socialist revolution. Tito had been warned in March 1941 that the revolution was still a long way off, and as the Yugoslavs embarked on their armed uprising against the occupier, the Comintern's position became even more categorical. The Yugoslavs were told on 22 June 1941, the very day of the Nazi invasion, that they should 'take into account that at the present stage, the issue is liberation from fascist oppression, and not socialist revolution'.[49]

However, the Yugoslav Communist Party's activities on the domestic front were indeed concerned with social revolution. Wherever partisans secured control, liberation committees were established which deprived any previously existing political authority of its power. While politicians of many parties became involved in the work of liberation committees, they did so as individuals. The committees were organized and dominated by the Yugoslav Communist Party: it was a united front from below rather than from above. This radical interpretation of the anti-Fascist front was shared by the Slovak Communist Party. In March 1942 the latter called for a guerrilla war to be led by anti-Fascist committees which were clearly dominated by the Communist Party and hostile to bourgeois parties.[50]

Dimitrov's messages to Tito suggest that the Comintern had returned to the deliberately ambivalent concept of the popular front favoured by Dimitrov in 1935.

The 'united front from below' had been abandoned, and with it the insistence of the Spaniard Diaz, endorsed by Tito, that for a popular front to work the old state apparatus had to be abolished. Dimitrov in 1941 clearly favoured a return to something closer to Togliatti's views on working within the capitalist state structure; while not yet advocating the 1938 policy of the 'united front from above', i.e. a straightforward coalition government, he wanted a return to his original concept of unity from above underpinned by unity from below. This meant no talk of imminent socialism, but equally no let-up in the struggle to win workers over to Communism.

The *Communist International* reflected this ambivalence and was quite prepared to take a critical view of potential partners in a national front government and of the Soviet Union's western allies. In the same spring 1942 article calling on all resisters to follow Yugoslavia's lead, the view that guerrilla warfare was impossible in the modern age was dismissed as a story put out by the reactionary leaders of the Second International. These leaders were blamed for the inactivity of the resistance movements in western and central Europe. The Czechoslovak socialists were singled out for particular criticism.[51]

In August 1942 the journal was equally dismissive of those who argued that the best tactic for resistance movements was to wait for an Allied invasion; only then did it make sense to begin a partisan war. The concept of a 'once and for all last minute uprising' was held up to ridicule. A partisan movement could not appear overnight. It would take months of preparation and active struggle to train cadres capable of establishing a national underground network and playing an active role in liberation. National liberation should, after all, be the work of the people themselves rather than the people of another country. The Yugoslavs had shown what could be done on their own initiative.

In describing the sort of political body which would be needed to organize such a partisan war, the same article clearly reflected Dimitrov's views on the popular front. 'A national front, firmly organized amongst the rank and file and supplemented by agreements between the leaders of all genuinely anti-Hitler parties and groups . . . represents the main weapon in this great struggle'.[52] But such a formulation, while accurately reflecting Dimitrov's views of the relationship between the united front from below and the united front from above, did not correspond to the sort of grand coalition of leaders which Stalin would soon insist should become Comintern policy.

Winston Churchill arrived in Moscow on 12 August 1942 for talks with Stalin. In August the Comintern Secretariat met and heard Dimitrov insist that all patriotic elements had to be allowed to take initiatives in the anti-Fascist struggle.

> There is no need for a narrow, sectarian policy. On the contrary, contact should be made with all who are opposed to the anti-people regimes. A programme suitable for a national front has to be worked out. That does not require a detailed programme for the future, concerning itself with questions that can be decided within the country after the war, but a programme for struggle against Hitlerite oppressors.

A resolution was then passed calling for unity between workers, peasants, intellectuals and the patriotic bourgeoisie.[53]

With this resolution a campaign against sectarianism in the international Communist movement was launched. Although the resolution appeared innocuous enough, it marked a return to the same type of anti-sectarian campaign seen after the events in Spain of spring 1938. The motive for the campaign was the same: the Soviet Union's once potential and now actual allies had to be accommodated. In his speech on the occasion of the twenty-fifth anniversary of the October Revolution, Stalin criticized those who argued that the different ideologies of the members of the Grand Coalition made genuine co-operation impossible. 'It would be funny if the ideological difference were denied', he said, 'but does that exclude the possibility of joint action against a common enemy? No it does not.'[54]

The *Communist International* now began to find and condemn elements of sectarianism in the approach of the other parties, notably the French and Italian.[55] In the same vein the Slovak party was instructed early in 1943 to open up contacts with the bourgeois parties,[56] and in February 1943 the Italian party established its National Action Front.[57] Not surprisingly the star of the Yugoslav party began to fall. While reports from Yugoslavia continued to appear, increased coverage was given to the French resistance. This began as early as September 1942, and continued into the spring of 1943. The new theme in reporting the resistance was the increase in partisan struggle in France, and the growing unity of the various resistance groups.

In spring 1943 much coverage was given to the visit paid by Grenier, a member of the French Party's Central Committee, to London to meet de Gaulle and the subsequent joint statement and increase in co-operation. The March 1943 joint appeal by French anti-Fascist groups was given particular prominence, and reproduced in full. The phrase used by Dimitrov at the August meeting now became a regular slogan on the pages of the journal: only when the enemy had been driven out could the people of occupied countries decide their future. Stalin's attention was turning from the Balkan sideshow to centre stage. Coverage of events in Yugoslavia, while still detailed, sought to contradict the view put out by the Nazis that the Yugoslav partisan movement was 'Bolshevik'.[58]

For all the prominence given to the Yugoslav partisans, the Comintern had remained suspicious of Tito's activities. Although as early as December 1941 the Comintern had asked for details of the partisan leaders so that their names could be publicized, they never were.[59] Unlike the French Communist leader, Thorez, Tito never wrote in the *Communist International*. The Yugoslav party was never referred to by name as the organizer of the partisans, who were always described as 'patriots'. Very few details of the partisans' social policies in liberated territories ever emerged, although when reporting greetings from the partisans to Stalin reference was made to the existence among them of political commissars. The only reference to Communist dominance came when it was denied.

This concern over the nature of events in Yugoslavia continued throughout 1942. In February the Comintern suggested that the Yugoslav partisans issue an appeal to the resistance movements in France and Czechoslovakia, but the idea was cancelled after protests from the Yugoslav government in exile. Subsequently Dimitrov appears to have been bombarded with stories originating from the government in exile about the 'Trotskyist' activities of Tito, and quizzed Tito as to whether it was not his radical policies which were responsible for the break with the četniks, rather than their preference for collaboration with the Germans. The tone of these exchanges suggests Dimitrov was as much baffled as angry about Tito's domestic policies.[60]

After the start of the sectarian campaign in autumn 1942, the Comintern began to interfere quite blatantly in Yugoslav party affairs. On 9 August Dimitrov instructed Tito to change the name of his 'proletarian' brigade since it was fighting for the people as a whole not just the workers. Similarly, Tito had made it clear that he favoured the establishment of a new government to replace the government in exile. However, on 13 November 1942 the party was told that its planned Anti-Fascist Council for the National Liberation of Yugoslavia (AVNOJ) could not act as a government. The future government of Yugoslavia would be decided after the war was over.[61]

That the future government of occupied countries would be decided after the war was over was the central message of Dimitrov's August speech; now it was being dictated by Moscow to the Yugoslavs for adoption at AVNOJ and then subsequently quoted in *Communist International* as one of the most important decisions taken at the assembly. To stress the non-governmental nature of AVNOJ in the eyes of the Comintern, the only report of its session was published alongside a report of the Anti-Fascist Conference of Women, as if the two were of equal standing.[62] In February 1943 the Comintern dropped a broad hint that Tito should form some sort of coalition government and open up negotiations with one of the Croatian Peasant Party leaders, Subašić.[63]

With a similar view to the diplomatic future of Europe, the Comintern resolved a dispute between the Yugoslav Communist Party and the Italian Communist Party in favour of the Italians. This requires some explanation. Until autumn 1942, the Yugoslav Communist Party continued to play the role of leading party which it had acquired in the period 1939–41. It was the only party with which the Comintern had secure and regular contact throughout the war, and via the Zagreb centre contact was maintained with central Europe and the Balkans.[64] Through Yugoslavia the Comintern also succeeded in sending agents into occupied countries. In July 1941 two Austrians were smuggled into their homeland, and while they could have been sent prior to June 1941, in February 1942 and April 1942 respectively the Comintern asked for Yugoslav help in sending agents to Bulgaria and Austria.[65]

The major party with which the Yugoslav party was still in touch was the Italian party. Relations between the two parties had been soured by the arrest of one of the Italian leaders based in Yugoslavia, Martini; for this the Italians naturally, if unreasonably, blamed the Yugoslavs. Nevertheless Yugoslavia remained the only route for contacts between the Comintern and the Italian Communist Party. It was via Tito that Togliatti sought to re-establish links with his party in December 1941 and Dimitrov clearly expected to receive reports from Italy from this source.[66]

During the spring of 1942 the Slovene section of the Yugoslav Communist Party handed over 30,000 lira to Martini's wife, presumably at the request of the Comintern. However, when the Yugoslav party requested a report on events in Italy which could be forwarded to Moscow, the Italian party leader Massola refused to comply. He insisted, citing Martini's arrest, that the Yugoslav party was full of police agents. Reporting this state of affairs to Moscow, Tito made it clear that he was prepared to cut off all aid to the Italian party if it did not take a more comradely attitude. He concluded his report: 'I think what is needed is for me to be given a mandate to control their work.'[67]

As well as the tension over the fate of Martini, who died in prison in September 1942, the two parties were not agreed about which of them should organize the population of Trieste and the nearby coast. To the Yugoslavs, Radio Free Milan seemed to be putting out chauvinist propaganda, as Tito made clear in the above-mentioned report. Sometime in September or October Tito sent a telegram to Massola outlining his views on Trieste, but the Comintern decided in November 1942 that the Italian party should be responsible for organizing resistance on that part of the coast claimed by Yugoslavia but part of pre-war Italy. Yugoslavia's brief spell as the Comintern's most favoured party was over and Tito's thoughts of running the Italian as well as the Yugoslav Parties remained a pipe-dream.[68]

Precisely what the anti-sectarian line might mean in the field was made clear in classes given at the Comintern School in Siberia in the late autumn of 1942 and early spring of 1943. Scarcely a day passed without lectures on the dangers of sectarianism, defined as 'a damaging political and ideological notion in the working class movement which seeks to deny the need for a policy of alliances between the working class and other strata and thus isolate the Party from the masses'. The party instead should set aside all its distinctive objectives and show itself the most vigorous of anti-Hitler forces. In that way it could still achieve 'decisive influence'.[69]

An incident recalled by W. Leonhard, one of the students at the school, shows just how far Communists were expected to go in sinking their differences with other groups. In one of the seminars, an Italian group suggested that, with liberation by the British and Americans increasingly likely, the Italian partisans should find safe hiding places for their weapons to avoid their having to be surrendered to the Allies. This 'sectarian' attitude was condemned in the strongest possible terms; it was nothing less than aiding and abetting Hitler, they were told.[70]

The dissolution of the Comintern was the logical consequence of Stalin's new diplomacy. Even with the campaign against sectarianism well underway, the *Communist International* could hardly help printing statements which sounded rather too revolutionary. Despite the commitment to a broad national front, the Comintern journal continued to stress that the working class would make a unique contribution to the operation and ultimately the success of such a front. An article on the Czechoslovak resistance in the issue for January 1943 stressed that the more quickly factory committees were established by the workers, the more quickly would victory be achieved. The factory-owning patriotic bourgeoisie might not have agreed.[71]

Similarly, the May Day issue for 1943 pointed out to readers that it was only with the involvement of the workers and 'vanguard anti-fascists', i.e. Communists, that the national fronts really became effective. The same issue reminded readers that in May 1939 the Communists had called for unity, both within states and internationally; they had been ignored and the war had followed. Self-righteous remarks of this kind were hardly conducive to the harmony of the Grand Alliance, and might also remind employers that the pre-war popular front had seemed a very frightening animal indeed. For Stalin it therefore made sense to give a clear sign to the world that the new national fronts and the old popular fronts were not one and the same thing.[72]

The idea of dissolving the Comintern was not entirely new. It had first been canvassed as early as 1938 in discussion about its future role in North and South America. The explanation put forward by Dimitrov then was similar to that used in 1943: it would disappear, as Marx's First International had disappeared, when it had served the purpose for which it had been created.[73] Dissolution was again discussed by Dimitrov in the summer of 1940, presumably in the context of a concession to the 'Anti-Comintern' powers; in November 1940 the US Communist Party, for example, actually left the Comintern.[74]

The resolution of the executive dissolving the organization was signed on 15 May 1943. All the circumstances suggest that whatever enthusiasm there might have been for dissolving the Comintern in the era of the anti-Comintern pact, Stalin's decision to dissolve it when the international climate was improving took the leadership by surprise. A month passed before a communiqué could be issued showing the support of thirty Communist parties for the decision.[75] The Yugoslav Communist V. Vlahović, present at the final meeting as the leader of the Youth International (KIM), recalled that the presidium was far from convinced of the necessity for the move, but would not and could not challenge Stalin.[76] But not all the Comintern officials opposed the decision. Fischer and Leonhard seem to have reflected the views of many when they expressed the hope that a decentralized Communist movement would be better suited to the post-war world.[77] Togliatti expressed views similar to these at the dissolution meeting itself. Talking of possible new forms of international co-operation, he mentioned the regional collaboration of parties with similar prospects and problems, 'polycentrism' before the event.[78]

The official explanation, that the Comintern had simply served its historical purpose, had a certain logic. Students at the Comintern school were told that the decision was actually the logical consequence of the Seventh Comintern Congress resolution giving Communist parties greater autonomy. The various Communist parties did indeed face very different tasks depending on whether they operated in Allied or Axis territory.[79] The Comintern had already changed. The wartime evacuation to the Siberian town of Ufa had resulted in a series of organizational changes which amounted to the dissolution of the old Comintern with its sections, secretaries, offices, paperwork, and agents. To quote Ceretti, one of the leading activists in Radio Free Milan, the evacuation meant that the Comintern as a collective organization for world revolution was dead. There remained in Ufa only radio stations. All the Comintern's Moscow-based activists spent the first two years of the war preparing radio broadcasts for occupied, Allied or neutral Europe.[80]

The dissolution occurred at the moment staff were to move back to Moscow from Ufa, when the question of whether the Comintern would continue to do no more than broadcast, or otherwise revive its former activities, was apposite. Ceretti assumed that Togliatti had been summoned to an 'important meeting' to discuss not the dissolution of the Comintern but to draw up plans to go beyond radio propaganda and start parachuting cadres into Europe to reinforce the party at home.[81] This was precisely what Stalin did not want to happen, not simply because this would upset his new allies, but because Stalin himself did not want a strengthened Communist movement to come under any sort of international control. After all, for the first time in his life it looked as if he would have to take seriously the prospect of successful revolutions elsewhere in Europe and in these circumstances an intermediary body like the Comintern would be a nuisance.[82]

In fact the dissolution meant that very little changed. Political cadres were transferred *en masse* either to the radio stations or to 'Institute No 205', which served as a centre for providing material to be used by all the foreign-language radios. Secretarial staff and typists worked for the Dissolution Commission which Dimitrov headed and operated for about two years. Dimitrov headed the Foreign Department of the CPSU Central Committee, responsible to Zhdanov as the Comintern had been ultimately all along. Dimitrov still sent advice to Communist party leaders, while representative of foreign parties served as the link between the individual parties and their country's specialists in the Foreign Department of the CPSU. Deprived of a forum for airing their common concerns, they would meet informally in the Hotel Lux where they still lived.[83]

The dissolution of the Comintern enabled Tito to declare AVNOJ the government of Yugoslavia and form a government based on the wartime liberation committees, the sort of new governmental structure called for in 1940 by Diaz. In France and Italy the parliamentary activity of the Communist parties was far closer to the tactics called for by Togliatti in Spain in 1938. In Greece the tactics to be pursued by the Communist party in this regard were obscured by the outbreak of civil war, a war seen by the Yugoslav party as no less crucial to the future of Europe than the Spanish Civil War had once been. Without the Comintern to guide them, Communist leaders were pursuing very different roads to socialism.

The decision to found the Cominform seems to have been as abrupt as the decision to dissolve the Comintern. Communist leaders were given hardly a week's warning of the decision to convene a founding conference in Poland in September 1947.[84] Although the Yugoslavs had requested a new co-ordinating body for the Communist movement in 1945 and 1946, and the Hungarians had made similar proposals,[85] it was once again the international situation which prompted Stalin to act. As Malenkov pointed out at the foundation conference, periodic bilateral meetings between parties were not enough when Britain and America were planning to use Marshall Aid to turn sovereign states into vassals.[86]

As in the era of the Nazi–Soviet Pact, 'sectarianism' suddenly ceased to be a dirty word, and the whole controversy about Togliatti's role in Spain was rehearsed again, only this time it was his policies in Italy from 1944–7 which were criticized, as were those of Thorez and the French Communist Party; the Yugoslavs now took the place of the Spaniards as prosecuting council. Their bitter denunciation of the Italian Communist Party was full of quotes from Togliatti. The Italians had been opportunist and had seriously believed in a peaceful parliamentary road to socialism even under imperialism. Instead of creating anti-Fascist unity 'from below' they had done so 'from above' based on a simple coalition with equal representation for different parties. While the Polish and Bulgarian communists had secured a dominant position in the armed struggle, the Italians had backed down.[87]

Their worst error had been to slow down the revolution in the north of the country ostensibly in order to prevent the north being divided from the south. However all this had achieved was the loss of all their positions in the resistance and the surrender of their arms. Worse still, the Yugoslavs had explained to their Italian comrades, both during and after the war, what insurrection was all about, but had been ignored. The Italians had simply been obsessed with the fear of being tricked into a 'provocation', a premature uprising which would divorce the party from the masses.

The Yugoslav case concluded by turning to the situation in Greece. Neither the French nor the Italian Parties had pulled their weight in supporting Greece while Yugoslavia, Albania, and Bulgaria had come under imperialist attack for their readiness to back a partisan war. The Greek party was actually in a better situation than the Italian and the French parties, however, because it was staging a counteroffensive. 'If every Party made Greece the concern of progressive humanity, if every Party rose up to defend Greece, that would create an obstacle to American intervention. One of the results of this conference should be to reinforce our aid to Greece.' The Yugoslavs could have been Spanish 'sectarians' denouncing the socialist policy of non-intervention in the Spanish Civil War.[88]

When briefing his delegation to the conference, Togliatti had warned that if the subject of Greece came up, the conference should be reminded that if Italy were turned into a second Greece the interests of the Soviet Union would not be served. That was indeed the case. While the Italian and French parties were made to eat humble pie at the foundation conference, and the Soviet representative Zhdanov rubbed home the point that they were being asked to make fundamental changes in strategy and not minor adjustments, the impassioned Yugoslav appeal for aid to Greece was not repeated by the Soviet Party and was quietly ignored. The future of Greece had, after all, been decided in Moscow between Churchill and Stalin. Stalin wanted to make use of the Yugoslavs' revolutionary fervour, but he did not share it.[89]

When, after the foundation conference, the Yugoslavs drew up plans for the absorption of Albania and began discussing with Bulgaria the possibility of a Balkan Federation which would include Greece, Stalin summoned Tito and Dimitrov to Moscow. This was Stalin's final intervention, There, on 10 February, they were told that Bulgaria and Yugoslavia could form a confederation at once, but any broader scheme was quite out of the question.[90] Dimitrov accepted Stalin's ruling, making the idea of federation with Bulgaria alone suddenly unattractive to the Yugoslavs. On 12 February the latter were forced to agree to undertake no foreign-policy initiatives without the agreement of the Soviet Union. The way was paved for the open break of June 1948 and Yugoslavia's expulsion from the Cominform.[91]

Between 1938 and 1948, then, the international Communist movement wrestled with two related issues: first, whether the struggle against Fascism should or could result in socialist revolution, and, second, whether the Communist Party could best prove its commitment to democracy, and thus earn the respect and support of the masses, by loyalty to a parliamentary system or the construction of new democratic forms. The Togliatti and 'sectarian' tendencies articulated these competing viewpoints.

During these years, however, the movement remained ultimately subservient to the foreign-policy dictates of Stalin who shifted support from one tendency to the other as the world situation changed. This use of the Comintern and Cominform for foreign-policy ends prevented either strategy from being pursued consistently enough for it to win the support of the broader public. Polycentrist Euro-Communism and self-managed non-alignment emerged later as different Communist responses to the Stalinist dead end, and both have their origins in this troubled decade.

NOTES

1 P. Spriano, *Stalin and the European Communists* (London, 1985); F. Claudin, *The Communist Movement from Comintern to Cominform* (London, 1975).
2 For Stalin's methods of rule, see J. Arch Getty, *The Origins of the Great Purge* (Cambridge, 1986). Dimitrov's ideas are most fully developed in his speech to the Seventh Congress of the Comintern: G. Dimitrov, *For the Unity of the Working Class against Fascism* (London, 1975).
3 M. T. Meshcheryakov, *Ispanskaya respublika i Komintern* (Moscow, 1981), p. 141.
4 E. Fischer, *An Opposing Man* (London, 1974), p. 289; E. Castro Delgado, *J'ai perdu la foi à Moscou* (Paris, 1950), p. 207.
5 P. Togliatti, *Opere*, IV, vol. I, pp. 327, 331 (Report of 12 March 1939) and 358 (Report of 25 May 1939); Meshcheryakov, op. cit., p. 118.
6 On the Spanish Communists' attitude to the elections, see Meshcheryakov, op. cit., pp. 116–20, 128 and M. T. Meshcheryakov, *Vsya zhizn – bor'ba* (Moscow, 1971), p. 151. On the attitude of Communist ministers, see Togliatti, op. cit., p. 361.
7 P. Togliatti, *Escritos sobre la guerra de España* (Barcelona, 1980), p. 197.
8 Fischer, op. cit., p. 17.
9 Togliatti, *Opere*, pp. 377, 384–6, 392.
10 ibid, pp. 330–1, 337.

11 Claudin, op. cit., p. 237–8.
12 ibid., p. 234.
13 This open reference to hegemony was made in spite of a letter from Togliatti to the Comintern in August 1937 asking for action to be taken against those calling for hegemony, a point made to a delegation of Spanish Communists then in Moscow. See K. K. Shirinya and I. N. Ksenofontov, 'Georgi Dimitrov i natsionalno-revolyutsionnata voyna v Ispaniya', in *Georgi Dimitrov i borbata za os'shchestvyavane na novata strategiya i taktika na Kominterna* (Sofia, 1972) p. 366 (hereafter *Dimitrov Collection*).
14 Meshcheryakov, *Vsya zhizn*, p. 153; J. Diaz, *Tres años de lucha* (Bucharest, 1974) p. 520 (report to November 1937 plenum of the central committee), and 539 (article in 'Nuestra Bandera', February 1938).
15 This was openly suggested in an article in the Madrid-based 'Mundo Obrero': see Meshcheryakov, *Ispanskaya respublika*, p. 141.
16 The majority of the Spanish Communist Party was in fact 'sectarian'. Togliatti's problems in getting the party to accept his views reinforce an impression of strength. According to Togliatti's own reports Diaz and Dolores Ibarruri acted as 'sectarians' on occasion. Madrid was a veritable nest of 'sectarians', while the problem was most pronounced among the rank and file. There were numerous discussions between the Politburo and the Comintern during April 1938. At an enlarged Politburo meeting 'bitter disputes' occurred on the subject before the famous '13-point' programme for democracy was agreed. The May central committee plenum, however, endorsed the programme unanimously. See ibid.; Meshcheryakov, *Vsya zhizn*, pp. 162–7; Togliatti, *Escritos*, p. 197; J. Hernandez, *La Grande Trahison* (Paris, 1953), pp. 136–46.
17 Togliatti, *Opere*, pp. 385, 395. The decision of the Politburo to support Togliatti on this matter became a source of great controversy. The decisions made on 6 March were contradictory. In the morning it decided on the orderly evacuation from Spain of as many cadres as possible. In the evening it met again, when Ibarruri and others had gone, and decided that Togliatti and a few others should stay on and try to negotiate. One of those evacuated, Manuel Taguena, felt that he had been tricked into leaving Spain, especially when he heard on reaching France that some Communists had defied Togliatti and were indeed fighting Casado. Had Togliatti wanted known 'sectarians' out of the way? Togliatti recognized in his own report that not many of those Politburo members present at the meeting had shared his point of view. See ibid., pp. 395–8; M. Taguena, *Testimoni de dos Guerros* (Mexico, 1973), pp. 315–19.
18 Meshcheryakov, *Vsya zhizn*, p. 180; J. Urban, *Moscow and the Italian Communist Party* (Ithaca, NY, 1986), p. 150; J. Estruch, *El PCE en la Clandestinidad* (Barcelona, 1978), p. 50. Santiago Carillo's suggestion that there were no great controversies (see his *Dialogue on Spain* (London, 1976)) is hard to accept.
19 Taguena, op. cit., p. 344; Estruch, op. cit., p. 50.
20 J. Diaz, 'Ob urokakh voyny ispanskogo naroda', *Bolshevik*, January 1940, p. 34. While Togliatti was not mentioned by name, the Casado affair was discussed in the following terms: 'In the face of an inevitable attack by the enemy, and concerned most of all with the situation at the front, the Party disregarded the question of mobilising the masses in the struggle against betrayal and did not put down the mutiny although it had the necessary force to do so.'
21 ibid.
22 Castro Delgado, op. cit., pp. 50–1; Carillo, op. cit., p. 66.
23 M. Adereth, *The French Communist Party: a Critical History* (Manchester, 1985), p. 92; G. Bocca, *Palmiro Togliatti* (Rome, 1973), p. 331; G. Cerreti, *Con Togliatti e Thorez* (Milan, 1973), p. 204; P. Spriano, *Il Compagno Ercoli* (Rome, 1980), p. 174.
24 D. E. Kunina and V. M. Endakova, 'Georgi Dimitrov i borbata za s'zdavane na natsionalni

frontove protiv fashizma v perioda na vtorata svetovna voyna', in *Dimitrov Collection*, p. 476.
25 'Die Kriegsverbrecher', *Communist International*, 10, 1939 (hereafter *CI*: references for the years 1939–May 1941 are to the German edition and from June 1941–1943 to the Russian edition). Despite the journal being dated October, this article was clearly written in September. Spriano dates the unpublished resolution as 7 September: see *Stalin*, p. 110.
26 'Ein Kriegziel wird gesucht', *CI*, 11, 1939; J. E. McSherry, *Stalin, Hitler, and Europe, 1939–41* (New York, 1970), p. 9.
27 W. Pieck 'Um was gebt es in diesem Krieg', *CI*, December 1939.
28 Statement by the German, Austrian and Czech Communist parties, *CI*, December 1939; and Kunina and Endakova, op. cit., p. 478.
29 The attacks on Leon Blum were particularly vituperative, see M. Thorez, 'Das ist Leon Blum', *CI*, 1, 1940.
30 P. Wieden (pseudonym), 'Einige Bemerkerkungen zur Frage des Imperialismus', *CI* 11–12, 1940; for Dimitrov's views, see Spriano, *Stalin*, p. 122.
31 Fischer, op. cit., p. 345; Castro Delgado, op. cit., p. 60.
32 McSherry, op. cit., p. 40.
33 For 'Soviet Bulgaria', see T. Angelova, 'Georgi Dimitrov i borbata na BKP za obedinyavane na demokratichnite sili protiv fashizma i voynata, za pobedata na sotsialisticheskata revolyutsiya v B'lgariya', *Dimitrov Collection*, p. 542; for 'Soviet Slovakia', see V. Mastny, *Russia's Road to Cold War* (New York, 1979), p. 90; for 'Soviet Slovenia' and 'Soviet Macedonia', see U. Massola, *Memorie* (Rome, 1972), p. 100, and *Izvori za Istoriyu SKJ: Dokumenti Centralnih Organa KPJ, NOR, i Revolucija 1941–45* (Belgrade, 1985), vol. 2, p. 38. (The *Izvori* started to be published in 1985, with many volumes envisaged over the years. For simplicity, documents for 1941 have been cited from the published volumes 1 and 2, and subsequent documents are cited according to the date of the original document to enable them to be traced in the volumes as they appear. Nothing is cited that was not marked 'for publication' in the relevant archive.)
34 Fischer, op. cit., p. 345; Kunina and Endakova, op. cit., p. 481.
35 Fischer, op. cit., pp. 357–8.
36 Adereth, op. cit., p. 102; Kunina and Endakova, op. cit., p. 483.
37 Adereth, op. cit., p. 102; Kunina and Ednakova, op. cit., pp. 485–8; Spriano, *Ercoli*, p. 190.
38 McSherry, op. cit., p. 110ff.
39 'Dokumente', *CI*, 5, 1941; K. Funk, 'Karl Liebknecht und Rosa Luxemburg: Internationalisten der Tat', *CI*, 2, 1941 (this article did not appear in the Russian edition).
40 Taguena, op. cit., p. 401; J. Bell, *The Bulgarian Communist Party from Blagoev to Zhivkov* (Hoover Institution, Stanford, 1985), p. 65.
41 The Yugoslav Communist Party–Comintern correspondence is reproduced in the appendices to vols 5 (p. 197) and 6 (p. 201) of Tito's *Collected Works* (Belgrade, 1977). For the Italian Communist Party incident, see Kunina and Endakova, op. cit., pp. 486, 489–90.
42 For Dimitrov's telegram to Tito, see the latter's *Collected Works*, vol. 6 (p. 215); for Tito's commitment to social transformation, see accounts of the 'May Meeting' of the KPJ Central Committee, in particular, in English, S. Clissold, *Djilas: the Progress of a Revolutionary* (London, 1983), p. 48.
43 V. Cenčić, *Enigma Kopinič* (Belgrade, 1983), vol. 1, p. 117.
44 ibid., p. 129; V. Massola, 'La direzione del Pci in Italia, 1940–43', *Critica Marxista*, March/April 1976, p. 157; Massola, *Memorie*, p. 90; E. R. Terzuolo, *Red Adriatic: The Communist Parties of Italy and Yugoslavia* (London, 1985). A short note on the tension between the two parties is in order. To the Italians it seemed that much of the promised

support from the Yugoslavs never materialized, or was of poor quality. However, there was also a point of principle at stake. The Yugoslavs argued that when the French Communist Party had played host to foreign communist parties, it had not kept close enough control over the operations. Close control was even more important in the case of Yugoslavia, where the host party was illegal. The Yugoslav request for details of all Italian safe houses was seen as interference by the Italians, but an elemental precaution against *provocateurs* by the Yugoslavs, who felt it was only in this way that they could fulfil the role given them by the Comintern.

45 *Izvori*, vol. 1, pp. 63–4. Tito was being slightly dishonest here. The uprising had already started.
46 V. Vlahović, 'L'internationalisme a l'oeuvre', *Est et Ouest*, 16–31 May 1959, p. 8; T. Angelova, op. cit., p. 543.
47 B. Voinich, 'Boevoy primer Yugoslavii', *CI*, 3/4, 1942. See also Castro Delgado, op. cit., p. 181.
48 'Edinyi antigitlerovski front narodov', *CI*, 5, 1942, and 7, 1942.
49 *Izvori*, vol. 1, p. 63.
50 J. Jablonicky, *Z Ilegality do Povstania* (Bratislava, 1969), pp. 71–5; F. Janaček *et al.*, 'KPC i politica narodnog fronta', in P. Morača *et al.* (eds), *Narodni front i komunisti* (Belgrade, 1967), pp. 221–3.
51 Voinich, op. cit.
52 'Bit' zakhvatchikov vo vsekh okkupirovannykh stranakh', *CI*, 7, 1942.
53 Kunina and Endakova, op. cit., p. 504.
54 *CI*, 10/11, 1942.
55 Urban, op. cit., p. 159.
56 Jablonicky, op. cit., p. 199.
57 Massola, 'La direzione', p. 172.
58 'Edinyi antigitlerovskii front narodov', *CI*, 2/3, 1943.
59 *Izvori*, vol. 2, p. 232.
60 *Izvori*, 13 February 1942; 22 March 1942; and June 1942. Yugoslav historians, anxious to find early examples of conflict between Tito and the Comintern, and thus precedents for 1948, have portrayed Dimitrov's correspondence with Tito in the spring of 1942 as direct criticism of Tito's policies: see P. Morača 'Odnosi izmedu KPJ i Kominterne od 1941 g. do 1943 g.' *Jugoslovenski Istorijski Časopis*, 1, 1969. The publication of this correspondence in full leaves this author with the impression that Dimitrov sincerely wanted to discover what was happening in Yugoslavia, and was unwilling to accept reports of Milhailovič's collaboration with Fascist forces until confirmed by other sources. Even before such confirmation arrived in April 1942 (*Izvori*, 19 April 1942), however, the tone of the exchange was comradely, even friendly. In one telegram (*Izvori*, early March 1942) Dimitrov urged Tito to be as flexible as possible and to remember the Soviet Union's diplomatic links with the government in exile, but ended 'I firmly clasp your warrior's hand'.
61 *Izvori*, 9 August and 13 November 1942.
62 'Edinyi antigitlerovskii front narodov', *CI*, 1 and 2/3, 1943.
63 *Izvori*, early January 1943.
64 Cerreti, op. cit., p. 261; Cenčić, op. cit., vol. 2, pp. 99, 65.
65 *Izvori*, vol. 1, p. 80; 17 February 1942; 29 April 1942.
66 ibid., vol. 2, p. 425; Terzuolo, op. cit., p. 19.
67 *Izvori*, 11 July 1942.
68 Terzuolo, op. cit., p. 19; *Jesen 1942: Korespondenca Edvarda Kardelia in Borisa Kidriču* (Ljubljana, 1963), pp. 24, 404, 559, 569; Cerreti, op. cit., pp. 255–6.
69 W. Leonhard, *Child of the Revolution* (Chicago, 1958), pp. 255–6.
70 ibid., pp. 260–1.

71 J. Shverma, 'Problemy natsional'no-osvoboditel'noy bor'by v Chekhoslovakii', *CI*, 1, 1943.
72 'K pervomu mayu', *CI*, 4, 1943.
73 E. Ravines, *The Yenan Way* (Connecticut, 1972), p. 260.
74 Spriano, *Stalin*, p. 137; Claudin, op. cit., p. 42; A. Kriegel 'La Dissolution du Komintern', *Revue d'Histoire de la Deuxieme Guerre Mondiale*, October, 1967, p. 38.
75 Kriegel, op. cit., p. 35.
76 Vlahovič, op. cit., p. 8.
77 Leonhard, op. cit., p. 276; Fischer, op. cit., p. 400.
78 Vlahovič, op. cit., p. 8.
79 Leonhard, op. cit., pp. 271–3; M. Burmeister, *Dissolution and Aftermath of the Communist International: Experiences and Observations, 1937–43* (New York, 1955), pp. 20–1.
80 Cerreti, op. cit., p. 261.
81 ibid., p. 279. According to Castro Delgado, some Comintern officials had already returned to Moscow, see op. cit., p. 207.
82 Taguena, op. cit., p. 464; Urban, op. cit., p. 155; Mastny, op. cit., p. 96 (quoting Hernandez).
83 Burmeister, op. cit., pp. 21–4; Bocca, op. cit., p. 355. As the *Izvori* show, Dimitrov continued to receive almost daily reports from Tito.
84 E. Reale, *Nascita del Cominform* (Milan, 1958), p. 17.
85 G. Boffa, *Storia dell'Unione Sovietica* (Milan, 1979), vol. 2, 347; Reale, op. cit., p. 122.
86 ibid., p. 64.
87 Claudin, op. cit., p. 383.
88 Reale, op. cit., pp. 121–2.
89 ibid., p. 147.
90 Boffa, op. cit., p. 397. Tito did not in fact go to Moscow, but sent Kardely in his place.
91 V. Dedijer, *The Battle Stalin Lost* (London, 1979), p. 33.

ABBREVIATIONS

AVNOJ   *Antifašističko veće narodnog oslobodjenje Jugoslavije* (Anti-Fascist Council of National/People's Liberation of Yugoslavia)

NKVD   People's Commissariat of Internal Affairs (The Soviet security service, precursor of the KGB)

2 The Parti Communiste Français and the French resistance in the Second World War

LYNNE TAYLOR

The question of the involvement of the Parti Communiste Français (PCF) in the resistance in France against the Nazi occupation still raises controversy. Of especial interest and debate is the PCF's degree of involvement in the resistance during the first year of the occupation, from June 1940, when the German forces swept through France, until June 1941, when the Germans invaded the Soviet Union and in so doing broke the Nazi–Soviet non-aggression pact. The pact had created a crisis of policy in the PCF, and the story of what the PCF did and did not do during this year is a complex one. A full appreciation of this story requires a brief recounting of the history of the party in the months preceding the invasion and fall of France.

By the last years of the 1930s, the popular front in France was in serious trouble. The broad unity of the front was falling apart over the dilemma of Munich and the mounting threat of Nazi Germany. The decrees of the Daladier government, issued in November 1938, further split the syndicalist movement. These decrees severely curtailed many of the gains made by the labour movement during the decade, and the attack on workers' rights was combined with official tolerance of a campaign against the Communist Party. However, it was the Nazi–Soviet pact which ended the popular front once and for all.

The Nazi–Soviet non-aggression pact of August 1939 took the majority of the French Communist Party by surprise, as it had other European Communist parties. In line with Comintern doctrine and the principles of the popular front, the PCF had been following a policy of aggressive anti-Fascism. Yet, without warning or explanation, the Fascists were now the allies and Moscow demanded that the French abandon their anti-Fascist tactics and programmes and focus their attack instead on the British and French, who were now to be held primarily responsible for the imperialist war being fought. The disillusionment and confusion of French Communists were profound, and militants left the party in droves. One-third of the party's parliamentary delegation resigned.

The French government had been waging a war against the syndicalist movement for months, with the November 1938 decrees, for example, and Daladier's harsh suppression of the general strike of 30 November 1938. The decrees were ostensibly a response to the Munich crisis and in the interests of national defence. In order to build up national production levels and to improve national defences, the 'décrets-lois visaient à démanteler le régime de la semaine de 40 heures, des conventions collectives syndicats-patronat, afin de restaurer les profits industriels'.[1] In response, the CGT called for a general strike on 30 November to protest at this severe curtailment of the gains workers had won during the popular front period. The worker response was overwhelming, the government's reaction quick and harsh, and the strike was suppressed brutally.

However, the Nazi–Soviet non-aggression pact provided the government with a perfect excuse to escalate the conflict. The pact was condemned as defeatist, and therefore treasonable, in spite of the fact that the remaining Communist deputies in the Chamber argued that support of it did not necessarily preclude a defensive war against the 'Hitlerite aggressor'.[2] Indeed, on 2 September, they had unanimously voted in favour of military credits for the government. Despite this demonstration of patriotism, the PCF was declared illegal on 26 September.

The reaction of the Communist deputies was to create a new party, the Workers' and Peasants' Group. This group was registered with the *Journal Officiel* on 29 September, and issued a formal protest against the banning of the PCF. On 1 October, the Communist deputies addressed a letter to the President of the Chamber of Deputies, calling for an accord with the USSR, pulling France out of the war and reaching a just peace. The government's response was to adjourn Parliament and to arrest the Communist deputies.[3] With this, the government's attack on the party began in earnest. The party was outlawed, its papers banned, its parliamentary representatives expelled and thousands of party members arrested:

> (l)es mandats électifs du communisme n'existent plus. Trois cents conseils municipaux communistes ont été suspendus. En tout, deux mille sept cent soixante-dix-huit élus communistes ont été déchus de leur mandat. Les deux quotidiens, *L'Humanité* qui tirait a 500,000 exemplaires et *Ce Soir* a 250,000 exemplaires, ont été supprimés, ainsi que 158 autres feuilles. 620 syndicats ont été dissous. 11,000 perquisitions ont eu lieu, 675 dissolutions de groupements politiques à tendance communistes ont été prononcées. En outre, les militants ont été traqués, 3,400 ont été arretés au mars. Il y a de nombreux internements dans les camps de concentration. 10,000 sanctions ont été prises contre les fontionnaires communistes.[4]

The PCF was thrown into total chaos, the organization shattered. By mid-October, the party leadership was split between Moscow (André Marty and the International), Belgium (where Eugene Fried, Maurice Thorez, and Jacques Duclos had fled), and Paris (Benoît Frachon and Charles Tillon).[5] Such a situation exacerbated the chaos and badly hindered the party's ability to reorganize itself and to coordinate efforts and policy. At this stage, the government's pursuit intensified, if anything, as the scope of the arrests expanded. Not only were those Communists arrested who were obviously leading figures in the Communist organizations, but all persons known to be Communist were subject to harrassment and arrest. Communists within all branches of the syndicalist movement, the CGT (Confédération Générale du Travail), specific trade unions, and any other workers' organizations, were sought out and interned. Given the relentlessness of the persecution, and the anarchic state of the party, it is small wonder that the party's stand on international affairs and its role in them was a little vague.

From September 1939 until May 1940, the PCF's stance with regard to the war went through a gradual shift. The alternatives available to the party were extremely limited. To begin with, it was directed by Moscow to change the nature of its campaign in a radical way, from the anti-Fascism of the popular front to opposition to the imperialist war being waged by the British and French governments. In addition, without a party organization or structure there was little of a practical nature that could be done. Finally, it was not clear exactly what the party should be doing. The PCF was left with little else but propaganda.

Adereth[6] identifies four principle themes in the PCF's propaganda during the *drôle de guerre*: a conscientious effort to prove that the party was not defunct, but rather was alive and well; denunciation of the government for allowing Fascism to continue to prevail in France; continued praise of the peaceful policy and the socialist system of the USSR; and condemnation of the ongoing war of the rich against the popular masses – in the form of the Daladier decrees, the steep inflation, and the loss of the gains made by the working class during the popular front.

Initially, the PCF's stance was one that did not object to the war itself (witness the Communist deputies' vote in favour of military credits on 2 September as noted above), but to the manner in which the French government was fighting it. It would be much better, the party argued, to enlist the aid of the unions and the people and to address the real threat, the Fascism that existed within France. This stance did not last long, and by the end of September 1939 the party's definition of the nature of the war had changed. The war was now seen as an imperialist one, imperialist on both sides. The party denounced the ruling class of France for its readiness to sell its country. In the same breath, it also demanded that the French government end French involvement in the war with a just peace, and that it sign an alliance with the Soviet Union. However, it was still unclear just exactly what the PCF rank and file were supposed to do. They had been told, when war broke out, that they were to join the armed forces and fight for France against the Fascist aggressors. They were still to join the armed forces, or remain there if already enlisted, but the cause for which they were to fight and the enemy they were to combat were less clear. They were told to fight against the war, for the peace, and against the French government, but not how they were supposed to conduct such a battle. Sabotage was not encouraged, which left them with propaganda, written and oral.[7]

Having been driven underground, the party had begun the slow process of regrouping and of building a small but efficient clandestine organization with an intelligence-gathering network and a propaganda machine. However, in the spring of 1940, a deeply demoralized and shattered PCF had still only just begun to rebuild itself into a clandestine structure when it was once again scattered before the wind by the German invasion in May.

The French government itself did not fare much better. Daladier, prime minister of France since 10 April 1938, was replaced by Paul Reynaud on 20 March 1940. With the German invasion and the swift collapse of the French forces, it was quickly obvious to the government and the military that a peace would have to be arranged. On 16 June 1940, two days after the fall of Paris, Marshal Pétain was selected as prime minister by the national assembly sitting in the spa town of Vichy. An armistice was signed with the Germans on 22 June. On 10 July, the national assembly authorized Pétain to assume full, autocratic powers pending a new constitution.[8]

The armistice effectively split France into four parts – the free zone to the south administered by the newly created Vichy government under Marshal Pétain, the occupied zone to the north under German occupation and Vichy administration, the prohibited zone (*zone interdite*) of Nord-Pas-de-Calais which was, from the moment of occupation, under direct German military administration as a part of the northern France–Belgium military district, and, finally, Alsace-Lorraine, which was annexed directly to Germany.

With the collapse of the French governmental administration in the face of the invading German forces, the persecution of the PCF subsided by default. However, the ensuing chaos and upheaval prevented the PCF from taking advantage of this. The breakdown in communications and transportation networks, and the major dislocation of population across the face of France in front of the German armies, all combined to rip asunder the clandestine organization the PCF had been so carefully reconstructing since being driven underground in 1939.

The historiography of what happened in the days preceding the fall of Paris is confused. Some Communist historians have, in the past, claimed that the party leadership approached the Reynaud government, using the Communist philosopher Georges Politzer as an intermediary, and offered to rally the masses in an armed defence of Paris. In return for their assistance, the Communists had five demands:

1 the character of the war was to become that of a national war of independence and freedom;
2 the government was to release from imprisonment all arrested Communist deputies and militants, as well as the tens of thousands of interned workers;
3 all enemy agents in Parliament, the ministries, and the General Staff were to be arrested;

4 a mass uprising was to be declared upon the fulfilment of the first three conditions; and
5 the people were to be armed and Paris transformed into an impenetrable fortress.[9]

However, it is far from certain that the offer was ever even made. The text of the conditions was not published until 1943 and the first account of the circumstances was published in 1951, in the novel by Louis Aragon, *Les Communistes*. According to Aragon's account, Frachon drafted the terms in the name of the central committee which was unable to meet due to police oppression. Apparently Anatole de Monzie, Minister of Public Works, had approached the Communists on 28 May. The PCF had been unable to reply until 6 June, due to the difficulties of communication between the government and the outlawed party. By that time de Monzie had been dismissed. Thus, according to Aragon, ended the proposal.[10]

Other historians are equally certain that it was not the Communists who called for one last stand against the Germans, but the French government. Edward Mortimer asserts that the French government considered sending Pierre Cot, the former Air Minister, to Moscow. The French were apparently hoping to persuade the USSR to provide them with aircraft, an idea that originated with de Monzie. He and Cot were on good terms both with the Soviet embassy and, if not with the PCF, then with individual Communists. In the end, Reynaud decided against the plan, for the USSR insisted on an official ambassador from France and to appoint Cot to that position would arouse right-wing opposition.[11] Rossi[12] also maintains that it was the French government who called for a last effort to resist the German invasion. The military governor of Paris, General Héring, called for such an effort when the Somme fell on 6 June. Rossi notes that the PCF journals said nothing of it at the time and several months later actually accused Héring of panicking the French population and aggravating the miseries of the mass exodus from the city with his vain appeals for resistance. The one man who could shed light on the incident, Georges Politzer, was executed by a Nazi firing squad in May 1942.[13] What is clear is that, in the absence of any encouragement from the government, the PCF failed to spark a revolt among Parisians against the German troops. On 14 June, the Germans marched into Paris unopposed.

As noted above, the PCF was only just beginning to rebuild its organization on a clandestine basis when the Germans invaded France. As the Germans moved through France, thousands of Communist prisoners of the Reynaud regime were moved south from prison to prison, ahead of the German advance. (Amouroux estimates the number interned to be approximately 18,000 by March 1940).[14] Although the PCF appealed to the French government to release the Communists and to allow them to assist in the battle against the Nazis, this appeal was ignored.[15] This dispersal of the Communists was further aggravated by the mass exodus from Paris, the centre of Communist activity and support, ahead of the invading army. Jacques Duclos writes that only about 200 Communists remained in Paris.[16] The PCF's membership was scattered throughout the country. Like all Frenchmen, the Communists were physically and psychologically exhausted. Their first preoccupations were food, shelter, employment, and locating friends and relatives. The leadership itself was dispersed: Thorez had fled to Moscow; Duclos' whereabouts at that time are not certain, and although there have been suggestions that he was in Paris, he remained uninvolved;[17] and the rest of the party's leading figures were arrested, prisoners of war, or on the run. With the breakdown in law and order and the chaos in the days after the German occupation, the nation's communications network had broken down. The outlying regions were cut off from Paris. For all of these reasons (the loss of leadership, members, and communications, as well as the general chaos) the PCF's organization once again fell apart.

The tasks facing the PCF were enormous. First and foremost, the party's entire organizational structure had to be recreated. Then, a programme of propaganda and of direct action had to be developed and launched. Once again, the organization had to be a clandestine one, a state with which the party already had some familiarity. The new structure was designed to maximize security. Each basic unit or cell was to consist of three people. Only one of these people was to act as liaison with other cells, while the other two members were left isolated.[18] The unoccupied zone was divided into ten sectors, each being autonomous.[19] Within every sector there were numerous *réseaux*, or cells, which reported to one of a number of *sections*, which in turn were part of one of several *fédérations*, all units established on the same principle of maximum security. At the peak of the organizational pyramid was the central committee in Paris. Each of these higher organizational bodies was directed by a leadership triangle. One person was responsible for propaganda, one for political work, and the third for mass work. The central committee (CC) retained ultimate authority over the party's activities.[20] At least, this was the structure in theory. Given the severe problems in communications and dislocation described above, the degree to which a system designed to be so highly centralized and closely controlled could properly function was minimal.

It was crucial that the PCF reach as many people as possible, and quickly. The support of the working class was deemed vital to the success of the party, so as early as August 1940 the party called upon Communists to form *comités populaires*. These were to operate at the municipal level and their ostensible purpose was to organize the care of the sick and the homeless and to help with the distribution of food.[21] The committees were also to take advantage of any issues that might be used to build opposition to the Vichy regime.[22] The popular committees were especially successful in the factories and in industrial regions, the traditional sources of PCF support. Their demands were simple, but impossible for the Vichy government to accept. They asked that the consumer goods factories be reopened, that the imprisoned militants be freed, that the food shortages be corrected, and that provision be made for 'des secours pour les chômeurs'. By the autumn, over 100 committees are said to have existed in the factories around Paris.[23] As well as using the popular committees as a way of reaching the masses, PCF members were encouraged to join legal organizations (the popular committees being illegal and in direct conflict with Pétainist organizations of the same nature) and to 'come out into the open', in an attempt to reach the general populace.

There were several risks involved in this approach. Although the Vichy police were also in the midst of reorganizing after France's defeat and had lost track of many Communists,[24] the breakdown in communications and the relative inexperience in clandestine activity of many of the party's new members made it easy for the police to infiltrate the newly-forming groups.[25] The Paris police especially were ardent in continuing to enforce the dissolution of the PCF and the battle against clandestine propaganda begun by Daladier in 1939. Thus, the reorganization was a costly exercise in terms of manpower for the party. In the first seven days of July 1940, in the region of Paris alone, ninety militants were arrested, nine clandestine propaganda organizations were destroyed and sixty-three Communists were interned.[26] In total, according to Amouroux's sources, from July to November 1940 there were 548 arrests, 328 administrative internments, and 35 propaganda organizations uncovered.[27] Ehrlich reports that from July to the end of the first week of September, the Paris police arrested 1,141 Communists and smashed 37 different propaganda groups.[28] Despite the disagreement in the literature as to the exact figures, all are agreed that the numbers were high and the cost to the party prohibitive.

The large number of arrests was also a result of the disastrous policy of fraternization advocated by the PCF in the first months of the occupation. It is uncertain whether Moscow dictated fraternization to the French Communist Party or not, although there is evidence to suggest so. In June, the PCF approached the German occupation administration with a request to be allowed to publish legally its newspaper *L'Humanité*, which had been banned by the French government in 1939 as a part of the general suppression of the Communist Party. Similar requests to legalize the Communist press were being made in other occupied countries at the same time, suggesting that the requests were initiated in Moscow.[29] It is generally accepted that the PCF did in fact make the request, despite the party's subsequent denial.

Amouroux provides the most detailed account of the request for authorization, based on the 5 December 1947 session of the PCF. One purpose of the meeting was to discuss the charges laid by Pierre de Chevigne against Denise Gillolin for her role in the fiasco of June 1940.[30] In June 1940, Denise Gillolin was secretary for the party's section in the 11th *arrondissement*.[31] On 20 June, she and two compatriots made contact with a printer, M. Dangon, who had printed *L'Humanité* in the past. They arranged for him to begin printing again and gave him 50,000 francs to cover initial costs. Gillolin's compatriots were Jeanne Schrocht and Maurice Tréand, a member of the party's central committee. At the hearing, Tréand confirmed that Gillolin was acting on his orders. He had believed at the time that, because there were similar Communist journals appearing in Belgium with the authorization of the German authorities, it would be simple to obtain permission for publication from the local authorities. Moments after the meeting with the local German *Propagandastaffel* to request authorization for publication, all three were arrested by the

French police for violating the September 1939 decree dissolving all Communist organizations and the August 1939 suspension of *L'Humanité*. Within days, the Communists were released at the express order of the German military administration. This move by the Nazis was part of a broader and short-lived policy of cautious cultivation of the Communists as potential allies.

As soon as Tréand and company were released, a second application was submitted. In the second application, Tréand specified the tasks that the new *L'Humanité* would undertake. Its objectives were to be to denounce British imperialism, pursue a European peace, and fight for a French–Soviet pact of friendship. It would contain nothing that would upset the German occupiers.[32] The second application was submitted on 25 June and signed by two members of the party's central committee, Maurice Tréand and Jean Catelas.[33] The application was rejected. Adereth suggests that the Germans broke off negotiations when it became apparent that they would not be able to control the publication's contents. Initially, the Germans had been receptive to the idea, as long as the articles were to be subject to German censorship. Instead, they created their own newspaper entitled *la France au Travail*, with a format similar to that of *L'Humanité*. Adereth contends that the PCF's application was a tactical move, an attempt to take advantage of all legal possibilities. He identifies their mistake as the assumption that the Germans would respond favourably to the application.[34] Mortimer believes the application's rejection was a result of pressure from the French authorities, who were strongly anti-Communist.[35]

The official PCF account places the burden of the blame on the shoulders of a few over-zealous individuals within the party. Tréand was ostracized soon after the war when it became necessary for the party to repudiate his actions.[36] It is not known for certain whether he was acting on his own initiative or for the party when he made the applications. Several pieces of evidence seem to suggest that he was acting on behalf of the party: he was a member of the central committee, and the second application was co-signed by another member of the central committee, Jean Catelas. It is difficult to believe, even given the confusion of the time, that the central committee was completely unaware of his actions, especially as Catelas obviously knew and approved the action. It is also difficult to conceive of the source of the 50,000 francs given to the printer if the party's resources were not available. It seems more plausible that the PCF did, in fact, make the request to the German authorities.

Although the request failed, *L'Humanité* was published clandestinely and it continued to promote fraternization between French workers and German soldiers. In the 13 July edition, *L'Humanité* contained an article calling for a period of tacit *entente* between the Communists and the occupiers. It noted with satisfaction the increasing fraternization between German soldiers and French workers. Even as late as September, the party continued to state that its objective was to shed its illegal status and emerge into the open as the only way of regaining contact with, and the trust and support of, the general populace.[37] Rossi maintains that just as collaboration with Hitler was of tremendous advantage to the USSR, as it enhanced Soviet territory and prestige, so Franco-German fraternization was not a deviation from the party line, but rather a logical consequence of the PCF's subordination to Russian interests. Fidelity to Stalin required collaboration with Hitler.[38] Courtois points out that the French Communists were merely following in the tradition of 1917 when Lenin appealed for fraternization between the soldiers of all imperialist lands in the interests of the revolution.[39] The official Communist history, in contrast, maintains that this approach was adopted in order to gain German support for the creation of a popular Communist government within the framework of the Nazi–Soviet pact. Although the party had the best of intentions, the tactic resulted in confusion and a loss of zeal amongst its members.[40]

The tactic was also unsuccessful. It was soon clear that the Germans were not going to work with the Communists, but rather with Pétain and the Vichy regime in the continued suppression of the Communists.[41] The numerous arrests mentioned earlier provide concrete evidence of that. As the Vichy government's administration and policies began to coalesce, and the dictatorship gained firmer control, Vichy–German co-operation improved and the suppression of the Communists was stepped up. Initially, as was seen in the case of the application for the legalization of *L'Humanité*, the German occupying forces remained aloof from the Vichy government's persecution of the PCF. However, as scattered resistance to the Germans in the occupied zone began to develop, the German repression became heavier. Punishments were severe. On 14 August, the town of Royan was fined 3 million francs for the death of a German 'matelot'. On 12 September, a mechanic by the name of Marcel Drossier was sentenced to death for having damaged military equipment.[42]

The Vichy police were the spearhead of the anti-Communist witchhunt. The French police, especially in Paris, were already accustomed to ferreting out Communists, something they had been doing for almost a year. The Laval government had now created special brigades within the force expressly to combat Communist subversion. The German occupiers found it simpler and politically wiser to use the French police system for their interests. This became easier once the few members of the police force who were part of the resistance had been expunged.[43]

In October 1940, the Vichy police launched a great sweep against the PCF. This *grand coup de filet* was intended to decapitate the newly burgeoning secret Communist organization, which it very nearly did. Noguères estimates that 300 Communists were arrested in the first part of October,[44] and Michel reports 760 arrests over September and October.[45] Such persecution made the tasks of renewing contacts, regrouping, and reorganization slow, dangerous, and repetitious as newly-formed cells of the PCF were smashed by the police and had to be rebuilt.

The French Communists realized that not only was it necessary to rebuild the organizational structure of the party, but also that it was necessary to rebuild the party membership's morale, shattered by a succession of events; the Nazi–Soviet pact, the persecution of the PCF by the French government, the war, and the defeat.

Thus, a vital condition for keeping the French Communist Party alive was the creation of a renewed sense of identity within the membership. So the means of propaganda (newspapers, journals, tracts, pamphlets, and leaflets) became a crucial element in the PCF's operations in the months following the occupation. The tracts served as a means of and focus for obtaining and maintaining contact and for regrouping. Their purpose was to 'inform, educate, clarify'.[46]

The classic example of the Communist propaganda tracts was the 10 July Appeal. Traditionally, Communist historians have offered the July Appeal as proof of the continuing existence and struggle of the PCF. It has been used as evidence that the Communist Party was part of the resistance almost from the moment of occupation. However, more recently, French Communist historians have had to acknowledge the limitations of the Appeal as a call to resist. The July Appeal was intended as a statement of the party's official position regarding the French political situation. The Appeal soundly condemned both the leaders of the Third Republic and the Vichy regime, and proclaimed that the Communists were the only ones truly fighting for peace.[47] It attacked both capitalism and imperialism, and praised both the USSR and the Nazi–Soviet pact. It also attacked all those who were responsible for French misfortunes and were benefiting from the occupation. The one party that was not mentioned in the tract's sweeping condemnations was the German occupying force. The Appeal, signed by Maurice Thorez and Jacques Duclos, was carefully worded in order to avoid any attack on Hitler or on the occupying forces. The authors attacked the Vichy leadership, not as collaborators, but as a government of plutocrats and war profiteers.

The tract offered a political programme as a solution. It proposed the formation of a people's government led by the PCF. It called for a free and independent France linked by a pact of friendship with the USSR. Only in that way could true peace be obtained. Finally, the Appeal called for the transformation of the existing imperialist war into a revolutionary class war.[48] Although it made grand appeals, it failed to offer any indication of how to achieve these goals. At best, the Appeal would have served as a warning to the Germans that they could expect some form of resistance if they persisted in supporting Vichy. The Appeal's emphasis, however, was on economic recovery, not sabotage.[49] Even if there were no other problems with the Appeal, it would still be difficult to believe that it was a serious call to resist the occupation. Its emphasis on economic recovery and the careful phraseology that avoided any condemnation of the Germans make the suggestion implausible. The other problems with it only serve to heighten the implausibility.

There are differing dates suggested by historians for the actual publication of the Appeal. One point they all have been able to agree on, even the Communist historians, is that the 10 July Appeal was not published on 10 July. Jacques Duclos maintains in his memoirs that the Appeal was printed and distributed over the course of the summer months as a means of contact between the isolated militants. The tract was periodically revised in the light of current developments.[50] The tract could have been written no earlier than 13 July because it names ministers not announced until that day.⁵¹ Some accounts have the Appeal being written in July and published in different editions carrying different dates, 15 August being the most common.⁵² Others question even that dating. Rossi believes that the July Appeal was not published until after the war because its attitude had nothing in common with either the appeal made in July 1941 or with the 1943 brochure Thorez wrote in Moscow. He maintains that the Appeal was published in a false first issue of *L'Humanité* which was itself only published *after* the Liberation. The language and rhetoric jar with that of the tracts ostensibly published immediately before and after it.⁵³ The history of the party published by the PCF's central committee seems to concur with Rossi.⁵⁴ Amouroux also agrees that it must have been backdated. Finally, as he rightly points out, even if it was a genuine appeal to resist, it still failed to motivate and therefore, to all intents and purposes, it might as well not have existed.⁵⁵

L'Humanité and the July Appeal were not the only means of propaganda used by the French Communists. *L'Avant-Garde*, the journal of the young Communists, and *Les Cahiers du bolchévisme*, a doctrinal review, were both restarted and published frequently. Such publications had an important role in uniting the party's ranks and reaching the masses. In October 1940, 100,000 copies of *Letter to a Socialist Worker* were published. It stated that the PCF wished to unite with the Socialist rank and file, who were leaderless now that the SFIO had virtually collapsed. In December 1940, *Letter of a Radical Working Man* was published, appealing to the patriotism of the peasantry and middle class.⁵⁶ In November, *Letter to Communist Militants*, signed by both Thorez and Duclos, was published. It attacked the Pétain government, declaring that France should fight neither the British nor the Germans. This brochure is an example of the precarious neutrality that the PCF was attempting to maintain.⁵⁷ The central committee's *Manifesto* was also issued in November. It adopted a slightly different, more strident tone than previous publications. It attacked the bourgeois governments of the west for having 'sold out' to Hitler and Mussolini. The tone was anti-Fascist and anti-Hitler, but only as a means of furthering the blistering attack on the western imperialist powers. The PCF proposed an alternative, a people's government that would liberate the national territory, sign a friendship agreement with the USSR, nationalize all large firms, and build a new democracy.⁵⁸ This was, however, one of the first attacks, if only a coincidental one, on Germany.

Finally, in what could be considered one of the last attempts to legitimize the PCF, on 19 December 1940, François Billoux, deputy from the Bouches-du-Rhône, wrote to Pétain from his prison requesting his release as well as the release of others. In return for their release, he offered his and his compatriots' testimonial against Reynaud, Daladier, and Blum at the Republican leaders' trial in the Supreme Court in Riom. Billoux argued that since Pétain was condemning those responsible for the war, he should release those who had been imprisoned for also condemning it. Pétain declined the offer.⁵⁹

From this point on, the nature of the party's attacks changed slightly. Vichy was still the focus and chief culprit, but was also now stated to be collaborationist. The

German occupying forces were now subjected to their share of abuse at the hands of the Communists. Splits within the party became apparent in the tracts being written. Two articles in particular illustrated the trend. The first article was published in the first 1941 issue of *les Cahiers du bolchévisme*. It was entitled 'la situation internationale au début de 1941'. The article basically reviewed the by now standard refrain against authoritarianism. It also reviewed the Germans' role in the imperialist war since October 1939. The author rejoiced in the obstacles facing Hitler: the strength of the Soviet Union, the weakness of Italy, and the problems that the Germans were facing in Europe. The article, however, also condemned Anglo-American imperialism. It remained unhelpfully vague in its proposals on how to achieve the national liberation for which it called.[60]

Another article of importance was Gabriel Péri's April 1941 brochure, *Non, le nazisme n'est pas le socialisme*. It did not break with the official line of the party, but did change the emphasis. Péri stressed the anti-Nazi aspects of the propaganda and de-emphasized the condemnation of de Gaulle, of his Free French movement, and of Anglo-American imperialism. Unlike all previous tracts, this one focused on the Nazis and not on the French collaborators. Péri levelled criticism at the Nazi exaltation of the principle of leader, contrasting it with the egalitarianism of the Communist leadership. He charged that to allow France to become a Nazi German protectorate was a betrayal of socialism. Péri's pamphlet was the closest the Communist propaganda machine ever came to advocating armed resistance before 22 June 1941.

On 18 May 1941, within a month of publishing the brochure, Péri was arrested on charges of infringing the decree of 1939 banning the Communist Party. He was executed by the Gestapo on 15 December of that year. The details of his arrest are unclear, but it has been suggested that he was framed by Maurice Tréand's assistant, the victim of a purge of dissidents by the PCF's leadership.[61] Interestingly, Péri's brochure had never been acknowledged by the central party journalistic organs. Courtois maintains that the brochure and article just noted were written by an opposition faction within the party, who disagreed with the central committee's stance of neutrality. Typically, a clandestine party would not tolerate the existence of a vocal opposition faction, but given the relative weakness of the party's organization and of its leadership, the opposition was able to voice its opinions.[62] Nevertheless, Nazi Germany was never openly or directly attacked by officially-sanctioned Communist propaganda until after 22 June 1941, when Germany invaded Russia and freed the PCF of the restrictions of the Nazi–Soviet Pact.

Interestingly, the shifts in the party's propaganda parallel the state of German–Soviet relations. In mid-1940, the Soviet Union held itself aloof from the European conflagration, and cultivated an image of neutrality. The PCF's propaganda reflected the same attitude. It was neither anti-German nor pro-German; if anything, it was anti-anti-German. Rather than having to deal with the confused problem of squaring the French Communists' patriotism and anti-Fascism with the Soviet need for a neutral PCF, it was easier to ignore the German presence and focus on something that could be justified in terms of both the USSR's interests and those of the local party. That something was Vichy. With the failure of the request for legal publication of *L'Humanité*, the Communist literature initially took on a recriminatory tone. However, with Molotov's reaffirmation of Nazi–Soviet co-operation in August 1940, the recrimination ended.[63] Despite Molotov's reaffirmation, however, the state of Nazi–Soviet relations deteriorated, as Germany established control in the Balkans and threatened Finland by moving troops into Norway and Sweden. By mid-November, relations had deteriorated enough to affect the PCF, and it was in mid-November and December that the first, cautious, limited attacks in print against the Germans were launched.[64]

If the party's propaganda proves a less than satisfactory source for the PCF's purported resistance efforts, one can turn to evidence of physical acts of resistance. One source of support for the PCF had traditionally been from students. Just as the Communist Party proper had been smashed after the Nazi–Soviet Pact, so too had the Communist student movements. And as the PCF rebuilt itself, so did the latter. Generally, the students' activities involved little more than writing graffiti on walls, distributing leaflets, and publishing a small newspaper. But two incidents do stand out in the history of the student movement of the time. The Communist student movement got an unexpected boost when François de Lescure, one of the movement's leaders, was appointed director of the Pétainist *Union Nationale des Etudiants Français* (UNEF) for the southern or Vichy zone of France.[65] Then, on 30 October, Professor Paul Langevin (a Communist) was arrested by the Gestapo. The Communist students, under Lescure, immediately organized a student rally that was held in front of the Collège de France on 8 November to demand Langevin's release. A second rally, organized by Pierre Daix, a non-Communist student, was held at the Tomb of the Unknown Soldier, at the Arc de Triomphe, on 11 November. Both rallies were dispersed by German soldiers, the second even more brutally than the first.[66]

Since then, some Communists have claimed that the two rallies were manifestations of the same sentiments and were both organized by the Young Communists.[67] At the time, however, the PCF denied responsibility for the second rally[68] and the Communist press contained no mention of either.[69] The party could hardly maintain its neutrality and claim responsibility. The non-Communist participants have since claimed that the second rally, on 11 November, was planned long in advance of the 8 November rally and was the result of a BBC appeal (by de Gaulle and the Free French) to visit the Tomb of the Unknown Soldier as a show of strength and solidarity against the occupation. They maintain that, although Communist students may have participated, their role was negligible.[70]

If the rallies were initiated by the PCF as a way of demonstrating the strength of its support base and of advertising itself, one would not expect the party to deny its involvement. If the denial was intended as a public gesture to placate the obviously irate Germans, one would still expect to see at least a veiled reference to the rallies in the Communist press. Their propaganda value would have been too good to ignore. But there was no mention of the rallies in any Communist journals. The only explanation that is consistent with all the known facts is that neither rally was PCF-inspired, rather each was the result of the exuberance of the city's youth, Communist or not. Whether one or both was unofficially organized by the Communist students is not important; the point is that the official PCF apparently was not involved.

One dimension of the party's reorganization included the collection and stockpiling of arms and munitions. The intention was to provide the material basis for future armed resistance.[71] A primary source was the arms discarded in the fields and woods of France by the French soldiers who had retreated hastily before the German invasion forces in May and June 1940. The arms also served a more immediate purpose. Due to the heavy persecution facing the Communists, it became obvious that the party's propagandists and activists needed some form of military protection. In the autumn of 1940, the party created l'Organisation Spéciale de Combat (OS) to collect arms and to protect its activists. Each region was ordered to organize its own team of OS shock troops, typically numbering six to eight men. The individual OS teams were to act independently of one another.[72]

Another ostensible function of the OS cited by some historians was the punishment and/or liquidation of traitors within the party.[73] Since the PCF was Stalinist in orientation as well as illegal, it could not tolerate dissension among its membership, the more so as dissension constituted a major security risk. Thus anyone who broke with the party's line of policy was deemed a traitor. Irwin Wall reports that, according to 'some knowledgeable sources', the OS had a list of Communist militants selected for execution. He does not know how many were actually executed. Interestingly, one local leader, Georges Guingouin, cut all contact between the guerrilla force he had created in the Limousin and the party until 1942, apparently because his men had intercepted an OS mission sent to assassinate him.[74]

By the end of 1940, there were several OS units involved in actual sabotage. This early involvement in active sabotage is often cited as an example of the party's early, pre-Barbarossa resistance. Certainly there were acts of sabotage and resistance, and some were undoubtedly the work of units of the OS. The question is whether they were acting on local initiative or on the initiative of the party. It is important to remember that the two did not necessarily coincide. Often, individual Communists were forced to make decisions and to act on their own initiative because of the poor state of communications with an extremely disorganized central committee. Others chose to act on their own and so avoid the neutralist stance dictated by the CC.

Thus, the redevelopment of the PCF was necessarily haphazard and shaped by the personalities involved.[75] Four independent centres of Communist-led resistance sprang up in 1940: in the Nord and Pas-de-Calais under Charles Debarge and Auguste Lecoeur; in Brittany under Auguste Havez, Robert Ballanger, and Marcel Paul; in the Limousin under Georges Guingouin; and in Bordeaux under Charles

Tillon.⁷⁶ In the northern prohibited zone especially, the desire and tendency to resist despite central party directives was stronger, and the CC's control and influence weaker. Roger Pannequin, a northern socialist who became a Communist after the war, pointed out the profound difference in the conception of resistance between the Communists of the two zones, prohibited and Vichy. The Communists of the Nord dismissed *L'Humanité* as inapplicable to them because Paris, where it was published, had to deal with the Vichy regime, and the Nord with the Germans. Therefore, the Communists of the prohibited zone preferred to write their own tracts and to act independently. After all, as Pannequin explained to two Parisian Communists, the Communists from the Nord believed that those in Vichy France (i.e. the occupied and free zones) 'ne comprennent pas qu'il faut tuer le maître avant de tirer sur le chien' (le maître allemand, le chien vichyssois).⁷⁷

As early as 18 June 1940, as the Germans swept across France, Charles Tillon called on the people to fight for national liberation, in leaflets inserted in the daily papers. In July he issued another circular denouncing the armistice and calling for a union of the people to free France from the capitalists and invaders. August Havez distributed a pamphlet declaring that there would be not rest until France was rid of the Germans. In August 1940, Georges Guingouin decried the Hitlerian occupation and appealed to the French people to prevent the institution of a Fascist regime in France. All three men rejected the passivity espoused by the central committee.⁷⁸ Certainly a large number of Communists ignored the party directives and either acted individually or joined the budding non-Communist resistance movements, especially as the Germans dropped their facade of neutrality and their attitude hardened towards the French population and, in particular, towards resistance.

There are numerous examples of unofficial Communist resistance from the beginning of the occupation. In July 1940, Maurice Romagon recovered guns in Troyes and Marcel Paul printed 2,000 copies of a tract in Brittany. In August, Henri Rol-Tanguy sabotaged the production of war materials in a Renault plant, and in September Marcel Paul recovered sixty firearms.⁷⁹ Charles Tillon, Auguste Havez, and Georges Guingouin used their forces for sabotage, primarily of communications and railroads.⁸⁰ The sabotage was sufficient to earn harsh reprisals from the German authorities in the form of crippling fines, arrests, mass internments, and outrageous penalties. Blake Erlich cites the example of 19-year-old Communist Pierre Roche who was arrested for cutting the phone cable to la Rochelle. He was sentenced to two years' hard labour by the French courts, but when he was then turned over to the German military courts, they ordered him to be shot.⁸¹

Before acknowledging what seems strong evidence of Communist resistance, it is important to remember that the occupation authorities were inclined to blame *all* sabotage on the Communists, whether they were responsible or not. This predilection on their part makes it difficult for the historian to distinguish between Communist and non-Communist acts of sabotage. In addition, as Henri Amouroux rightly points out, it is important to put the Communist record of resistance in perspective. In July 1940, long before Communist resistance was active, the Free French landed their first agent, Jacques Mansion. Within days he had formed an embryo network. Tracts written by Edmond Michelet unambiguously calling for resistance were distributed. Michelet also forged papers for anti-Nazi Germans. Intelligence services were organized, cables sabotaged, the *Conseils à l'Occupé* published, and networks established in Paris and Rouen. In August 1940, Captain Fourcaud arrived in France and established contact with Frenay, leader of one of the various interior resistance movements. In September General Cachet, chief of the Second Bureau (Military Intelligence) and head of the airforce of the Fifth Army of France, signed appeals to resist. Frenay created the national movement, Libération. The Seventh Column was created in Alsace, and the Free French established contact with the exiled Polish government in London. The accomplishments of the Communists seem less spectacular when compared to these and other achievements of the Free French and non-Communist movements.[82] There was indeed a small Communist resistance movement operating prior to 22 June 1941, but the indications are that it was at the initiative of individuals and that the party's central hierarchy was not involved.

Another area of traditional activity for the Communists was among the working class. In September 1939, the Communists had been banned from the trade unions. With the fall of France and the massive upheaval of the nation's population, the unions had disintegrated. Part of the PCF's reorganization in July of 1940 included organizing popular committees (as mentioned earlier). These committees soon formed on union lines, once the unionists returned. The conditions were ideal for the party, the old unions having disappeared and nothing having emerged to replace them. Communist involvement in union activity would serve to renew the party's contact with the workers and would provide a vehicle for keeping the workers' discontent alive and directed against the government. In addition, by participating in legitimate unions, the PCF could hope to regain a degree of legal status. Therefore, the party's platform was designed to appeal to the workers. It was a call to the bewildered and leaderless militants to join the Communists in protest against repression and in the traditional demands for bread and for employment. The Communists' activity was intense, and by mid-August 1940 the workers' journal *La Vie Ouvrière* was in print and seventy popular committees were active in the Parisian region.[83]

There were heavy costs involved in this organizing effort. The Communists had to take a great many security risks in their efforts, to the advantage of the police. The authorities became increasingly worried about the increased union activity and planned a countering move. That move was part of a massive sweep by the police in October 1940. In a matter of days, the police smashed three months' work by the Communists.[84] Although the movement was badly hurt, such was its strength that by November there were again 100 popular committees in the Parisian metal industries.[85]

However, despite the success of the Communist Party's organizational efforts, there was little in the way of strike activity and none before the end of the year. There were numerous brief protests but all demands were settled through negotiation. The metalworkers especially were carefully watched by both police and government. Any militant Communists who became involved in the legal unions were soon identified and marked for arrest if they caused trouble. Although the Communists had achieved a great deal, their hold in the factories was still not strong enough to enable them to foment a general strike. Unemployment among the metalworkers was too high for them to consider seriously any grand, and probably costly, gestures. The workers were more concerned with immediate needs, such as food and employment. The PCF had been decapacitated twice in as many years, once in 1939 and again in October 1940, and had hardly been in a position to agitate for general strike activity.[86] However, by the end of 1940, everything was in place for a major strike action. After the losses of October, the unionists had retrenched and although the repression was still severe in the southern zone, the police were much less successful in the occupied zone.[87] Yet there was only one strike of any magnitude in the Parisian area, at *L'Incombustibilité d'Issy-Les-Moulineaux*, a plant employing 3,000 workers producing camouflage nets for the Wehrmacht. The workers succeeded in shutting down the plant for a day, on 17 April 1941, in a dispute about salaries and new rules governing working conditions.[88]

Following this, on 15 May 1941, the PCF issued an Appeal for a National Front of Struggle for the Independence of France. The objective was to maintain France's neutrality between the two rival imperialisms, German and Anglo-American. The Appeal did not seek to bring France back into the war on the British side, but rather to prevent France from slipping into it on the German side. The 15 May Appeal did not explain the strategy underlying the proposed struggle,[89] although Stéphane Courtois reports that a second text detailing the strategy was published at the same time. In this text, the PCF proposed to install the necessary infrastructure for the fight, a popular government. The fundamental force in the fight was to be the working class with the PCF at its head. The party appealed for the unity of all French peoples, excluding the traitors and capitulators who collaborated with the occupiers. It was ready to assist all those in government and in any organization who were willing to join the stuggle. The war of national liberation was to consist of two parts, a class struggle within the imperialist countries and the emancipation of the colonies. Thus the imperialist war was now to be reshaped into an international revolutionary movement.[90]

On the heels of the 15 May Appeal came the miners' strike of May and June 1941. The miners' action is significant for a number of reasons. It was the only general strike in France which occurred before Barbarossa, thus making it the sole case of open mass resistance to the occupying forces before Germany invaded Russia. If it could be shown that the strike was organized and initiated by the Communists, the PCF would have gone a long way to proving its pre-Barbarossa participation in the resistance. For this reason, the proximity in time between the 15 May Appeal and the eruption of the strike is often pointed out, implying that the one led to the other.[91] Before that assertion can be accepted, it would pay to examine the strike and the conditions surrounding it more carefully.

Since the end of 1940, the Communist press had been reporting evidence of unrest among miners across France. In its 3 December issue, *L'Humanité* reported that the miners of St Etienne and the Gard had struck and were demanding soap and food. In Braxières-les-Mines, they struck over the arrest of several Communist comrades. *La Vie Ouvrière* reported on 29 March 1941 that the iron miners at Moutiers had won a 30 per cent increase in their wages by protesting. On 5 April, the Bédarieux mines in Hérault struck for 600 grammes of bread a day. The Béraudière pits in St Etienne came out demanding food on 22 June. In St Louis, they struck after a fatal accident.[92]

The two *départements* of the Nord and Pas-de-Calais have a long history of intense Communist activity and of strong anti-German feeling. The occupation was the second the regions had had to endure within twenty-five years. It was also an important one for the Germans, for the regions were a major coal-producing district, crucial to the German industrial war machine and thus subject to close German intervention. The Germans had signed contracts with the mines to purchase the coal, and the owners consequently wanted to increase production and decrease costs, especially labour costs. In order to reduce the cost of labour, they installed a new wage system. The new system effectively eliminated all the gains the miners had won since 1936 and, furthermore, badly undermined their purchasing power, for inflation was now a serious problem in France.

On 2 January 1941, the miners at seven pits in L'Escarpelle came out on strike. Around 28 January there were rumblings of discontent in the pits of Aniche. There was unrest in Dourges and Courrières from the 1 to 11 February.[93] In March, there was another strike in L'Escarpelle. The first of May was a day of great union activity across the whole of the Nord and Pas-de-Calais.[94] For months, then, spontaneous movements had been erupting, almost exclusively over economic matters – the need for adequate food and wages.

It appears that the May miners' strike erupted for the same reasons. Rather than being an insurrection against the German occupation, it was a protest concerned with 'surtout de beurre, de viande et de savon'.[95] Initially, it was a spontaneous strike with little direction, but the local Communists soon became involved and organized it. Chief among these was Auguste Lecoeur, supported militarily by two OS units.[96] Lecoeur's involvement is often offered as living proof that the PCF was involved in anti-German resistance before Barbarossa. However, it seems that there was a significant difference in attitudes between the local Communists led by Lecoeur and the central committee. The CC's purely economic slogans could not have inspired such a strike.[97] The strike was not acknowledged in *L'Humanité* until 20 June, well after it had ended and then only in an article discussing it as an example of the party's 'glorious efforts'.[98] The records of the Vichy regime show that they understood the nature of the strike to be a miner-instigated affair in which neither the Gaullists nor the Communists were heavily involved.[99]

Furthermore, the party's writings have since played down the strike and Lecoeur's role in it, suggesting that not only was the strike not instigated by the central committee, but also that it was not in keeping with PCF policy of the moment.[100] Auguste Lecoeur himself notes the difference between the local and the executive Communists at the time. The executive used *L'Humanité* to warn the miners not to be deluded by their apparent success, and reminded them that 'ce n'est pas dans la victoire d'un impérialisme sur un autre que réside notre salut commun'.[101] The miners' local press took a slightly stronger anti-German tone, declaring that they would not tolerate national oppression. Thus it appears likely that the failure of similar strikes to erupt in the Parisian region was because the Parisian workers were restrained by the central committee, unlike the miners of the north.[102]

With the German invasion of the USSR in June 1941, the PCF was freed of the restrictions imposed by the Nazi–Soviet pact. It could direct its energies into an attack on the Germans without any qualms, and the party threw itself into the task of resistance wholeheartedly. Its first move was to formalize its military organization. As explained earlier, the PCF had created special guerrilla units (the OS) whose purpose was to protect party activists and to deal with dissension within party ranks. In February 1942 these OS units were brought together into a more organized and formalized military organization, called les Francs-Tireurs et Partisans (the FTP). It was headed by a three-man committee: Charles Tillon, who acted as director of the organization; Eugène Hénaff, in charge of recruitment; and Raoul Vallet, who was in charge of military operations (he was arrested in March of 1942 and thereafter replaced by Albert Ouzoulias). It was this organization which was to wage the battle against the enemies, both German and Vichyite, and to provide protection when necessary for party members.

The PCF also created le Front National (FN). Its purpose was to unite all the resistance movements, both Communist and non-Communist, under one umbrella organization, thus creating a more effective resistance against the occupiers and the Vichyites, as well as bringing independent organizations under closer Communist influence and control. Although efforts to this end were made in both sectors, occupied and free, the organization only really gained a hold in the occupied zone. There it came to dominate the resistance.

The resistance movements, both Communist and non-Communist, burgeoned after 1941, for several reasons. Initially Pétain had been hailed as the saviour of France, but as time passed his appeal wore thin. The Nazi repression became increasingly harsh and open, and Vichy's claim to be acting as a cushion for France from the effects of a fully-fledged Nazi occupation was proving hollow. However, what galvanized a veritable flood of new recruits to the *maquis* was the imposition of the forced labour laws. On 21 March 1942, Sauckel, the Nazi labour chief, demanded 350,000 workers from France to replace German workers who were conscripted to fight on the Russian front. The Vichy government launched a programme called 'La Relève', promising to obtain the release of a French prisoner-of-war for every three workers who went to Germany. In July, Laval promised the Germans 350,000 more men.

The voluntary system never worked very well, however, and in September Laval introduced new labour laws, promising a further 250,000 men to Germany. In November 1942, the German Army was annihilated at Stalingrad and 300,000 German troops were lost. The decision was made to replenish the German forces with German factory workers who had previously been excused from service and to man the factories from the occupied territories.[103] On 16 February 1943, the Service du Travail Obligatoire (STO) was decreed in France, calling up all Frenchmen of mobilizable age as if for compulsory military service. As a result, 250,000 men were sent to Germany and Sauckel then demanded a further 100,000. The reaction of the general populace was to resist, to strike, and to disappear into the forests and countryside and join the resistance.[104] The *maquis* were flooded with new recruits, all needing to be fed, clothed, armed, and housed surreptiously. The strains on the underground organization were enormous, but the gains in manpower and general popular support invaluable. From this moment onwards, the underground resistance was truly a force to be reckoned with.

Up until this point, the PCF had basically ignored Charles de Gaulle and his London-based Free French movement, notwithstanding the common goals of the two organizations, and the USSR's recognition of the Free French Committee in September 1941. (Recognition from Great Britain and the United States came later.) The disagreement was over the relative worth of internal resistance and the value of armed resistance against the occupying forces, de Gaulle arguing that the harsh costs imposed by the Germans and by Vichy for acts of armed resistance far outweighed the possible gains made through such acts.

However, by the spring of 1942 it had become apparent to both sides that there was a need for some sort of *rapprochement*. It was also obvious that, as the two continued to expand, they increasingly would come into conflict unless some sort of accommodation was arranged. By 18 April 1942, de Gaulle's position on internal resistance had changed, as evidenced by his adoption of the PCF's slogan, that 'national liberation cannot be separated from national insurrection'.[105] However, the *rapprochement* was far from close or amicable. Indeed, it could be argued that the tensions between the two organizations were exacerbated by the increased interaction, because the struggle became one over day-to-day strategy, rather than one over the purpose and value of internal resistance.

In September 1942, the USSR recognized the Comité National Français (CNF), created by de Gaulle, as the

> Directing organ of Fighting France, alone qualified to organize the participation of citizens of France and its territories in the war and to represent, before the Government of the U.S.S.R., French interests, insofar as they are affected by the conduct of the war.[106]

In recognition of the need for improved communications, the PCF sent Fernand Grenier to London to represent the PCF on the CNF. The first evidence of joint action was a tract condemning the newly imposed STO, the forced labour draft described above. The tract was distributed in factories in the southern zone and signed jointly by Combat, Libération, Francs-Tireurs (the three resistance movements of the southern zone which comprised the Mouvements Unis de la Résistance (MUR)), the PCF, and the Front National.[107]

The process of uniting the Gaullist and the Communist resistances was gradual, in large part due to the antipathy and suspicion on both sides. It was a move born of necessity, not of desire. For de Gaulle, whose objective was to put his organization and himself in control of the post-war French government, it was necessary to neutralize, if not eliminate, the threat the PCF posed to his plans, a goal most readily achieved by co-opting the Communists into his organization. For the PCF, it was obvious by late 1942 that de Gaulle was going to dominate a post-war government, and that if they wished to be part of the decision-making process and the power structure after the war they would have to join him.

An example of this attitude may be seen in the PCF's support of de Gaulle's efforts to establish a French provisional government in Algiers following the Anglo-American invasion of North Africa in November 1942. When the Allies successfully completed the landing, the Americans made Admiral François Darlan head of French administration in North Africa. De Gaulle had been hoping to establish a Free French provisional government there. The appointment of Darlan came as a major shock, as Darlan had until recently been Commander-in-Chief of Vichy's land and sea forces. The Americans had installed a Vichyite. On 24 December, Darlan was assassinated, and General Giraud replaced him. This was an improvement in so far as Giraud at least was not a Vichyite, but de Gaulle was still furious at the appointment of his military superior. On 3 June 1943, the Comité Française de Libération Nationale (CFLN) was established in Algiers, with de Gaulle and Giraud as joint chairmen. The CFLN was, in effect, the provisional government, although it was not officially recognised as such by the Allied powers. By November, de Gaulle had effectively asserted his control of the CFLN and manoeuvred Giraud out of the way.[108]

In all of this, the PCF supported de Gaulle. Its purpose was simple. In September, the CFLN had created a Consultative Assembly in Algiers, to be composed of representatives of the resistance, former deputies who had not voted for Pétain and others. De Gaulle also invited the PCF to participate in the CFLN, which was distinct from the Consultative Assembly and was the key policy-making body. There was a decided advantage for de Gaulle in having the PCF in his own organization where he could control the situation. For the PCF, in turn, not to participate would effectively exclude them from the newly-forming post-war government.

However, there were conditions to their acceptance of de Gaulle's offer. Chief of these was the PCF's desire to choose who was to represent them on the CFLN and which posts those representatives were to fill. De Gaulle, however, was not interested in letting anyone but himself appoint his ministers. The negotiations lasted for months, until April 1944, when Fernand Grenier and François Billoux accepted, on behalf of the Algiers delegation of the PCF, the posts of Commissar of Air and

Commissar of State, which had just been offered by de Gaulle. Until the early spring of 1944, the Communists had been adamant in their demands for Communist appointments to various key ministerial posts, despite de Gaulle's intransigence. What induced the PCF to back down was probably the apparent imminence of national liberation; if the party wanted to be a part of the provisional government when the liberation took place (a position of decided advantage), then it had to gain a foothold quickly.[109]

Together with this slow amalgamation of Free French and Communist forces there had been a gradual unification of internal resistance. In May 1943, after long negotiations, the Conseil National de la Résistance (CNR) was created. It was a union of all the resistance groups, all the anti-German political parties (chiefly the PCF, the SFIO, the Christian Democratic groups, and the Radicals), the main trade unions (CGT and CFTC), and also included a representative of de Gaulle's Free French organization. Each member group or party retained its own separate identity.[110] A military arm, the Comité d'Action (COMAC), was created to co-ordinate the various paramilitary efforts of the resistances. Although COMAC's composition was heterogeneous, it was dominated by the Communists.[111]

From 1943 to 1944, there was increasing debate over how to co-ordinate the FTP (the dominant force in COMAC) and de Gaulle's Armée Secrète. All were agreed on the need for co-ordination; the difficulty lay in what the strategy was to be and under whose direction. In this case, the Communists were much more reluctant to surrender their independence or to buckle under to the Gaullists. The two strategic alternatives were to continue the guerrilla warfare (the strategy advocated by the FTP) and to reorganize the paramilitary units along the lines of the massive units controlled by London, a formation more akin to a regular army.[112]

The differences over the organizational form of the paramilitary forces merely reflected the difference of opinion between the Communists and the Gaullists over the ultimate objective of these units. The Gaullists maintained that the resistance fighters should wait for the Allied and French regular forces to arrive before rising up against the Germans and against Vichy. They were concerned that if the Communists acted independently, they might be able to seize control before the Gaullist forces arrived. The Communists, on the other hand, argued for local, spontaneous uprisings once the Allied forces started to move across France, to throw the occupying forces into disarray and therefore ease the way of the Allied forces. They argued that the action should be independent and determined by particular local circumstances.[113] The dispute over strategy was never resolved; the Communists had a solid, well-established, and by then well-armed clandestine organization which they were loath to sacrifice on the altar of co-operation with the Gaullists.

The issue became an especially acute one as the Allies moved into France. The Communists, and indeed many of the non-Communist resistance groups in France, ignored de Gaulle's directives and staged uprisings anyway. The most serious of these insurrections happened in Paris. The Allies were not expected to reach Paris until September 1944. The month of July was marked by increasing tensions in the

The PCF and the French resistance 75

city. There were hunger marches and a strike by railwaymen. On 14 July, Bastille Day, there was a demonstration numbering 100,000 strong that the police could not disperse.

Charles Tillon, leader of the FTP in Paris, was waiting impatiently for orders to launch the insurrection, orders which never came. Unwilling to wait any longer, Tillon called for a general strike by the members of the CGT and CFTC and began the insurrection. The PCF central committee quickly endorsed the *fait accompli* on 18 August, and on 19 August the Gaullist representative in Paris, Rol-Tanguy, decreed a general mobilization. Once it was launched and unstoppable, the Gaullists were compelled to support the insurrection or lose any claim to control of the situation or its outcome. The Germans, faced with an impossible situation, offered to withdraw from the city in exchange for a truce. The Gaullists were willing to consider such a deal, but the insurgents were not. On 21 August, with most of Paris liberated, the CNR officially rejected the truce. At this point, de Gaulle sent in an armoured division of Free French forces under Leclerc, effectively neutralizing the insurgents. On the 25th, the Germans in Paris surrendered to Leclerc and Rol-Tanguy and on the 26th de Gaulle entered Paris in a triumphal parade.[114]

By the end of September 1944, most of France had been liberated, but the war actually lasted until 8 May 1945. During these intervening months of 'mopping up', the PCF and de Gaulle continued to clash over the 'irregular' guerrilla units. The PCF wanted them to become a part of the new French army and de Gaulle insisted that they be disbanded. Reluctantly, the Communists agreed to disband them, in an effort to maintain a position in de Gaulle's government.[115]

By the time of the liberation of France and the installation of de Gaulle's government in France, the PCF's strategy was clear. In fact, its options were severely limited. It could either attempt to foment a revolution and create 'a people's government', or it could accept de Gaulle's control as a *fait accompli* and work within that framework. As is obvious from the preceding discussion, the PCF chose the second alternative, and opted for the role of a government party. The obstacles to launching a successful revolution were formidable. The French people were heartily tired of war, fighting, hardship, and deprivation and were anxious to return to some semblance of normality. France was full of Allied troops who were unlikely to stand idly by in the midst of a Communist revolution. Finally the USSR was in no position to lend support. The Yalta Conference was impending and the Soviets could not afford to antagonize their allies. Nor did the USSR have the resources to assist the French Communists in a revolution. Thus, almost from the first, the Communists concentrated on the effort to free France from Fascist hands, be they German or French, and were willing to work with anyone in order to achieve that goal.

Thus the story of the PCF during the years of France's occupation can be seen as consisting of two parts. The first part of the story is the shorter, spanning the year from June 1940 to June 1941, from the fall of France to the Nazi invasion of the USSR. However it is by far the more interesting, for it remains the subject of a never-ending debate as to the nature and extent of PCF and Communist involvement in the newly-forming resistance.[116] With the shattering of the Nazi–Soviet pact in June 1941, the story simplifies tremendously. It quickly becomes a tale of two dominant political forces jostling for control of the resistance and of the post-war government as the latter was being planned during the war itself. After June 1941, the focus of attention shifts from the domestic to the international scene, with the course of events within France being shaped to a large degree by the needs of other nations. More particularly, the actions of the PCF became once again dependent on the policy needs of the USSR, as they had been in the late 1930s. Thus, the subsequent motivations and actions of the PCF are best examined in the light of international tensions and the needs of the USSR, a task beyond the scope of this essay.

NOTES

1 S. Courtois, *Le PCF dans la guerre* (Paris, 1980), p. 20.
2 M. Adereth, *The French Communist Party: A Critical History (1920–84)* (Manchester, 1984), pp. 92–3.
3 Comité Central du Parti Communiste Français, *Histoire du parti communiste français (manuel)* (Paris, 1964), vol. 1, p. 375.
4 ibid., pp. 378–9.
5 S. Courtois, op. cit., p. 60.
6 Adereth bases his conclusions on a review of *L'Humanité* for the period in question, arguing that it is the chief source of information regarding the PCF during the period that it was illegal. Adereth, op. cit., pp. 96–100.
7 ibid., p. 96.
8 For a good account of Vichy France, see Robert O. Paxton's *Vichy France: Old Guard and New Order (1940–1944)* (New York, 1972).
9 Edward Mortimer, *The Rise of the French Communist Party* (London, 1984), p. 293.
10 ibid.
11 ibid., pp. 293–4.
12 A. Rossi, *Les Communistes français pendant la drôle de guerre* (Paris, 1951), pp. 310–11.
13 ibid., p. 313.
14 H. Amouroux, *La Grande histoire des français sous l'occupation* (Paris, 1977), vol. 2, p. 452.
15 A. Werth, *France: 1940–55* (London, 1956), p. 191.
16 J. Duclos, *Mémoires: dans la bataille clandestine* (Paris, 1970), vol. 3(1), p. 72.
17 Courtois, op. cit., p. 134.
18 F. Knight, *The French Resistance 1940–1944* (London, 1975), p. 63.
19 Mortimer, op. cit., p. 302.
20 Adereth, op. cit., p. 108.
21 H. R. Kedward, *Resistance in Vichy France* (London, 1978), p. 91.
22 Adereth, op. cit., p. 112.
23 Comité Central du PCF, op. cit., p. 392.
24 Courtois, op. cit., p. 145.
25 Kedward, op. cit., p. 61.
26 Comité Central du PCF, op. cit., p. 390.
27 Amouroux, op. cit., p. 452.
28 B. Ehrlich, *Resistance: France 1940–1945* (Boston, 1965), p. 27.
29 I. Wall, *French Communism in the Era of Stalin* (London, 1983), p. 20.

30 Amouroux, op. cit., p. 415.
31 Courtois, op. cit., p. 133.
32 Amouroux, op. cit., pp. 417–20.
33 Mortimer, op. cit., p. 294.
34 Adereth, op. cit., pp. 109–10.
35 Mortimer, op. cit., p. 294.
36 Wall, op. cit., p. 20.
37 Mortimer, op. cit., pp. 295–6. A. Lecoeur, Le parti communiste français et la Résistance (Paris, 1968), p. 90.
38 Rossi, op. cit., p. 325.
39 Courtois, op. cit., p. 137.
40 Editions Univ, Histoire du parti communiste français (Paris) (n.d.),vol. 2, p. 32.
41 Mortimer, op. cit., p. 297.
42 Duclos, op. cit., p. 87.
43 H. Nogueres, Histoire de la Résistance en France de 1940–1945 (Paris, 1967), vol. 1, p. 146.
44 ibid., p. 143.
45 H. Michel, Vichy: Annee 40 (Paris, 1966), p. 139.
46 Kedward, op. cit., p. 60.
47 J. Touchard, La Gauche en France depuis 1900 (Paris, 1977), p. 256.
48 Kedward, op. cit., p. 60.
49 Mortimer, op. cit., p. 297.
50 Duclos, op. cit., p. 73.
51 Mortimer, op. cit., p. 297.
52 Courtois, op. cit., p. 139; Kedward, op. cit., pp. 49–50.
53 Rossi, op. cit., pp. 308–9.
54 CC of PCF, Histoire, vol. 2, pp. 34–5.
55 Amouroux, La grande histoire, p. 427ff.
56 Adereth, The French Communist Party, pp. 113–14.
57 Adereth, The French Communist Party, p. 112.
58 Comité Central du PCF, op. cit., vol. 2, pp. 34–5.
59 Mortimer, op. cit., pp. 297–8.
60 Courtois, op. cit., pp. 162–3.
61 Mortimer, op. cit., pp. 303–4.
62 Courtois, op. cit., p. 164.
63 ibid., p. 161.
64 ibid., pp. 158–9.
65 Nogueres, op. cit., p. 123.
66 Amouroux, op. cit., p. 443.
67 Courtois, op. cit., p. 152.
68 Amouroux, op. cit., p. 443.
69 Courtois, op. cit., p. 152.
70 Nogueres, op. cit., pp. 172–5.
71 Adereth, op. cit., pp. 112–13.
72 ibid., p. 113.
73 Wall, op. cit., p. 21; Lecoeur, op. cit., p. 83; Nogueres, op. cit., pp. 147–8.
74 Wall, op. cit., p. 22.
75 Kedward, op. cit., pp. 62–3.
76 Wall, op. cit., p. 21.
77 Amouroux, op. cit., p. 442.
78 Courtois, op. cit., p. 141; Mortimer, op .cit., pp. 301–2.
79 Amouroux, op. cit., p. 442.

80 Lecoeur, op. cit., pp. 80–1.
81 Ehrlich, op. cit., pp. 26–7.
82 Amouroux, op. cit., pp. 428–9.
83 Courtois, op. cit., pp. 147–8.
84 ibid., pp. 150–1.
85 ibid., p. 148.
86 ibid., pp. 176–7.
87 ibid., p. 174.
88 ibid., pp. 177–8.
89 Mortimer, op. cit., p. 300.
90 Courtois, op. cit., pp. 191–2.
91 Nogueres, op. cit., p. 286.
92 Courtois, op. cit., p. 195.
93 ibid., pp. 195–6.
94 Lecoeur, op.cit., p. 67.
95 Nogueres, op. cit., p. 384.
96 Adereth, op. cit., pp. 114–15.
97 Mortimer, op. cit., p. 304.
98 Amouroux, op. cit., p. 439.
99 ibid., p. 445.
100 Lecoeur, op cit., p. 62.
101 Quoted in ibid., p. 77.
102 ibid., pp. 78–9.
103 R. du Jonchay, *La Résistance et les communistes* (Paris, 1968), pp. 50–1.
104 Knight, op. cit., p. 114.
105 Adereth, p. 122.
106 C. de Gaulle, *Mémoires*, vol. 2, p. 371, as quoted in J. Sweets, *The Politics of Resistance, 1940–1944* (DeKalb, Illinois, 1976), p. 124.
107 Note that the Francs-Tireurs was a separate, non-Communist organization, and was not affiliated with the Communist paramilitary organization, the Francs-Tireurs et Partisans.
108 Sweets, op. cit., pp. 75–8.
109 A. J. Rieber, *Stalin and the French Communist Party (1941–1947)* (New York, 1962), pp. 56–8.
110 Adereth, op. cit., p. 119.
111 du Jonchay, op. cit., pp. 130–1.
112 Knight, op. cit., p. 151.
113 Adereth, op. cit., pp. 124–5.
114 ibid., pp. 125–6.
115 ibid., pp. 126–7.
116 It is interesting that the debate was replayed in detail at the conference held in October 1983, the results of which are published in the volume entitled *Le Parti communiste français des années sombres, 1938–1941*, ed. J.-P. Azéma and J.-P. Rioux (Paris, 1986). The main lines of the debate were reaffirmed, with little new coming to light.

ABBREVIATIONS

CC   Comité Central (du Parti Communiste Français)
CFLN   Comité Français de Liberation Nationale
CFTC   Confédération Française des Travailleurs Chrétiens
CGT   Confédération Générale du Travail
CNF   Comité National Français

CNR	Conseil National de la Résistance
COMAC	Comité d'Action
FN	Front National
FTP	les Francs-Tireurs et Partisans
MUR	Mouvements Unis de la Résistance
OS	l'Organisation Spéciale de Combat
PCF	Parti Communiste Français
SFIO	Section Française de l'Internationale Ouvrière
STO	Service du Travail Obligatoire

3 Communism and resistance in Italy, 1943–8

DAVID TRAVIS

INTRODUCTION

The Italian experience of resistance and revolution followed a much different path from that of Yugoslavia or Greece. Unlike the Communists grouped around Tito, who based a social revolution on their strength in the war, and unlike their Greek counterparts, whose revolution failed when it became a civil war, the Italian Communists emerged from the resistance with a new and non-revolutionary definition of the Marxist project for social change in their country.

This essay first considers how and in what ways the Italian resistance (1943–1945) influenced the Partito Comunista Italiano (PCI), both in the development of its organization and in the formulation of some strikingly new ideas about Communism. The discussion then focuses on how anti-Fascism and resistance determined the policies and actions of the PCI during the early years of the post-war Italian republic (1945–8).[1]

The starting point for the discussion, however, lies in the years before the Second World War. Unique to Italy in the history of Mediterranean Communism was the experience of domestic Fascism.[2] The period of illegality for the PCI, from 1926 to 1943, nearly twenty years (the Fascist *ventennio*) of imprisonment, clandestinity and exile under Mussolini, exerted a powerful influence on the young Communist Party. Therefore, in order best to understand the PCI and its role in the period of resistance and revolution, we need first to consider briefly exactly what Italian *Fascism* meant in the early history of Italian *Communism*.

Contrary to the prevailing view, the early history of the Italian Communist Party *must* be read in domestic terms. This may seem a peculiar assertion given that most of the PCI was effectively excluded from Italy for at least seventeen of its first twenty-two years of existence. But it was precisely the party's own spectacular failure to understand and resist Fascism which profoundly influenced the PCI in the years after 1943.

The Communist Party of Italy emerged from the ranks of radical dissidents within the Socialist Party after the First World War. At the National Congress of the Partito

Socialista Italiano (PSI) in Livorno in 1921, one-third of the delegates left the PSI; this was the culmination of several years of growing differences within the Socialist Party (the country's largest after the war) on the possibility and timing of revolution in Italy. The question of adherence to the new Communist International in Moscow sparked the final split at Livorno: the dissidents favoured full acceptance of Lenin's 21-point programme for membership in the International; the Socialists objected to the Soviet demand for a purge of the reformist elements in their party.

The dissidents' breakaway from the Socialists was a particularly bitter one. Controversy surrounded the foundation of the Communist Party, because the Livorno schism occurred during the period that Fascism was at its most violent stage, intent on defeating a much-feared bolshevik revolution in Italy. These were the years of the Fascist squads, the beatings and murder of prominent opponents, and the violent destruction of the Left's powerful trade union movement, particularly in northern Italy. The split at Livorno hastened the rise of Mussolini to power as the Communists and Socialists devoted more time to arguing among themselves about who was 'right' at Livorno than in joining together to resist most effectively the real threat to Italy – the *fascisti*.

The political Left – both the Socialist and Communists – were defeated quite rapidly. Fascist squads beat the Left out of existence in the streets and the trade unions by the end of 1921. The Communists and Socialists lost the crucial parliamentary contests in 1922 which saw Mussolini assume the prime ministership after the Fascists' 'March on Rome'. The Left failed to regroup sufficiently to block the 1924 plebisicite vote which gave the appearance of wide popular support to Fascism and handed absolute control in Parliament to Mussolini. The last chapter in this tragic decline was written in 1926 when the Fascists banned all opposition parties, removing the last elements of the Communists' and Socialists' fragile political existence.

The Communist Party realized much too late the threat that Fascism posed, not just to the political Left, but to all of Italy. Their defeat provided the leaders of the PCI with much to think about during the twenty years that followed. Three important facts figured among the lessons learned by the Communists.

First, its rapid destruction seriously called into question the young Communist Party's understanding of events in Italy. Formed at the peak of revolutionary expectations in Italy, the PCI collapsed only four years later, defeated by an enemy which, according to Marxist analysis, represented only a transitory phenomenon associated with the 'last stage' of capitalism. The Communist Party's early history can thus only be read as one of theoretical shortcomings and strategic misjudgement, and this bitter lesson would be remembered.

Secondly, Mussolini's victory highlighted how important the unity of the political Left was in the face of an all-out assault by the Fascists. The senseless sectarian infighting against the Socialists would not be waged again in Italy by the Communists. Finally, though the Fascist revolution was carried out in the name of saving Italy from bolshevism, its real accomplishment was the elimination of parliamentary democracy in the country. The end of most civil, legal, and economic rights revealed to all opponents of Fascism, not just the Communists, the very real advantages that 'bourgeois' democracy provided in liberal Italy. Never again would the PCI so lightly dismiss parliamentary democracy; indeed, the party became one of its major champions after 1943.

The lessons of defeat were to figure prominently in the PCI's policies when it was able to return to Italy. But that did not occur until 1943. In the meantime, the party faced a very difficult period of repression and isolation. What kind of party was the PCI in 1926?

First, it was very young, with only four or five years of formal political activity between its foundation in 1921 and its effective elimination in 1926. It was also quite small. Only a minority at Livorno supported the Communists' position and the party did not grow much larger in the years before Mussolini's seizure of power. Additionally, the PCI did not play a truly significant role in Italian politics before 1926; it had not been a major party in Parliament, but rather a vehicle for the expression of social revolutionary sentiments and propaganda in a reactionary period. So the Communist Party was not particularly strong even before the Fascists moved against it, and imprisonment made the PCI almost completely irrelevant within Italy by 1930. None the less, the Italian Communist Party survived Fascism and later was the foremost political organization in the resistance. How did this young, small, propaganda group manage to emerge from the Fascist period and assume such an important role?

The arrests of most Communist leaders and much of the party's membership began immediately after the ban on political parties in 1926. One of the founders of the party, the theoretician and parliamentarian Antonio Gramsci, was imprisoned in October 1926. Gramsci spent the next ten years in Fascist jails and was released for reasons of poor health in 1937; he died only a few months later.[3] The treatment given to Gramsci, an extreme example of the Fascists' determination to silence their opponents, was symbolic of the fate awaiting those in the PCI who remained in Italy. By 1928, 2,500 of the Communist Party's total enrolment of 7,500 were already in jail.[4] By 1934, the Fascists had imprisoned a further 2,800 Communists, leaving only 2,400 still free in Italy.[5] Party membership remained well below 3,000 for the next ten years.[6] These approximate figures reveal the rapid decline of the Communist Party from a propaganda group to the mere skeleton of an organization. Imprisonment created a tightly knit leadership within the PCI, however. The Communists were most commonly incarcerated together in the jails of Ponza, Ventotenne, Lipari, and Civitavecchia; they formed their own study groups and read the same classic texts of socialism.

Confino, or domestic exile, was an alternative to jail for many opponents of the Fascist regime. Most commonly, political and intellectual figures who spoke out against Mussolini were sent deep into the south of Italy where their ideas about democracy or social revolution were completely irrelevant to the misery of backward, almost feudal Calabria. Internal exile was an extremely effective way of silencing the opposition.

Carlo Levi's *Christ Stopped at Eboli* is a moving portrait of the experience of *confino* for one person (although not a Communist).

The life of those few Communists within Italy who avoided jail and *confino* was one of clandestinity. Ignazio Silone's book, *Bread and Wine*, eloquently captures the frustration and fear of a life passed between ineffective proselytizing and imminent arrest. Palmiro Togliatti, the leader of the PCI, described the traits developed among the Communists during the clandestine period:

> We became accustomed to working in little groups. We had to meet in the smallest numbers possible. All contacts had to be organized in such a way as to expose the organization to the minimum risk. All individuals joining the party had to be thoroughly considered and examined, according to particular criteria, so as not to expose the illegal body to the risks of penetration, not only by enemy but even by uncertain elements, since uncertainty was enough to compromise everything. It was in this way, then, that certain habits of work developed.[7]

These 'habits' would later count in the Resistance.

Imprisonment, *confino*, and clandestinity effectively dismantled the Communist Party on Italian soil. The only way that the PCI survived the years of Fascism was by leaving the country. Most of the national leaders as well as many of the local figures in the Communist organization spent the *ventennio* in France, particularly in Paris, where the PCI set up its main foreign headquarters. The Communist Party continued to publish its own newspaper, *l'Unita'* (Unity), though circulation was largely restricted to the exiled community outside Italy. The Communists developed strong ties with their French counterparts; indeed, many Italians later fought with the French resistance after 1943.

A significant group of Communist leaders spent many of their exiled years in Moscow. The most important of these individuals was Palmiro Togliatti, the PCI's general secretary from 1927. Togliatti had been a revolutionary activist within the Socialist Party and one of the founders of the Communist Party in 1921. Arrested by the Fascists in 1925 and released early the next year, he travelled to Moscow to represent the PCI. Fascist repression in Italy forced Togliatti to remain abroad and he took up the leadership of the PCI from the Soviet Union.

Moscow was, in a sense, the 'logical' location for the PCI to concentrate its highest leadership – after all, the Communists had first proclaimed their loyalty to the bolshevik revolution in 1921. Exile forced the Communist Party to develop further its ties to Moscow. As the PCI grew weaker and weaker within Italy, its connection to the international Communist movement simply became indispensable to the Italians, for it gave the Italian Communist Party the appearance of strength and permanence which Fascism had so thoroughly undermined.

The years abroad in Paris and Moscow affected the PCI in many ways. Most importantly, the longer the Communists stayed in exile, the poorer became their understanding of the Italian situation. Increasingly ignorant of what was taking place within their native country, the Communists gradually lost contact with Italian reality. The decline in the quality of their thinking is best revealed in the major theoretical and strategic debates among the exiled Communists in the 1920s and 1930s.

At the PCI's Third National Congress, held outside Italy in Lyon, France, in 1926, the Italian Communists devoted most of their attention to considerations on the socialist revolution they still believed possible. They then passed the late 1920s in sterile argument about whether resistance to Fascism should take the form of a proletarian (i.e. Marxist) or a popular (i.e. national) revolution, unable to see that an anti-Fascist uprising of any sort was quite unlikely at that time. But perhaps most revealing of how exile had weakened the Communists' analytical powers was their decision in 1936 to promote a policy of national reconciliation with the *Fascists* based on Mussolini's original programme of 1919 with its anti-capitalist rhetoric and advocacy of major social reforms. The Communists were unaware of the confusion that an alliance on these terms would create among the opponents to Fascism; the PCI leaders also showed a poor appreciation of the difficulties a strategy designed only to reform Mussolini's regime would be likely to face within Italy. The Soviets, acknowledging the protests of the incredulous Italian Socialists (also in exile), forced the PCI to back down on this confused and ill-advised tactic.

Exile also increased the influence of the Soviets within the Italian Communist Party. The very fragility of the PCI after its expulsion from Italy made it increasingly dependent on affiliation with the Comintern. But recognition from Stalin carried a price – the Italian Communist Party had to submit to Soviet discipline. This resulted in the PCI's acceptance of the many policy shifts of the Third International: the Italian Communists first supported the 1928 'social fascism' programme and later, in 1934, they reversed their policy in recognition of the United Front strategy. The combined effects of exile and dependence on the Comintern, then, virtually eliminated accurate and independent thinking among the Italian Communist leaders, at least until the Spanish Civil War.

If exile increased the PCI's reliance on its Comintern connection, to what extent could the PCI be considered a 'Stalinist' party in the 1930s? The answer may at first seem relatively simple: no one and no party survived those years in Moscow without becoming 'Stalinist'. The establishment of the PCI's leadership in the Soviet capital, the purges within it (by 1932, five of the nine members of the PCI's central committee had been expelled from the party on the orders of the Comintern, although none were assassinated), and Togliatti's position on the Secretariat of the Comintern (from 1927) are the most striking examples of the absorption of Italian Communism into the Soviet system.

But another factor makes it more difficult to maintain that the Italian Communist Party was *thoroughly* 'Stalinized' in the 1930s. It must be remembered that the PCI was an extremely weak member of the international Communist movement. The exiled community of Italian Communists was hardly central to the Comintern's concerns, unlike their comrades in Germany, France, and Spain. Furthermore, precisely because the PCI no longer existed as anything but an organizational shell, it could not be oriented to Soviet interests as a mass movement. As a result, the allegiance of Italian Communists to the Soviet Union was different to that of their European counterparts (especially the French); ties to the USSR were less rigid and less doctrinaire in Italy because they were largely formed during and after the Second World War, not at the high point of the Soviet crisis in the 1930s. Thus Mussolini's destruction of the PCI paradoxically 'saved' Italian Communism from the worst effects of Stalin. The PCI's leadership could (and did) shed much of its formal Stalinist trappings later when it found itself directing a spontaneous mass resistance movement in Italy.

Though it may have escaped the worst effects of its dependence on the Soviet Union, the PCI was still in poor shape in the 1930s: it was a small group of exiles largely arguing about their own insignificance. This sterile period only ended with the outbreak of the Spanish Civil War in 1936. After the dramatic collapse of Communism in Nazi Germany, the Comintern endorsed the united front policy and promoted a broadly-based resistance by all political and social groups against Fascism. Spain was the first nation where this strategy was put to the test, and the Italians participated wholeheartedly in the defence of the republic against Franco's insurgents.

Oggi in Spagna, domani in Italia! ('Today in Spain, tomorrow in Italy!') was the rallying cry for the Italian Communists who joined the PCI's Garibaldi Brigades as part of the international volunteer forces fighting for the Spanish Republic. A number of Communists gained considerable military experience during the Civil War; later, in the early 1940s, they put that experience to work in the Italian resistance to Fascism. The PCI leadership also involved itself actively in the Spanish struggle. Togliatti was the principal Comintern observer in Spain and directed relations between the Communists and the other political forces defending the republic. The experience in Spain matured in Togliatti many ideas about the role of a Communist party in an anti-Fascist resistance: the need for moderation in order to ensure the social and political unity necessary to defeat Fascism and the desirability of defending bourgeois democracy as a crucial element of that national unity. Togliatti's pamphlet, *'For the Salvation of Italy, for the Reconciliation of the Italian People'*, which appeared in August 1936, included many of the ideas which would later be used in Italy. The Civil War in Spain, then, developed both an anti-Fascist, democratic strategy for the Italian Communist Party and prepared many of its exiled members for the armed struggle which would later be waged in Italy.

The collapse of the Spanish Republic ended this period of fruitful activity for the Italian Communists. The PCI abroad was further weakened in 1939 in the wave of the arrests by the French police which followed the declaration of the Nazi–Soviet non-aggression pact; Togliatti himself was briefly imprisoned, but concealed his identity and was soon released. The PCI, though, was forced to re-establish its offices in Moscow, where it remained for the next four years.

In the spring of 1940, Fascist Italy entered the war on the side of Germany and seized the south-eastern region of France. Immediately after this initial victory, however, the alliance with Hitler and participation in a world war became too costly for a weak Italy. Italian troops joined the disastrous Russian invasion, they fought and were defeated in north Africa, and they had to be rescued by the Germans in Albania and Greece. Within Italy, civilian discontent with the war effort rose at the same time. Food shortages, rationing, the draft, and military defeat abroad all undermined the passive tolerance Italians had given to Mussolini's regime throughout the 1930s.

The PCI was not particularly active in Italy during the first years of the Second World War. The Communists attempted to establish an operating centre in Milan in 1941, but this group remained largely ineffective. A wave of factory strikes in March 1943 saw the PCI playing a prominent organizational role, but the protest lasted only a short time and was strictly limited to a few industrial cities in the north. The Communists largely spent the period up to 1943 waiting for an opening. Indeed, the Comintern sharply criticized the PCI for its 'opportunist passivity' as early as 1939; however, there was very little that the Italian Communists could do. Though the party had an idea of the anti-Fascist struggle it wished to wage in Italy, conditions in the country were not yet ripe.

That situation changed suddenly and quite unexpectedly in July 1943. Shortly after American and British troops invaded Sicily, the King of Italy, Victor Emmanuel III, announced the dismissal of Mussolini and the assumption of governing powers by an Army officer, Marshall Badoglio. Victor Emmanuel's act caught the exiled opponents of Mussolini by surpirse. Fascism seemed to have ended overnight; the Italian Communist Party was nowhere to be seen.

RESISTANCE 1943-5

The 'palace coup' of the king on 25 July 1943 opened a curious period in Italian history.[8] The royal dismissal of Mussolini followed a vote of no confidence in the Duce by his own Grand Council of Fascist Ministers. Mussolini was taken into custody and sent to prison for his own safe-keeping; the king appointed Marshall Badoglio, hero of the 1930s African campaigns, as the Duce's successor to the prime ministership. The new state would last for only a month and a half – the so-called 45-day summer government of Badoglio.

Italians greeted the announcement of Mussolini's dismissal and Badoglio's assumption of power with joy. The population filled the streets in spontaneous demonstrations celebrating the end of the war. Lost in the general enthusiasm of the moment were the concluding words of Badoglio's radio message to the nation: 'The war continues.'

The job facing Pietro Badoglio was monumental. He had to find a way to 'neutralize' without sacrificing Italy. This required secret negotiations for an armistice with the Americans and British – who crossed the channel from Sicily to the Italian mainland during his time in office – while simultaneously appearing not to renounce Italy's obligations to her German ally – who had some troops already stationed on Italian soil. The task was far too great for a man of Badoglio's limited capabilities; the collapse of his government was a tragedy for the nation which also had a crucial effect on the resistance.

Though the 45-day summer government was a failure, the Badoglio period was quite profitable for political groups of all sorts. These included the Communists, the Socialists, the 'Justice and Liberty' group (later the Action Party), the forerunners to the Christian Democrats (DC), and the Liberals. The manner and speed with which Mussolini fell from power stunned all the opponents of Fascism, but, more importantly, Fascism ended in Italy without their participation in any significant fashion. The king's decision thus showed the irrelevance of anti-Fascism in the Italian political system at that moment. The opposition parties, particularly the PCI, determined never again to be 'left out' of the political arena as they had been on 25 July.

The summer of 1943 was a prolific time of organization for the anti-Fascist movement. While genuine political parties remained illegal during the 45-days, Badoglio's government did permit the formation of 'groups' and committees which could represent the interests of the populace to the state. The Italian Communist Party seized this opportunity. The PCI was able to capitalize on the partial return of political rights under Badoglio far more than other groups for three major reasons.

First, the organizational shell of the Communist Party had remained intact during the years of Fascism, even though the individuals who held leading posts in the party had been incarcerated or exiled. The Communists, therefore, already had an organization, and their task was simply to fill it; the other political groups had first to create their organizations. Additionally, by 1943 the Communists had a long history of determined anti-Fascism, reinforced by Mussolini's propaganda which had defined all opposition as 'Communist'; the PCI immediately drew on this tradition in its recruitment efforts. Thirdly, an amnesty granted to the political prisoners of Fascism in August returned the very best and most dedicated of the PCI's arrested comrades to the party; filling the organizational structure became that much easier. For all these reasons, then, the PCI was able to make more out of the opportunities for political action presented during the 45-days than all of the other political groups combined.

The 45-day period ended ignominiously. Italy's need for an armistice with the Allies became all the more obvious when the American and British forces crossed the channel separating Sicily from the Italian peninsula and began to work their way north. Badoglio's secret armistice talks resulted in an agreement on 3 September, but fear of German reprisals led him a few days later to attempt a change in the treaty's terms. This action prompted General Eisenhower to announce the armistice on 8 September. Italy was unprepared for its new neutral status.

The Germans, however, had not been deceived by Badoglio's declarations of loyalty. The army divisions already in Italy were reinforced and preparations were made for the complete occupation of the country. The German invasion of Italy took place immediately after Eisenhower revealed Italy's armistice with the Allies. By 10 September, Germany fully occupied most of the mainland and faced the Allies in the south.

The Badoglio government did not stay in Rome to see the German occupation. On the announcement of the truce, Badoglio, the king, and most of the government's highest officials fled the capital city and made their way south to the areas already held by the Americans and British. Badoglio left ambiguous instructions to the Italian Army, calling for a resistance to 'aggression' and promising further orders. Those instructions never came. As a result, virtually all of the Army capitulated to the invading Nazi forces.

The manner in which the 45-day government ended had several important effects for the anti-Fascist resistance movement which was soon to develop. First and foremost, the flight of the king and the government thoroughly destroyed whatever popular allegiance to the monarchy and state had managed to survive twenty years of Fascism. A gaping political vacuum opened which the political 'groups' of the Badoglio period were eager to occupy. Compounding the crisis of state legitimacy was the Army's capitulation to the Germans. The military was thoroughly discredited and as a result never played a formal role in the later resistance to Fascism. Italians were thus remarkably free of allegiance to state and armed forces in a way uncharacteristic of the other Mediterranean nations occupied by Germany during the war. This made resistance, in some ways, a less divisive proposition.

The invasion by Germany also set the stage for resistance as national liberation; the Nazis' installation of Mussolini in a 'new', Fascist Republic of Salò did not confuse the issue – the Duce's thorough reliance on foreign troops was obvious to all Italians. After 10 September, the liberation of the nation from both foreign occupation and an imposed Fascist regime became the primary concern of Italian anti-Fascism. All political actors – foremost among them the Communists – adopted a strong focus on national liberation as part of their resistance programme. In response to the conditions in Italy, then, nationalism found its way into the programme of the Italian Communists.

The significance of the manner in which the Badoglio government fell – the end of traditional loyalties and the inauguration of a movement for national liberation – would become more obvious over the next twenty months. Most immediately clear was that Italy had suffered a major defeat; all anti-Fascist groups were forced back underground after the short period of somewhat open political activity during the 45-day parenthesis between two Fascisms. The end of political freedoms, however, was least traumatic for the PCI, which already had twenty years of experience in clandestinity. The PCI returned to the familiar terrain of illegality and took up its old 'habits', newly reinforced and expanded by the brief period of relative liberty during the summer of 1943.

Between 25 July and 8 September 1943 the stage was set for the generation of a mass, popular resistance to foreign occupation and domestic Fascism. This, however, took several months to develop. The belief that the war was nearly over initially blocked the rise of a national resistance movement. The liberation of Naples in October, which followed several bloody days of popular insurrection against the German forces, and the Allied advance up the peninsula seemed to announce the end of the Italian campaign within the year. However, the Allies stopped for the winter just north of Naples, and the front did not move until the following spring. In the meantime, the political organization of the resistance took shape.

The first step was the formation of a Committee for National Liberation (the CLN). Participating in the CLN were all the major political opponents of Fascism: the Communists, the Socialists, those in the newly formed Action Party, the Christian Democrats, and the Liberals. The CLNs, which also existed at regional and local levels, brought all these groups together in a programme whose common denominator was opposition to Mussolini's Fascism and German occupation. Agreement on this basic programme guaranteed the minimum unity of all the national anti-Fascist forces – including the PCI – for the duration of the war. Unity was also expressed concretely: all decisions had to find unanimous agreement within the CLNs.

The Allied advance obviously played the most crucial role in Italy after September 1943. Most importantly, the liberation of southern areas in 1943 (that is, before the resistance actually began) recreated an age-old problem in the history of Italy: the division of the peninsula between the north and the south. From Rome northwards, the CLNs focused on the military organization of the resistance; from Naples southwards, they concerned themselves with problems of administering an Allied-occupied Italy. The two experiences were vastly different and the political perspectives of north and south in the post-war years reflected that difference: southern Italy remained largely unaffected by the resistance and therefore unsupportive of the movement for political reform generated by the anti-Fascist struggle. The results would be seen in the first post-war elections in 1946 when the conservatism of the south tended to block a fundamental renewal of political institutions in Italy as a whole.

In the German-occupied areas of Italy, the hint of what the national liberation movement would become was first seen in the small, armed groups which appeared spontaneously after the fall of the Badoglio government and the reinstallation of Mussolini at Salò. Most commonly, local anti-Fascists found weapons among the supplies left behind in the barracks of the Italian military. They took up a precarious existence in the more remote areas of the country, particularly in the Apennine mountains and the foothills of the northern Alps. Communist Party members participated, and occasionally led, these first small bands. By the end of 1943, there were at most 9,000 men in these groups; their resistance was largely limited to graffitti on village walls, sabotage, and the assassination of individual Salò officials.

But conditions in Italy were laying the groundwork for a mass resistance at the same time. Life in German-occupied and Fascist-administered Italy grew more difficult during the winter of 1943–4. The sacrifices required of the population to sustain the war effort increased: food rationing and the deportation of men to Germany as a source of labour contributed greatly to popular discontent. Most important for the resistance movement itself was the introduction of a military draft by the Republic of Salò. The desperate nature of Italy's situation was obvious to all, and the young men called to arms under Mussolini after November 1943 increasingly refused to report for induction. Many opted for concealment in the northern regions of Italy and there, in hiding, they came into contact with the small bands of determined political anti-Fascists. The nucleus of the Italian resistance formed in this manner; draft evaders, whose first political act after a lifetime spent under Fascism was the decision to save their own lives, became anti-Fascist *partigiani*. Indeed, it was young men with an average age of only 22 years who made up most (perhaps 80 per cent)[9] of the fighting forces in the armed anti-Fascist movement.

The 'real' Italian resistance appeared when political direction and military orientation were brought to the spontaneous anti-Fascism of popular discontent and draft evasion. This began during the spring and summer of 1944. One of the earliest indications of what this combination could accomplish was the wave of factory strikes in the north of Italy in March. In Turin, Milan, Genoa, Bologna, and Florence nearly 500,000 workers put down their tools in what was the first and largest strike in all of German-occupied Europe. The industrial action was a protest against conditions in both the factories and the cities. The Italian Communist Party played the key role in organizing this mass demonstration which clearly revealed the extent of popular discontent with the war. Civilian and industrial protests continued and intensified in the months that followed.

As discontent increased and spread throughout German-occupied Italy, the people and the *partigiani* gradually moved closer together. Initially, this occurred because the partisans were most often themselves natives of the small mountain villages. Indiscriminate German reprisals against innocent civilians living in the areas of resistance activity only strengthened the ties between the populace and the anti-Fascists. A close relationship soon developed: the *partigiani* acted in ways to help the local population by disrupting German requisitions of food and livestock, by burning draft and civil records in Fascist town halls, by distributing foodstuffs to the people, and by monitoring their own partisan forces to protect civilians against bandits; the local population provided food, shelter, clothing, and vital information to the partisans. A truly mass anti-Fascist movement developed in this manner.

Organization combined with the discontent of the Italians to produce an increasingly serious and armed anti-Fascist resistance in central and northern Italy from the spring of 1944. The Communist Party played the most significant role in forming the first large partisan groups. The party's Garibaldi Brigades, seen earlier in the Spanish Civil War, with their Communist commanders and political 'commissars' appeared in Italy in September 1943; initially, the military command was solely in the hands of the PCI. By June of the following year, the *Garibaldini* were the largest and most effective fighting forces in Tuscany, Emilia-Romagna, Piedmont, Lombardy, and Liguria.

How large and important was the armed resistance movement at this time? Estimates of the strength of the *partigiani* vary enormously, but the Republic of Salò's own figures put the total in the summer of 1944 at approximately 80,000 armed partisans in the centre and north of Italy.[10] What is much more certain than the actual numbers was the growing scale of partisan activities. June 1944 saw the establishment of the first 'free' zone within German-occupied Italy – the short-lived Republic of Montefiorino, nearly 1,200 square kilometres of mountainous land in the Emilian provinces of Modena and Reggio-Emilia. The partisans, under the leadership of the Communist Party, liberated Montefiorino from German and Italian Fascist control and administered the 'Republic' until the end of August.[11] The late summer and early autumn of 1944 also saw the armed resistance movement spread out of the hills and into the flat countryside in northern Italy. The *partigiani* engaged in their first major battles in open terrain with German troops. Perhaps as many as six of the twenty-five German divisions in Italy were eventually diverted from the war against the Allies to contain the partisan movement.

Aid began to reach the partisans once the resistance assumed such significant proportions. American and British secret service officers parachuted behind German lines and established contact with the *partigiani*, providing military expertise and organizing the first air drops of supplies and weapons. Official Allied policy in Italy was strongly influenced by the English desire for the restitution of the monarchy and strong suspicions of Communism. However, the British and Americans in the field appear to have paid very little attention to the politics of the resistance forces; their help went to those most able to fight the Germans and the Italian Fascists, and that commonly included the partisans enrolled in the Communist Party's Garibaldi Brigades.

To what extent was this early resistance Communist? The answer to this question rests quite heavily on how 'being Communist' is defined. Actual members of the Communist Party were always a small minority within the partisan forces. In July 1943 membership stood at roughly 5–6,000; the party grew to perhaps 50,000 by September[12] and it remained at that approximate level to the end of the war in April 1945. These individuals were most often the leaders of the *partigiani*; those whose anti-Fascism had been formed in prison and exile and who brought to the movement military experience gained during the Spanish Civil War.[13] There is little doubt, then, that a significant percentage of the local leaders of the Italian resistance were communists.

But enrolment in the PCI was far from the most important consideration during the months of the resistance. The conditions of guerrilla warfare discouraged official membership. There was quite simply no time for political education or enrolment; indeed, there were barely enough resources available to arm and feed the partisans during the resistance. But it is important to stress that there was really no need for either political education or formal membership at any time during the resistance. Thousands of young men and women considered themselves 'Communist' because they supported or fought in the Garibaldi Brigades under the leadership of Communist Party members; the Brigades were open to any person regardless of political ideas, religious beliefs, or social standing willing to take up arms against domestic Fascism and foreign occupation. The strength of these people's loyalty was seen every day in the risks they took to free their country.

These observations suggest that a general Marxist definition of 'Communism' inadequately describes the specific National Communism developing in Italy during the 1940s. The PCI's role in the resistance and its earlier history during the 1920s and 1930s increasingly made Communism and anti-Fascism synonymous terms. New conditions, those of an armed struggle whose strength lay in the support of the Italian people, then created a very new 'Communism'.

The leadership of the PCI did everything it could do to encourage the identification of Communism with anti-Fascism. The lessons gained painfully in the defeat by Fascism plus the experiences in the Spanish Civil War laid the foundations for a new Communist strategy in Italy in the years 1943–5. The crucial development came in the early spring of 1944 when Togliatti, the PCI's general secretary, returned to Italy to lead the party in the resistance struggle. This important watershed in the history of the Italian Communist Party is referred to as the *svolta*, or 'turning point', of Salerno.

In early March 1944 the Soviet Union unexpectedly recognized the Italian government led by Badoglio which had taken refuge after the German invasion in the Allied-occupied south. On the 28th, Togliatti reached Italy, landing at Salerno after a month-long journey from the USSR. In his first statement on Italian soil in nearly twenty years, Togliatti announced that the Communists would collaborate with Badoglio and the monarchy in the interest of mobilizing the country most efficiently in the fight against Fascism. He furthermore indicated the Communists' willingness to postpone the all-important 'Institutional Question' – the decision between monarchy or republic – until after the end of the war.

Togliatti's dramatic change in policy recognized the supreme importance of defeating Fascism in 1944. He spelled out the implications of the *svolta* in a June 1944 pamphlet entitled *Instructions to All Comrades and to All Party Cadres*. It included the following two important points:

2. ... The insurrection we are aiming for must not be that of a political party or of a section only of the antifascist front. It must be the insurrection of the whole people of the nation.
3. Always remember that the aim of the insurrection is not the imposition of political and social transformations in the socialist or communist sense. Its aim is national liberation and the destruction of fascism. All other problems will be solved by the people through a free popular consultation and the election of a Constituent Assembly when the whole of Italy will have been liberated.[14]

These words express quite clearly the moderation of the PCI's highest leadership at least until the end of the war. On other occasions in 1944, Togliatti spoke of the need for the party to make 'political sacrifices' and to avoid 'useless disorder' as ways to guarantee national unity for the duration of the resistance.[15] What did this new orientation to the problems of Italy really mean and what considerations lay behind the *svolta* of Salerno?

There was little about the 'turning-point' that was truly new. In essence, the PCI's willingness to work with the current government and postpone other major questions (monarchy or republic; parliamentary democracy or social revolution) until after the war was the statement in Italian terms of the Comintern's earlier 'united front' strategy.

But the *svolta* did indeed mark a major change in at least two ways. First, it broke a stalemate in the political organization of the anti-Fascist movement. The Italian anti-Fascists, including many of the Communists already in the country before Togliatti's return, had consistently refused to acknowledge Badoglio's claim to govern Italy; they felt quite deeply about the betrayal by the state and the monarchy on 8 September 1943. In the spring of 1944, their hostility to Badoglio had become a major obstacle blocking the unification of the entire country in the struggle against Fascism. Togliatti's decision immediately altered this situation. The *svolta* forced the other political parties – the Christian Democrats, the Socialists, the followers of the Action Party, and the Liberals – to follow the Communist lead speedily or find themselves isolated in their intransigence.

Furthermore, the *svolta* marked a new direction within the Communist Party itself. Togliatti's own position was far from certain after twenty years in exile, and his policies were not immediately adopted. Debates about the *svolta* assumed dramatic proportions within the Communist Party itself; however, Togliatti's decision, reinforced by the prestige of the Soviet Union, was eventually accepted for it did make sense of the current situation in Italy and matched the outlook of the newest recruits to the PCI. Therefore, the real turning-point intended in the *svolta* was twofold: first, it ended the political stalemate facing Italian anti-Fascism; secondly, it returned centralized decision-making to the Communist Party after twenty years of illegality, exile, and clandestinity.

Many factors 'explain' the *svolta* of Salerno: international, military, domestic, and party considerations entered into the complex matrix from which Togliatti's decision emerged. However, one element is particularly worth emphasizing. The decision at Salerno was a clear response to the party's early history of defeat and exile. The failure to resist Fascism in the 1920s, expulsion from Italy in 1926, and, more recently, the irrelevance of the PCI (along with the other anti-Fascist forces) in the dismissal of Mussolini in 1943, convinced the Italian Communists of the absolute importance of remaining within the government. Twenty years in the political wilderness developed a pragmatic view among many in the Communist leadership; the *svolta* presented them with the opportunity not only to return to Italy and end their exile but also to take up a leading role in the government. Togliatti's decision to work with Badoglio moved the PCI from the margins into the political centre, placed the party in a commanding position, and opened the path towards a government of national unity for the duration of the war. The Communist Party's role in the growing resistance movement only reinforced its newly achieved political status.

The *svolta* was intended as a pragmatic reaction to the conditions existing in Italy in 1944, but it was not only that. The Salerno 'turning-point' also began to redefine the nature of Italian Communism. Official entry into the government on 21 April 1944 tied the PCI to temporary collaboration with the monarchy, established the party as a responsible actor on the Italian political scene, and committed the PCI immediately to the defence of both nation and democracy (and not to the advancement of social revolution). These were remarkable positions for a Leninist political party to adopt and no one, including Togliatti, could foresee their eventual implications. Once accepted as official policy, the Salerno decision encouraged further changes in the Communists' perspective on Italy and the country's future. Conditions different from those which lay behind the *svolta* would further develop these new ideas about Communism in the years after 1945.

The Allies liberated Rome in the early days of June 1944. The city again became the centre of national politics. The war appeared to be drawing to a close and the Committee of National Liberation, established in the capital, began to play a more active role. It refused to endorse Badoglio for a further term; instead, it selected Ivanoe Bonomi, a Liberal from pre-Fascist days, as the new head of government. The CLN promoted the unity of the Italian trade union movement by sponsoring the Rome Pact which created a single working-class economic organization, the General Confederation of Italian Workers (CGIL). The Committee also developed better relations with the Allied occupation forces, reaching at the end of 1944 an agreement with the Allies in which the CLN gave up its claim to govern all of Italy in exchange for Allied recognition of CLN local administrators in the newly liberated areas.

Of course, the war did not end in 1944. The Allies reached Florence in August 1944 but went no further that year as their advance was bogged down in the rains and mud of the autumn. Northern Italy remained separated from the liberated centre and south by the German defences on the 'Gothic Line' running along the crest of the Apennine mountains between Florence and Bologna. In November, the British general Alexander told the partisans, poised for a popular insurrection in the north, to return home and await the Allied spring offensive. Thus began the harshest winter in the Italian resistance.

German troops took advantage of the Allied halt to organize expeditions against the Italian *partigiani*. For most of the winter of 1944–5, the partisans managed to stay only a few steps ahead of the enemy. Groups most commonly disbanded or crossed the German lines only to be disarmed by the Allies and sent to work repairing the damage in newly liberated Tuscany. Few partisan divisions were able fully to carry on the fight during the winter.

The spring, though, saw both the renewal of the Allied advance and the resurgence of the partisan movement in northern Italy. Once the Allies were under way and the end of the war was in sight, the resistance movement grew enormously in the final weeks before liberation. Armed partisans now operated freely in the hills and the flat countryside. Civilian demonstrations assumed massive proportions, with the Communist Party organizing women's protests against food rationing and forced deportations; these demonstrations became a serious problem for the local

Italian Fascist administrators. In the last weeks of April, with the Allies across the Apennines, the *partigiani* and populace arose in a general insurrection, harassing the German withdrawal and liberating Italian cities in advance of the British and American troops. Partisans captured and killed Mussolini as he attempted to leave Italy for Austria. By the end of the month, all of the north had been liberated. The war in Italy was over.

At the head of most of the triumphant partisan forces in the liberated areas was the Italian Communist Party. The party had reason to celebrate. The PCI had promoted armed resistance from its beginnings in 1943. Its contribution to the movement was greater than any other single party: perhaps as many as 50 per cent of the *partigiani* had enrolled in the Garibaldi Brigades. The Communist Party had made sacrifices, too: more than 42,000 of the approximately 70,000 partisan casualties during the war of liberation came from the divisions of the PCI.[16] There was no question of the major role played by the Italian Communist Party in the national defeat of Fascism.

The implications of the Communists' success were many. Most obviously, the PCI had become a mass movement during the twenty months of the Italian resistance. Though actual membership figures remained quite modest until after the April liberation, popular support for the Communist Party increased dramatically during the war. That support was soon expressed in official figures: membership in the PCI soared from a few thousand in April 1945 to over 1,750,000 by the end of the year, and to over 2 million by the middle of 1946.[17] Anti-Fascism brought these people to the PCI; the resistance had given the Communist Party what it had sought since its foundation twenty-five years earlier: mass support.

Additionally, the identity of resistance with Communism, which was the foundation of the PCI's enormous and rapid growth, had some significant effects on PCI thinking. First, the resistance was partially a struggle for national liberation from Germany. The Italian Communist Party was therefore 'reborn' with a strong national identity. This meant that the PCI in 1945 was no longer only a political party of the working-class. Togliatti faced this issue six months before the liberation when speaking about the national 'character' of the PCI:

> What do we marxists mean when we speak of the nation? We mean the working class, the peasantry, the mass of intellectuals, the mass of workers not only by hand but also by brain – clerical workers, professional workers. We exclude from the national community only those selfish groups, those reactionary, property-owning classes who are politically incapable – and have demonstrated this to the whole of the Italy and the whole continent of Europe – of rising above the consideration of their own shabby interests, but have instead put these above the general interests of the people of their country.[18]

Nationalism in the PCI thereby created not only a mass party, but also a movement in most sectors of Italian society.

Representation throughout Italian society was not the only result of the Communists' expanded definition of their legitimate constituency. A primary characteristic of the resistance was its broad social unity in pursuit of one goal common to the whole of the country. This lesson informed both the PCI's leadership and its mass membership. Formation during the years of anti-Fascism encouraged the Communists in their belief that such single goals did in fact commonly exist and could provide the basis for future political action. The Communists were unable to see that there might be very little left on which to stand united once Fascism had been defeated in Italy.

For these reasons, success in the resistance meant that the PCI in 1945 only poorly resembled a 'traditional' Marxist party. The Communists were well aware of the originality of their situation. Togliatti noted:

> The reality . . . is that we Communists in Italy, perhaps first among the Communists in the whole of Western Europe, find ourselves faced with a new problem which never confronted us in past years, either when we were a legal force, or much less in the harsh years of illegality and persecution. We Italian Communists, first among the Communists of all Western Europe, are faced with the new and serious task of creating a Communist party in completely new conditions, with tasks completely new and different from those we were posed in the past.[19]

Realizing that the resistance had both changed the meaning of Communism *and* provided possibilities for different policies in Italy, the Communists began to talk of the PCI as the *partito nuovo* – the 'new party' – a mass, national, broadly-based, and innovative movement.

The resistance, however, was not 'just' a movement for national liberation. Fundamental to the anti-Fascist appeal was the idea of renovation in Italy which would make the reappearance of Fascism impossible. The Communist Party defined its commitment to renewal in terms of support for a 'progressive democracy'. The content of this new democracy was presented in the following manner:

> We speak of progressive democracy as the form of political and social life which is distinguished from the old, prefacist democracy to the extent that it is formed on the self-government of the popular masses. Therefore, it is not a democracy which exhausts itself in periodic electoral consultations; rather it is a form of social and political life which assures, through the free associations of the people, a pre-eminent weight to popular participation in government.[20]

The forms that progressive democracy were to take would be decided upon later. It is important to note, however, that these words, as vague as they were, did not include a call to social revolution.

Why not? Togliatti had hinted that the PCI faced 'new tasks', but what had become of revolution in the Communist Party's programme? One answer popular in the late 1940s maintained that the PCI's leadership engaged in a tactic of deception, playing down its real revolutionary aspirations while awaiting a more appropriate moment for the uprising. There is no doubt that there were men and women genuinely committed to social revolution within the Communist Party; they could read between the lines of 'progressive democracy' and find an endorsement of their own point of view. But given that we shall never know who or how many of these people were active in the Communist movement in 1945, it seems more important to stress that the majority of those who supported Italian Communism did so on the basis of the party's own propaganda, which consistently gave primary importance to anti-Fascist, and not revolutionary, goals.

Even if those with radical aspirations had been able to influence Communist Party policy, there were very good reasons for not advancing social revolution in Italy in the spring of 1945. Foremost among these was the Allied presence on the peninsula. British and American troops remained in Italy as an occupation and administration force until the end of 1945. The civil war then raging in Greece was proof of the Allies' determination to block social revolution in the Mediterranean, and Communist Party leaders in Italy specifically cited the 'Greek example' when urging restraint on more radical supporters. Additionally, the partisan movement was simply not strong enough to make a revolution immediately after the war: its numbers were too few and its military capability too limited. But the most important reason remains the fact that by April 1945 the PCI was no longer the party of social revolution it had been in 1921.

Togliatti was always ambiguous on the issue of revolution, hoping not to split the party at a crucial moment when the Liberation offered the PCI a real opportunity for concrete, if not revolutionary, political action. But a more satisfactory response to the question of revolution within the Communist Party must look beyond the PCI leadership to the conditions existing in Italy at the time of the liberation. The resistance developed out of mass discontent with war, German occupation, and Mussolini's second Fascist republic. For certain historical reasons (not peculiar to Italy), the Communist Party was best equipped to articulate the spontaneous anti-Fascism of the population and provide the organization necessary to create an armed resistance movement. In the process, Communism and anti-Fascism became inextricably linked; the victory of the resistance was therefore a victory also of Italian Communism. But the resistance's primary task was the defeat of Fascism; it was never intended, nor did it gain mass support, as a movement for social revolution. The identity of resistance and Communism in the particular situation existing in Italy, then, continued the transformation of the PCI begun in the years of Fascist repression and exile. The resistance simultaneously created Communism in Italy as a mass movement and set the *partito nuovo* new, non-revolutionary tasks; both aspects amounted to a major redefinition of Marxism during the period. The Communist Party returned to Italy as the leading advocate of anti-Fascism, an important proponent of democracy, and a prominent party of government.

THE REPUBLIC, 1945–8

1945–8 was a period of transition for Italy and its new democracy.[21] It was in these years that the 'wind from the north', the spirit of renewal which arose during the resistance, finally exhausted itself, lasting only a few months longer than the armed anti-Fascist movement itself. Even after Fascism and the disaster of war, many of the institutions which had traditionally led Italy (with the notable exception of the monarchy) found their way back into power. Curiously enough, the Communist Party – which arguably had the most to gain from genuine renewal in Italy – acted in ways which only hastened the end of this transitional period and ensured the survival of conservative elements in Italian society. That the 'wind from the north' eventually blew itself out may not be all that surprising; that the Communist Party played an important role in obstructing the renewal is, at first sight, quite curious.

The Italian Communist Party expanded enormously throughout the immediate post-war period. By November 1945 its membership stood at just over 1.7 million; at the year's end that figure reached nearly 1.8 million. Growth continued during 1946, passing the 2 million mark by the autumn; membership in the party continued to increase, reaching 2.3 million by the end of 1948.[22] Electoral support for the Communists in 1946 approached 20 per cent, equivalent to 4 million votes. In many areas, their support was far higher. An 'electoral machine' for Communism had been created in Italy.[23]

These figures reveal a simple fact: Togliatti's *partito nuovo*, with its vision of a progressive democracy for Italy, its support for a government of national unity to enact much-needed economic, social, and political reforms, and its open admissions policy, was quite clearly received with enthusiasm by a significant (and ever growing) percentage of Italians. The numbers, in essence, were the strongest confirmation of the popularity of the party's strategy.

By 1946, then, the PCI had become a major force in the country. The party also played an important role in the Italian economy through its domination of the major trade union organization, the CGIL. The PCI leadership had therefore fully succeeded in its immediate task – that of establishing the party's presence in many sectors of Italian society. There was little on the political horizon to trouble the Communists; strong and growing stronger, they looked forward to conquering new terrain.

Success encouraged the PCI in its policies. The party leadership, validated by the immediate post-war boom in Communist fortunes, attained an even greater degree of control. At the very top of the hierarchy, Togliatti remained the PCI's general secretary. His conciliatory style ensured that the central committee of the party included all of the leading figures in the Communist movement – even those most reluctant to accept the *partito nuovo* orientation.[24] Togliatti thereby guaranteed unity and a wide diversity of political opinion within the party, avoiding the creation of an outspoken opposition to his leadership. Togliatti also enjoyed the approval of the Soviets, and the prestige of the USSR within the PCI was quite high immediately after the war.[25] The advancement of younger members, whose political formation was intimately tied to the resistance period, into leadership positions in the rapidly expanding organization guaranteed that Togliatti's vision of Communism gained further support. For all these reasons, Togliatti's views on the *partito nuovo* gradually overcame the reservations expressed by the older generation whose primary political experience was the bolshevik revolution and exile.

Success in the first years after the war also gave the Italian Communist Party a greater interest in the 'system'. Democratic politics served the PCI quite well (until 1948) and the party's support of the Parliament, initially offered in the interest of resisting Fascism most effectively, took on a more permanent character. Participation in government, crucially important to a party exiled for twenty years under Mussolini, gradually became the only political 'strategy' of the PCI; and in this respect, the Communists came increasingly to look like other political parties in the new Italian democracy.

Indeed, the first disturbing sign of the PCI's absorption into the Italian political system, with its tradition of alliances based on expediency rather than principle, appeared remarkably soon after the end of the war. In the autumn of 1945, a political crisis created by conservative parties brought about the fall of Italy's first (and as it turned out only) government based squarely on the spirit of renewal generated by the resistance. Prime minister Parri, the leader of the Action Party and head of a government which represented the Committee for National Liberation, was forced to resign after only six months in office. The Communists were eager to arrive at early elections and establish a three-party governing coalition (PCI, DC, and PSI). They chose not to oppose the Christian Democrats and the much smaller Liberal Party in their efforts to put an end to the experimental CLN-government.[26] The fall of the Parri government weakened the 'wind from the north'; the discrepancy between the Communists' words on political and social unity and their failure to act decisively to save the CLN formula was striking.

One unexpected development encouraged the Communist Party in its focus on participation in the government. Life in Italy, especially in the recently liberated north, remained exceedingly difficult immediately after the war. Food supplies were low, unemployment was high, and, despite a general demobilization of the partisan forces, there was still a tremendous quantity of weapons in circulation. These were the ingredients for a frightening crime wave which lasted for more than a year after liberation.

Violence first erupted in a bloody settling of scores between the *partigiani* and ex-Fascists in the spring and summer of 1945. 12–15,000 people died between April and June 1945;[27] among these were, undoubtedly, the innocent and marginal collaborators with Fascism. A leap in the rate of common crime, particularly armed robbery, occurred in these same months and continued for the next year. National and local police forces concentrated their efforts on removing as many weapons as possible from circulation; hundreds of people were arrested and huge caches of hidden arms discovered during 1947.

Most often those found with concealed weapons were ex-partisans, and in the north that meant they were most commonly ex-partisans in the divisions of the Communist Party. For this reason, the police attempt to demilitarize the northern provinces very quickly took on the appearance of an anti-Communist crusade. The arrests put the PCI on the defensive and the party rushed to protect the resistance heritage from what it considered harassment and slander.[28] But the Communists also quickly discovered that while protest and legal action could correct the worst errors, participation in the government was the only way to restrain the police.

Alcide De Gasperi, the head of the Christian Democratic Party, became the new prime minister of Italy in December 1945. The PCI accepted a DC-led government with hopes of moving quickly towards a national vote in which the Communists and Socialists expected to do particularly well. But the PCI seriously underestimated the capabilities of the Christian Democratic leader; De Gasperi, in fact, held the prime ministership without interruption until August 1953.

The Left, though, initially got what it wanted. Elections, the first since 1924 (and the first in which women voted in Italy), were scheduled for the spring. The elections for local administration came in March and April, and with these the Left did particularly well in the northern and central areas where the resistance had been the strongest. But more important was the national vote in June 1946, which combined a referendum on the Institutional Question with elections to a Constitutional Assembly.

The popular referendum on the Institutional Question – the choice between monarchy or republic – was an epic electoral campaign. The political forces most tied to the resistance – the Communists, Socialists, and 'Actionists' – all publicly supported a vote for a republic; indeed, the Communists altered their resistance propaganda and spoke of a vote for 'Republican *and* progressive democracy'. The Christian Democrats prefered not to offer an official recommendation to their supporters. In a last-minute effort to save the monarchy, Victor Emmanuel abdicated six weeks before the vote and handed the throne to his son. The king's gesture, however, was too little and too late.

The results of the 2 June 1946 vote on the Institutional Question were quite close. Despite the complicity of the monarch in Mussolini's rise to power and Italy's disastrous involvement in the Second World War, the republic won only a narrow victory. Just over 2 million votes decided the Institutional Question: 54 per cent of the population endorsed the Republic, 46 per cent the Monarchy.[29] The vote revealed the importance of the different experiences in German-occupied and Allied-occupied Italy between 1943 and 1945. The north and centre – the heartland of the resistance – voted in favour of a Republic by nearly two to one while the south – largely unaffected by the armed anti-Fascist movement – supported the monarchy in the same proportion. It was clear that there was a great reservoir of conservatism in the south and that the unification of the 'two' Italies would once again be a major problem in the post-1945 period just as it had been since the 1860s.

However close the final vote, the victory of the republic was still a major achievement. The referendum ended eighty-five years of monarchy in Italy – the enormity of this change makes it impossible to dismiss it as merely a reform. After June 1946, Italy set out as a republic on a new course with a tremendous potential for further innovation. The end of the monarchy was also the direct result of the anti-Fascist movement, and again, as a victory of the resistance, it was also an important and prestigious success for the Italian Communist Party.

Elections for members to a Constituent Assembly were held concurrently with the referendum on the Institutional Question; Italians therefore voted for the men and women who would write the new constitution before knowing whether Italy would be a parliamentary republic or monarchy. Despite this confusion, the voting figures were high (over 90 per cent) and the vote revealed the political preferences of the Italians: 35 per cent for the DC, 21 per cent for the PSI and 19 per cent for the PCI. The combined forces of the Left, therefore, received a majority of just over 40 per cent. The Action Party of ex-prime minister Parri gained less than 2 per cent of the popular vote. The remainder was split among eleven smaller parties.[30] The Communists saw their policies and history validated by over 4 million votes, establishing the PCI as the nation's third largest political party.

The Communists had reason to celebrate after the June elections. Nearly 2 million members, over 4 million votes, control of local administrations in Emilia-Romagna, Tuscany, Piedmont, and Lombardy — all of these were major achievements for a party which had never before exercised a real impact on Italian politics. Progress, and quite possibly even progressive democracy, seemed guaranteed. 1946, however, turned out to be the high-water mark of Italian Communism in the immediate post-war period. In only a few months the Communists would be on the defensive; by April 1948 it appeared as if they were again heading towards political insignificance.

An important issue arose immediately after the 2 June vote. One policy common to all the political parties of the resistance was an insistence on a thorough purging of Fascism from Italian society after the war; this 'cleansing' was seen as the important first step in a true renewal of the country. Even before the final liberation of the north, the CLN had established its own commissions of inquiry in many local areas. These bodies gathered information and prepared for the removal of Fascists and collaborators in politics, business, government, and society.

Its origins in the armed struggle ensured that the PCI strongly endorsed a thoroughgoing purge in Italy. During the war, the party had even included as legitimate targets of the purge those who had 'helped' Fascism to gain power in the 1920s and had later profited during Mussolini's rule in the 1930s. 'We consider these people, just as much as the [Fascists] . . . co-responsible for the catastrophe that Italy has undergone', Togliatti announced in Florence in October 1944.[31] The PCI had furthermore put some of its best people to work on the CLN's commissions in the liberated areas. However, the issue of collaboration was an extremely complicated one in a country which had been Fascist for over twenty years. In addition, the 'unofficial purge' seen in the spontaneous wave of killings in the first months after liberation greatly alarmed the country's political leaders — including those of the PCI — and encouraged the search for a new solution to the difficult question of collaboration. It gradually became clear, even while the Communists continued their speeches, that the wide purge envisaged during the resistance was probably undesirable and quite possibly impracticable.

It was Togliatti, the Minister of Justice in the DC-led government which followed Parri, who, late in June 1946, drafted the law granting amnesty to all Fascists not actually convicted of crimes. This step marked a major reversal of Communist Party policy; though the PCI leaders tried hard to present the amnesty as an act taken in the best interests of the country, they largely failed to convince the organization's mass base. Disillusion ran high within the party. The resolution of the purge issue, though, was seen as a necessary step to ensure the PCI's presence within the government. The amnesty effectively extinguished the 'wind from the north' by allowing the many individuals and major institutions which had clearly collaborated with Fascism to continue to occupy important positions in post-war Italy. Amnesty also marked the death of the CLN spirit, already mortally wounded by the fall of Parri's government and the results of the June vote for the Constituent Assembly.

A second PCI initiative made even clearer the Communists' determination to stay in the government. 1947 opened with the Assembly hard at work on the constitution. One of the most sensitive issues concerned the status of the Roman Catholic Church in the new Italian republic. Church and state relations had been a constant problem since national unification in 1870; a resolution had come only in 1929 when the Fascists and the Church found enough common ground to sign a concordat, the Lateran Pacts. This agreement had established the principle of a Catholic Italy and granted full legal and diplomatic status to the Vatican in exchange for the Church's recognition of the Italian nation and government. By 1947, however, the Church was concerned that the 'northern wind' might blow away the many privileges which the Lateran Pacts had guaranteed for nearly twenty years. Pope Pius XII launched the Church's crusade in defence of its status on 22 December 1946, speaking out against the Communists to 250,000 people in St Peter's square. As the Pope saw it, Italians were 'either with Christ or against Christ; either for the Church or against the Church'.[32] It looked as if the religious question was about to resurface in Italian politics.

This greatly concerned the Communists. As part of its resistance programme, the PCI had suspended the intransigent rejection of religious sentiments associated with traditional Marxism. The Communist Party had accepted all those who wished to enter its organization, insisting only on a commitment to anti-Fascism during and immediately after the war. To some extent, this was only practical politics for a Communist party in as Catholic a country as Italy; however, it also reflected the PCI's commitment to the unity of all Italians in the fight against Fascism. The Pope's attack on the PCI, then, threatened to raise a very unwelcome issue for the Communists.

In order to forestall a potentially explosive and certainly divisive debate on religion, the Communist Party instructed its members in the Constituent Assembly to join with the Christian Democrats in their endorsement of the renewal of the Lateran Pacts as the basis for regulating Church and State relations after the war. This put the PCI in sharp contrast to its closest ally, the Socialist Party, which, along with the smaller Republican Party, strongly opposed the continuation of the Fascist concordat in republican Italy. The Communist Party's support was crucial: the PCI's 104 votes in the Assembly guaranteed the inclusion of the Lateran Pacts as Article 7 in the new constitution.

Togliatti had warned the party that 'political sacrifices' would have to be made in order to remain in the government, but the PCI's support of Article 7, coming after the amnesty for Italian Fascists, shocked many of the most dedicated Communists. More damaging than the dissatisfaction within the party, though, was the fact that the Communists' many sacrifices did not guarantee their presence within the governing coalition. The Cold War was heating up in Italy by 1947. The spread of Communism elswhere in the Mediterranean – in Turkey, in Yugoslavia, and especially in Greece (where the civil war continued) – sounded an alarm in the United States. Italy assumed greater significance to American foreign policy-makers, and early in 1947 the US began to explore ways of minimizing the perceived Communist threat in that country. The Church's hostility to Italian Communism was clear. At the same time, coalition with the Communists was becoming an increasingly uncomfortable proposition for the Christian Democrats. De Gasperi returned from a short visit to the United States in January convinced that American anti-Communism could serve his political party well. Several months of government instability from February 1947 encouraged both the Americans and De Gasperi to act: the United States ambassador to Italy tied American assistance, especially a renewal of Marshall Aid money and $100 million in an export–import bank loan, to the formation of a more stable government without Communist participation; on 13 May, De Gasperi submitted the resignation of his third government and two weeks later he formed a new coalition without the Communists and Socialists.

In contrast to the amnesty for the Fascists, votes for the Lateran Pacts, support for a Christian-Democrat-led government or any of the other sacrifices made by the PCI to remain in government, the party could offer no response to an anti-Communist crusade. The combined weight of American economic pressure, De Gasperi's desire to eliminate the Left from government, and the Church's influence was more than the *partito nuovo* could bear. And few, if any, of the lessons from the resistance could help the Communists once the underlying commitment to the unity of all anti-Fascist forces had been broken; however, it is important to note that the Communists themselves had undermined that fragile unity by granting an amnesty, weakening the CLN government, and preserving the privileges of the Vatican. The Communists' only solution was to join with the Socialists in opposition to De Gasperi's fourth government and to form an electoral alliance, the Fronte Democratico Popolare, in preparation for the national vote scheduled for the following spring.

The American anti-Communist crusade had a curious effect on the nature of the PCI's attachment to the USSR.[33] The PCI had previously shown little in the way of a slavish reliance on the Russians. Communist Party propaganda prior to 1947 included obligatory references to the achievements of the Soviet Union, but membership in the international Communist movement was not central to the concerns of the PCI until the Cold War reached its height after May. And even when the Americans, the Catholic Church, and the Christian Democrats made a major propaganda point of the PCI's rather weak affiliation with the Soviet Union in 1948, idolization of Soviet Communism *per se* lacked deep roots within the PCL. However, the need to maintain its position during the Cold War led the Communist Party to develop its connection with the USSR. This emphasis, in turn, set the stage for a severe ideological crisis in 1956 when Khruschev inaugurated the destalinization campaign and the Soviet Union showed its own imperialist leanings with the invasion of Hungary.

Criticism rained down on the Italian Communists from abroad following their expulsion from the government in May 1947. The newly established Cominform permitted the Yugoslavs to launch an attack on the PCI: the Italians were condemned for having accepted parity within the CLNs, for not attempting a revolutionary seizure of power at the end of the war, and for engaging wholeheartedly and exclusively in parliamentarianism. The Communist Party of the Soviet Union continued the criticism later, chastizing the PCI for its failure to remain in the Italian government and for not having taken full advantage of the great opportunities of the post-war transitional period. The PCI had to admit the fairness of these criticisms, for the party had failed at the very task it had set itself.

The national elections of 18 April 1948 were a watershed in Italian post-war history. Cold War rhetoric dominated the campaign propaganda on both sides. The Communists were accused of ties to the Soviet Union, revolutionary aspirations for Italy, and atheism; the PCI charged in return that the Christian Democrats had violated the 1946 popular mandate for a government of national unity and had made Italy a slave of American imperialism.

The results of the vote were a resounding defeat for the Left and an endorsement of the Christian Democrats. The new Democratic Popular Front received only 31 per cent of the vote – this was *less* than the 40 per cent that the Communists and Socialists had polled separately in the 1946 elections to the Constituent Assembly. The Christian Democrats, on the other hand, received 48 per cent, gaining nearly 4 million votes over their 1946 total. The DC gained an additional 100 seats in the Chamber of Deputies, establishing their effective control of Parliament. The magnitude of its defeat stunned the Communist Party and threw the PCI into a serious crisis.

As long as both party membership grew (which it would continue to do, at a decreasing pace, until 1953) and the Communist share of the popular vote rose, the PCI had been confident that its support of parliamentary democracy was still in some way 'truly' Communist. But once defeated by the very political system it had helped to rebuild, the PCI could no longer maintain such optimism. An anti-Communist, conservative government had nothing in common with the PCI's goals for a progressive democracy. The unexpected result of the April elections forced the party to face the fact that it had very little effective strategy remaining. The Communists continued their attempts to broaden the base of the PCI, but this policy had been devised for a party of government, not of opposition.

Three months after the April elections, on 14 July 1948, a young man fired four times at Togliatti as the PCI general secretary left the Parliament building. Togliatti's wounds were serious. He was rushed to hospital and it was not immediately clear whether he would survive. Within a few hours, a spontaneous, mass uprising began in the north of Italy. For two days areas of Emilia, Tuscany, Lombardy, and Piedmont were in the hands of the Communists. They occupied public buildings and factories, barricaded streets, defied the authorities, and declared a general strike. The protest was a clear expression of the Communists' frustration with recent events in Italy; however, the general strike also looked very much like revolution.

The PCI did everything it could to restrain and control the uprising. Even those in the Party with a reputation for favouring more radical policies worked night and day to defuse and contain the protest. The party mobilized fully its trade union organization, the CGIL, in these efforts. Fortunately, Togliatti's condition stabilized and he appeared out of danger. On 16 July, the PCI and the CGIL called off the strike they had never promoted and the situation in the north returned to normal.

The July general strike was perhaps the clearest sign of the dilemma facing Italian Communism in 1948. The PCI had consistently lost political ground, even though it continued to grow, from liberation in April 1945 to the defeat at the polls three years later. In July 1948, the leaders of the PCI proved their unwillingness to support a movement whose strength lay in the streets, not in Parliament, even after the party appeared to have lost the parliamentary 'game'. At the same time, the mass base of the Communist Party manifested a spontaneous desire to change the terms of the political contest while demonstrating their continuing reliance on the leadership of the PCI. The party had reached an impasse.

CONCLUSIONS

The history of the Communist Party in Italy in the years of resistance and revolution has sometimes been recounted with an air of regret. The political party which had given the most to the liberation of the country from domestic and foreign Fascism, willingly postponing other issues until after the country's liberation, received none of its 'just' rewards in the post-war years. After 1945, struggling to maintain its position, the PCI compromised on many important principles and yet still found itself expelled from the governing coalition in 1947 and rejected by the voters in 1948.

There is obviously more to the history of the party than this interpretation allows. First, the PCI was not an innocent victim of history. Though it may not have received the permanent position in government it (arguably) deserved, the party created many of its own problems. The defensive and short-term nature of party policies, the post-war focus on Parliament as the exclusive theatre of political action, the willingness to help powerful opponents – all these elements of the Communists' electoral strategy left the party particularly vulnerable after April 1945.

However, these policies did not miraculously appear nor were they imposed upon the PCI. The Communists' political programme in post-war Italy was the result of the long years of exile, rapid formation in the resistance movement, and experiences in the armed, anti-Fascist struggle. The complicated interplay between the spontaneous anti-Fascism of the Italian people and the organizational abilities of the PCI figured decisively in the generation of the Communists' strategy. The conditions existing in Italy suggested certain tactics or required that policies be fitted to the Italian situation. Strategy had no existence apart from this reality; nor was policy forced upon the Communist mass membership. The thousands who enrolled in or supported the Communist Party did so because the PCI's view of the world made sense to them. Therefore, it would be a misleading simplification to view the policies of the Communist Party, both during and after the resistance, as the products only of its highest leadership.

So, if the PCI suffered after 1945, it did so with policies of its own invention, tested and proved successful in an earlier period. But there is another fundamental issue to consider as well. The premise of this chapter is that the fortunes (both good and bad) of the Italian Communist Party were inextricably tied to the resistance. After the liberation of Italy, the Communist Party was trapped by its own success in the resistance. Its only real strategy of electoral advance required that the conditions generated by anti-Fascism in Italy, particularly the unity of the nation's political forces, would continue after the war.

Could the 'wind from the north' have lasted longer? Could the national unity forged in the resistance have survived after Fascism was defeated? Neither event was preordained, even if highly desirable. The resistance, after all, was a very brief period of only twenty months in the much longer history of unified Italy; furthermore, resistance was confined to the central and northern regions. Given these important limitations, there is little reason to maintain that the mass anti-Fascist movement could have changed Italy permanently. Under sorrowful versions of Communist Party history, then, lies an assumption that the peculiar conditions of the resistance in Italy could have continued after the liberation. This is the same error that the Communists committed in April 1945.

The history of the PCI in the 1940s is a contradictory one of both success and failure. It is commonly accepted that the resistance was the Communists' major victory. The party guided Italy in the defeat of Fascism, and in the process became a mass movement of great importance in Italian society and politics. That the PCI fared much less well in the tasks it set for itself after the war is not a particularly controversial issue either. Given that social revolution was neither part of its programme nor crucial to its mass support (and that Italy was occupied by the Allies until 1945), it is hardly surprising that the PCI chose not to adopt a radical course in the years immediately after the war; however, what is remarkable is that the Communists failed even in the more modest goal of remaining within the government.

Nonetheless, the historical record must be favourable to the Italian Communists. The PCI was instrumental in many of the most important achievements of the nation between 1943 and 1948. It was a key actor in the anti-Fascist resistance, the turning-point in contemporary Italian history. The party emerged from the war as one of the principal champions of democracy; its support ensured the inauguration of a parliamentary republic and a democratic constitution in Italy. The Communists were instrumental in the resurgence of an active and potent trade union movement. The PCI itself became a mass organization and as such played a major role in Parliament, first as a party of government and then as the leading opponent to the political Catholicism of the Christian Democrats.

These are substantial accomplishments for any political party. And though these achievements may have little to do with a 'traditional' or revolutionary Communist programme, they did mark the end of twenty years of Fascism and the beginnings of a lively parliamentary republic which continues today. The PCI, therefore, deserves much credit for its important contribution to the modern Italian nation. The history of Communism in Italy followed an extremely complex path through the turbulent years of a reactionary seizure of power, Fascist dictatorship, world war, and national resistance. These experiences transformed the PCI; the new ideas about Communism's tasks in the present and its goals for the future were distinctly related to the victory over Fascism in 1945. Only an understanding of the effects of the party's development during this complicated time resolves the apparent paradox of how a *Communist* party made the decisive contribution to the return of *democracy* in the very centre of the Mediterranean.

NOTES

1 The history of the Italian Communist Party is best recounted in: G. Amendola, *Storia del Partito Comunista Italiano* (Milan, 1976); G. Amyot, *The Italian Communist Party: The Crisis of the Popular Front Strategy* (New York, 1981); D. Sassoon, *The Strategy of the Italian Communist Party: From the Resistance to the Historic Compromise* (London, 1981); P. Spriano, *Storia del Partito communista italiano*, 5 vols (Turin, 1967–75); J. Urban, *Moscow and the Italian Communist Party* (Cornell, 1986).
2 Italian Fascism is the subject of much recent historiography. Some of the better general accounts are: M. Clark, *Modern Italy, 1871–1982* (London, 1984); D. Forgacs (ed.), *Rethinking Italian Fascism* (London, 1986); A. Lyttleton, *The Seizure of Power* (London, 1973); D. Mack-Smith, *Italy: a Modern History* (Ann Arbor, Mich., 1969), and *Mussolini: A Biography* (London, 1981); C. Seton-Watson, *Italy from Liberalism to Fascism 1870–1925* (London, 1967).
3 On Gramsci's life and works, see: J. Cammett, *Antonio Gramsci and the Origins of Italian Communism* (Stanford, Cal., 1967); A. Davidson, *Antonio Gramsci and the Revolution that Failed* (London, 1977); G. Fiori, *Antonio Gramsci: Life of a Revolutionary* (London, 1970); Q. Hoare (ed.), *Selections from the Prison Notebooks of Antonio Gramsci* (New York, 1971).
4 Urban, op. cit., p. 44.
5 ibid., p. 125.
6 D. Blackmer, *Unity in Diversity* (Cambridge, Mass., 1968), p. 7 n. 9.

7 P. Togliatti, 'Tasks of the party in the actual situation' (3 October 1944), in D. Sassoon (ed.), *On Gramsci and Other Writings* (London, 1979), pp. 68–9.
8 Among the many works on the Italian resistance are: C. Delzell, *Mussolini's Enemies* (Princeton, NJ, 1969); D. Ellwood, *Italy 1943–1945* (Leicester, 1985); G. Quazza, *Resistenza e storia d'Italia* (Milan, 1978); L. Valiani *et al*, *Azionisti, Cattolici e communisti nella Resistenza* (Milan, 1971). English-language readers interested in the resistance should not overlook three novels: S. Hood, *Pebbles in My Skull* (London, 1971); E. Newby, *Love and War in the Apennines* (London, 1971), and I. Origo, *The War in Val d'Orcia* (London, 1956).
  The term 'palace coup' is Ellwood's (p. 13).
9 Quazza, op. cit., p. 105.
10 Ellwood, op. cit., p. 157.
11 On the Republic of Montefiorino and the history of the Communist Party in one province during the resistance, see D. Travis 'Communism in Modena: the provincial origins of the PCI, 1943–45', *Historical Journal*, 29, 4 (1986), pp. 875–95.
12 Urban, op. cit., p. 166.
13 P. Secchia, *Il Partito Comunista Italiano e la Guerra di Liberazione, 1943–1945* (Milan, 1971), pp. 1064–5. This appendix includes a profile of over 1,600 Communist leaders in the resistance. More than 1,500 had been jailed, sent into *confino*, fought in Spain, or participated in the French resistance before returning to Italy and takini command of partisan groups there.
14 Sassoon, op. cit., p. 18.
15 Togliatti, op. cit., pp. 78, 81.
16 Sassoon, op. cit., p. 29.
17 P. Togliatti, 'Il programma dei comunisti per la Costituente', *l'Unita'* (30 December 1945), p. 3; M. Einaudi, *Communism in Western Europe* (Ithaca, NY, 1955), p. 200.
18 Togliatti, 'Tasks . . .', p. 73. Even the connection with the Soviet Union did little to dispel the nationalist sentiments in the party; the wartime propaganda of the PCI most commonly portrayed the USSR as the country which had made the greatest contribution to the defeat of Hitler and Fascism; much less common and much more ambiguous were references to the socialism of the Soviet Union.
19 ibid., p. 68.
20 Cited in Quazza, op. cit., p. 180.
21 The history of these post-war years in Italy is best told by: A. Gambino, *Storia del dopoguerra* (Bari, 1978); N. Kogan, *A Political History of Post-War Italy* (New York, 1981); G. Mammarella, *Italy after Fascism* (Notre Dame, 1966). See also the general works on modern Italy listed in n. 2.
22 Einaudi, op. cit., p. 200.
23 Urban's term, op. cit., p. 213.
24 Indeed, for the next ten years, until 1956, the central committee and the directing executive committee of the PCI remained largely unchanged.
25 See. n. 18.
26 Gambino, op. cit., p. 98.
27 Clark, op. cit., p. 317.
28 Both sides were 'right' on this issue. The national and local police forces were often led by men whose hostility to the Communists was quite clear (and who themselves had much to fear from partisans intent on settling scores with Fascist collaborators). On many occasions, these officials used the discovery of concealed weapons to arrest and detain (sometimes for up to a year) many innocent people. Haste led the PCI, however, to take up a blanket defence of *all* ex-partisans in the Garibaldi Brigades. As a result, the party was left defending many men who were quite clearly guilty of robbery and other crimes; these mistakes did not help the PCI in its protests against the government's police operations in the north.

29 Istituto Centrale di Statistica (ISTAT), *Annuario Statistico Italiano 1944–1948* (Rome, 1949), pp. 154–5.
30 Gambino, op. cit., p. 224n.
31 Togliatti, 'Tasks . . .', p. 70.
32 Gambino, op. cit., pp. 292–3.
33 One of the best sources on the PCI's relations with the Soviet Union is Blackmer's study cited in n. 6.

ABBREVIATIONS

CGIL Confederazione Generale Italiana di Lavoro (General Confederation of Italian Workers)
CLN   Comitato per la Liberazione Nazionale (Committee for National Liberation)
DC   Democrazia Cristiana (Christian Democrat Party)
FDP   Fronte Democratico Popolare (Democratic Popular Front of Communists and Socialists for April 1948 elections)
PCI   Partito Comunista Italiano (Italian Communist Party)

4 Pariahs to partisans to power: the Communist Party of Yugoslavia

MARK WHEELER

On 13 Feburary 1942 the Comintern executive suggested to Tito that the Partisan Supreme Command issue a short proclamation to the peoples of occupied Europe, and especially to those of France and Czechoslovakia, calling upon them to emulate the heroic example of the Yugoslavs' fight for freedom and independence: to deny food and raw materials to Hitler's war machine, to disrupt its operations in every possible way, and to organize partisan movements against the 'mortal enemy of all the countries of Europe – German fascist imperialism'. Moscow promised to give the proclamation 'the widest publicity' on radio and in the press.

The proposal reached the Yugoslav Communists through both the secret Comintern radio station established in Zagreb in June 1940 and their own newly operational wireless link at Tito's Foča headquarters in south-east Bosnia. The partisan leaders were, as Tito wrote to Politburo members Edvard Kardelj and Ivo-Lola Ribar on 23 February, 'delighted' at this mark 'of the trust which Grandpa [i.e. *Djeda*, the Comintern] places in us'. Kardelj and Ribar, who were in Zagreb reorganizing the Croatian party leadership when the telegram arrived, had immediately signalled their assent to Moscow, as did Tito when he received the message ten days later. The proposal was, as Tito enthused in a letter to Moša Pijade in Montenegro on 25 February, 'really a great honour for our Party and our Partisan movement'. Pijade needed the encouragement. He was then beginning what would prove a thirty-eight-night vigil in the snow on Mt Durmitor awaiting Soviet aircraft that never came.[1]

However heartened Tito may have been by Moscow's recognition of the leading role won by the Communist Party of Yugoslavia (KPJ) in the European anti-Axis struggle since June 1941, he assumed the Comintern would itself prepare the proposed proclamation. In his radiogram agreeing to the idea on 23 February he asked merely for the text to be broadcast either in Serbo-Croat or in English so that the KPJ could use it in its own propaganda. He was therefore surprised to receive a reminder on 4 March that his draft was anxiously awaited. He produced a proclamation which was despatched to Moscow on 6 March.

Georgi Dimitrov, the Comintern general secretary, replied on 10 March that Tito's text possessed too much of 'a party tone' to have the effect desired. He proposed amendments which emphasized the grand alliance of 'England', America, and the USSR (which Tito had neglected to mention), removed Tito's reference to the KPJ's leadership of the partisan movement, and excised the concluding slogans hailing the Red Army, Comrade Stalin, and the Soviet Union. Dimitrov also suggested that Valter (Tito's Comintern pseudonym) sign the proclamation with his real name (Josip Broz) rather than 'Tito', and that other members of the Supreme Command sign it as well.[2] Tito promptly agreed to Dimitrov's 'corrections', but demurred that any mention of his name would endanger many people in his native Croatia. His new alias 'Tito' was, he reported, already well known throughout the Yugoslav lands.

KPJ expectations that the proclamation would now be issued were disappointed. Tito was informed on 22 March that 'in the interests of the cause' publication would be postponed until various matters affecting relations between the Soviet and Royal Yugoslav governments had been resolved. The proclamation was never made.[3]

This characteristic episode in the Yugoslav Communists' wartime relations with Moscow has generally been interpreted as an illustration of Stalin's reluctance to worry or antagonize his western allies in any matter peripheral to Soviet state interests. Foreign Commissar Molotov was about to travel to London to sign the Anglo-Soviet alliance and the Soviets were soon to propose a mutual assistance pact to the Yugoslav government in exile, which was widely regarded as a creature of the British. As far as the Yugoslav Communists were concerned, at least after their expulsion from the Cominform in 1948, the Soviets' behaviour in the matter of the proclamation was symptomatic of their disregard for and misunderstanding of the Yugoslav revolutionary struggle. Just as they had been misled that same month to expect the arrival of Soviet aid and advisers, so too had they been set up to flatter themselves Stalin's favoured pupils, a trap into which they would fall again after the war. For not only had the proclamation come to naught, but the Comintern also chose March to launch an inquisition into the truthfulness of Tito's reports on the treachery of the partisans' rivals for resistance leadership and the appropriateness of his party's military and political strategy.

In fact, the contretemps over the proclamation came in the midst of what would later be recognized as a crisis in the partisan movement. At issue, besides the fealty of the KPJ to the first country of socialism, were the nature, aims, and prospects – if any – of the Communist-led resistance. In the spring of 1942 it was to be impressed upon Tito and his colleagues that the successful defence of Moscow did not herald their imminent deliverance by the Red Army, that their efforts to crush the suddenly ascendant četniks of General Draža Mihailović must not implicate the Serb nationalists' sponsors in London, and that their seizure of power was more likely to be achieved by constructing a patriotic front equivalent to the great Allied coalition that it was by provoking or embracing class war.

The partisans' 1942 crisis and their difficulties with their mentors in Moscow are worth stressing at the outset in order to show that the Yugoslav revolution was neither inevitable in its success nor predetermined in its form. The popular uprisings of 1941 had given the KPJ leaders cause for hope. The large-scale Axis offensives they endured and the Allied recognition they won in 1943 would make their triumph likely; and the liberation of Belgrade in autumn 1944 and the rest of the country in spring 1945 would see them ensconced firmly in power. But in 1942 it was their sheer survival that was remarkable.

Two features set the KPJ apart from the other parties considered in this volume. The first, obviously, is that it achieved power. Like the Albanian Communist Party, itself begotten and nurtured by the Yugoslavs during the war, the KPJ accomplished its takeover without the benefit of decisive intervention by the Red Army, a circumstance which distinguished it also from the parties of the future people's democracies of east-central Europe. The second respect in which the KPJ was unique among Mediterranean parties was that it fought for and successfully resurrected a multinational state which, owing to Hitler and two decades' failure to establish a viable political system, appeared dead beyond recall in 1941. Of course most interwar European states had national minorities; certainly all those discussed here did so. But none was composed, as was Yugoslavia, entirely of minorities more or less dissatisfied with their lots. It was the good fortune of the KPJ to be in a position to turn Yugoslavia's previously debilitating national question to its own advantage, skilfully harnessing the nationalisms of the defunct state's peoples to its own revolutionary and unitary ambitions.

There was, then, a causal relationship between the two features: the KPJ's projected resolution of the national question contributed mightily to the making of its revolution. This will be a principal theme in the essay that follows. Many other ingredients, however, went into the making of the KPJ's strategy and its ultimate triumph. These included: the discrediting and disintegration of the old order in 1941; the rivalry, chaos, and barbarism which characterized the Axis 'new order' that succeeded it; the inherent disunity, political shortsightedness, and military ineptitude of the Communists' anti-Axis rivals; the assistance the partisans received after 1942 from both the Anglo-Americans and the Soviets; and the KPJ's own organizational genius, tactical finesse, functional ruthlessness, military valour, and moral hegemonism – all of which enabled it to mobilize in the name of liberation and renewal the energies and enthusiasm of Yugoslavia's most determined minorities. Such a turn of events, and such a series of accomplishments on the part of the Communists, would have been impossible to predict and difficult to imagine in the early months of 1942, let alone during the previous twenty years.

THE BACKGROUND (1918–34)

The KPJ was born within six months of the creation of the Kingdom of Serbs, Croats, and Slovenes (Yugoslavia from 1929) on 1 December 1918.[4] The party represented an amalgamation in whole or in part of the pre-existing socialist parties in the South Slav lands; but its leadership and programme were derived mainly from the doctrinaire intellectuals of the Serbian Social Democratic Party, who joined it *en masse*, rather than from the trades union leaders and 'Austro-Marxists' of Slovenia and Croatia, who split on the issue of embracing bolshevism. The party promptly affiliated with the Third International. Serb dominance of the KPJ reflected what was happening in the kingdom, but with the twist that the party's ex-Habsburg adherents supported an integrated Yugoslav state out of ideological conviction and nationalistic zeal, whereas the Serb Communists merely took the extension of Serbian power and institutions over the other Yugoslav peoples for granted. The 'national question' was for them the business of the bourgeoisie, not of the proletariat or its vanguard. Neither were they interested in the peasantry from which they had themselves usually sprung and which constituted more than three-quarters of the population. They saw their role, rather, as to taunt the establishment, stir up trouble, and await the inevitable European-wide revolution, all the while trusting their class enemies to abide by the rules of bourgeois legalism.

With the tide of industrial strife and rural disorder running as high as revolutionary euphoria in 1919 and 1920, the Communists drew encouragement from their soaring membership (more than 50,000 by May 1920) and electoral successes, both in municipal elections and in the November 1920 poll for the Constituent Assembly. They won 12 per cent of the votes in the latter, coming fourth in the popular vote and third in the number of mandates secured. They did best in the most backward parts of the country and in those areas where there was no other party to give vent to national and/or confessional dissent. The party's popular support was thus less 'principled' than it appeared; while its leadership was divided between proponents of an electoral course and those favouring revolutionary adventures. In neither case, however, were they prepared for the government's assault upon them, initiated in December 1920 with the so-called *Obznana* (Decree). Alarmed by Communist-led miners' strikes in Bosnia and Slovenia, and citing the existence of a revolutionary plot, the cabinet banned KPJ agitation, dissolved its organizations, and seized its funds, archives, and premises pending enactment of the constitution.[5]

Possessing no underground cells or theoretical conceptions on which to fall back, with no support among the bourgeois opposition parties it had reviled as roundly as those in government, and with a membership only tenuously committed to its cause, the KPJ fell apart. The passivity of its disoriented leaders proved as dysfunctional as the desperate activism of certain of its younger elements. Assassination plots were hatched in the summer of 1921 against Prince Regent Alexander (who survived) and the former interior minister responsible for the *Obznana* (who succumbed). The unitary *Vidovdan* (St Vitus Day) constitution having been passed in the meantime (on 28 June), the government proceeded to complete the work of the *Obznana*. The Communist deputies were excluded from the National Assembly in July and the KPJ banned in August with the passage of the 'Law for the Defence of the State'. Party and union leaders were jailed or fled the country. As a recent party history puts it: 'Under the terror of the bourgeoisie the members of what had been until then one of the most broadly-based sections of the Comintern massively deserted its ranks.'⁶ By 1924 the party could claim only 688 members, and this was considered an improvement on the previous two years.⁷

As much a victim of its early heady successes as of its subsequent proscription, the KPJ floundered in its first fifteen years of illegality. Objectively, conditions in an underdeveloped, semi-colonial, and poverty-stricken land like Yugoslavia, where one of the peoples of state (the Serbs) rode roughshod over the others (the Croats and Slovenes) in the name of 'national oneness' (*narodno jedinstvo*), denied even a separate tribal identity to Macedonians, Montenegrins, and Slav Muslims, and ignored when it did not oppress the many non-Yugoslav national minorities (Albanians, Germans, and Hungarians being the most numerous), might have been thought made to measure for a Leninist party. But the KPJ was as yet no such party; and opposition to the real and perceived effects of Serb hegemony had been pre-empted by all manner of nationalist, clericalist, and peasantist parties, by terrorist groups like IMRO (Internal Macedonian Revolutionary Organization) and, later, the Croatian Ustaše (Rebels), and, among the exiguous working class, by a reborn Socialist Party endowed with a privileged position in the trades unions. Attempts initiated by Moscow in 1924 to link the Communists with the masses of the Croatian Peasant Party (HSS) and the gunslingers of IMRO were embarrassing fiascos. On the other hand, the party's marginalization at home and growing subjugation to the Comintern abroad did compel it to examine and re-examine its stance on the national and peasant questions, even if the practical meaning of Stalin's dictum that 'the national question is in essence the peasant question' long remained impenetrable and factional infighting consumed most of the party's energies.

Tito was later to attribute much of the notorious intensity with which Right fought Left for leadership positions to the scramble for the high salaries paid by the Comintern.⁸ Although no doubt part of the truth – and typical of Tito's disdain for theoretical disputation – the KPJ did try, whether resisting or accommodating the Comintern's successive orders, to find a means whereby the state's multinational essence and the party's natural inclination to regard that state as its proper sphere of activity could be married in the interest of revolution. The result, according to one Croat scholar, was that 'the KPJ programmatically tested all the viewpoints that are at all possible about Yugoslavia and about the national question in Yugoslavia' in the inter-war years.⁹

Although the KPJ's tangled history in the 1920s and early 1930s need not be reviewed here, its changing attitude towards the Yugoslav state and the place of non-Serbs in or outside it does need summarizing. Walker Connor has offered the following periodization:

> (1) from 1919 to 1923, a refusal to endorse secession; (2) from 1923 to 1926, periodic endorsement by the left wing, but continued rejection by the right wing; (3) from 1926 to 1928, endorsement by the entire party, but little or no attempt to convert it into a catalyst for action (in Soviet terminology, this might be described

as propaganda without agitation); and (4) from 1928 through 1935, the high-tide period, during which 'Secession now!' became the party's rallying cry for all non-Serbian peoples.[10]

The party thus moved from wholehearted endorsement of 'national oneness' and its corollary, unitarism, to obligatory separatism as the Comintern gradually managed to impose both its men and its assessment of Yugoslavia as an artificial creation of the Treaty of Versailles, a prison-house of nations, and a vital link in the anti-Soviet *cordon sanitaire* upon a surprisingly refractory KPJ. Along the way the party had sought refuge in programmes favouring constitutionally guaranteed autonomies, Yugoslav or Balkan–Danubian federations, and self-determination by some or all of a varying list of the state's nations and national minorities, but without compulsory secession. Such intermediate formulations would come in handy later on. For neither extreme, according to the Slovene historian Janko Pleterski, served the Communists' ends:

> They lost political ground when they defended the idea of a united Yugoslav nation, and lost it again when they rejected the idea in such a manner as to interpret the right of the Yugoslav nations to self-determination as requiring secession. Had they stood fast on either the first or the second position we would not today be living together in Yugoslavia, especially in a socialist one.[11]

Salvation was to come in the shape of the popular front. Meanwhile the left-wing sectarian adventurism which accompanied the KPJ's adoption in November 1928, at its Fourth Congress in Dresden, of the theses of that summer's Sixth Comintern Congress on the imminence of war against the Soviet Union – and the consequent urgency of destroying one of imperialism's most militarized bastions in Yugoslavia – led the newly Stalinized party into fresh disasters. Interpreting King Alexander's proclamation of a personal dictatorship on 6 January 1929 as proof that a revolutionary situation was at hand, the KPJ summoned the workers, peasants and oppressed nations to rise in arms in a 'united front from below'. The party postulated a two-stage revolution: a bourgeois-democratic revolution for national freedom would usher in its proletarian successor. These were also notions which would reappear, both before and after the KPJ next proclaimed an uprising in 1941.

The response in 1929 was virtually nil. Communists, few in number and isolated from those they were meant to unite, were arrested distributing leaflets or killed in backstreet shootouts with the police. The result was the effective dissolution of the party as anything other than a coterie of *émigré* 'leaders', themselves subjected to annual replacement by the Comintern. By 1932, when the call to revolt was revoked and the remnants of the KPJ at home began to knit together and to benefit, especially among university students, from a relaxation in the rigours of the dictatorship and a growing disenchantment with its ideology of Serbocentric integral Yugoslavism, the party's membership stood at between 300 and 500.

The KPJ was on the mend in 1934. Although still committed to the early destruction of a state now held to be one of imperialism's weakest links, the party was also toying with anti-Fascism, abandoning Left sectarianism to the extent of penetrating the socialist trades unions, and, perhaps most importantly, expressing the idea that its proper place was at the head of each of the non-Serb peoples' national movements. Yet if the 1934 agreement among the Yugoslav, Italian, and Austrian Communist Parties to promote Slovene unification and independence had both anti-Fascist and national liberation components, the simultaneous KPJ efforts to form 'national revolutionary groups' with the likes of the Croatian Ustaše and Montenegrin separatists reflected continuing delusions about the uses that might be made of the radical right.[12]

The Fourth National Conference, held secretly in Ljubljana in December 1934, illustrated these contradictions. Organized by Tito, who had been released from five years' imprisonment in March and co-opted onto the Vienna-based central committee in August, the conference determined to unmask Fascism's claims to set the non-Serbs free, but also to continue efforts to build bridges to their reactionary separatist movements. Worker-peasant republics were demanded for each of the Yugoslav lands, but now in the context of Soviet power 'in all the countries of Yugoslavia' rather than as part of a Balkan federation. Immediate secession by these 'countries' and self-determination for the non-Yugoslav minorities were off the agenda; but the Comintern's orders that separate Communist parties be formed for Slovenia and Croatia – and soon for Macedonia as well – were endorsed. This last decision, by the time it was carried out in 1937 for Slovenia and Croatia, had however become part of the party's policy of national affirmation among those peoples whose 1918 unifications were regarded as incomplete rather than an expression of separatism.[13]

TITO AND THE POPULAR FRONT (1935–9)

The revival in the KPJ's fortunes in the second half of the 1930s is naturally associated both with the introduction of the popular front in 1935 and with Tito's assumption of provisional leadership in 1937. The first development, although foreshadowed by events in 1934, would put the party in a position to break out of its sectarian ghetto and revert to its more congenial, pro-Yugoslav instincts; and Tito, although personally at risk during his several long sojourns in Moscow and with his party under threat of disbandment until late 1939, would succeed in remaking the KPJ in Stalin's image, but with its own interests increasingly to the fore. The repatriation of the central committee, the termination of most Comintern subventions, the installation of a leadership devoted to Tito, and the purging of factionalists, nationalists, liquidationists, and other elements inimical to democratic centralism would make the party an instrument fit to face the trials and opportunities ahead.

With elections in which a united opposition bloc was due to participate scheduled for May 1935, the Comintern instructed the KPJ in March to correct the resolutions of its Fourth Conference, emphasizing anti-Fascism and anti-sectarianism. In June a central committee plenum, meeting in Split, removed secession as an obligatory concomitant of national self-determination. The ground was thereby prepared for the smooth assimilation of the popular front strategy decreed by the Seventh Comintern Congress in August. By the end of 1935 KPJ membership had climbed to 4,500, its highest since 1921.[14]

The party's adoption from 1935 of a progressively more positive attitude towards the Yugoslav state did not mean, however, that it ceased trying to align itself with the grievances of non-Serbs, nor that it renounced its commitment to the transformation of Yugoslav society. Indeed, it was only through revolution that the national question could finally be superseded. In its stress on the revolutionary possibilities of anti-Fascism the KPJ was faithfully reflecting the decisions of the Seventh Comintern Congress.[15] What was not so clear was whether or not the KPJ envisaged establishing its popular front 'from above' (that is, by creating a legal workers' party which might ally with the burgeoning bourgeois opposition) or 'from below' (that is, by infiltrating the unions and various cultural, sporting, and fringe political associations). In the first case, revolution would be postponed; in the latter, it could be close at hand. Certainly no popular front was to be formed. The parties of the United Opposition, convinced that the dictatorship would not long outlast its creator's death at the hands of Ustaše–IMRO assassins in October 1934, and unimpressed by the KPJ's claims as an ally, refused to have anything to do with the party. The experience of being frozen out by the opposition in the 1935 elections was enough to persuade the leadership that the popular front would have to be constructed from below.[16]

The struggle to maintain the party's own precarious unity also appeared to dictate such a course. Wholesale arrests of Communists in late 1935 and early 1936 pointed to the risks of going public. There were other dangers then and later: in Slovenia Communists showed themselves vulnerable to infection by parochial nationalism; in Croatia the comrades resisted orders to establish a legal front party for fear of crossing swords with the dominant Peasant Party; in Dalmatia and among members of the Communist Youth League (SKOJ) enthusiasm for the popular front led to liquidationism, that is to abandonment of the KPJ's vanguard role and internal discipline; while among the left-wing intelligentsia in Zagreb there was unwonted tergiversation over the Moscow show trials. Manifestations such as these reinforced the party's fear of submersion in any genuine national front.

The issue was complicated further by the obscure manoeuvrings that would lead to the ousting and execution in Stalin's terror of the party's general secretary since 1932, Milan Gorkić (né Čižinski), and his replacement by Tito. Gorkić had apparently chopped and changed on the nature of the popular front, confusing and annoying the rank and file at home and setting off at the party summit a new bout of the factional infighting which had long discredited the KPJ. A central committee plenum, held in April 1936 during Gorkić's absence from Vienna and unbeknownst to the Comintern, passed resolutions critical of the popular front and dismissive of the Fascist threat in and to Yugoslavia. The Comintern reacted decisively. Party leaders were summoned to Moscow in August and condemned for departing from the policies of the Seventh Congress, Dimitrov insisting that conditions in Yugoslavia were in fact favourable to the formation of a popular front with the opposition parties, whereas the KPJ had worked exclusively to create one from below. The party was also told that it must, in view of the international situation and the Yugoslav government's increasing tilt towards the revisionist powers, repudiate dismemberment more categorically, counterposing the demand for a democratic and republican federation of equal nations. (This, of course, was just the sort of formula which the KPJ had tried and Moscow rejected in the mid-1920s.) The Comintern decided to install a new central committee which was ordered to move its seat to the country. In the meantime Gorkić would operate abroad as general secretary and link-man with the Comintern, while Tito was named organizational secretary with the task of preparing the return home. In January 1937 the central committee named in November, which had recently transferred its headquarters to Paris, published a proclamation consonant with Dimitrov's August strictures: the Yugoslav state in its present boundaries, constitutionally reorganized in accordance with the right of each of its peoples to self-determination, was hailed as the ideal framework for their common existence in a world menaced by Fascism.[17]

The next two years present the paradox of the KPJ continuing, as a result of Hitler's successive conquests in central Europe and Tito's energetic reorganizations and purges at home, to recover its relevance while becoming almost a non-party in the eyes of the Comintern. When Tito journeyed to Paris in August 1937 to take charge of a rump central committee again embroiled in factional strife following Gorkić's summons to Moscow and subsequent disappearance, the KPJ's stock stood lower than ever. Not only was the enforcement of democratic centralism far from complete in Yugoslavia – where the Montenegrin Petko Miletić was mounting a campaign against Tito's alleged Trotskyism from inside Sremska Mitrovica prison – but ructions among the Yugoslav volunteers in Spain, students and exiles in France, and apparatchiks and NKVD agents in Russia, were compromising the party's existence and costing hundreds of lives at a time when Stalin's fear and loathing of his foreign tools were at their height.

Ignored by the Comintern and deprived of its moneys, Tito decided in March 1938 to return home. There he nominated a provisional leadership, about which he kept Moscow informed, despite the absence of any feedback. Although he had apparently rebuffed an ominous invitation to Moscow in October 1937, by the following June he was back in Paris and keen to go on to the Soviet capital in order to clear up the uncertainty surrounding the party and his leadership. He flew to Russia at the end of August for what would prove a five-months' stay. Besides waiting many weeks to report to Dimitrov and completing his translation of Stalin's short history of the Bolshevik Party, Tito seems to have worked hard at remaining inconspicuous. He later gave Dimitrov and Wilhelm Pieck, head of the Comintern's Balkan section, much of the credit for both his and his party's survival, even though the former affected to doubt the existence of any domestic KPJ organization when they did eventually meet. Tito's ability to offer convincing assurances on this score, and the defeat for collective security represented by the betrayal of Czechoslovakia at Munich, gave him confidence that the Soviets would not sacrifice lightly his increasingly influential party. When Dimitrov did offer him the permanent appointment as general secretary in October, Tito reportedly vowed 'to wash away the stain' besmirching the KPJ. Only in January 1939, however, was the offer confirmed and a mandate extended to form a central committee.[18]

This was not the end of the matter. On his way home in January Tito found that rumours were rife in Paris that the KPJ had been wound up. Dimitrov had to intervene with officials of the French Communist Party to secure the help Tito needed to impose his authority on his fractious comrades in France. In his absence the party in Yugoslavia had also shown less than monolithic unity in the run up to the December 1938 elections. The Croats had refused to endorse the independent participation of the KPJ's legal arm, the Party of the Working People, in competition with the opposition bloc led by the HSS. This was yet another instance of the KPJ's inability to cope with the popular front from above. (The Croatian leadership would be purged after it stepped out of line again in 1939 by responding with what had suddenly become inappropriate patriotism to the outbreak of war.)

Although Tito had agreed to return to Moscow in the spring for a review of his stewardship, he won a postponement when the invitation arrived in May. He was thus on board a Baltic liner when the Molotov–Ribbentrop pact was signed in August. The pact and the war it facilitated simplified his quandary over how to make use of the popular front, and probably contributed to the inquiry's positive outcome in late November. For the Comintern now reverted to a line with which the KPJ was in any case more comfortable: class war and the popular front from below, combined with popularization of the USSR as the bastion of peace and defender of small nations against the ravening imperialists.

IMPERIALIST WAR (1939–41)

At home there was initially confusion in the ranks over the meaning of the Nazi–Soviet pact and a pronounced tendency on the part of some regional leaderships to make their response too defeatist for a party which still touted its readiness to defend its own version of Yugoslavia. The party's embarrassment seems, however, to have been brief. Discipline was ever Tito's watchword, and lapses were now the exception rather than the rule. The abandonment of vocal anti-Fascism and the heaping of odium on the western democracies were, of course, unpopular outside the party, but a certain freedom from intrusive second-guessing by Moscow seems to have been a welcome accompaniment to the outbreak of war. The defection of Vladko Maček's HSS from the opposition, and its entry into Dragiša Cvetković's government following the August 1939 *Sporazum* (Agreement) establishing an autonomous Croatia, had already scuppered any lingering KPJ hopes of forging a united front with the bourgeois opposition, as well as depriving the party, for the time being, of its ability to play the nationalist card in the country's most important disaffected region. What was left was agitation for peace, for reliance on the USSR, and for working-class solidarity in a 'revolutionary national democratic movement' based on the party's now dominant position in the trades unions.[19]

Tito, who spent nearly three months stranded in Istanbul awaiting a convincingly forged passport and visas, did not reach Yugoslavia until late March 1940. Taking up residence in Zagreb, he acted both to relaunch the party by convoking a national conference for the autumn and to dampen down the exaggerated defeatism which had accompanied efforts to sabotage army mobilization in Montenegro, Kosovo, and Macedonia after September 1939. Opposition to the imperialist war was not to be understood as support for the Axis powers. Communists had worked since the *Anschluss*, Tito wrote in the revived party newspaper, *Proleter*, that spring, to remove all obstacles to the defence of Yugoslavia's independence, the most harmful of which was the absence of a 'true people's government'. A more robustly anti-Axis line was adopted in June. The fall of France had shaken traditionally Francophile Serbs, while Italy's entry into the war added to the menace felt by Slovenes and Croats. The Soviets' seizure of Bessarabia and northern Bukovina, and the belated establishment of Soviet–Yugoslav diplomatic relations that same month, indicated that Stalin was not prepared to give Hitler a free hand in south-east Europe. More Yugoslavs were coming, perforce, to believe the Communists' warranty that reliance on the USSR – or Russia – was their country's only hope of staving off incorporation in Germany's 'new order'. The Balkan Communist parties were ordered to revive their slogans in favour of anti-Fascist popular fronts, albeit from below. In this endeavour the KPJ had notable success now, as later, in Slovenia.[20]

The emergence of Soviet–German rivalry in the Balkans reinforced the new-found importance of the KPJ, which was now also acting as the conduit for Moscow's communications with the underground Italian, central European, and Balkan parties. And although the presence of numerous Comintern, NKVD, and Soviet diplomatic personnel in Yugoslavia might have been expected to inhibit exercise of the greater autonomy Tito claimed to have won from the Comintern, it seems instead to have buttressed his confidence that he enjoyed the Soviets' full support.

The Fifth National Conference was both a logistical triumph certain to impress the Comintern and a timely opportunity for affirming the party's revolutionary strategy based on anti-Fascism, resolution of the national question, and emulation of and reliance on the CPSU and the USSR. More than 100 delegates, representing some 7,000 members, assembled secretly in a Zagreb suburban villa between 19 and 23 October to celebrate the party's recovery of nationwide cohesion and influence, and to confirm the leadership which Tito had put in place since 1938. Described by Milovan Djilas as 'not only politically unanimous but personally intimate and friendly', Tito and his colleagues were convinced that the imperialist war had reopened the prospect of new victories for socialism, and that a revolutionary tide was rising in Yugoslavia as well. Whether or not the country escaped direct involvement in the war, the likely exacerbation of economic distress and national disharmony offered opportunities to the Communists. They alone, Tito told the conference, possessed the cure to Yugoslavia's 'chronic malady' in the example of the multinational Soviet state and, with it, a presumptive right to rule. He went on to declare, according to Stephen Clissold's reconstruction of his speech:

> That is why the Party now stands at the moment of its historic destiny. We are not interested in the bourgeois ideal of a fatherland to be defended, but of a world revolution to be carried through. Remember this. The greatest revolution for the Yugoslav State – a revolution which I am confident the mass of the people will accept – will be a revolution which brings national equality to Serbs, Croats, Slovenes, Macedonians, Montenegrins. And that, comrades, will in turn make possible the greater social revolution which we plan and of which the Soviet Union is our glorious model.[21]

The defence of Yugoslavia, whether against Nazi–Fascist aggression or western capitalist warmongering, thus presupposed its revolutionary transformation under the KPJ.

The published resolutions of the Conference were less categorical about the national solution envisaged by the party. The Macedonians (who gained their first ever central committee member in the person of the pro-Bulgarian Metodi Šatarov-Šarlo) ought, like the Montenegrins, to have equality and the right to self-determination. An autonomous government should be considered for the peoples of Bosnia and Hercegovina (Serbs, Croats, and Slav Muslims), so extricating their lands from the perfervid contention of the Serb and Croat bourgeoisies. The ethnic minorities, meanwhile, were asked to content themselves with equality and freedom from national oppression. In all these cases, however, the party stressed the need to expose as bogus the inducements of Italian, German, Bulgarian, and Hungarian reactionaries and imperialists. The Croats and Slovenes were promised merely 'a true settlement' of their national questions. While, as far as the Serbs were concerned, no national question was as yet apparent to the KPJ. None the less, as Paul Shoup has written, this set of propositions 'was remarkably successful in anticipating much of the line to be followed during the war, taking a position in defence of the unity of the Yugoslav peoples, but dissociating the Party from the efforts of the non-Communist groups to solve the national problem'.[22]

Consulting the Comintern that autumn about its more immediate tactics, the KPJ pointed to the increasing likelihood of an Axis-initiated partition in which the national bourgeoisies could be expected to take part. It asked if the party should not now make the overthrow of the Cvetković–Maček government and its replacement by one of the workers and peasants an action slogan. The Comintern disagreed: introduction of a proletarian dictatorship would serve only to isolate the party and promote imperialist intervention. The party must free itself of 'speculation' about possible help from the Red Army, struggling instead for peace, independence, and resistance to Axis demands. On the other hand, slogans calling for the defence of inviolable frontiers or an armed rising in which Communists might also find themselves isolated were inappropriate. The party should work instead to shore up the masses', the bourgeoisies' and the army's will to resist. Should Yugoslavia nonetheless fall victim to dismemberment, it would be the party's task to organize the masses against bourgeois treason and Fascist violence.[23] The Comintern's advice made it plain that there was already some tension between the KPJ's inclination to seize its chance and the more subtle calculations of Soviet diplomacy.

The other powers were pursuing policies in the region that were far from subtle. Within a week of the Fifth Conference, Mussolini invaded Greece. This act, and the formidable Greek resistance it evoked, put paid to Hitler's plans for exercising a strictly economic and diplomatic dominion over south-east Europe. His resolve to attack the Soviet Union in the spring now made it urgent that he secure his southern flank: by rescuing the Italians in Greece and so denying the British the chance to re-establish a continental foothold within striking distance of the Rumanian oilfields vital to the Nazi war machine. The ability of the Yugoslav government to maintain its neutrality was coming to an end. Hitler initiated a campaign of threat and blandishment to compel Prince Regent Paul and his ministers to adhere to the Tripartite Pact, thereby eliminating any uncertainty about their stance when German forces advanced from Bulgaria into Greece. The British, meanwhile, by exerting pressure simultaneously on the personally Anglophile Prince Paul and on anti-Axis Serbs in or near the opposition and military, were seeking to confound the Germans' plans. By February 1941, when inadequate British forces began landing in Greece, their expectations had risen: the million-strong Yugoslav army would now be required to make the defence of Greece tenable by attacking the Italian rear in Albania. Thus by early spring both Britain and Germany were resolved that Yugoslavia should stand aside no longer.

In the short run German power proved more persuasive than British sermons. Yugoslavia joined the Tripartite Pact on 25 March. Yet thirty-six hours later a coup d'état mounted by Serbian airforce officers – some of whom had been encouraged by the British – overthrew the Cvetković–Maček government, declared the 17-year-old King Peter II of age, and sent Prince Paul packing. What the new cabinet led by General Dušan Simović did not do was repudiate the Tripartite Pact. The country's fragile strategic and internal positions did not permit this. A coup which brought rejoicing crowds onto the streets of Belgrade, and allowed the Communists in their number to provide appropriate chants, was greeted with sullen resentment in Zagreb. In order to ensure that Maček and the HSS entered the coalition government rather than accept Axis offers to establish an independent Croatia, Simović agreed to regard both the Pact and the *Sporazum* as valid, notwithstanding the explicitly anti-Axis and implicitly anti-Croat origins of the putsch. Such equivocation made no impression on Hitler. He determined within hours of the coup to obliterate Yugoslavia as well as the British presence in Greece.[24]

The Soviets maintained a cautious attitude in these months. The Yugoslav government had been offered the opportunity to buy arms when Hitler became importunate, but was kept at arm's length when such fillips appeared either unnecessary or a pointless provocation of Berlin. Dimitrov ordered the KPJ on 22 March to stand decisively against capitulation to Germany, but to seek also to create the widest possible opposition to the pro-British 'war crowd'. Reliance on the USSR would somehow square the circle. Soon after the coup Moscow insisted that Communists withdraw from the delirious demonstrations in which they were figuring prominently: the final reckoning with the enemy was far off and the party must not endanger its avant-garde status. Tito, on the other hand, concluded at a meeting with the Serbian leadership on 29 March that war was both imminent and justified. The Simović cabinet was a step forward and its preparations for war should be supported. The party expected legalization and the release of its political prisoners in return. But it continued to assail the warmongering of the 'English' and the 'Serb chauvinists' and to demand an alliance with the Soviet Union. Simović, while trying to discover through staff talks what help the British might provide (the answer was: help yourselves in Albania), was keen too on signing a mutual assistance pact with Moscow. The Soviets, however, would offer no more than a friendship and non-aggression treaty, assuring the Germans in the process of their desire to contribute to Balkan peace. This treaty was announced on the morning of 6 April as the Luftwaffe devastated Belgrade.[25]

THE DESTRUCTION OF YUGOSLAVIA (1941)

The April War was over before it began. A gulf yawned between the Wehrmacht and the Yugoslav Army that no amount of fighting spirit on the part of the latter could have bridged. As it was, there was little inclination and few opportunities for heroics. Not only were the Yugoslavs organized and equipped according to the standards of a bygone era, but they were only half-mobilized for fear of provoking the invasion they now confronted. Their overwhelmingly Serb officer corps was hidebound in its conceptions and paralyzed by German might. Their conscript ranks were riven by demoralization, disaffection, and a 'fifth column' whose rumoured presence was more insidious than its capacity for real subversion. Their war plan, envisaging the maintenance of a corridor for eventual withdrawal from the mountainous interior towards Greece, was invalidated at the outset by the Germans' deep penetration from Bulgaria. It took the Germans longer to locate a general with authority sufficient to sign an instrument of surrender than it did to produce the conditions of chaos and disintegration that made capitulation imperative. The Independent State of Croatia (NDH) was proclaimed by the Ustaše on behalf of their absent *Poglavnik* (Leader), Ante Pavelić, on 10 April. The Italians and Hungarians entered the war the next day to claim their portions of the spoils. The Bulgarians were to have a share merely for undertaking its occupation. King Peter and most of his ministers fled the country on 14 and 15 April, Simović leaving behind orders to seek an armistice and castigating the Croats for having made one necessary. An armistice amounting to an unconditional surrender was concluded in Belgrade on 17 April. This was no simple military defeat. It was the fracture and destruction of an entire ruling order and of the political and national conceptions that underlay it.

The system of partition and occupation improvised by Hitler aimed to assure to Germany its needs (control over the north-west–south-east lines of communication and the production of Yugoslavia's mines and richer agricultural areas), to give expression to Hitler's prejudices and Nazi racial doctrines (punishment for the Serbs, Germanization for many Slovenes, satellite status for the 'Aryan' Croats), to reward Germany's allies while exploiting their manpower, and to eradicate the very idea of a Yugoslav state. The system was in fact to prove a principal cause both of the subsequent resistance and civil wars, and of the Axis powers' inability to extirpate the former while making use of the latter. The satisfaction of those rewarded was brief; the opposition of those consigned to helotry or oblivion was assured. Hitler's allies wanted more. The Italians, especially, felt cheated. Despite their long-term investment in the Ustaše, Pavelić soon repudiated their patronage for that of the Nazis. Instead of dominating all of the western Balkans, Mussolini's legions found themselves policing and provisioning the barren Dinaric regions behind the Adriatic. The Bulgarians mourned the 'loss' of western Macedonia to the Italians' Greater Albania (which also acquired Kosovo), and the Hungarians resented having to yield Banat to the local *Volksdeutsche*.

Nor were the Axis collaborators or favoured peoples among the Yugoslav population long content with their lots. The nationalistic pretensions of the Ustaša regime were undermined by the cession of much of the Adriatic littoral to Italy and Pavelić's agreement to the designation of a prince of the House of Savoy as Croatia's future king. Bosnia, Hercegovina, and Srem were not regarded as adequate compensation, particularly since all of the NDH was divided longitudinally between German and Italian zones of occupation. The reign of terror inaugurated by the Ustaše in May and designed to produce an ethnically and ideologically pure Croatia (Serbs, Jews, Gypsies, and Communists were to cease to exist) was eventually to sicken and its effects to alienate the many Croats who had rejoiced at Hitler's destruction of Serb tyranny and Croatia's recovery of its 1,000-year-old statehood.

The Montenegrin separatists who had looked to Italy for deliverance discovered they were to be but despised satraps in a diminished and militarized colony. The mass uprising that greeted the Italians' proclamation in July of a Montenegrin kingdom in dynastic union with Italy emphasized their isolation.

Macedonians who for thirty years had pined or fought for liberation by their Bulgarian brothers found the reality less pleasing than the prospect. One set of alien and overweening officials, gendarmes, and teachers was replaced by another, overlaid by a brutal military occupation for which Macedonians were also expected to pay. The small number of Macedonians concerned with matters of national identity and inclined to believe that they might be something other than Bulgarians was to grow under the impact of Bulgarian tactlessness and Yugoslav Communist success.

Would-be Slovene collaborators were quickly disabused of their hopes that a tributary but united Slovenia might emerge from the collapse. The Germans annexed the northern two-thirds of the Slovene lands (which were earmarked for German colonization and Slovene assimilation or expulsion); the Italians created a Province of Ljubljana in the south which was joined to Italy; and the Hungarians incorporated the north-east corner. Only in the Italian zone was a collaborationist Slovene administration and militia established.

The Germans' most important Serb servant, General Milan Nedić, who from August presided over what he called a 'government of national salvation', occupied an especially unenviable position. Pared down to roughly its pre-1912 frontiers, Serbia was to remain under direct German control, notwithstanding Nedić's puppet administration and an expanding Bulgarian share in its garrisoning. As well as seeking to secure Serbs' acquiescence in their humiliation with the threat that worse would otherwise befall them, Nedić attempted to invoke traditional Serb symbols, to stimulate anti-Communist and anti-Semitic feeling, and to persuade the Germans to detach the eastern portions of the NDH and add them to rump Serbia. In none of these endeavours was he successful. As the uprising that summer was to show, large numbers of heartland Serbs could accept neither the finality of the April catastrophe nor the enormity of what diaspora Serbs were suffering.

Besides those citizens of the former Yugoslav state who continued to serve the Axis out of conviction or self-interest, or who later came to do so from dread of Communism, only four groups of people found Hitler's order an improvement for any very lengthy period: the Albanian, German, and Hungarian minorities (who were 'restored' to their motherlands or allotted a privileged role in the new dispensation), and the Muslims of the NDH (who as the 'purest Croats' were wooed and aroused by the Ustaše to murder Serbs and who were subjected, in turn, to Serb reprisals). For the bulk of Serbs, Slovenes, and Montenegrins, and eventually too for Croats and Macedonians, the regimes imposed by the Axis powers had nothing positive to offer. Their problem was to find tolerable alternatives.

REVOLUTION THROUGH WAR (1941)

The KPJ leadership, impressed by the 27 March *coup d'état* and the demonstrations that accompanied it, had expected the Army to put up a convincing fight and its own members to assume a prominent part in it. Tito was disappointed on both counts. Communists had not known any better than the generals how to arrest the German *blitzkrieg*. Nor had the military and political establishments proved more willing *in extremis* than in the past to accept the proffered co-operation of a party claiming superordinate status. On the other hand, the new situation was pregnant with revolutionary possibilities. The bourgeois state and its institutions were dead, the manner of their dying offering confirmation of the Communists' earlier and instinctual assessment of their rottenness. Yet the KPJ endured, not unscathed, but unique in possessing both an extensive underground organization and a vision of itself as continuing to operate in an all-Yugoslav framework and for all-Yugoslav ends. At a time when loyalty to and obsession with the fate of one's own nation – as well as hatred for one or more of the others – were in the ascendant, both in the dismembered Yugoslav lands and in the councils of the exile government, the Communists' devotion to the Yugoslav idea was exceptional.

Meeting in Zagreb on 10 April as the Ustaša state emerged and German troops arrived to an enthusiastic welcome, the Politburo decided to transfer its seat to the greater safety of Belgrade, to establish a military committee under Tito, and to issue a manifesto proclaiming the continuance of the struggle. Although there would be temporary defeats, Yugoslavs were exhorted not to lose heart 'because a new world will arise out of this horrible imperialist massacre, the roots of imperialist wars and national oppression will be removed forever and a free fraternal community based on the genuine independence of all Yugoslav peoples established.'[26]

Party leaders assembled again in Zagreb at the beginning of May for a central committee consultation. Among several absences the most notable was that of the Macedonian representative, Šatarov. He had led the regional committee into the Bulgarian Communist Party on the pretext that party and state boundaries should coincide. Insisting that Fascist conquests must not be recognized by Communists, Tito would be required to wage a summer-long dispute with the Comintern and the Bulgarians to get back the right to restart operations in Macedonia. (He was not to be so punctilious about pre-war frontiers when it came to the KPJ's own claim to organize the Croats and Slovenes of Istria, Trieste, and Venezia Giulia.) It was by May also apparent that the party had been eliminated in Albanian-occupied Kosovo and Hungarian-occupied Bačka, while in Croatia a large proportion of the leadership was in Ustaša prisons.[27]

The May consultation was important for Tito's enunciation of what Djilas called 'a new thesis', namely that the party could expect to come to power as a direct result of the war, bypassing the bourgeois-democratic stage of revolution. The party must organize itself militarily so as to be in a position to seize control when Germany and its minions were defeated. This meant, according to Djilas, 'that we had abandoned earlier schemes for democratic and national revolution, as well as the idea of collaboration with allies in a transitional period'. In its enthusiasm for revolution through war – and Tito is reported to have been reading Edgar Snow's *Red Star Over China* that spring – the KPJ was not just reaffirming its preference for the popular front from below, but positing a political vacuum in which non-Communist alternatives to the Axis had ceased to exist, at least on a nationwide level. For, as Djilas went on to write, 'there were no such parties any longer, or such power, unless we Communists, in our fear of an armed struggle for power, were to invent them'.[28] However accurate the diagnosis, what the KPJ leaders did not foresee was that by embracing Christ's (and Stalin's) precept that 'he who is not with me is against me' they would, in effect, help create (or invent) the rivals they depreciated.

Nor did the KPJ yet foresee the possibility that it might find itself waging a large-scale and basically independent struggle before the Axis collapse. Subsequent accounts of the May consultation which portray the party as already envisaging a protracted national liberation war, and a novel form of revolution under conditions of occupation, are wise after the event. In the first place, until Germany invaded the Soviet Union the war would remain imperialist in character. Secondly, even though Tito and his colleagues probably did, as they claimed, anticipate Hitler's betrayal of Stalin and the war's consequent transformation, they also expected the Red Army to make short shrift of the Germans. Their own seizure of power would thus be swift in coming, but it would do so as part of a chain reaction of proletarian revolutions throughout the Balkans and central Europe. The attention lavished in this period on vain attempts to suborn Axis soldiers in the name of working-class unity, and the plans laid for liquidating bourgeois 'traitors' (including both the Ustaše and the royalist officers already in the hills), illustrate the party's expectations. So too do the organizational forms adopted and the nomenclature employed to describe them: at the head, Tito reported to the Comintern, were 'military–revolutionary committees' which, under firm party control, were composed of *desetina* (tens) designed mainly for urban diversions and *coups de main*.[29]

But if the KPJ was planning to launch no uprising or mass resistance struggle at its May consultation, it was seeking to tailor its programme and structure to the varying requirements of each detached Yugoslav nation and region. Open advocacy of social revolution was out of the question for a conspiratorial party of some 8,000 members, while overt appeals for the reconstitution of Yugoslavia would have been met with incredulity in the recrimination-filled atmosphere of spring 1941. Instead the party sought to attract subservient allies and a mass following by adopting a nation-by-nation approach. In each case the party would present itself as the champion of that people's national and social liberation, adding or subtracting pan-Slav and Yugoslav grace notes, and making greater or lesser play of local patriotism, anti-Fascism, social radicalism, and Italo- and Germanophobia. As Walker Connor has noted, neither of the party's slogans (soon to be ubiquitous) – 'Brotherhood and unity!' and 'Death to fascism, freedom to the people/nation!' – contained specific endorsements of Yugoslavia. They could be understood that way, but also as exhortations on behalf of local–national unity and freedom. Yet the party's own high degree of cohesion would, it was assumed, permit it to bring forth unity out of notional diversity. The forms would be Croat or Slovene or Montenegrin, but the content would be socialist and Yugoslav. From the autumn each nation or region would have a military headquarters of its own, staffed by the party's central or regional committees. These, plus the full panoply of fronts for women and young people and organs of local and regional self-government that were evolved, would serve to enhance the sense of equality, to assuage the hurt of historical wrongs, and, ultimately, to replace formal acts of national self-determination.[30]

The Slovenes' strong urge towards solidarity had already found expression in the formation of an Anti-Imperialist Front in late April. Renamed the Liberation Front (OF) after 22 June, its programme demanded both Slovene self-determination ('including the right to secede and unite with other nations') and 'unity and harmony' among 'the enslaved peoples of Yugoslavia and the entire Balkans' in their struggles for national liberation and social emancipation against Italo-German and Anglo-American imperialism.[31] Ranging Christian socialists, members of the Sokol athletic society, and 'progressive intellectuals' alongside the Communists, it carried over into wartime the closest Yugoslav approximation of a genuine united front. For the Slovenes, as for the Croats, a principal plank in the party's platform was national unification, i.e. acquisition of their remaining irredenta from Italy and Austria. (Eventually Macedonians would also be attracted on this basis.) Outside Slovenia the dissolution of the traditional political parties, the continuing hostility of their remnants towards the KPJ, and the Communists' insistence on their own absolute hegemony in any front or pact, left the party few potential allies among the various national establishments. Individual dissidents from the bourgeois parties and assorted luminaries from cultural life were to become highly prized ornaments on the KPJ's numerous fronts, but only the tiny (Serbian) People's Peasant Party of Dragoljub Jovanović contemplated accepting at this state the Communists' terms for anti-Axis unity: its own evisceration and a 'soviet' Yugoslavia.[32]

THE ORIGINS OF RESISTANCE (1941)

Resistance began in Yugoslavia before Hitler's invasion of the Soviet Union impelled the KPJ to summon its compatriots to rally to the defence of the embattled workers' state. Traditions of both organized rebellion and spontaneous popular revolt against alien oppressors were long-established and still-living parts of the South Slav heritage. They were especially marked aspects of the Serb and Montenegrin self-images. Shame at having caved in so easily in April, anger over their present plights, and fear for their future fates combined to produce a widespread hunger for a rematch. The withdrawal of front-line German divisions for service in the east and their replacement by over-age garrison units had, simultaneously, shortened the odds against such a venture. There were, besides the Communists, other groups who refused to accept the finality of the April cataclysm and who intended to organize militarily in the interest of Yugoslav restoration. Foremost among these was the nascent movement of Serb officers who had eluded capture and deportation to prisoner-of-war camps in the Reich and who, taking up a clandestine life in the hills, were to become known as četniks, the appellation (meaning members of a četa or company) an evocation of the Serb irregulars who had fought the Turks in earlier Balkan wars.

Like the KPJ before 22 June, the officers who came gradually to acknowledge the command of Colonel Draža Mihailović did not anticipate fighting the Axis powers until such time as they began to crumble. Their recent experience of the Wehrmacht was too overpowering for them to believe that their movement could play more than an ancillary role in liberating their country. But whereas the Communists envisaged a revolutionary seizure of power guaranteed by the arrival of the Red Army, Mihailović's četniks aimed to take control in the name of King Peter and on behalf of suffering Serbdom as soon as the western Allies appeared on the scene. In the meantime their intention was to organize a secret army founded on the continuity of the Yugoslav kingdom and to offer what protection they could to Serbs imperilled by Ustaša genocide and the depradations of their Croat and Muslim neighbours. The goals of the two movements, then, were antithetical, even if their similar initial strategies and common dependence on Serb and Montenegrin recruits, as well as their respective headquarters' proximity in western Serbia, kindled hopes at home and abroad during the summer and autumn of 1941 that a united patriotic resistance was emerging.

That the četniks and the Communist-led detachments which adopted the Russian name 'partisans' during the summer were to find themselves fighting the Axis and its helpmates – and occasionally doing so together – was the result not only of the Soviets' entry into the war (an important boost for most would-be Yugoslav resisters), but also because of the stark choices confronting the nearly 2 million Serbian Orthodox inhabitants of the NDH. The implementation by the Ustaše of their threefold scheme to rid Croatia of its 'oriental' minority (by expelling a third to rump Serbia, forcibly converting a second third to Roman Catholicism, and slaughtering the remainder) was met first with terror and dumb acquiescence, and soon after with flight and armed revolt. Spontaneous risings of Serb villagers and townspeople began in eastern Hercegovina in mid-June and spread westwards to the former Habsburg military frontier between Civil Croatia and Bosnia where Serbs were numerous and warlike. Although the KPJ later asserted that its waxing influence helped foment these revolts, their elemental and indiscriminately anti-Croat and anti-Muslim character would have made them more amenable to eventual četnik direction had it not been for Hitler's great miscalculation.

PARTISAN WAR (1941)

Tito and the central committee moved to Belgrade immediately after the May consultation. Whether a desire to escape meddling by the Comintern's ambiguously empowered radio operator, Josip Kopinić, and the chief NKVD agent in Yugoslavia, Ivan Srebrenjak-Antonov, played any part in this decision is uncertain. Kopinić's attempt during July to oust the Croatian central committee and to replace it with the Zagreb city committee under his own direction – although ostensibly based on the Croats' inadequate response to the Soviets' desperate plight – lends some credibility to suppositions either that Tito's leadership had begun to displease Moscow or that the USSR had been preparing to recognize the NDH's 'independence' and to hive off the Croatian party. In any case, the famous Comintern injunction to the KPJ to 'bear in mind that, at this present stage, what you are concerned with is liberation from fascist oppression, and not socialist revolution' that accompanied the late-June summons to form 'a united national front' in support of the Soviet war effort certainly indicated that Moscow had serious reservations about the Yugoslavs' Leftist course since April.[33]

The KPJ's florid appeal to Yugoslavs on 22 June to regard the Soviet peoples' heroic struggle as their own, and to do nothing to assist the Fascist hyenas, had also asked them merely to make ready to fight themselves. The leadership, although convinced, in Djilas's words, 'that armed guerrilla actions were in the offing', was not prepared to take such a momentous step without explicit orders from the Comintern.[34] The late-June message from Moscow quoted above had not specified what the party was expected to do to develop the liberation struggle with which it was now charged. The Politburo had none the less converted itself into a chief headquarters of the National Liberation Partisan Detachments of Yugoslavia on 27 June. Tito informed the Comintern at the end of the month that 'we are preparing a people's uprising against the occupiers because there is a great readiness for struggle among the people'. He asked both for Moscow's opinion and, if possible, for the urgent shipment of arms.[35]

'For once', Djilas wrote, 'Moscow did not delay'.[36] The second and last Comintern radiogram in this period (at least for the entire KPJ leadership) was dated 1 July, and presumably represented an answer to Tito's request for help and advice. After repeating that the Soviets' 'fatherland war' was also a fight for Yugoslav freedom, the message continued:

> The hour has struck when communists are obliged to raise the people in open struggle against the occupiers. Do not lose a single minute organizing partisan detachments and igniting a partisan war in the enemy's rear. Set fire to war factories, warehouses, fuel dumps (oil, petrol, etc.), aerodromes; destroy and demolish railways, telegraph and telephone lines; prohibit the transport of troops and munitions (war materials in general). Organize the peasantry to hide grain, drive livestock into the forests. It is absolutely essential to terrorize the enemy by all means so that he will feel himself inside a beseiged fortress.[37]

An enlarged Politburo met in Belgrade on 4 July to put these instructions into effect. A headquarters for Serbia was to be formed immediately under Sreten Žujović; while Svetozar Vukmanović-Tempo and Djilas were delegated to proceed to Bosnia and Montenegro respectively to seek to impose the party's direction on the revolts already brewing or erupting. Vladimir Popović and Edvard Kardelj, who were on their home grounds in Croatia and Slovenia, were entrusted with those less promising commands. The Homolje massif to the south-east of Belgrade was originally considered the most favourable terrain for the struggle in Serbia, it being assumed that the Red Army would soon be crossing the Danube from Rumania. In the event, the more centrally located region of western Serbia – where Mihailović already had his headquarters – was selected. Some of the leaders present at the 4 July meeting lamented the fact that the shortness of the war would deprive the party of opportunities to demonstrate its revolutionary maturity. Only Tito, it seems, believed the war was likely to be long and arduous.[38]

The KPJ's faith in the invincibility of the Soviet Union had no doubt been reinforced by the terms of Moscow's orders to commence 'partisan' warfare. For this implied – and the distinction was drawn explicitly in Tito's enquiry at the end of June about launching a people's uprising – diversionary, sabotage, and small-scale guerrilla operations, not the mobilization of a popular army, the liberation of whole provinces, and the elaboration of revolutionary political institutions. Bidding farewell to Djilas, Tito cautioned against inciting a general rising in Montenegro. The party was strong there, but prone to sectarian extremism; while the Italians appeared well organized. He should begin slowly, with minor actions. Yet if partisan war signified the Yugoslavs' relegation to the role of auxiliaries to the conquering Red Army (and in Vojvodina the KPJ devoted itself to setting up first-aid stations for the expected Soviet paratroops), it also meant accelerated preparations for the seizure of power in Belgrade and other cities. It was notable, for instance, that when the eighty-odd Communists imprisoned at Kerestinec were sprung in Kopinič's badly organized action on 14 July they made immediately for Zagreb and the waiting Ustaše.[39]

Events, in fact, were to compel the party both to embrace all-out struggle in the countryside and to postpone thoughts of taking power in the cities. As Djilas was to discover in Montenegro, the popular will to revolt could neither be stayed nor confined to predetermined channels. 'The people's uprising', as he called it, had to be accepted by the party, even if that meant sharing leadership with royalist officers and arousing expectations of permanent liberation or sweet revenge that were destined to be dashed or turned bitter. Otherwise the KPJ would lose any chance later to impress upon the struggle its own tactics and goals.[40] The cities, meanwhile, remained bastions of Axis power, from which it was necessary to try to extract workers and party members, if only to leaven the party's ideologically dubious dependence on an insurgent peasantry. Tito himself did not abandon underground life in Belgrade until mid-September, when he joined the Serbian headquarters near Valjevo.

It is probable that the Kopinič affair reinforced the lessons being learnt by the KPJ in Montenegro and Serbia. Representing himself as possessing a special directive from the Comintern, Kopinic's frantic efforts to spur the Croatian party into action, even at the cost of destroying its cadres, must have shaken the Politburo's priorities. Kopinič, after all, made no bones about the fact that he held Tito responsible for the Croats' failure to rise up immediately in defence of the USSR. And however inept he may have been in forming a counter-party or inciting his followers to sabotage transports of men and materiél to the eastern front, his activity certainly underlined the message that what Moscow required was the maximum possible diversion in the enemy's rear, not preparations for the seizure of power.[41]

The party's re-evaluation of the nature of the war and of the tasks before it can be seen in the differences between the two proclamations put out by the central committee during July. The first, dated 12 July, summoned Yugoslavs to come to the aid of the USSR in terms identical to the Comintern's 1 July message. Britain and America were invoked merely for their expressions of sympathy for the Soviets' crusade against Nazi Germany. By 25 July, when the second manifesto was issued, the war had been nationalized. Yugoslavs were called upon to live up to their ancestors' freedom-fighting pasts. They must not heed the cowards and traitors who advised that the time for revolt was not yet ripe, but fight to win their own liberty. The party offered all-national leadership in a spirit of self-sacrifice, not because it aspired to post-war power. Yugoslavs must unite 'regardless of political conviction and religious creed, and drive out the detested invaders from their country by their joint efforts', just as the Soviet Union, 'England', and America were uniting to destroy Fascism.[42]

The KPJ had by no means abandoned its revolutionary ambitions, but it was amending its tactics and vocabulary in order to create the liberation front Moscow decreed. Moreover, as Djilas noted, 'words later had an important effect on deeds.'[43] Until its left turn at the end of the year, and then again from the spring of 1942, the party would pursue 'differentiation' on grounds not of class – for neither the masses' weak class consciousness nor the international environment allowed of such a confrontation – but on the basis of whether people were for or against the anti-Axis struggle in its Communist recension. In any case, the more successful that struggle, the more obvious the bankruptcy of the old regime and its remaining proponents would become. During the summer the Politburo ordered the Croatian party to initiate talks with Maček's followers in the HSS and with the Independent Democrats (the party of Croatian Serbs) about forming joint national liberation councils. Besides facilitating resistance by Croats as well as Serbs in the NDH, such councils were envisaged as a step towards 'some sort of central people's government' which would both confound those who contended that the war was a purely Communist enterprise and offer a counter to the exile government. Tito informed Moscow on 23 August of plans to set up a clandestine 'National Liberation Committee which will include well-known representatives of various democratic factions together with our people' and appeal to Yugoslavs 'to join the nationwide struggle'. The re-establishment of Soviet–Yugoslav diplomatic relations in late August put an end to the wider scheme, while the bourgeois politicians' continuing refusal to have truck with the KPJ meant that its narrow aims also remained unfulfilled.[44]

The party's decision to seek co-operation with groups, and not just with individuals prepared to accept its prerogatives, was also evident in the better-known case of Serbia, where from July a *modus vivendi* was sought with Mihailović. The četniks too had been forced to adapt. Surveying the spreading rebellion and the Communists' increasingly prominent part in it, Mihailović concluded that he could not afford to stand aloof if he intended to maintain his claims to embody traditional Serb values, to command the officers' movement, and to preside over the apotheosis of both at the end of the war.[45] As will be seen below, however, his belief in the efficacy of active resistance, and his willingness to tolerate the partisans' practice of it, were as highly conditional as were their terms for working with him. Thus despite taking longer to fail in the case of Milhailović than of Maček, the KPJ was to be stymied yet again in trying to create the semblance of a popular front from above. Moscow's disinclination to credit Tito's explanations meant that the KPJ would also once more find itself at odds with the Comintern, despite having tried to conform.

The insurrection that swept Montenegro immediately after the Italians' proclamation of its 'independence' on 12 July, and which quickly confined the occupiers and their adherents to a few beseiged towns, had not been preceded by any pact or alliance among the KPJ, the many royal officers native to the country, or the clans with which the well-armed Montenegrins still identified. It crumpled as soon as the Italians brought in reinforcements, including the Montenegrins' inveterate Albanian and Slav Muslim foes, and proceeded to mete out punishments. Peasants went home; royalist officers concluded that the rising was premature; and party stalwarts, desperate to keep the revolt going, indulged in summary executions in the name of what they termed the 'anti-Fascist revolution'. As the most vehement proponents and visible organizers of the uprising, the Communists bore the brunt of the blame for its suppression, as well as for their own excesses. The officers began to organize themselves against the Communists and to enlist the support of the Italians. They also sought affiliation with Mihailović. The people's uprising was degenerating into civil war.[46]

The Serbian uprising, meanwhile, had smouldered before taking flame in August, affording partisans and četniks ample opportunity to take each other's measure. More than their antithetical ends, the two movements' incompatible strategies were to make their co-operation and, eventually, their coexistence impossible. Yet because neither side could afford to be seen as the wrecker of anti-Axis unity, and because each possessed moral and material assets coveted by the other, it would take several months for rivalry to become civil war. Although the Communists had worked to provoke the uprising and Mihailović to avoid it, he was as much its progenitor as they, since the widely reported presence of a shadow army in the woods had been as effective an incitement as any offered by the KPJ. By mid-August the Communists disposed of twenty-one partisan detachments with some 8,000 members.[47] Mihailović probably had call on a larger force, but then, as later, his ability actually to deploy his (in)subordinate local commanders and their immobile peasant conscripts was limited. Even worse for his plans for an eventual 'grand finale', many of these men were refusing to wait. The successes of the partisans in attacking communications, gendarme posts, and German patrols, and then in liberating market towns and the resources they contained, seemed to be proving that the immediate and implacable resistance demanded by the KPJ was both feasible and popular. As četniks hastened to join the fray, Mihailović, against his better judgement, but for the sake of his position and his ability subsequently to tame or put down the partisans, followed suit.

As far as the Communists were concerned, Mihailović was both a typical product of the old order they were bent on burying and a legatee of the Serb nationalist tradition they were endeavouring to arrogate. He had to be nobbled or neutralized: forced to commit himself to the struggle (in which case he might have a leading military role in Serbia) or compelled to show that his loyalty was to class over nation (in which case he would be destroyed). By 18 September, when Tito arrived on liberated territory in the company of a party of supposed picnickers, the need to define relations was becoming urgent. Mihailović had lately succeeded in making radio contact with the British, and highly romanticized accounts of his movements were beginning to appear in the Allied press. Word spread at home that he was London's agent and had been promised full support. The military and popular preponderance which the partisans assumed they had won in Serbia by this time might be in jeopardy, for the Communists had a preternatural fear of the reach of the 'English' and their intelligence service. Tito proposed a meeting which took place the next day near Mihailović's headquarters at Ravna Gora, and at which he rehearsed his arguments for unrelenting struggle. Mihailović countered that only carefully planned sabotage was appropriate. Their sole agreement was to maintain a non-aggression pact concluded in August.

In the five weeks that elapsed before their second and final meeting the prospects for even limited co-operation deteriorated. Conflicts over the governance of the 4,500 square miles of west-central Serbia they shared (dubbed the Užice Republic by the partisans after their 'capital'), over the booty to be had from it, and over projected operations to extend its eastern frontiers became more frequent. At the end of September the Germans took the offensive with troops brought in from Greece, France, and the eastern front. At Hitler's command they also initiated a policy of savage reprisals against civilians: 100 hostages were to be shot for every German killed and 50 for every German wounded. In the cities of Kragujevac and Kraljevo on 20–1 October as many as 10,000 men and schoolboys may have been executed in conformity with this order. Like others who had survived the carnage and epidemics that wiped out a quarter of Serbia's population between 1912 and 1918, Mihailović was haunted by premonitions of their biological extinction, a dread which the mass murders in the NDH had already revived. His doubts about the wisdom of the uprising, his assessment of the Communists as an anational and criminal rabble for their provocation and conduct of it, and his assumption – fortified by messages from his government and the arrival of an Anglo-Yugoslav liaison mission at Ravna Gora on 23 October – of his right to compel the partisans' obeisance or destruction were all confirmed.[48]

The exercise of Communist power in Serbia to which Mihailović took such exception – he was especially outraged by the appearance of women in the partisans' ranks and the burning of tax and land records from town halls – had developed according to central party directives, illustrating both the KPJ's precocious commitment to institutionalizing its rule and Tito's organizational flair. Unlike the wretched survivors of Ustaše butchery and rebellious peasants out of whom the party was attempting to mould an army in most other areas, in Serbia it disposed of a good many disciplined KPJ and SKOJ members. The regulations of the partisan detachments promulgated on 10 August had ordained that while Communists were 'fighting in the front ranks', the partisans were not to be regarded as a party force, but as the army of all patriots. Correcting its earlier and more limited understanding of partisan warfare, the regulations stated further that the task now was to develop a nationwide uprising 'lest the Partisans isolate themselves from the masses'.[49]

The people's liberation councils which began to be established in August were entrusted with responsibility for local government and military support services in liberated areas. They were also conceived of as fronts (or transmission belts) in which the party would enlist the masses and through which it would demonstrate that there could be no return to the old regime, but without making its own control either overt or exclusive. Striking the right balance was difficult. Overly-zealous comrades in Montenegro and the Serb pale of Croatia were already setting up organs of revolutionary self-government inspired by – and sometimes proclaiming themselves to be – Soviets. This was as impermissible as the Bonapartism of partisan commanders who treated the councils as subordinate entities, rather than, as Tito and Kardelj explained to the Montenegrins in December, deferring to them as

> the basic organizational form through which the masses are rising in a people's uprising, through which the political leadership of the party in that uprising is being achieved, and through which the national masses are realizing their democratic-revolutionary power under the guidance of the party.[50]

Concerned over the differential pace at which their movement was developing, as well as over its sectarian excesses in some areas and passivity or total absence in others, party leaders gathered in the west Serbian village of Stolice on 26–7 September. They agreed to stimulate uprisings everywhere, and not to rest content with mere 'guerrilla' warfare. Each nation and historic province would have its own staff save Serbia, where the renamed Supreme Headquarters under Tito would remain, but every staff would replicate a common command structure, complete with political commissars. They also confirmed the people's liberation councils as the germs of the future people's power: they would make of the liberation struggle in its separate national manifestations a unified and seamless transition to socialism. Already the Supreme Plenum of the OF had transformed itself into a National Liberation Council with the attributes of a Slovene provisional government, and 'incorporated' its partisan detachments in the Yugoslav partisan army. On the other hand, the need to forge the widest possible wartime unity, including an operational agreement with Mihailović, was reaffirmed.[51]

When Tito met again with Mihailović on 26 October the differences between them had come to centre on the question of overall command. Neither side would yield this to the other, and so no more than a series of technical agreements and pious resolutions to avoid conflict could be made. Having formed the impression that Tito was a Russian, Mihailović made free with imprecations against the Croats and Muslims, declaring his intention to settle accounts at the end of the war. Such talk was no more likely to win over the Communists than were Mihailović's invocations of the king, the British, and his officers' greater experience in support of his claim to supreme leadership. Concluding immediately after the meeting that only force would do, Mihailović resolved to approach the Germans, utilizing his previously established links with Nedić, and offering his services against the Communists in return for weapons and a free hand in their use. In fact open partisan–četnik warfare began before Mihailović was able to meet representatives of the Abwehr (military intelligence) and occupation regime on 11 November. Mihailović, who had overestimated his forces' ability to deal the partisans a decisive knockout blow, then found the Germans unwilling even to consider a temporary anti-Communist alliance. They had agreed to talk only to present a demand for the četniks' unconditional surrender. They intended to rid Serbia of all its rebels by themselves.

Rebuffed by the Germans, his headquarters surrounded by the partisans, and unable to expect timely or adequate help from the British (who, while supporting his waiting strategy and claim on command, were also preaching resistance unity, but without disposing of the means to induce compliance), Mihailović had no alternative but to break off attacks on the partisans and propose a resumption of negotiations. That Tito agreed to cease his counteroffensive and to renew talks was the result of several factors, including the mounting German threat, fear of being held responsible by Serbs for the outbreak of civil war and, perhaps most importantly, Radio Moscow's rebroadcast of British news items lauding Mihailović's leadership of Yugoslav resistance. Negotiations between partisan and četnik emissaries led on 20 November to the signature of an agreement providing for the cessation of mutual hostilities, their rededication to the anti-Axis struggle, and a mechanism for the peaceful resolution of other sources of conflict. Given the impending liquidation of the uprising by the Germans, the expulsion of the partisans from Serbia, and Mihailović's decision to disband or 'legalize' his forces in collusion with Nedić lest his movement suffer the same fate, this agreement was to be taken seriously only by the British and Soviet governments.[52]

Djilas, who had been recalled from Montenegro for his 'errors' in launching and leading an inadequately prepared revolt, arrived in Užice in mid-November both chastened and keen to discover whether or not the party was presiding over a revolution. He sought out Kardelj, already the KPJ's chief theoretician. They agreed that a revolution had begun, more obviously so in socially diverse and politically disunited Serbia than in patriarchal Montenegro. Although national rather than proletarian in form, its essence was being made 'unequivocably' clear in the Užice Republic. Later, in 1943, Kardelj told Djilas that 'sectarian errors' had also been committed in Serbia in 1941, by which Djilas understood him to mean 'the narrowness of our propaganda and perhaps also of our organization, with its exclusively Communist commanding cadres and insignia, etc. – the red star, the clenched fist salute'. Djilas thought one such error had been the parade staged to mark the anniversary of the Bolshevik Revolution, at which Tito took the salute in imitation of the proceedings in Red Square. He felt their principal mistake, however, had been to entertain illusions about their own strength.[53]

CLASS WAR (1941–2)

These illusions were now to be tested: by the Germans' assault on Užice which sent Tito and some 2,000 partisans reeling south-eastwards into Italian-occupied Sandžak at the end of November; by the apparent coming together of the partisans' enemies in an unholy and counter-revolutionary alliance supported, it seemed, by both Britain and the Axis powers; and by the Soviets' inability and/or unwillingness to send material aid, provide propaganda support, or comprehend the nature of the partisans' war. Tito had reported regularly to the Comintern on the progress of the uprising and asked repeatedly for arms and specialist advisers. By late November he was so angry at the tenor of Soviet broadcasts (whether in its own voice or in that of Radio Free Yugoslavia, which started transmissions from Tbilisi on 11 November) that he simultaneously ordered Kopinič (whom he had accused earlier of failing to relay his messages to *Djeda*) to tell Moscow the truth about Mihailović and to remove himself and his radio station to Supreme Headquarters.[54]

Although the partisans claimed to have raised an 80,000-strong army across the length and breadth of Yugoslavia by the end of 1941, their situation was in fact dire. The movement had been effectively eliminated in Serbia; and despite high hopes and repeated attempts to reinfiltrate units, Mihailović would hold virtually undisputed sway there as the nominal resistance leader until early 1944. In Montenegro the partisans' position went from bad to worse. Their reign of terror, which continued through the spring of 1942, far from inciting a recrudescence of rebellion, was solidifying the četnik–Italian condominium. The Slovenes' militancy, meanwhile, had yet to produce a commensurate military struggle; but it was stimulating the consolidation of an Italian-backed and clerically inclined Slovene Alliance (*Zveza*) with its own 'White Guard' forces. In Macedonia the KPJ had won back the right to organize resistance, but would generate no action worthy of note until 1943. Conditions in the NDH were complex and depressing. The party's identification with the Serbs' struggle for survival and revenge vitiated its appeal to Croats and Muslims, above all in German-occupied eastern Bosnia, where local co-operation with the četniks lingered on into 1942. This was not, however, to the benefit of the Communists, since it was the četniks who ruled the roost, absorbing and dispersing partisan units following the latters' expulsion from Serbia. Efforts to save the movement in east Bosnia would be Tito's first priority in the new year. In the Italian zone, on the other hand, the occupiers had considerable success in winning over the Serb populace and četnik bands by offering protection against the Ustaše and arms and money for the fight against the Communists. Eventually the falling out among the Serbs would enable the KPJ to enlist large numbers of Croats (including deserters from Pavelić's ineffectual regular army, the *Domobran*) and some Muslims, but in the first half of 1942 the party maintained only a precarious hold on a few liberated islands in the former military frontier.

The full extent of the crisis was not apparent when the Politburo met on the night of 7 December in the corner of a stifling room full of sleeping soldiers in the village of Drenova near Nova Varoš. The reverses in Serbia, Montenegro, and east Bosnia of which the leadership was aware seemed serious but remediable. Although out of touch with the Comintern, the news from the eastern front was exhilarating: the Germans had been stopped before the gates of Moscow and the Red Army had taken the offensive. Five months of despair on account of the Russian front turned to elation. The war would surely be won during 1942. Linking its own and the wider wars, and dusting off the two-stage model of revolution, the Politburo concluded that Soviet and KPJ successes were, in analogous fashion, forcing both the western imperialists and their Yugoslav adherents (the exile government, Mihailović, the HSS, the Slovene clericals, etc.) to regroup. The contest between the forces of revolution and reaction was opening before the end of the war. Having done little if anything to aid the Soviets, the British were now backing the collaborator Mihailović. The anti-Fascist war was obviously yielding to the class war. How else could their own sudden reversals at the hands of a previously disunited and debilitated bourgeoisie be explained?

The party must strengthen itself ideologically and organizationally, relying on the working class and the poorer peasants. The units which had retreated from Serbia would be merged to form a brigade capable of being sent into action wherever it might be needed as 'the armed force of the party'. (The 'First Proletarian People's Liberation Shock Brigade' was duly formed with a majority of Serbian and Montenegrin party and SKOJ members – if not of workers – on Stalin's birthday: 21 December.) Yet if the KPJ was eager to wage the class war it considered to have been forced upon it, Tito was alarmed by its present association with military failure. He offered his resignation to his colleagues, suggesting that Kardelj replace him as general secretary. All present rejected Tito's gesture, not only because his apparent intention to carry on as commander made it nonsensical, but also because Moscow would inevitably conclude that the party was in an advanced state of disintegration.[55]

The conclusions of the Drenova meeting were translated into directives for the various national and provincial parties as Tito and the Supreme Command fought their way north-westwards into Bosnia over the next few weeks. The Serbian leaders, most of whom had fled with the partisans into Sandžak, but who were trying now to return home, were informed on 14 December that Hitler's 'imminent' downfall and the consequent efforts of the imperialists to disarm Europe's national liberation movements and to dissipate the 'tremendous revolutionary energy' they had generated made the struggle against the emergent 'centre' of Serb reaction their primary task. Mihailović personally should be treated with circumspection, but they must no longer attempt 'to rally the greater-Serbian reactionary elements on any basis whatsoever'. They were 'the future archenemy' of all the Yugoslav peoples. The party, meantime, 'must assume the dominant role in the process of differentiation', strengthening 'the worker-peasant core within the Liberation Front' and thereby 'preventing the reactionary bourgeois elements from profiting by the results of the people's struggle for their anti-popular purposes'.

The Slovene central committee, with which Tito had been out of contact for over a month, was sent similar instructions on 1 January. It was clear that the reactionaries were consolidating in Slovenia as in Serbia. Geography, however, imposed special responsibilities on the Slovenes, who must do their utmost to aid their Italian and Austrian comrades as Hitler's 'débâcle' and the arrival of the Red Army drew nigh. Tito condemned their recent efforts to appeal to reactionaries – by denying their links with and reliance on the USSR, by equating Moscow and London, by submerging the party in the OF, and by playing down the Yugoslav component of their struggle:

> These are dangerous symptoms. It is necessary to correct these errors promptly if you wish to prevent the greater Serbian-cum-clericalist clique from London from pulling the carpet from under your feet. You will not preserve unity by making concessions to reactionary elements, but by fighting against them with the utmost determination, by isolating them from the masses. It is of a fundamental importance today to work among the masses which have rallied within the Osvobodilna Fronta, to preserve unity from below, while concurrently exposing all elements hostile to the people, even if within the OF. You are doing exactly the opposite: by making concessions you are formally preserving unity in the top echelons of the OF, while losing the masses.[56]

The zeal with which the Slovenes embarked upon class war was such that, by May 1942, Kardelj would write to Tito about a Montenegrin-style reign of terror 'in miniature', during which an average of sixty people were 'liquidated' each month. Not only was tyranny becoming the hallmark of the prospective new regime, but bureaucracy and moral decay had also made their appearance in partisan commands.[57]

It was ironic that the Politburo's 22 December directive advising the Montenegrin provincial committee of the Drenova line of 'sharper class differentiation' should have been concerned mostly with rebuking them for their 'new "ultra left" and still worse errors', the purport of which had been to liquidate the leading role of the party. Djilas received a copy of this letter, which he recognized as the work of Kardelj, when he was in Nova Varoš with the forces charged with what was turning out to be the impossible assignment of returning to Serbia. In that little mountain town he could see no one against whom 'the spirit of a sharper class differentiation' might be applied. The comrades in Montenegro had no such difficulty, and the rise of the četniks continued apace. Still smarting from his chastisement for earlier Montenegrin 'errors', Djilas was surprised to be asked by Tito at the beginning of March to go back. His efforts to stem the partisans' decline, first by overseeing a more selective use of terror and reprisals, then by calling a halt to the burning and executions, were to fail, and he was to earn a second reprimand. The brutalized, hungry, and war-weary country would be largely abandoned to Italo-četnik rule between the summer of 1942 and spring 1943; but the party's disasters there and in neighbouring Hercegovina were to play a large part in compelling the leadership to reassess its policy of class war.[58]

An even larger part was played by the Comintern. Kopinič's arrival at Supreme Headquarters in Rogatica late in December bearing call signs and ciphers permitted Tito's radio operators to try to raise Moscow direct. They apparently succeeded on 7 January in sending a message dated 29 December in which Tito reported on the loss of Serbia, the formation of the First Proletarian Brigade, the consolidation of the četniks and other Serb reactionaries around the occupiers, and the partisans' troubles in east Bosnia, and concluded with another appeal for help: 'The arrival of your assistance would put an end to all that as this would have a tremendous moral value for the continuance of our Liberation Struggle.' Regular radio links were established only after Tito took up a more settled existence in Foča at the end of January.[59] It was through this channel that the Comintern, after raising Tito's hopes that aircraft would soon be on their way and paying him the compliment of suggesting a proclamation to the peoples of occupied Europe, weighed in on 5 March with its criticisms:

> Upon reviewing all your communications the impression is gained that from certain reports obtained by the English and the Yugoslav Government one might suspect that the Partisan movement is acquiring a Communist character and is aiming at a Sovietization of Yugoslavia. For instance, why did you have to form a special proletarian brigade? At the moment the basic, immediate task is to unite all anti-Hitler elements, to defeat the invader, and win national liberation. . . . It is difficult to accept that London and the Yugoslav Government are going along with the occupiers.[60]

The KPJ was told to reconsider its actions and tactics, particularly over whether or not it had done everything possible to forge a united front. A second message sugared the pill. Pointing to the USSR's treaty relations with the exile government on the one hand, and to the paramountcy of the Big Three alliance on the other, the Comintern asked the Yugoslavs 'to show political elasticity and some ability to manoeuvre' before going on to hail their example and to cite its own efforts to popularize their cause. The message also implied, however, that no planes would be coming.[61]

'Baffled and upset', according to Djilas, Tito sought to refute the Comintern's 'mistaken conclusions', to discipline those of his colleagues who, like the querulous and underemployed Pijade, inclined to take Moscow's side, and to quash henceforth any public expressions of dubiety in the solidity of the grand alliance. Suspecting that the Comintern's intervention was the result of some intrigue by the British, he also determined to overwhelm Moscow with daily reports on the partisans' war and the četniks' treachery. In a radiogram to *Djeda* on 9 March he insisted that most of London's followers were indeed collaborating with the Axis, but he minimized their significance (especially that of Mihailović) while exaggerating his own forces' strength by at least twofold. Not only were all 'honest patriots' to be found in partisan ranks (including 'even generals'), but peasants were clamouring to join the proletarian brigades (a second had just been formed) in such numbers that volunteer units had been set up to accommodate them. The people's liberation councils were not 'any kind of soviets'. As he would do in 1948, Tito asked the CPSU to send observers to see conditions for themselves. The surest way to form an effective liberation front, he deftly concluded, would be for the partisans to get the arms they needed in order to enlist all those who longed to fight the invaders.[62]

Tito's reluctance to admit wrongdoing was becoming as fixed as his habit of concealing certain complex and unpalatable facts from the ignorant busybodies in the Comintern. But that did not mean that Moscow's strictures did not have an immediate impact on the making of KPJ tactics and strategy. This particular dispute seems to have been quickly patched up. *Djeda* denied in 'his' next telegram any intention of making 'reproaches' and reaffirmed 'his' confidence in Tito. The object, rather, had been to seek an explanation of Tito's 29 December report. On one thing, however, Moscow insisted: since for policy reasons the Soviet media made no references to the četniks, it was not 'opportune' for the partisans to contend that their principal struggle was against them. As far as the public was concerned, resistance to the occupiers must have precedence over unmasking the četniks.[63]

Djilas had found Tito dissatisfied with their sectarian line and its effects in Montenegro when he arrived in Foča at the end of February. Pijade had already re-emphasized in a manual dealing with the people's liberation councils that they were not to be regarded as the property of any one party, but should be open to all 'good sons [and daughters] of their people.' Moscow's intervention was, therefore, perhaps as much a catalyst as a cause of change. Vladimir Dedijer recorded in his diary a party meeting in Foča on the evening of 9 March (i.e. four days after receipt of the Comintern critique) at which he and others spoke about the new international constellation but were advised that they had 'got things wrong! Leftist deviation. Djilas put things in their proper perspective. The alliance between the USSR and Britain is strong and will become stronger.' Djilas went on to reveal – expressing ideas he and Tito had been discussing – that they must abjure class war, which was what the invaders sought to impose upon them, and hold fast to the concept of a war of national liberation.[64]

The fluctuating complement of central committee members that composed the wartime Politburo met in Foča on 4 and 6 April to repudiate the left sectarian course pursued since Drenova.[65] Djilas had reported to Tito in the meantime on the boon their hunt for 'fifth columnists', summary executions, and incendiary reprisals had represented for the četniks in Montenegro.[66] The leadership remained convinced, none the less, that the rise of a formidable četnik movement outside Serbia could not have occurred without British instigation or connivance (a belief reinforced by the unheralded arrival and inexplicable behaviour of several British and Anglo-Yugoslav intelligence missions that spring). Tito was prepared publicly to overlook Britain's apparent double-dealing, not only because the Soviets insisted upon it, but also – and now more importantly – because by doing so they would, as he advised the Montenegrins on 12 April, frustrate the plans of the occupiers and reactionaries 'to break the unity of the national liberation struggle so that it would turn into a civil, class war'.

Maintenance of the party's discipline and the assertion of its hegemony of leadership were, as always, central to Tito's calculations. The comrades in Montenegro were informed that by their own sectarian blunders, their failure to strengthen the party's leading role, and their political and military negligence they had abetted the consolidation of their enemies. They must disabuse themselves of the ideas either that there had been any attenuation of the Big Three alliance or that 'we are entering a "second phase of the battle" '. Conceptions such as these, Tito now wrote, 'are dangerous deviations from the KPJ political line and can only aid the occupier and his lackeys in their attempts to destroy the unity of the popular ranks and provoke a civil war in this country'. All those who had proved hesitant, unreliable, or 'liable to panic' should be purged and replaced by battle-tested partisans.[67] These were the people on whom the party must rely. As Djilas was to reflect much later, 'a new revolutionary ideology merged with a heritage', revealing in the process Lenin's 'main link' which 'now had to be grasped in order to set the chain in motion'. The reassertion of the primacy of the anti-Axis struggle was thus a means of fortifying the party, as well as of enlisting non-Communist patriots and consigning to perdition all those who opposed it. 'From that time until the end of the war', Djilas wrote, 'nothing essential was changed in the party line and tactics: the revolution had been born in the struggle against the invader'.[68]

Tito elaborated on the new line over the remainder of the month in a series of articles in *Proleter*, open letters to the party faithful (such as the one quoted above), and secret directives to the partisan commands and party leaderships. To Moscow he offered a concise statement of the partisan platform on 21 April which, he noted, 'is likewise the political programme of the KPJ': 'to fight the invaders and their agents, to fight for the liberation of the Yugoslav peoples, for the unity and brotherhood of all the peoples of Yugoslavia. All political and economic activities undertaken by the People's Liberation Committees must be subordinate to this objective.'[69] The notion of a two-stage revolution was finally set aside. It had become clear that the national liberation struggle was itself, in the words of Branko Petranović, 'sufficiently broad that through it – and without sharpening class conflicts – a change of political power could be realized'.[70] The Stalinist dilemma of the single alternative was relaxed: he who is not against us is potentially with us – at least until we decide otherwise. To that end there would be increased emphasis on the mobilizing role of the national liberation councils, more propaganda play of the fact that non-Communist notables (priests, officers, and intellectuals) were to be found in partisan ranks, and greater efforts to enlist peasant youths and women in them. The short-lived experiment with the so-called volunteer units was a case in point. The leadership regarded these as a halfway house for Serb peasants who appeared keen to defend their villages, but whose aversion to partisan discipline and Communist indoctrination might make them vulnerable to četnik recruitment.[71]

The party's commitment to destroy its domestic rivals – above all the četniks – had neither weakened nor lost its precedence, whatever gloss might be put on the matter for the Comintern. They were to be fought, however, not because they were anti-Communists engaged in a civil war, but as 'agents' of the Axis powers who had wantonly sabotaged the patriotic struggle. Tito issued explicit orders to the Croatian command on 7 April: 'Liquidate četniks throughout the territory under your staff. Only when you have liquidated these bands will you be able to fight the invader more successfully.'[72] On the other hand, the Croatian central committee was advised the next day to try again to establish contact with 'all honourable supporters' of the HSS and the socialists, to work with them to form national liberation councils, and to nominate a few of their number as potential Croatian representatives on an all-Yugoslav national liberation council.[73] In both its resolve to extirpate the četniks and its revived effort to challenge the exile government the party showed its determination to advance its claims on post-war power, even while wading out of the 'communist waters' Moscow and many Yugoslavs found too deep.[74]

Tito explained the new course and some of the considerations that lay behind it in his 8 April directive to the Croatian central committee. Although the middle portions of this letter (castigating the British for helping to create the četniks, predicting that they intended to land in Dalmatia to save the country from 'chaos' when the Italians surrendered, and counselling extreme caution towards their intelligence missions) are well known, the opening and closing paragraphs are more relevant to the development of KPJ strategy and merit quotation:

> It is evident to us today that all the reactionary forces in Yugoslavia are concentrating beneath the occupier's cloak, and are fighting us jointly. Generally speaking, the situation here is very complicated. On the one hand, this concentration, and on the other, the great contradictions that exist between these different groups, oblige us to be extremely prudent in our assessments, not to draw premature conclusions in such matters. One thing is clear to us, and continues to be pertinent, and that is: 1) Combat, relentless combat against the invader, is for us irrevocable. 2) By the same token, relentless combat against the occupier's henchmen, against traitors to our people. These include all who have openly taken up arms against us, who are striking bargains with the occupiers at the expense of the national liberation struggle. But here there are different groups such as the leadership of the Croatian Peasant Party, various so-called London sympathizers, etc. who must also be opposed through exposure to the masses, differentiation in their ranks, and the insistence that these groups should decide once and for all whether they are with the people and against the occupier, or with the occupier, because there is no middle course, because any kind of appeal to remain passive, to wait for better times, etc. is tantamount to helping the invader. One must be very careful not to generalize, not to lump the entire Croatian Peasant Party together with certain leaders who absolutely refuse any cooperation whatever with us, that is to say with the people in the present struggle. Elements that are still hesitating should be drawn away from the Croatian Peasant Party to our side and won to the national struggle. . . .

We must continue to stress the alliance between the Soviet Union, England and America; we must also emphasize the last two as our allies, but within the country we must strike their hangers-on and agents as lackeys of the occupier and enemies of the people, who are undermining the national liberation struggle.

As regards the Yugoslav Government in London, it is pursuing a policy of pure Greater-Serbian hegemony. It does not express this over the London radio, but its representatives in the country, such as Draža Mihailović and others, are operating wholly in this spirit and unhesitatingly talk quite openly of establishing Serbian hegemony after the liberation, of complete subservience of Croats and other peoples of Yugoslavia upon liberation . . .

The most important assignment of the moment lies ahead of you: work ceaselessly to form a National Liberation Front for the struggle against the occupier, enlist all patriotic elements, rally to it the broadest popular masses, for only a strong National Liberation Front of this kind is a guarantee of a victorious battle against the occupier and Pavelić's bands, a guarantee against all attempts at intrigue from outside elements which for various reasons spread discord and incite civil war in our country.[75]

NATIONAL LIBERATION WAR (1942–5)

By the end of April 1942 the KPJ's basic strategy for seizing power was complete. The unrealistic expectations of early deliverance by the Red Army that had animated both its efforts to provoke resistance in July and its left turn in December 1941 could no longer be sustained. It was obvious that the party was on its own for the foreseeable future. The ambiguity about whether it should be attempting to construct a liberation front from above or below that had marked its dealings with the HSS, the četniks, and its fellow travellers in the Slovene OF in the summer and autumn had been resolved, predictably, in favour of the latter course. (Not until early 1943, however, were all vestiges of a genuine coalition expunged from the OF when, in the so-called Dolomite Declaration, the Communists' partners were forced to acknowledge the KPJ's hegemony.) The abortive inauguration at Drenova of a second, 'proletarian' phase of the revolution had been shown to be misconceived, counterproductive, and unnecessary, alienating just those people on whom the struggle had come to depend – the country's peasant majority. Renewal rather than revolution, resistance rather than resignation: these were to be the principal elements of the party's line until such time as international recognition was won and its domestic opponents were co-opted, sidelined, or destroyed. As Paul Shoup has observed, 'What the partisans offered, in effect, was a fresh start, utilizing the conditions of backwardness to build up support among the peasantry, and appealing to the most elemental national feelings associated with the desire to expel foreign powers from the homeland.'[76] This they did as proponents, simultaneously, of each nation's cause, of reconciliation among the nations and national minorities, and of a reformed Yugoslav state. In the meantime they would push as far and as fast as circumstances at home and abroad allowed to institutionalize their alternative order and to usurp the prerogatives and legitimacy of the exiled king and government. All this was made possible by the party's revived commitment in spring 1942 to making implacable war on the Axis powers and their servants its absolute propaganda priority, and very nearly its first real priority.

Militarily, by early 1942 the party had learnt that it could afford neither to offer frontal opposition to inherently superior Axis forces nor to hold static territories against them. It must, above all, preserve the core of its mobile units by timely withdrawal, but leaving behind wherever possible the rudiments of a military and political presence in the areas and populations abandoned. This lesson, drawn from the costly experience in Serbia, was being reiterated by an Italo-German offensive against the partisans' south-east Bosnian redoubt between April and June. Although loath to admit defeat in Montenegro and to relinquish hope of an early return to Serbia (always perceived as crucial to the winning of power), Tito decided in mid-June to make for western Bosnia, where there were again free territories of considerable size. The hungry and devastated triangle between Serbia, Bosnia, and Montenegro could no longer sustain and would no longer support a movement contaminated by the stench of decomposition.[77]

So began the 200-mile 'long march' by some 3,000 partisans from east Bosnia to the borders of Croatia along the demarcation line separating the Italian and German zones of occupation. This trek, which took three months to complete and offered the partisans abundant opportunities to replenish their forces and rehabilitate their image *en route*, represented one of the major turning-points in their war. By late autumn they had knitted together a liberated territory of approximately 20,000 square miles centred on the town of Bihać. The Soviets, meanwhile, and despite raising their legation accredited to King Peter to embassy rank, had finally begun to transmit news critical of Mihailović (the king's war minister since January) over Radio Free Yugoslavia and to mount a concerted attack on četnik collaboration with the Axis in the foreign Communist press. Tito protested furiously at the former act while continuing to complain about the content and extent of Soviet reporting of the partisans' struggle. He would have been thoroughly alarmed had he known that during the autumn the Soviets proposed sending a mission to Mihailović, a suggestion spurned by the exile government on account of Moscow's newly hostile propaganda.[78]

On 1 November Tito proclaimed the partisans' transformation into the People's Liberation Army of Yugoslavia and the start of the proletarian brigades' expansion into divisions. The consolidation of a 'state' larger than Switzerland also permitted him to proceed to give the movement the explicitly political dimension to which he had long aspired. He informed the Comintern on 12 November of the Politburo's decision, taken two months before, to 'set up something like a government'. Moscow supported the initiative but rejected its essence, telling Tito that the proposed body must on no account be regarded as a government in opposition to London or the monarchy. The Comintern further advised him to make sure his national liberation committee had an all-Yugoslav, all-party, and anti-Fascist character. The latter piece of advice was redundant, although Tito reported that he accepted it, while the former warning was illogical. Tito said as much when he replied that, since the exile government was considered 'traitorous' even by non-Communists, and the partisans and their people's liberation councils constituted the only uncompromised public authorities, the new executive would necessarily be obliged 'to look after all state business'.[79]

When Tito sent this radiogram on 29 November the fifty-four delegates to the first session of the Anti-Fascist Council of People's Liberation of Yugoslavia (AVNOJ) had already assembled in Bihać (on 26 November), applauded the patriotic orations laid on for them, confirmed the prearranged resolution and appointment of an executive, and dispersed (the next day). Despite the fact that the 'V' in AVNOJ stood for *Veće*, the Serbo-Croat equivalent of Soviet, moderation had reigned, and the party leadership remained largely in the background. 'It was as if', Djilas wrote, 'now that the revolution had found its vital concrete path, it could conceal itself.'[80]

As a celebration of success the convocation of AVNOJ was premature, even though the partisans now claimed to have 150,000 men and women at arms. AVNOJ and its executive were not yet to have the chance to challenge the exile government or to play the state-building role the party envisaged for them. In January the first of the two great Axis offensives of 1943 against Tito's forces (*Weiss* and *Schwarz* to the Germans) drove them back across Bosnia, accompanied by thousands of refugees and wounded. Tito had time first to oversee the formation of mass organizations for women and young people, to attend to the long-mooted foundation of a Macedonian Communist Party, and to write an article on the national question for *Proleter* which contained more than a hint of the federal solution the party had in mind. Attributing the movement's successes to both its anti-Fascism and its repudiation of the old regime, Tito went on:

> The words national liberation struggle would be a mere phrase, or even a deception, if they did not have, in addition to their all-Yugoslav meaning, a national significance for each people separately, that is, if they did not signify, in addition to the liberation of Yugoslavia, the liberation also of the Croats, Slovenes, Serbs, Macedonians, Albanians, Moslems, etc., if the national liberation struggle were not genuinely imbued with the aim of bringing freedom, equality and fraternity to all the nations of Yugoslavia. In this lies the essence of the national liberation struggle.

Tito commended the Serbs for having done the bulk of the fighting, despite the past sins of their reactionary rulers, and summoned the other peoples to follow their example. Only with 'gun in hand' could they earn the right to an equitable solution of their national questions.[81]

Weiss (January–March) and *Schwarz* (May–June) were successes for the partisans because they survived them. In both offensives more than 90,000 German and Italian troops, plus Croat and četnik auxiliaries, sought to encircle and obliterate the Supreme Command and its forces. Of the approximately 40,000 partisans who set out with Tito from western Bosnia in January, only a few thousand emerged from the cauldron of the Sutjeska valley in late June. The battles on the Neretva and Sutjeska rivers became the epics of the partisan war, but they also had profound political implications. During the attempt to break out across the Neretva in early March Tito initiated negotiations with the Germans designed, in the first instance, to exchange prisoners, but then to secure belligerent rights for his forces and their accompanying trains of wounded and to explore the possibility of a truce. His aim was to gain a respite during which the partisans might finish off the četniks in Hercegovina and Montenegro, already reeling from their defeat on the left bank of the Neretva, and thereby obviate the risk that they would one day link up with British forces landing on the southern Adriatic coast. The partisans intended then to make for Serbia.

Treating with the Germans was politically explosive, and Tito told the Comintern only about his proposal to exchange prisoners. When asked by Djilas what the Russians would say if they knew the truth, Tito, who had for weeks been sending desperate appeals for help, replied, 'Well, they also think first of their own people and their own army!' In fact, Moscow seems to have plumbed what was afoot; certainly an angry protest arrived almost immediately. Tito's reply was sharp: 'If you cannot understand what a hard time we are having, and if you cannot help us, at least do not hinder us.' The idea that a revolution other than the Great October Revolution might legitimately command a Communist's first loyalty was now alive at the top of the KPJ. The dissolution of the Comintern in May thus met with the Yugoslavs' wholehearted approval. They expected as a result to be able to conduct their relations with the Soviet Union on a direct, state-to-state basis, albeit on terms of filial devotion enriched by a shared ideology. Little had come in the meantime of the partisans' talks with the Germans. Prisoners were duly exchanged, but Hitler forbade any more substantive arrangement. Tito, for his part, lost interest in a truce once *Weiss* came to its appointed end and it became clear the Montenegrin četniks could be vanquished without one.[82]

At the same time as the Communists were surviving *Weiss*, defeating the principal četnik force outside Serbia, and testing their ties with Moscow, the reactionaries they feared most, the British, were preparing to send them missions. Probing teams were dropped into Croatia and north-east Bosnia in April. They were followed by a fully-fledged mission to Tito in Montenegro in late May, just as *Schwarz* reached its climax. Although it would take until the end of the year, the process whereby the British and – more reluctantly – the Americans switched their backing from Mihailović to Tito was begun. This was important not only because the partisans eventually derived substantial material, logistical, medical, and propaganda support from the western Allies, but also because the British commitment to seeing that King Peter got his throne back (or at least that some monarchical water was added to Tito's Communist wine) compelled them to seek a political settlement with him once they had become convinced that he and the KPJ were likely to be Yugoslavia's future masters. The report in November of Churchill's 'daring Ambassador-leader' to Tito, Fitzroy Maclean, stressed both the military value of the partisans' struggle to the Allies and their by then unstoppable progress towards power.

That it was the British imperialists rather than the Soviets who first sent missions and arms to the partisans, and then effectively recognized their political pretensions, was perhaps paradoxical, especially in view of what was happening concurrently in Greece and Italy; but it was also explicable. In the first place, Yugoslavia was not a country in which the British either aspired to or felt themselves capable of playing a decisive political and military role. The Americans, for their part, still regarded south-east Europe as an insignificant area of the world and a ridiculous place in which to contemplate prosecuting the war, which was what they feared the British sought to do. Churchill did periodically nourish such ambitions, but what mostly concerned him, as he delighted in repeating, was who was killing the most Germans. The partisans were lucky in being able to impress their well-connected British liaison officers (and through them the prime minister) with their valour during *Schwarz*, their quick recovery and establishment of a new 'republic' in west-central Bosnia thereafter, and their ability to claim a munificent inheritance in arms, equipment, territory, and recruits from the Italians' surrender in September. They were briefly able to control about one-third of the country, including most of the coast. More important for the western Allies was that the partisans' activity, however remote from centres of population and main lines of communication, obliged the Germans to maintain divisions in Yugslavia that would otherwise have been available for service in Italy.[83]

Speculation that the Yugoslav Communists' generally amicable and definitely profitable relations with the British and Americans after mid-1943 may have had some impact on their world view, if not on their immediate policies, remains just that. Tito was doubtless flattered by Churchill's initiation of a personal correspondence in January 1944 and by their meeting near Naples in August (he met Stalin for the first time a month later), but such fripperies hardly altered the KPJ leaders' intentions, ideology, or susceptibility to Soviet reinforcement of their already profound suspicions of the imperialists. The Soviet mission which finally arrived at Supreme Headquarters in February 1944 was accorded a welcome and intimacy which bore no comparison with the treatment of the British and Americans. What Tito wanted from them was political recognition: a short cut to power and a means of overcoming what he and virtually everyone else still assumed to be Mihailović's dominance in Serbia. The determination of the British to discharge their obligations towards King Peter gave him his chance.

The second session of AVNOJ met on 28 and 29 November 1943 in Jajce, capital of the fifteenth-century Bosnian kingdom and now the partisans' seat of power. Celebrated since as Yugoslavia's rebirth, the conclave had been preceded by meetings of the political fronts in Croatia, Slovenia, Montenegro, Bosnia-Hercegovina, and Sandžak. Moscow, however, was given only two days' notice of the KPJ's intention to reorganize AVNOJ as a provisional government and Parliament, and none whatsoever of the plan to appropriate the rights of the exile government, prohibit the king from returning home until such time as the people decided on the fate of the monarchy, adopt the federal principle, and make Tito a marshal. The Soviets were furious and initially refused to publicize the Jajce resolutions. Stalin referred to them as 'this stab in the back for the Soviet Union and the Teheran decisions'. (The Big Three had been agreeing at the same time to increase the support of the partisans, recognizing them *de facto* as an Allied force, though Molotov had again proposed sending a mission to Mihailović 'in order to get better information'!)[84]

The British were less annoyed, but more determined than before to extract the maximum possible benefit for King Peter and their own post-war influence in the region by making their severance of all ties with Mihailović conditional on Tito's agreement to 'work' with the king. To that end Churchill cajoled Tito by letter and Eden browbeat King Peter in person to dismiss his current government and appoint one 'not obnoxious' to the partisans. This game went on through the first half of 1944. The last British missions left the četniks in May. (Aid to them had ceased before the end of 1943.) By June the king had been prevailed upon to name the former *ban* (governor) of Croatia, Ivan Šubašić, as a one-man government and Tito had overcome his colleagues' scruples about dealing with royalist exiles supposedly overthrown at Jajce. Stalin's encouragement of the idea, even while warning the KPJ against the duplicity of the British and their capacity to do away with Tito in an aeroplane crash such as they had allegedly arranged for General Sikorski, no doubt helped. Tito was certainly attracted by the instant recognition which the revolution would win by virtue of a deal with Šubašić. He was, however, less needful than the British thought he was of the king's imprimatur in overcoming the monarchist Serbs' presumed devotion to Mihailović. Not only were the partisans at last making headway in their efforts to re-enter Serbia, but it had begun to look as if the Red Army would be available to help. When Šubašić travelled to the Supreme Command's new, British-protected seat on the island of Vis in June the resulting agreement to unify in due course the royal and AVNOJ governments was a triumph for Tito. As elaborated in liberated Belgrade in the autumn and amended and endorsed by the Big Three at Yalta in February, it provided for a regency council to exercise the king's nominal rights and for AVNOJ to be supplemented by non-compromised deputies from the last pre-war parliament. This made no difference whatsoever to the realities of power.

Early in July Tito had written to Stalin, asking that the Red Army should not bypass Yugoslavia on its way into central Europe. In mid-September he 'levanted' from Vis (in a Soviet Dakota) in order to make arrangements at the Rumanian front for its entry into Serbia. He then flew on to Moscow. Stalin counselled him to proceed slowly, as the Serbian bourgeoisie in particular was strong. Tito disagreed. It was weak and rotten with collaborationism. Stalin urged him to let the king come home, for it would always be possible later to stick a knife in his back. Tito replied that the people would never tolerate Peter's return. Stalin tested him by passing on a false report that British troops were landing in Dalmatia. Tito vowed to fight them. These were signs that the KPJ's regime would be both militantly revolutionary and potentially troublesome for the USSR now that its need to dissimulate had nearly passed. Neither then nor at any time before 1948 was there any idea of deviating from what they understood to be Stalin's path on the part of the KPJ leaders. They considered themselves his best pupils, and went out of their way in 1944 to secure glowing report cards from him and Dimitrov. Their problem – and Stalin's – was that they also believed in themselves, their own power, and their own revolution. Time was to show that Communists desirous of keeping in communion with Moscow were permitted to believe in only one revolutionary incarnation.[85]

Belgrade was freed on 20 October in a combined Red Army–partisan operation that was not without its frictions. The rape and pillage that attended liberation by the Red Army came as a shock to the puritanical and hero-worshiping partisans. Fortunately for the KPJ's current reputation and future survival, if not for the raw conscripts now hurled into what became a bloody war of attrition on the Slavonian front, the Soviets soon decamped for Hungary. They had served their principal purpose: Serbia was won and Mihailović's četniks disintegrated, although he and other would-be leaders of anti-Communist insurgency were to remain at large for more than a year, undermining the party's sense of security while justifying its maintenance of bloated military and secret police establishments. The only serious rebellion against the new regime occurred among the Albanians of Kosovo, who resisted reincorporation in the Yugoslav state at the end of 1944 and beginning of 1945. Meanwhile the Yugoslavs fought to liberate the north and west of the country – or, to be more exact, to take over as the Germans retreated while putting most of their own efforts into seizing Croat and Slovene irredenta. The frustration of their ambitions to win all these territories reinforced the KPJ's anti-western militancy and paranoia.

The united government in which Tito became premier and war minister, and Šubašić minister of foreign affairs, but which was overwhelmingly dominated by Communists, was installed on 7 March 1945. Known as Democratic Federal Yugoslavia, this would be the shortest-lived and most perfunctorily pluralistic of any of the transitional regimes in the emerging Soviet bloc. A People's Front, established in August, was to be the party's peacetime cloak and united front from below. Its slate of candidates ran unopposed in the November elections, although roughly 10 per cent of electors did vote 'no'. The new bicameral and Soviet-inspired assembly abolished the monarchy and made Yugoslavia a Federal People's Republic before the end of the year. In January 1946 it enacted a constitution modelled on Stalin's 1936 document. Such industry as survived, the savings of the urban middle classes and richer peasants, and 'excess' agricultural land and residential property had already been nationalized or expropriated on the grounds of wartime collaboration.[86]

Churchill, who had presumed to agree with Stalin in Moscow in October 1944 on a 50 : 50 division of influence in Yugoslavia, was soon crying foul. From the time of the Trieste and Carinthian crises in May 1945 until June 1948 Yugoslavia would serve as the 'worst case' model for westerners contemplating the present fate of eastern Europe and the possible fate of the whole continent. Not only was KPJ rule itself abhorrent, but Tito's truculent and expansionist foreign policy appeared inconceivable except as the product of Soviet support and direction. Few westerners imagined that the Yugoslavs' schemes to swallow Albania, federate with Bulgaria, and help the Greek Communists to power could be anything other than parts of a Soviet masterplan, let alone that they should have dared to shoot down overflying American transport planes or to mine the Corfu Channel without Moscow's approval. Stalin did not enjoy being blamed for the revolutionary ardour, impetuosity, and crudity of his Yugoslav imitators.

Yugoslavs paid dearly for their multifarious wars between 1941 and 1945. A recent statistical analysis puts the death toll at 1,014,000. This is lower by some 700,000 than the officially propagated and widely accepted figure, but still places the country in the same lamentable league as the Soviet Union and Poland.[87] The political and psychological salience of carnage on such a scale was all the greater because most of those who perished did so at the hands of other Yugoslavs. The wartime ubiquity of death, destruction, hatred, and fear explains in some measure why the Communists came to power, why their regime assumed the shape it did between 1945 and 1948, and why amelioration and systemic reform followed the traumatic split with Stalin. During the war the party offered a way out of the literal dead ends into which Yugoslavs had strayed or been plunged, and which the Communists' enemies and rivals promised only to perpetuate. After the war the imposition of a hard-boiled dictatorship, a millenarian ideology and an enforced forgetfulness put a stop at last to the killing. By fighting to expel the invaders and destroy their helpmates, to recreate the Yugoslav state and reconcile its peoples, and to overcome centuries of poverty and backwardness, the KPJ made its revolution. The outcome did not live up to the expectations of either its creators or supporters, but an autochthonous revolution at least possessed the power to transform itself.

NOTES

1 Fabijan Trgo (ed.), *The National Liberation War and Revolution in Yugoslavia (1941–1945): Selected Documents* (Belgrade, 1982), pp. 254–62, 266–7. (Hereafter *Selected Documents.*)
2 ibid., pp. 276–8, 280–2.
3 Stephen Clissold (ed.), *Yugoslavia and the Soviet Union 1939–1973: A Documentary Survey* (London, 1975), pp. 28–9, 156–7.
4 At its birth in April 1919 it was styled the Socialist Workers' Party of Yugoslavia (Communist), being renamed the KPJ at the Second (Vukovar) Congress in June 1920. The initial appellation reflected a compromise between Left and Centre socialists; the new name the victory of the Left faction. The use of 'Yugoslavia' in both names illustrates the party's positive assessment of South Slav unification. For a convenient and incisive account of the party's first years see Ivo Banac, 'The Communist Party of Yugoslavia during the period of legality, 1919–1921', in I. Banac (ed.), *The Effects of World War I: The Class War after the Great War: The Rise of Communist Parties in East Central*

Europe, 1918–1921 (Boulder, Col., and New York, 1983), pp. 188–230. See also Ivan Avakumovic, *History of the Communist Party of Yugoslavia* (Aberdeen, 1964). The best English-language account of inter-war Yugoslav politics is Joseph Rothschild, *East Central Europe between the Two World Wars* (Seattle, 1974), pp. 201–80.
5 Janko Pleterski et al. *Povijest Saveza komunista Jugoslavije* (Belgrade, 1985), pp. 75–6. (Hereafter *Povijest SKJ*.)
6 ibid., p. 87.
7 Banac, op. cit., p. 205.
8 Josip Broz Tito, *The Struggle and Development of the CPY between the Two Wars*, 2nd edn. (Belgrade, 1979), p. 20.
9 Jozo Ivicević as quoted by Banac, op. cit., p. 206.
10 Walker Connor, *The National Question in Marxist–Leninist Theory and Strategy* (Princeton, NJ, 1984), p. 142. See also Wayne S. Vucinich, 'Nationalism and communism', in W. S. Vucinich (ed.), *Contemporary Yugoslavia: Twenty Years of Socialist Experiment* (Berkeley, Col., 1969), pp. 236–84, and Paul Shoup, *Communism and the Yugoslav National Question* (New York, 1968).
11 Janko Pleterski, *Nacije-Jugoslavija-revolucija* (Belgrade. 1985), pp. 182–3.
12 ibid., pp. 300–1; *Povijest SKJ*, pp. 105–18; Pero Moraća, *The League of Communists of Yugoslavia* (Belgrade, 1966), pp. 15–17.
13 Pleterski, *Nacije-Jugoslavija-revolucija*, pp. 321–9; *Povijest SKJ*, pp. 122–6; Shoup, op. cit., pp. 39–40. No Macedonian party was created until early 1943, and no Serbian party until 1945, after which the other federal units also got parties of their own.
14 *Povijest SKJ*, p. 141.
15 Paul Shoup, 'The Yugoslav revolution: the first of a new type', in T. T. Hammond (ed.), *The Anatomy of Communist Takeovers*, (New Haven, Conn., 1975), pp. 246–7.
16 *Povijest SKJ*, p. 131.
17 ibid., pp. 143–4; Shoup, *Communism and the Yugoslav National Question*, pp. 40–3. Ironically, in view of his subsequent espousal of the popular front from below, Tito's 'Letter for Serbia' formed the basis of the manifesto. This lectured the unobliging opposition in the following terms: 'There is no democracy without national freedom (it is necessary to reiterate this for the Belgrade component of the United Opposition) and no national freedom without democracy (this, again, for Zagreb).' The well-taken point was that the Serbs in the opposition were keener to see parliamentary rule restored than they were to dismantle the unitary state, while the Croats were prepared to sacrifice Yugoslav democracy if autonomy could be won for Croatia. This was the basis on which Prince Regent Paul would ultimately split the opposition in August 1939; yielding home rule to Croatia in order to maintain the dictatorial 1931 constitution in other respects.

By summer 1936, and under the impact of events in France, the outbreak of civil war in Spain and the gathering pace of terror in the USSR, the Comintern's freedom to propagate revolution through the popular front and to allow its sections a measure of autonomy were at an end. See Jonathan Haslam, 'The Soviet Union, the Comintern and the demise of the popular front, 1936–39', in H. Graham and P. Preston (eds), *The Popular Front in Europe* (London 1987), pp. 152–60. The whole question of KPJ–Comintern relations and the proper nature of the popular front is the subject of a forthcoming article by Geoffrey Swain, provisionally entitled, 'The battle Tito won: The KPJ and the Comintern, 1935–41'. I am grateful to Dr Swain for allowing me to read his draft and to incorporate its insights.
18 *Povijest SKJ*, pp. 152–6; Phyllis Auty, *Tito: A Biography* (Harmondsworth, 1974), pp. 138–61; Tito, op. cit., pp. 50–60.
19 *Povijest SKJ*, pp. 156–9; Clissold, op. cit., pp. 5–6, 115–16; Shoup, *Communism and the Yugoslav National Question*, pp. 42–5; Tito, op. cit., pp. 58–63; Swain, unpublished article (see n. 17).

20 *Povijest SKJ*, pp. 160–1; Branko Petranović, *Revolucija i kontrarevolucija u Jugoslaviji (1941–1945)*, (Belgrade, 1983), I, pp. 141–2; Shoup, *Communism and the Yugoslav National Question*, pp. 48–50; Auty, op. cit., pp. 179–83.
21 Stephen Clissold, *Whirlwind: An Account of Marshal Tito's Rise to Power* (New York, 1949), pp. 20–1; Milovan Djilas, *Memoir of a Revolutionary* (New York, 1973), p. 353; *Povijest SKJ*, pp. 164–6. Clissold, who worked in Zagreb at the time and served later as a British liaison officer with the partisans, may have had access to what Tito actually said as opposed to what he wrote beforehand and which has been published. For an English-language record of the conference see Josip Broz Tito, *The Party of the Revolution: Fifth Conference of the Communist Party of Yugoslavia 1940* (Belgrade, 1980).
22 Shoup, *Communism and the Yugoslav National Question*, p. 50; Connor, op. cit., pp. 146–8; Petranović, op. cit., I, p. 153; Tito, *Party of the Revolution*, pp. 72–3; Djilas, op. cit., p. 354. The party would backtrack during 1941 and 1942 on the idea of autonomy for Bosnia-Hercegovina when it found it more important to cultivate the Serbs of the provinces than the Muslims or Croats. Contrary to Connor, *samoodredjenje* and *samoopredelenje* both mean self-determination.
23 Petranović, op. cit., I, pp. 155–6.
24 Mark C. Wheeler, *Britain and the War for Yugoslavia, 1941–1943* (Boulder, Col., and New York, 1980), ch. 2.
25 Petranović, op. cit., I, pp. 157–8, 461; Djilas, op. cit., pp. 367–74; Clissold, *Yugoslavia and the Soviet Union*, pp. 7–9; *Povijest SKJ*, p. 171.
26 *Selected Documents*, pp. 13–17; Petranović, op. cit., I, pp. 158–9; *Povijest SKJ*, pp. 171–2; Djilas, op. cit., p. 387.
27 Petranović, op. cit., I, pp. 163–4; *Povijest SKJ*, pp. 177–8.
28 Djilas, op. cit., p. 388; *Povijest SKJ*, pp. 178–9.
29 Radomir Vujošević (ed.), *Izvori za istoriju SKJ: Dokumenti centralnih organa KPJ: NOR i revolucija (1941–1945)*, I, (Belgrade, 1985), pp. 13–17, 64; Petranović, op. cit., I, pp. 163, 172–3; Djilas, op. cit., p. 389; Pero Morača, 'Elaboration of the political platform of the CPY', in Novak Stugar (ed.), *War and Revolution in Yugoslavia 1941–1945*, (Belgrade, 1985), pp. 21–5.
30 Connor, op. cit., p. 151. Connor, however, exaggerates the extent of the KPJ's efforts to distance itself from the Yugoslav idea, mistaking apparent diversity for reality. On the other hand, for encomia to the party's pro-Yugoslav line at this juncture see *Povijest SKJ*, p. 180, and Petranović, op. cit., I, pp. 164–5.
31 *Selected Documents*, p. 60.
32 Vujošević, op. cit., I, p. 48. Clissold, following Dedijer, erroneously places in late September Tito's early June report to the Comintern on what was to prove a stillborn agreement with Dragoljub Jovanović: *Yugoslavia and the Soviet Union*, pp. 23, 145.
33 Although usually reported to have reached the KPJ late on 22 June, the Comintern directive seems in fact to have arrived in Zagreb on 24 or 25 June, and not to have been passed on to Tito in Belgrade until the end of the month. Ivan Jelić, *Tragedija u Kerestincu: Zagrebačko ljeto 1941* (Zagreb, 1986), pp. 159–60; Clissold, *Yugoslavia and the Soviet Union*, pp. 10–11, 96, 128.
34 Milovan Djilas, *Wartime* (London, 1977), p. 4; *Selected Documents*, pp. 61–5.
35 Vujošević, op. cit., I, p. 64; Djilas, *Wartime*, pp. 7–8; Petranović, op. cit., I, pp. 173, 177, 464.
36 Djilas, *Wartime*, p. 4.
37 Jelić, op. cit., pp. 64–5; Clissold, *Yugoslavia and the Soviet Union*, p. 129.
38 *Povijest SKJ*, p. 184; Petranović, op. cit., I, pp. 177, 180; Djilas, *Wartime*, pp. 5–7.
39 Vujošević, op. cit., I, p. 64; Djilas, *Wartime*, p. 8; Morača, op. cit., p. 26; Jovan Marjanović, *Ustanak i Narodnooslobodilački pokret u Srbiji 1941 godine* (Belgrade, 1963), p. 86.

40 Djilas, *Wartime*, pp. 21–5.
41 The Kopinić affair has become an historical and polemical growth industry. Ivan Jelić's recent and scholarly attempt in *Tragedija u Kerestincu* to demystify the matter and to defend the Croatian party against accusations of passivity, incompetence, and Croatian nationalism is the best introduction and guide to the literature. Tito was unable to secure Kopinic's dismissal by the Comintern, and soon came to harbour serious doubts about whether Kopinić was in fact sending his reports on the Serbian uprising to Moscow.
42 *Selected Documents*, pp. 65–9, 79–83; Moraca, op. cit., p. 26.
43 Djilas, *Memoir of a Revolutionary*, p. 389.
44 *Povijest SKJ*, p. 195; *Selected Documents*, pp. 96–8; Moraca, op. cit., pp. 29–31; Petranović, op. cit., I, pp. 187–9.
45 Wheeler, op. cit., pp. 80–1. For full accounts of the Četnik movement see Matteo Joseph Milazzo, *The Chetnik Movement and the Yugoslav Resistance* (Baltimore, 1975), and Jozo Tomasevich, *War and Revolution in Yugoslavia 1941–1945: The Chetniks*, (Stanford, 1975). The latter is the first volume of a projected trilogy. Tomasevich has produced a brilliant introduction to this massive undertaking in 'Yugoslavia during the Second World War' in Vucinich, op. cit., pp. 59–118.
46 Besides Djilas's own extensive account in *Wartime*, see *Povijest SKJ*, pp. 202–4, and Stephen Clissold, *Djilas: The Progress of a Revolutionary* (London, 1983), pp. 54–70.
47 Marjanović, op. cit., pp. 97–8.
48 Wheeler, op. cit., pp. 80–90.
49 *Selected Documents*, pp. 83–7.
50 Petranović, op. cit., I, pp. 214–7, 471–2; Vujošević, op. cit., II, p. 243.
51 *Selected Documents*, 113–14, 117–25; *Povijest SKJ*, pp. 190–1, 194–5.
52 Wheeler, op. cit., pp. 87–120; *Selected Documents*, pp. 145–51.
53 Djilas. *Wartime*, pp. 95–9; *Selected Documents*, pp. 134–5.
54 Vujošević, op. cit., I, pp. 209–11; II, pp. 63, 156–7; Clissold, *Yugoslavia and the Soviet Union*, pp. 129–32.
55 Djilas, *Wartime*, pp. 118–23; Petranović, op. cit., I, pp. 313–27; *Povijest SKJ*, pp. 211–14.
56 *Selected Documents*, pp. 164–70, 191–200.
57 Petranović, op. cit., I, pp. 323–4, 487.
58 Vujošević, op. cit., II, pp. 240–6; Djilas, *Wartime*, pp. 122–4 and *passim*; Clissold, *Djilas*, pp. 80–9.
59 Vujošević, op. cit., II, pp. 288–9, 494–5; *Selected Documents*, pp. 178–9.
60 Clissold, *Yugoslavia and the Soviet Union*, pp. 145–6; *Selected Documents*, pp. 278.
61 ibid.
62 Djilas, *Wartime*, pp. 141–4; *Selected Documents*, pp. 278–82; Clissold, *Yugoslavia and the Soviet Union*, pp. 123, 99, 146–7.
63 ibid.
64 Djilas, *Wartime*, p. 142; *Selected Documents*, pp. 246–53; Clissold, *Djilas*, pp. 81–2. Pijade's *Fočanski propisi* of early February are invoked by establishment historians to demonstrate that the KPJ was abandoning sectarianism before the arrival of the Comintern critique. Djilas's supporting testimony is, of course, not cited. See *Povijest SKJ*, pp. 213–4.
65 ibid., pp. 214–15; Petranović, op. cit., I, p. 339.
66 ibid.; Clissold, *Djilas*, p. 85. 'How', Djilas wrote to Tito, 'is one else to explain that on territory cleared of Četniks by the Partisans, such panic has been aroused that the Partisans do not encounter a single soul?'
67 *Selected Documents*, pp. 298–303.
68 Djilas, *Wartime*, p. 143.
69 *Selected Documents*, p. 322.
70 Petranović, op. cit., I, p. 339.

71 *Povijest SKJ*, pp. 215–16.
72 *Selected Documents*, p. 292.
73 ibid., p. 297.
74 ibid., p. 280. The phrase 'communist waters' was used by Tito in his 11 March letter to Pijade.
75 ibid., pp. 294–7.
76 Shoup, 'The Yugoslav revolution' in Hammond, op. cit., p. 271.
77 Djilas, *Wartime*, pp. 173–7, 183; *Povijest SKJ*, pp. 226–7.
78 Clissold, *Yugoslavia and the Soviet Union*, pp. 24–5, 139–40, 149–50.
79 ibid., pp. 150–1; *Povijest SKJ*, pp. 233, 238–9.
80 Djilas, *Wartime*, pp. 207–9.
81 *Selected Documents, pp. 394–402*. The best English-language account of the tangled Macedonian issue can be found in Stephen E. Palmer, Jr, and Robert R. King, *Yugoslav Communism and the Macedonian Question* (Hamden, Conn., 1971). Also useful are Elisabeth Barker, *Macedonia: Its Place in Balkan Power Politics* (London, 1950), and Shoup, *Communism and the Yugoslav National Question*, ch. 4.
82 Clissold, *Yugoslavia and the Soviet Union*, pp. 26–8; Djilas, *Wartime*, pp. 229–50; Walter R. Roberts, *Tito, Mihailović and the Allies, 1941–1945* (New Brunswick, 1973), pp. 106–12.
83 For accounts of Allied policy-making see: Phyllis Auty and Richard Clogg (eds), *British Policy towards Wartime Resistance in Yugoslavia and Greece* (London, 1975); Elisabeth Barker, *British Policy in South East Europe in the Second World War* (London, 1976); Roberts, op. cit.; Wheeler, op. cit. An analysis of British efforts to save the Yugoslav monarchy is Mark Wheeler, 'Crowning the revolution: The British, King Peter and the path to Tito's cave', in Richard Langhorne (ed.), *Diplomacy and Intelligence during the Second World War: Essays in Honour of F. H. Hinsley* (Cambridge, 1985), pp. 184–218. The British memoir literature relating to Yugoslavia is outstanding. See especially F. W. D. Deakin, *The Embattled Mountain* (London, 1971); Fitzroy Maclean, *Eastern Approaches* (London, 1949); Basil Davidson, *Partisan Picture* (Bedford, 1946), and *Special Operations Europe: Scenes from the Anti-Nazi War* (London, 1980); Jasper Rootham *Miss-Fire: The Chronicle of a British Mission to Mihailovich, 1943–1944* (London, 1946).
84 Clissold, *Yugoslavia and the Soviet Union*, pp. 27–33, 151–2.
85 For a recent elaboration of the idea and a justification of the terminology see Ken Jowitt, 'Moscow "Centre" ', *Eastern European Politics and Societies*, I, 3, pp. 296–348.
86 A fascinating if mechanistic account of the party's devouring of its allies is to be had in Vojislav Koštunica and Kosta Čavoški, *Party Pluralism or Monism: Social Movements and the Political System in Yugoslavia, 1944–1949* (Boulder, Col., and New York, 1985). The Serbo-Croat original appeared in Belgrade in 1983.
87 For a convincing statistical demolition job on the multiple cults of death which most Yugoslav peoples have embraced see Bogoljub Kočović, *Žrtve drugog svetskog rata u Jugoslaviji* (London, 1985).

ABBREVIATIONS

AVNOJ Antifašističko veće narodnog oslobodjenje Jugoslavije (Anti-Fascist Council of National/People's Liberation of Yugoslavia)
CPSU Communist Party of the Soviet Union
Djeda Grandpa, i.e. the Comintern
HSS Hrvatska seljačka stranka (Croatian Peasant Party)
IMRO Internal Macedonian Revolutionary Organization
KPJ Komunistička partija Jugoslavije (Communist Party of Yugoslavia)
NDH Nezavisna Država Hrvatska (Independent State of Croatia)

NKVD People's Commissariat of Internal Affairs
OF Osvobodilna fronta (Slovene Liberation Front)
SKOJ Savez komunističke omladine Jugoslavije (Alliance of Communist youth of Yugoslavia)

5 The Greek Communist Party: in search of a revolution

HARIS VLAVIANOS

FROM FORMATION TO BOLSHEVIZATION

On 10 November 1918 a small number of Marxist workers, trade unionists, and intellectuals representing various socialist organizations and groups in Greece founded the Socialist Labour Party of Greece (Sosialistikon Ergatikon Komma Ellados).[1] After the establishment of the Third International in March 1919, the national council of SEKE decided in May 1919 to 'break all formal ties with the Second International which had betrayed the socialist ideology' and 'prepare the ground' for the party's adhesion to the new organization.[2] By the time of the Second Congress of the SEKE which was convened on 5 April 1920, the pro-Comintern faction within the party had gained control and the Congress, accordingly, voted unanimously in favour of 'organizational integration' with the Third International, and accepted 'all its principles and resolutions'. The Congress also voted for 'affiliation with the Balkan Communist Federation' (BCF), an association of the Balkan sections – Bulgarian, Greek, and Serbian – of the Third International and modified the name of the party adding to its title the word *kommounistikon* in brackets.[3] Four years later, at the Third Extraordinary Congress, SEKE(K)

> accepted unanimously all the resolutions of the World Congresses of the Comintern and the BCF and especially the resolutions of the Second World Congress which adopted the Twenty-One Conditions for the admission of new parties to the Communist International and in accordance with these Conditions, changed the name of the party from *Socialist Labour Party of Greece (Communist)* to *Communist Party of Greece (Greek Section of the Communist International)*.[4]

The Third Extraordinary Congress, by embracing the Comintern thesis of bolshevization, marked a turning-point in the party's history. From then onwards Comintern delegates laid down the KKE's (Communist Party of Greece) policies and directly or indirectly appointed the KKE's leaders. In addition, the Congress introduced fundamental changes in the party organization by establishing for the first time the system of 'cells' and 'fractions'.[5] In January 1926 the KKE was formally outlawed for the first time. In line with Comintern instructions which advised its 'sections' to combine 'legal with illegal work', the leadership decided that the party should assume the form of an 'illegal organization' operating on the principle of 'democratic centralism'. This did not rule out the formation of 'legal organizations' which could be used 'for propaganda and agitation among the masses'.[6] During the next five years the KKE suffered from numerous leadership crises until the Comintern decided to put an end to the endless personal feuds by appointing the trusted and dynamic Moscow-trained Nikos Zachariadis as secretary of the party. He was officially 'elected' secretary only in 1934, and secretary-general and 'Leader of the Party' in 1935 by the Sixth Congress.

Throughout this period (1918–31) the KKE remained on the sidelines of Greek political life, with no significant political power. There are four factors that explain the KKE's failure to raise the membership of the party and its share of the national vote in the elections of 1923, 1926, 1928, and 1929.[7] First, Greece was an agrarian and underdeveloped country. The landowning peasants found nothing to attract them in Marxist doctrine and even those few thousands of industrial workers who could qualify as 'proletarians' were generally too close to their village origins easily to abandon the traditional peasant frame of mind. Moreover, they were less interested in exhortations regarding the nobility and brotherhood of the proletariat than in climbing the social ladder as artisans or shopkeepers. As the Greek historian Svoronos notes, 'the numerical weakness of the industrial proletariat and the absence of a long standing syndicalistic and political tradition did not allow for the development of a proletarian consciousness, nor, therefore, for the spreading of such a consciousness among the working class to any considerable extent'.[8] What is more, the Communists were inhibited by their own doctrinaire priorities from seeking support among the peasants. By espousing an ideology of *ouvrierisme*, the KKE chose to ignore the radical potential of the peasantry and followed a course of political and organizational isolation. Even if the party's recruitment objectives had been different, however, the results would probably have been meagre. As Stavrianos argues, 'when Greek peasants were forced by overpopulation and the current crisis to leave their ancestral village, they sought their fortune in glamorous America rather than in a nearby city'. As for the strongly nationalistic and property-minded bourgeoisie they remained conspicuously unimpressed by Communist appeals to 'join the struggle against the capital yoke'.[9]

Secondly, this bourgeoisie, with its individualistic and entrepreneurial values, its belief in progress and economic opportunity, found a leader in the person of Eleftherious Venizelos, who had enacted during 1912–13 a sweeping reform programme that satisfied both the middle and lower classes. The Communists were thus left without an audience, as even the workers (with the notable exception of those working in the radical and organized tobacco industry), impressed by Venizelos' charismatic style and his proof that a modified liberalism could be effective in Greece, followed his banner. The majority of the bourgeoisie, moreover, invoked social Darwinism to support Venizelos' expansionist ambitions in Turkey, arguing that Greece had a right and a duty to retake Constantinople from the Turks and create a 'Greater Greece' similar to the Byzantine empire. Even after the Asia Minor disaster in 1922, when anti-Communism became the official ideology of the state – the 'threat of Communism' providing the endangered bourgeois parties with a useful device to rally mass support – the KKE had little success in mobilizing the industrial proletariat against the legislation that was adopted to suppress the labour movement. Its call, for example, in August 1929 for a mass demonstration against Venizelos' notorious (*Idionymon*) Law (which authorized the persecution of all those whose acts and thoughts were judged to undermine the existing order) was ignored by almost 95 per cent of the labour force, which throughout this period continued to remain deeply divided and aligned to the two dominant traditional parties.[10]

Thirdly, and following from the second, the KKE's subordination to the Comintern and the mechanical application by its leadership of all of the Comintern's resolutions and programmes contributed to the KKE's inability to appeal to the two socio-economically frustrated, but strongly nationalistic, groups, i.e. the peasants and the refugees from Asia Minor who flooded Greece after the disastrous Greco-Turkish war of 1922. The endorsement by the KKE, in 1924, of the Comintern resolution for a 'united and independent Macedonia and Thrace', at a time when 700,000 Greek refugees from Asia Minor had already settled in Greek Macedonia, and the Greek element there formed a majority of more than 95 per cent of the total population, isolated the party and provoked a strong nationalist reaction. (The Comintern, in an effort to assist the powerful Bulgarian Communist Party, supported the Bulgarian demand for a united Macedonian state, comprising the territories of Greek, Yugoslav, and Bulgarian Macedonia.)[11]

Finally, the perennial quarrels and the constant changes in its leadership and political orientation could not but lessen the party's effectiveness as a political force. By 1931 the KKE had gone through eight leaders, most of whom were also eventually expelled from the party. As Zachariadis himself admits in his *Theses on the History of the KKE*, the crisis of the KKE in the period 1918–31 'was basically and principally the crisis of its leaders'.[12]

When Zachariadis took over the leadership of the KKE, the membership of the party had dropped to 1,500. By 1936, before General John Metaxas established a dictatorship, the membership had reached 15,000. This growth in the strength of the KKE can be attributed to the organizational skills of its new leader and his determination to build a strong party organization capable of operating efficiently under legal or illegal conditions. Preparedness for the latter requirement proved, of course, invaluable to the KKE during the German occupation.[13] Three more factors, however, contributed to the KKE's success. The first was Zachariadis' decision to change the KKE's official line on the 'Macedonian Question'. In December 1935, at the Sixth Congress, the slogan for a 'united and independent Macedonia' was abandoned and replaced with the slogan of 'complete equality for the minorities'.[14] The resolution adopted by the Congress stated:

'Marxism–Leninism requires that the communist parties base their policy and their slogans on *firm and realistic grounds*. In the part of Macedonia which Greece holds, Greek refugees have been settled. Today, in the Greek part of Macedonia, the population, in its majority, is Greek. And in the present circumstances, the Leninist–Stalinist principle of self determination demands the substitution of the old slogan.[15]

Secondly, the adoption by the KKE of the anti-Fascist 'popular-front' policy, promulgated officially by the Comintern at its Seventh Congress in July–August 1935, helped the party to emerge from its political isolation. By establishing a common front with the leaders of non-Communist trade unions and political groups, the KKE managed to increase the party's following from 14,000 (in the elections of 1928) to almost 100,000 (in the elections of 1935), that is, to raise the percentage of the votes from 1.41 per cent (1928) to 9.59 per cent (1935). That this increase in pro-Communist votes was not entirely the result of the abstention of the Venizelists from the elections of 1935 is proven by the fact that in the elections of 1936 the KKE alone received 5.76 per cent of the votes and sent fifteen MPs to Parliament, enough, as we shall see, to hold the balance between the two major parties of the day. Free from the burden of the 'Macedonian Question', the KKE could turn its attention to the task of strengthening its 'alliances' with all democratic forces, especially the Socialists (the 'social Fascists' of two years earlier) and the Liberals, and seize the historical opportunity offered by the failure of the two bourgeois parties to reconcile their differences.[16]

The third factor that explains the growth of Communist influence during this period was the economic depression that hit Greece in the 1930s as a result of the world economic crisis. High unemployment, rampant inflation, political instablility, a debt-ridden agricultural sector, and heavy taxation all furnished the KKE with fuel for their expansionist drive. Moreover, Venizelos' failure during his last term in office (1928–32) to implement structural changes in the Greek economy and satisfy the urgent needs of the peasants and the refugees offered the Communists the possibility of making further inroads into Venizelist popular support, especially among the refugees, whether urban or rural.[17]

Thus, by 1936 the KKE under Zachariadis' leadership had increased its support and its political power was steadily growing. The establishment in August 1936 of the Metaxas dictatorship, however, interrupted the KKE's revolutionary programme.[18] The process was to resume in 1941 when the German occupation had smashed the bureaucratic and military carapace of the traditional order. It was during Metaxas' Fascist rule that the KKE was shaken to its foundations and Greece, having been attacked by Italy in October 1940, entered the war on the side of the Allies. Any discussion though, of the reasons that brought about this dictatorship requires in turn a brief summary of the major political developments that shaped Greek history in the 1920s and early 1930s.

THE FAILURE OF THE REPUBLIC AND THE METAXAS DICTATORSHIP

Parliamentary democracy in Greece during the inter-war period was plagued by the *Ethnikos Dichasmos* – 'the National Schism' – a continuous feud between the two dominant political factions of the era, the (Republican) Liberal Party of Eleftherios Venizelos, and the 'Anti-Venizelist' bloc led by the (Royalist) Popular Party of Panayis Tsaldaris. With the outbreak of the First World War, Greece found herself divided over the fundamental issue of intervention or neutrality. For Venizelos, the architect of Greece's territorial expansion during the Balkan Wars of 1912–13, and his supporters, the choice was a clear one: since the Ottoman Empire and Bulgaria were allied to the Central Powers, Greece should enter the war on the side of the Entente, in order to further its irridentist aspirations in Asia Minor and Macedonia. King Constantine I, however, effectively the leader of the predominantly Germanophile 'Anti-Venizelists', convinced that the Entente would be vanquished by the Central Powers, and because of his family connections with the German Kaiser, wanted Greece to cling to neutrality. Unable to agree on a common national policy, the country lapsed into acute party strife. The unity of purpose and effort achieved during the Balkan Wars was destroyed. Greece found herself torn between two contending factions hating each other and bent on totally exterminating the other. In 1917, a year after Venizelos had formed a 'revolutionary government' in Salonica, Britain and France intervened and forced Constantine to abdicate. Greece finally joined the Entente, but the tug of war between the two men had crystallized into a schism that was destined to affect Greece's internal political development for decades to come. Despite Venizelos' impressive diplomatic accomplishments at the Paris Peace Conference, the decline in national strength and consensus culminated in disaster – the military débâcle of 1922 in Asia Minor.

In May 1919, while the Peace Conference was discussing the future of Turkey Venizelos persuaded the Allies to allow Greek troops to occupy Smyrna in Asia Minor. The Turks bitterly resented the violation of their territory and from this resentment a widespread movement of national revolt was born under the leadership of the powerful Mustafa Kemal. Within a year the Kemalists had swept the whole country, and only the presence of an allied garrison kept a puppet Turkish government in being in Constantinople. Undeterred by this warning, the Allied Powers signed at Sèvres a treaty of peace with the Constantinople government in August 1920. Any faint chance which remained of the enforcement of the Treaty of Sèvres was, however, destroyed by events in Greece. In the 1920 general election, Venizelos was swept from power and ex-King Constantine returned triumphant following the plebiscite of 5 December 1920. This development alienated the sympathy of the Allies – a sympathy largely achieved through Venizelos' magnetic personality – and although the Greek army had boldly advanced from Smyrna into the interior of Asia Minor, it became clear that it could no longer count on the effective support of the Allies. In these conditions a débâcle was inevitable. The Greeks were driven back; and in September 1922, after some particularly savage fighting, Kemal drove the last Greek troops from the soil of Asia. In Greece, a revolutionary committee headed by Colonel Plastiras forced the king to abdicate in favour of his son George and to go into exile. Constantine left Greece in disgrace, never to return, cursed by 1.5 million impoverished refugees who flooded the country. The search for scapegoats culminated in the summary execution of six leading anti-Venizelist leaders, including the ex-premier Gounaris. The *Ethnikos Dichasmos* had been sanctioned with blood. The dream of a Greater Greece in the image of Byzantium had now turned into a nightmare.

Following an unsuccessful military coup (in October 1923), and the boycott of the December 1923 elections by the royalists, the revolutionary committee obliged King George to leave the country. In May 1924 Greece officially became a republic, remaining one until 1935. During the period 1924–8, eleven military coups or *pronunciamentos* and a succession of weak republican governments destroyed normal party alignments, confirmed the military as a powerful but divided force, added many more prominent names to the list of the purged, and discredited the parliamentary system in the eyes of the public. Venizelos' last attempt to save the ailing and frail republic during his final period of office (1928–32), came to nothing. Although this government proved to be the longest and most stable one of the interwar period, the Great Depression of the early 1930s further aggravated the country's severe economic problems, while the rising tide of Fascism in Germany, Italy, and the Balkans gave a new impetus to undemocratic tendencies. When the Venizelist–Republican camp boycotted the elections of June 1935, protesting against the sentencing to death *in absentia* of Venizelos and Plastiras for their involvement in the unsuccessful coup of March 1935, General Kondylis established a dictatorship and forced a rump assembly to proclaim the abolition of the republic and the restoration of the monarchy. This decision which was taken against the will of all politicians including the royalist Tsaldaris, the Populist premier, was ratified by a plebiscite (in November 1935), which produced a vote, with the manipulation of the military, of 98 per cent in favour of the monarchy.[19]

The restoration of the monarchy paved the way for dictatorship. The efforts of the young and inexperienced king to bring about unity and order proved totally ineffective. New elections were held in January 1936 resulting in a parliamentary deadlock between the two major parties: the Liberals won 142 seats; the Populists, 143. Neither party won an absolute majority and neither could thus govern without the support of the fifteen Communists MPs in Parliament. When it was discovered that the Liberals were prepared to negotiate a secret deal with the Communists,[20] the army (under General Papagos) declared that it would not tolerate a government resting on Communist votes. To prevent yet another coup, the king appointed the leader of a small monarchist party, General John Metaxas, well-known for his totalitarian views, his loyalty to the Greek monarch, and his admiration of the Nazi regime, to be the Minister of War. On 13 April, the nonpolitical prime minister, Professor Demertzis suddenly died, and on the same day the king appointed Metaxas premier, without consulting the party leaders, although he had only seven followers in Parliament. Almost the entire political world challenged the legitimacy of the king's choice, but in vain. Populists and Liberals began at long last to discuss forming a coalition, but took no immediate action. The KKE insisted that the Metaxas government be overthrown by passing a vote of no confidence. The Liberals, however, refused on the grounds that this

The Greek Communist Party 163

might antagonize the army and precipitate a coup. Instead, Sofoulis, the leader of the Liberals and successor of Venizelos (who had died in March 1936), eased through a resolution adjourning Parliament for five months and allowing Metaxas to govern by decree. The Parliament did not meet again until after the end of the Second World War.[21]

Events were hastened by an internal crisis. With the disintegration of the parliamentary system, the KKE decided to act more directly. It strengthened the anti-Metaxas front by signing a pact of co-operation with the Socialist–Agrarian party of John Sofianopoulos,[22] and organized a number of strikes, demonstrations, and street fights demanding higher wages, release of political prisoners, and withdrawal of the anti-Labour legislation which declared strikes illegal. In May 1936, a general strike in Salonica was brutally suppressed. Thirty workers were killed and over 400 wounded by Metaxas' police.[23] A national general strike was proclaimed for 5 August, and Metaxas seized his chance: hundreds of labour leaders were arrested and deported. On 22 July, Sofoulis approached the king with the new leader of the Populists, John Theotokis, offering to form a coalition government, which would have commanded a large majority in Parliament. But the king had other plans. On 4 August, he signed decrees declaring a state of emergency, suspending the constitutional provisions for personal liberties, and dissolving parliament, without fixing a date for new elections. A police state soon began to impose a carefully controlled reign of terror directed primarily against the Communists, trade unionists, intellectuals, and others known for their strong republican leanings. Monarchy had been transformed into Crown-sponsored dictatorship. The king emerged as the symbol of an oppressive dictatorship which presided over the death of democracy in Greece. The stigma of his association with the Metaxas regime was to prove indelible.

THE KKE UNDER THE DICTATORSHIP

The only organized force that tried to react to the dictatorship was the KKE, but without the support of the non-Communist democratic forces its party organization soon disintegrated under the repression of the Metaxas security police.[24] The single most important factor in this development was that long before the establishment of the dictatorship, agents belonging to the security police had succeeded in infiltrating the KKE's underground organization. Their information led to the arrest of Zachariadis, in September 1936, and of Mytlas, a member of the central committee, in whose house the KKE archives were found. Information in these archives led to a large number of arrests of prominent KKE members. By May 1938, all remaining members of the political bureau (Vasilis Nefeloudis, Dimitrios Partsaldis, and Stylianos Sklavenas) had been arrested, with the exception of George Siandos, who formed a new political bureau by including in it the members of the central committee – Nicos Ploumbidis, Dimitrios Papayannis, and Grigoris Skafidas.[25] In November 1939, Siandos and Skafidas too were arrested.

Only Papayannis, Vagelis Ktistakis, and Christos Kanakis remained at liberty and without waiting for the approval of Zachariadis, who was in prison in Corfu, they formed a central committee which was later to be labelled the 'Palaia Kentriki Epitropi' (old central committee – OCC).[26] The leader of the OCC was Ploumbidis who, even though interned in a sanatorium, kept in touch with the committee and directed it.[27]

The total disintegration of the Communist Party under the Metaxas dictatorship must also be attributed to the methods and tactics employed by Constantine Maniadakis, Metaxas' shrewd Minister of Public Security, described by some as the Himmler of Greece.[28] Maniadakis concentrated his efforts on destroying the KKE's party machine by uncovering and neutralizing its leadership and by smashing the party's internal cohesion. He succeeded in doing so by introducing the so-called 'repentance declarations' and by creating his own 'Communist Party'. The first tactic was successful in undermining party morale: under extensive psychological and physical pressure arrested KKE members were induced to sign statements denouncing their ideology and their party. These 'repentance declarations' were then published in the censored press. Almost 45,000 such declarations were signed during the four years of the dictatorship (1936–40), a number far exceeding the actual membership of the party at that time.[29] Although not all Communists who signed these declarations were 'spies' and 'traitors' (some did so after being ordered to do so by the party leadership so that they could resume underground activity), a few did in fact become active police collaborators. It was with the assistance of these collaborators that Maniadakis proceeded to break up the party by establishing a police-controlled KKE. Early in 1940 Maniadakis formed his own central committee, known as *Prosorini Diikisis* (Temporary Administration – TA), nominally headed by two political bureau members Michalis Tyrimos and Yannis Michailidis who had become collaborators.[30] With two central committees in existence, each publishing its own *Rizospastis* (the KKE daily), each accusing the other of being a 'traitorous' organization, and each claiming to draw its authority from Zachariadis himself, the interned KKE leadership was thrown into total confusion. Maniadakis' central committee was so successfull in fooling the KKE leaders, that until December 1942, most Communists considered the 'old central committee' a police-created organization and its members as 'traitors' and 'fifth columnists'.[31] This error occurred because Michailidis, who was the head of the 'Temporary Administration', had signed a 'repentence declaration' on the orders of Zachariadis, and was thus his 'trusted man'. Although in his *Official History of the KKE*, Zachariadis claims that he always knew that 'the Temporary Administration was in the hands of Maniadakis', it was not until January 1941, almost a year after the TA's founding, that the KKE leader discovered its true nature.[32] Likewise, the well-organized Communist detainees in the Akronafplia prison camp, under the instruction of Yannis Ioannidis, a member of the political bureau, expressed more trust in the TA than in the OCC. However, in November 1940, Michailidis became a double agent and, in a secret letter to Ioannidis, warned the Akronafplia Communists of the TA's role and

Maniadakis' methods. Ioannidis reacted by instructing Spyros Kalodikis, a Communist who had just escaped from Akronafplia, to form an 'independent organization' in Athens. This organization and the OCC, although denouncing each other as tools of Maniadakis, successfully prevented many party members from joining the TA and thus being arrested.[33] None the less, the existence of all these rival organizations and the declarations of repentance had spread so much confusion and suspicion among the party members that the KKE throughout the dictatorship remained a paralysed force unable to challenge Metaxas' regime.

THE FIFTH PLENUM AND THE COMINTERN DIRECTIVE OF JULY 1939; THE NEW COMINTERN LINE OF SEPTEMBER 1939 AND THE GREEK–ITALIAN WAR

In February 1939, as war was beginning to engulf Europe, the Fifth Plenum of the central committee of the KKE under the chairmanship of Siandos (who had escaped from exile) declared: 'Our Party struggles to secure the independence and integrity of Greece, but at the same time it states that the greatest enemy of our country's independence and integrity is found in Athens – it is *the monarcho-fascist dictatorship*'.[34] The plenum went on to criticize the Greek–Bulgarian treaty, signed by Metaxas and the Bulgarian Foreign Minister, Kiosseivanoff, in July 1938, as Greek submission to the Axis.[35] This resolution, however, was soon superseded by a new Comintern directive. In July 1939 the Comintern's political secretariat castigated the KKE's position and urged the party to support the Metaxas government in its struggle against the 'Axis forces' and particularly the 'Italian Fascists'. They were the main enemy, not Metaxas. Moreover, the executive committee of the Comintern urged the KKE to support the Greek–Bulgarian treaty because the treaty was 'a step in the direction of peaceful Balkan coexistence'. The duty of the KKE was to work for the creation of a strong Balkan alliance.[36]

In August 1939, the Nazi–Soviet non-aggression pact was signed. By September a new Comintern line began to emerge, reaching its final formulation in Dimitrov's article on the 'Tasks of the working class in the war' of 7 November 1939.[37] The Comintern now altered its 'anti-Axis' stand and urged all European Communist parties to put an end to the 'imperialist war', by agitating for peace, and if necessary, by direct sabotage of the imperialist armies in their own countries.[38]

Almost a year after the September 1939 Comintern resolution. Mussolini's armies invaded Greece (28 October 1940). Three days later, Zachariadis, who was being held in an Athens prison, handed Maniadakis his famous 'open letter', which was promptly published in the Metaxist censored press. In this letter the KKE leader said that 'in this war which is directed by the Metaxas Government, all of us should give our whole strength without any reservation'.[39] Zachariadis' 'patriotic' position was endorsed by the Akronafplia Communists, who on 29 October, two days before the publication of Zachariadis' letter, had sent a similar letter to the Metaxist authorities.[40] The old central committee, however, in strict accordance with the

September 1939 Comintern directive, denounced Zachariadis' letter as a 'forgery'. On 7 December 1940, and again on 18 March 1941, it issued two statements declaring that 'this war which has been caused by the Royalist–Metaxist gang, and which has been ordered by the English imperialists, cannot bear any relation whatsoever to the defence of our country, nor is it a war "against fascism"...'.[41] Needless to say, Maniadakis' brain child, the Temporary Administration, immediately endorsed Zachariadis' letter.

The question of whether Zachariadis in fact knew of the Setpember 1939 Comintern directive when writing his 'patriotic letter' is a crucial one but still a matter of controversy.[42] If Zachariadis did know of the September 1939 directive, and chose to ignore it, following instead the outdated July 1939 directive, then his 'bold' initiative constituted at the time one of the few incidents of a 'nationalist deviation' committed by a European Communist party.[43] On the other hand, if Zachariadis did not know of the September 1939 directive, but only of the July 1939 one (which was probably passed on to him by Maniadakis' agent Michailidis when Zachariadis was transferred from Corfu to Athens in January 1940[44]), then his stand in October 1940 was not in the least remarkable, since his letter is in strict accordance with the line laid down by the Comintern, which, as already noted, was at that point urging the KKE to adopt a nationalist position and support Metaxas.[45] In the *Voithima ya tin Istoria tou KKE* (the *Official History of the KKE*), written by Zachariadis himself after the end of the Civil War (1952), the KKE leader's 'antifascist, nationalist appeal' is characterized as a 'historic political act, which showed *courage, perspicacity* and *initiative*'.[46] Moreover, according to Vasilis Nefeloudis, the secretary of the central committee from 1935 and Member of Parliament in 1932–3 and 1936 (Nefeloudis was in Corfu prison with Zachariadis), the KKE leader came to know about the September 1939 directive from Chronopoulos, an OKNE (Federation of Communist Youth of Greece) cadre who in December 1939 had been arrested at the frontier on returning to Greece from the Soviet Union and had been interned in Corfu. Nefeloudis also claims that, while in Corfu prison, Zachariadis had defended the correctness of the September 1939 Comintern line but changed his mind when he was transferred to Athens.[47]

His decision to follow the outdated July 1939 directive may have been influenced by the following four factors: first, Zachariadis could have claimed that under the confused conditions of his captivity (he had been in jail since 1936) he did not know the exact 'content' of the September 1939 Comintern directive and that in choosing to follow the July 1939 one, which after all applied specifically to the KKE, he thought he was acting in strict accordance with Comintern views and wishes.[48] Secondly, the fact that Greece was at war with Italy and not with Germany, with whom the Soviets had concluded the non-aggression pact, may have provided the KKE leader with a useful alibi. Thirdly, the pursuit of the September 1939 line would have, as in the case of the 'Macedonian Question', offended the nationalist-minded Greeks. Zachariadis knew only too well what would have been the consequences for the party if at the time of the Italian attack he had advocated an 'anti-patriotic' policy.[49] Finally, in supporting

Metaxas Zachariadis may have hoped that the Greek dictator would free all the interned Communists and allow them to join the common struggle against the enemy. This was something that the Akronafplia Communists had also demanded in their letter to the Metaxist authorities. If the KKE leader had been successful in gaining this concession from Metaxas, and there were strong indications at the time that Metaxas was indeed considering freeing the Communists,[50] then he would have found additional grounds to justify his 'open letter' to the Comintern.

Whatever the reasons, the historical importance of Zachariadis' October letter cannot be underestimated. As Karas notes in his short biography of Zachariadis,

> this letter constitutes one of the most important documents in the history of the KKE ... because it gave the Party a clear direction at a time when the Soviet–German non-aggression pact of 1939 had given rise to conflicting interpretations regarding the character of the general war.[51]

What is more, Zachariadis' letter gave the KKE the necessary 'national and patriotic' credentials which proved invaluable during the occupation.[52] Even the anti-Zachariadist P. Nefeloudis had to admit that Zachariadis' letter 'raised the prestige of the party to a great extent in the eyes of the Greek people' and thus 'laid the most solid foundation for the creation of the National Resistance epic'.[53] Despite the unquestionable value of the letter, one should remember, however, that Zachariadis had been appointed to the leadership of the KKE by the Comintern and that the KKE was for him nothing else but 'the Greek section of the Comintern'.[54] It is quite unreasonable to assume that he would have acted against the views of the Comintern. If he did so in October 1940, it was only because the July 1939 directive offered him a good 'alibi' with which to defend his 'nationalist deviation'. But a few weeks after the publication of his 'open letter', Zachariadis in a 'second letter' changed his position, adopting instead a stand half-way between his first letter and the September 1939 directive. Zachariadis, the Comintern appointee, worried over the repercussions of his daring act, had decided to conform again with his 'masters'.

The KKE leader's new position was set-out in a 'second letter', dated 26 November 1940, which he smuggled out of jail and sent to the Maniadakis-controlled 'Temporary Administration', which he still trusted, instructing it to publish it in *Rizospastis*. In this 'second letter', the war against the Italians is characterized as 'imperialist'. Since the Italians had been expelled from Greek territory, 'Greece', Zachariadis argued, 'has no place in the imperialist war between England and Italy–Germany'. 'The Greek people', Zachariadis claimed, 'want one thing: freedom and neutrality'. The British forces should withdraw from Greece and through the mediation of the government of the USSR an armistice should be signed.[55] This letter, naturally, was not published by Maniadakis. Zachariadis finally realized that the 'Temporary Administration' had been in the services of Maniadakis all along and decided to write a 'third letter', addressed this time to OKNE, the Communist Youth Organization.

In this 'third letter', dated 15 January 1941, which fell into the hands of the police and was only published after the end of the war, Zachariadis, after denouncing the Temporary Administration as a tool of Maniadakis and its leader Michailidis as a traitor, gave full endorsement to the September 1939 Comintern line, accusing Metaxas of waging 'a war of conquest'. 'Since Metaxas is refusing to secure the peace and is conducting an imperialist war, he (and not Italy) remains the main enemy of the people and the country', Zachariadis argued.[56] After analysing the reasons for writing his 'first letter',[57] for which 'he took full responsibility before the KKE and the Comintern', Zachariadis went on to attack the Temporary Administration for 'reducing his [first] letter to a social-patriotic document' and hence for trying to 'stain the honour of the KKE'.[58] Obviously, Zachariadis had been alarmed by the fact that the Fascist authorities had been using his October letter, through the good offices of the Temporary Administration, to urge the KKE to support Metaxas. This meant that he was in danger of being castigated by the Comintern for assisting, albeit unintentionally, the war effort and the policies of a Fascist government.[59] It is no coincidence, therefore, that Zachariadis ends his 'third letter' with the slogan 'Hail the Communist International', something that he 'forgot' to do, incidentally, in his previous two letters. Having for a brief moment put on the 'antiCommunist' mantle of patriotism, Zachariadis, the faithful disciple of internationalism, found it necessary to proclaim again his unabashed loyalty to the Comintern. There is little doubt that had Zachariadis' 'second' and 'third' letter been published in the Metaxist press, the image of the KKE as a 'heroic nationalistic party' would have been shattered. But Maniadakis, judging their content to be 'subversive', banned their publication. So by a complex twist of providence the arch-enemy of the KKE became suddenly the redeemer of its sins. When on 27 April 1941 the German troops entered the city of Athens, the KKE, 'the party of the people', was ready to take the lead in organizing the resistance.[60]

THE KKE DOMINATES THE RESISTANCE

After the defeat of Greece by Germany in May 1941 (when German airborne troops finally captured Crete), King George II, accompanied by his new prime minister, Emmanuel Tsouderos (Metaxas died suddenly on January 29 and his successor, Alexander Koryzis, committed suicide two days before the Greek forces surrendered to the Wehrmacht), and a handful of mostly Metaxist figures, fled to Egypt where his government-in-exile soon began its 'inactive' existence. During the following three and a half years, until October 1944, Greece remained under Axis rule. Although the Italians and the Bulgarians participated in the administration of the country together with the Germans, the latter retained real control. A series of collaborationist cabinets functioned under the Axis authorities,[61] while the *de jure* government recognized by the Allies was the government-in-exile of King George II.[62]

Resistance began as a spontaneous movement carried out by individuals and groups of different political persuasions. The first act of overt defiance toward the invader was the blowing up of two Bulgarian ships loaded with munitions in Piraeus harbour on 30 May 1941 by a Venizelist who had been supplied with explosives by the Special Operations Executive (SOE). The same night a young student, Manolis Glezos, who later joined the KKE, removed the swastika from the Acropolis and the next day a German munitions dump was destroyed in Thessaloniki. The lead in organizing resistance, though, was taken by the KKE, which soon set up a number of secret organizations. In May the Communists founded the National Mutual Aid (EA) and two months later the Labour National Liberation Front (EEAM). In July the Sixth Plenum met under a 'new' central committee, recently reconstituted by a number of KKE cadres who had escaped from the Akronafplia camp. It endorsed a national front policy and called on 'the Greek people, the parties and their organizations to form a *national liberation front*'.[63] By the end of August the old central committee and all the parts of the KKE organization that had survived under Metaxas had adhered to the 'new' central committee.[64] Early in September the Seventh Plenum convened and a few weeks later, on September 27, the National Liberation Front (EAM) was formed.

Although during these occupation years a number of resistance groups appeared in Greece, EAM remained by far the most important. Towards the end of the occupation period it reached such proportions that it became virtually a *de facto* government and consequently a rival of the regime in exile. Efforts to create such a front had begun even before the Sixth Plenum had launched its appeal. Dimitrios Glinos, the KKE's intellectual ideologist, had in June 1941 contacted most of the leaders of the traditional bourgeois parties in an effort to persuade them to join such a national front. Most of these politicians, however, which included republican leaders like Kanellopoulos, Papandreou, Sofoulis, and Kafandaris, refused, distrusting the political aims of the KKE. The KKE was, nevertheless, successful in winning the support of several left-wing political leaders. Three small socialist parties, SKE (Socialist Party of Greece), ELD (Union of Popular Democracy), and AKE (Agrarian Party of Greece) headed respectively by Stratis, Tsirimokos, and Voyatzis, accepted the KKE call and formed EAM.[65] The inclusion of these small parties in EAM, and the fact that AKE was itself Communist-controlled, ensured that the KKE's role in EAM would be predominant.[66] The KKE, through its principal organization EAM and its armed forces ELAS (National Popular Liberation Army), formed in April 1942, soon emerged, therefore, as the dominant resistance power. The party which had almost disintegrated under the Metaxas dictatorship had become an organization with almost 300,000 members by the time Greece was liberated. As for EAM/ELAS these had some 2 million members between them, almost 30 per cent of the population.[67] There are five factors that account for this dramatic rise in Communist strength.

First, the failure of the king, his government-in-exile and the traditional political parties to deal with the problem of organizing a resistance. Based on a network of personal relations and with their activities geared mostly towards winning elections or participating in the government itself, the bourgeois parties found themselves totally devoid of the infrastructure necessary to organize a mass struggle.[68] Moreover, the old politicians' intense concern with the 'constitutional question' (the monarchy versus republic issue) and their general defeatism led them to adopt a negative attitude on the need to conduct an armed resistance. As C. M. Woodhouse, who succeeded Brigadier Myers as Commander of the British Military Mission, observed, 'communism was blamed for the provocation of German reprisals, and the threat of anarchy in Greece. As rumours from the mountains seemed to confirm the worst fears of patriotic conservatives, both republican and royalist leaders intervened against the Resistance'.[69] On the other hand, the government-in-exile, completely cut off from developments within Greece, lived and functioned within its own small world of intrigue and machination in Cairo, while the king, having made his home at Claridge's in London, entertained his small circle of 'sophisticated' Greek *émigrés*.[70] Thus, at the outset of the occupation, the traditional political world, deeply divided and demoralized, seemed to be in a state of permanent eclipse. New centres of power, new leaders, new mass movements, and new political aspirations were needed in the struggle that was about to begin. While the traditional leaders acted as though Greece was still in the 1920s, the KKE stepped in and filled the political vacuum by skilfully mobilizing the urban and rural population of Greece for the needs of the resistance.

Secondly, the absence of effective parliamentary democracy during the inter-war period and the resultant Metaxist dictatorship had discredited the king in the eyes of the Greek people (for giving his blessing to the dictatorship and maintaining it in power) as well as the traditional political parties (for acquiescing in it when it was established and for their ineffectiveness against it once its real nature was perceived). Moreover, the inability of the Liberal and Populist parties during the inter-war and occupation period to solve basic socio-economic problems (such as the poverty of the refugees who had flooded into Greece in 1922, or the famine of 1941–2 in which almost 300,000 people died) because of their fanatical preoccupation with the 'constitutional question', meant that in the eyes of the disillusioned Greek public EAM represented a real political alternative. It offered both a way to resist the enemy and a promise to establish a more democratic and just regime in post-war Greece. What is more, the Greek government-in-exile formed in 1941 was not only perceived by the majority of Greeks to be Metaxist in nature but because of the dictatorship itself it was also a non-elected government. Its legitimacy was thus challenged by the KKE and EAM who by virtue of their popular following could claim to represent the only legitimate power in Greece.[71]

Thirdly, of all the protagonists on the political stage, the KKE was the best able to survive and operate in the harsh conditions of occupation. Although Zachariadis had been handed over to the Germans by the Athens police and then transferred to Dachau, most of the party cadres had managed to escape prison on the collapse of the Metaxas dictatorship.[72] Their organizational experience in clandestine work and their zeal and dedication to the cause of the resistance proved invaluable assets in the struggle against the occupying powers. By contrast, the bourgeois parties totally demolished under Metaxas and deeply divided after the death of their leaders, Venizelos and Tsalderis, were ill-equipped to take the initiative in a clandestine reorganization of the national forces. The basic components of the traditional Greek party organization were the personal clientelist structures built up by local politicians.[73] Thus, when the occupation took place the leaders of these traditional parties, who under Metaxas had been 'neutralized', could not re-establish their customary direct contact with the masses. In December 1942 the traditional parties tried to create a resistance movement under their aegis (EDAM: National Democratic Liberation Front) but they soon discovered their organizational incapacity for mass mobilization and gave up the idea.[74] Their only act of 'resistance' was to sign a statement in March 1942 declaring that the king must await the result of a plebiscite before returning. The purpose of this statement was clear: by presenting a common front which transcended the inter-war republican/monarchist divisions, the traditional politicians wanted to capitalize on the antimonarchist popular sentiment that had developed in reaction to the king's collaboration with Metaxas and thus challenge EAM's growing power and monopoly of the republican cause that threatened to relegate them to permanent obsolescence. When they discovered that this strategy had failed to produce the expected results they turned to the British for help, who in their determination to establish in Greece a reliable pro-British and anti-Left parliamentary government gave them their support.

Fourthly, there were significant organizational differences between the various resistance movements. The principal resistance groups, other than EAM/ELAS, were the National Democratic Greek League, or EDES, led by General Zervas, and the National and Social Liberation, or EKKA, led by Colonel Psarros.[75] These two organizations, as well as several other minor groups, differed from EAM in certain basic respects: first, EAM strove to operate on a nationwide scale. The other groups were purely regional in their activities, EDES operating in Epirus and EKKA in Rumeli; secondly, EAM developed a comprehensive political and social programme and established numerous subsidiary organizations designed to enlist the support of all sections of the population. The other groups were primarily military in character and in recruiting followers were dependent on the personalities of their respective army leaders.[76] In contrast with EAM/ELAS, both EDES and EKKA, despite their socialist complexion, were not integrated or bound to any particular party and therefore were unable to put forward a political programme which might win wider support for their cause. The KKE, nevertheless, had by 1942 circulated such a programme, written by the party's ideologist and noted intellectual Glinos, entitled *What Is the EAM and What Does It Want.*[77] In addition, while EDES and EKKA were independent units free to follow whatever policy they wished, ELAS was created by EAM and remained its subordinate military branch to the end. All political decisions were taken by the EAM central committee and although military matters were entrusted to the ELAS central committee, it was EAM's central committee that appointed the members of this body. Leading each ELAS unit were a military commander, a *Kapetanios*, and an EAM political representative; the military commander, usually a regular army officer, decided on military matters; the *Kapetanios* took care of propaganda and morale within the unit and directed relations between the unit and the civilian population and organizations; the EAM representative dealt exclusively with political affairs and ensured that ELAS followed EAM's instructions. Since both the *Kapetanios* and the EAM representatives were Communists and as the military commanders gradually became party members, ELAS was firmly under the control of the KKE, which could then use its political organizations as powerful recruiting agencies for its resistance army;[78] finally, the policies of both EDES and EKKA were partly determined by the British, whose support was essential for their continual existence. This was not the case with EAM/ELAS which had established itself as the major resistance movement long before the British and the SOE had appeared on the Greek scene.[79] This brings me to the last factor, namely, the failure of the SOE and the British Foreign Office to agree on a co-ordinated military–political policy towards the Greek resistance movements. I shall examine this last point in more detail.

BRITISH POLICY TOWARDS THE GREEK RESISTANCE MOVEMENTS

As Woodhouse has himself admitted, the story of British policy towards the various Greek resistance movements 'does not command admiration even allowing for the lack of first-hand knowledge on which it was based', and as Elizabeth Barker has argued, 'it seemed a matter of muddle, inconsistency and conflict'.[80] This conflict was typically one between long-term (post-war) political interests and short-term military objectives. The basic problem facing the British policy-makers was that SOE, by supporting the anti-royalist EAM/ELAS for resistance activities, was in fact building up an opposition to the Greek king and his government-in-exile whom Churchill and the Foreign Office had pledged to support. The British felt a sense of obligation towards the Greek monarch for his personal role in bringing Greece in on to the side of the 'allied cause'. More importantly, though, they believed that the king, who was pro-British, could be expected to secure for Britain, after the war, a friendly and dependable Greece. This was particularly true of Churchill who was adamant in the view that monarchy afforded the best guarantees of political stability and of a post-war Greece well-disposed to British interests, and that the British must, therefore, do everything in their power to 'sell' the king to the Greeks as a democratic constitutional monarch. Despite the fact that George II had been recalled to the throne in 1935 on the basis of a rigged plebiscite, and despite his association with the Metaxas dictatorship, both of which meant that it would have been impossible for any king of Greece to dissociate himself from the monarchist faction and act as an 'arbitrator' between royalists and republicans, Churchill and

The Greek Communist Party 173

the Foreign Office were determined to restore George II to the throne after the war. At the same time reports from Leeper, the British ambassador in Cairo, and from the SOE Harling Mission which had been established in the Greek mountains under Brigadier Myers at the end of September 1942, stressed that all resistance groups were strongly anti-monarchist and were demanding that a plebiscite concerning the king should take place before his return to Greece.[81]

This situation led to the establishment of two contradictory positions within the British establishment. The military authorities, to whom the SOE was directly responsible, wanted full priority to be given to the expansion of guerrilla activity against the German occupation in order to pave the way for an invasion of the Balkans. When in November 1942 the Gorgopotamos bridge was blown up by the Harling mission in collaboration with ELAS and EDES, thus cutting the Salonica–Athens railway and preventing the dispatch of Axis reinforcements to north Africa, the Chiefs of Staff felt that SOE's left-wing anti-monarchist contacts had proved their value, and ordered Myers to stay behind in Greece to help co-ordinate resistance activities as head of a British military mission which would develop guerrilla forces, assisted by British liaison officers (BLOs), attached to different guerrilla groups. This was a major decision, with obvious political implications.[82]

Churchill and the Foreign Office, on the other hand, were afraid, as I have already indicated, that the build-up of anti-monarchist groups within Greece would lead to the creation of a strong movement which might be able to take control of Greece at liberation, and prevent the return of the king and his government-in-exile. Their fears were reinforced by the fact that the most powerful resistance movement, EAM/ELAS, which was under the control of the KKE, was staunchly anti-monarchist and anti-British. Although a new policy directive was formulated in March 1943 to accommodate the differing views of the military and the Foreign Office, the result of this interdepartmental conflict was the dispatch of contradictory instructions to the British military mission in Greece. This is illustrated in a directive sent by Churchill himself to the SOE in April 1943 which reads:

> In view of operational importance attached to subversive activities in Greece, there can be no question of SOE refusing to have dealings with a given group merely on the grounds that political sentiments of the group are opposed to the King and Government, but subject to special operational necessity SOE should *always veer in the direction of groups willing to support the King and the Government* and furthermore impress on such other groups as may be anti-monarchical the fact that the King and Government enjoy the fullest support of H.M.G.[83]

At the end of April Myers received his final directive from SOE Cairo which was similar to that sent by Churchill, but added rather desperately that since 'it appeared impossible to separate ELAS from EAM, whose political aims run counter to those of the more moderate Movements in Greece, civil war after the liberation of Greece was almost inevitable'.[84] Myers, however, argued that civil war was not inevitable, if only the British government persuaded the king to announce publicly that he would not set foot on Greek soil unless and until the people of Greece had, in a free plebiscite under conditions of tranquillity, expressed their wish for him to return as their constitutional king.[85]

Although the Foreign Office had gradually come to believe that such an unequivocal statement by the king would be a major means of weakening EAM's and the KKE's appeal, it still insisted that the king should return to Greece at the moment of liberation and before such a plebiscite was held. Churchill too wanted the king to set foot on Greek soil as soon as possible; any delay, he cabled Eden, would be 'an insult to the monarchy. He should go back as he left as King and General'.[86] In this way he would prevent EAM from gaining political predominance in Greece at the time of liberation.

On 4 July 1943, the king made a public statement to the effect that within six months of the liberation of Greece, free elections would be held for a constituent assembly which would determine 'the institutions by which Greece should endow herself'. The word 'plebiscite' was not used and the king made no reference to himself; he still intended to return to Greece with the Allied troops and with the Greek troops then training in the Middle East.[87] The promise of elections failed, however, to satisfy the parties and resistance organizations in Greece. It was against this background that an event occurred in Cairo which brought the relationship between the Foreign Office and SOE close to a breaking point and led to the 'first round' of the civil war in Greece.

FROM THE 'MILITARY AGREEMENT' TO THE 'FIRST ROUND' OF THE CIVIL WAR

In August 1943 Brigadier Myers, leading a delegation of six representatives of the resistance movements (three of whom were Communists), went to Cairo to try to obtain recognition of their status as part of the armed forces of Greece by the Greek government-in-exile. His visit was designed to provide the guerrilla movements with 'moral and material stimulus' which would avert the dangerous drift towards civil war.[88]

A few months earlier, Myers, in an effort to 'harness ELAS to the allied effort without yielding entirely to the KKE's ambitions to secure complete control of the resistance',[89] had developed the idea of forming a network of independent, non-political 'national bands' throughout the country, which would act in accordance with instructions from GHQME (General Headquarters Middle East). In March he presented the three major resistance organizations, EAM/ELAS, EDES, and EKKA with a draft proposal for a 'National Bands Agreement'. EDES and EKKA signed it at once but EAM/ELAS, realizing that the British had quite different intentions for the guerrilla movement from their own, objected to the term 'national bands' and counter-proposed their own draft agreement. The most important changes for

The Greek Communist Party 175

which EAM/ELAS struggled tenaciously and in the end successfully were essentially two: that there would be a Joint GHQ responsible directly to the Commander-in-Chief Middle East in Cairo; and that the function of the BLOs should be limited to liaison without any power of issuing orders.[90] The British, reluctant at first, eventually accepted the EAM/ELAS proposals and the final agreement, renamed 'Military Agreement', was signed on 5 July 1943.[91] The British acceptance of EAM's proposals was clearly the result of military necessity, as EAM/ELAS was indispensable for Operation *Animals* of June–July, which aimed at distracting German attention from the Allied landing in Sicily. For the KKE and EAM, the greatest success in the negotiations was the allocation of three seats to EAM in the Joint GHQ; EDES, EKKA, and the Commander of the BMM shared between them the other three seats. This, in effect, meant that EAM/ELAS was officially recognized by the British as the largest Greek resistance movement.

When Myers discovered, after the news of the Allied success in Sicily, that Greece was not to be liberated in the summer of 1943, he immediately proposed to his superiors a temporary visit to Cairo by himself and three representatives of the resistance (one each from ELAS, EDES, and EKKA, the three signatories of the 'Military Agreement'). Besides the broader aspects of morale, already mentioned, Myers was concerned that the prospect of relative military inactivity by the guerrillas for many months on end, following the postponement of the liberation of Greece, would result in civil war. As he notes in his book,

> if their belief in their importance to the Allies was at any time to wane, the extremist leaders would take even less interest in the requirements of the Middle East Command, and would concentrate correspondingly more on their political aims . . . it would be almost impossible for me to stop widespread clashes occurring between the rival movements.[92]

On the eve of departure, three more members were added to the delegation, all of whom belonged to EAM, two being members also of the KKE. But the resistance representatives did not focus their attention on military matters, as Myers had hoped. They raised instead purely political questions demanding that the king should not be allowed to return to Greece prior to the conduct of a plebiscite, a view backed by most republican cabinet members. Premier-in-exile Tsouderos himself urged the king to accept their demand.

Under the stress of such pressure, the king turned for support to Churchill and Roosevelt. They both came rapidly to his rescue, declaring that they supported his contention that he was to return to Greece before the plebiscite.[93] Following these developments the cabinet resentfully and only temporarily acceded to Churchill's and Roosevelt's ruling; the resistance representatives were sent back to Greece and Myers, who was accused by Leeper and the Foreign Office of triggering off the crisis, was replaced by Woodhouse as head of the BMM in Greece.

The KKE delegates however, did not simply raise the issue of the king's return to Greece. They also demanded that the resistance organizations should hold three portfolios within the government, those of Interior, War and Justice, exercising their powers on Greek territory. But this demand was also rejected by the cabinet and Leeper, who, as Clogg writes, 'despite his earlier enthusiasm for a coalition, was not prepared to give an encouragement to such proposals'.[94]

The Cairo crisis of August 1943 was clearly crucial in determining the subsequent course of events. Myers' sudden 'replacement' and the onslaught on SOE by the Foreign Office signified that 'in future, considerations of long-term policy would take precedence over short-term military requirements'.[95] After Cairo, attitudes on both sides hardened. The six Greeks returned to Greece ill-content and in a most disappointed frame of mind. As Clogg notes, 'the total failure of their mission and the ignominious treatment to which they have been subjected, coupled with the evidence that they had received of the strong commitment of the British government to the support of the King, was certainly a factor contributing to the outbreak of civil war between the rival groups'.[96] Myers himself recorded on 30 October 1943:

> EAM started the civil war for various reasons ... the fact that the Greeks believed that we, by our silence, intended to enforce the return of the King, led EAM to think that the time was ripe to strike ... such little confidence that EAM had in the British has been lost only because the Foreign Office for the past two and a half months have been exaggerating the Communist menace in Greece to suit their own policy and have refused to face the facts as they really are.[97]

The facts that the Foreign Office chose to ignore, but which Myers and David Wallace (a Foreign Office representative sent to Greece to make an independent investigation of the anti-royalist feeling in Greece) repeatedly underlined in their reports, were that the sentiment in Greece against the king was so strong that a new policy was called for.[98] But the Foreign Office's own policy, as already noted, consisted of using the Greek king as a rallying point in an effort to prevent EAM from gaining political predominance in Greece at the time of liberation.

When civil war broke out on 9 October 1943, the above policy was modified, without abandoning its basic principle of support for the king. It now meant a complete break with EAM/ELAS; also in an effort to win over the moderate rank and file of EAM/ELAS the king was to declare publicly that he would not return to Greece until invited to do so by a properly constituted and representative government, and to appoint Archbishop Damaskinos as Regent.[99] The question of the plebiscite had also been raised by Myers and the six resistance representatives in their August mission to Cairo but the Foreign Office had turned it down with indignation.[100] The new proposal, however, as it was combined with a decision to break with EAM/ELAS, was meant to win over the moderates from EAM and unite them under the influential figure of Damaskinos.[101] Accordingly, the war cabinet authorized Churchill and Eden, during their visit to the Middle East for the Cairo and Teheran Conferences, to press the king to agree to this plan. Unfortunately President Roosevelt, who also saw the king in Cairo, recommended him not to accept it, for reasons that are still obscure.[102] Having thus found support, the king refused to make the desired public statement and accept the creation of a regency council – possibly to Churchill's personal satisfaction, certainly to Eden's great annoyance and frustration.[103] Following the collapse of this plan, Leeper and the Foreign Office began to work on an alternative plan: to secure an armistice between ELAS and EDES.

As a direct result of the Cairo events, civil war between ELAS and EDES raged througout Greece during the winter of 1943–4. In the south the security battalions, special units raised by the government-of-occupation and commanded by German officers, scourged the countryside in their pursuit of EAM/ELAS sympathizers. In the north, ELAS failed to score a quick victory over EDES. Colonel Zervas secretly arranged a ceasefire with the German occupation forces.[104] He then turned the whole of his army against ELAS, and succeeded in repulsing the latter's offensive after bitter fighting. Finally, following an appeal for an end to the hostilities from Britain, the United States, and the Soviet Union, an uneasy truce was concluded between ELAS and EDES in February 1944 at the Plaka Bridge. The chief provisions of the 'Plaka Agreement' were that both sides accept the 'final cessation of hostilities', agree to exchange prisoners and hostages, and confine themselves to the areas which they occupied at the time of the truce. Article 7 requested the Allied military mission to provide 'the maximum possible supplies for the forces of all organizations in Greece, on the basis of their operations against the Germans and in proportion to the real requirements of the war'.[105] For EAM/ELAS the position was wholly unsatisfactory. EAM made two demands during the Plaka negotiations, attended also by EDES, EKKA, and BMM representatives, that a 'provisional committee' composed of representatives from the three resistance organizations should commence negotiations with the government-in-exile with the purpose of forming a government of 'national unity' and that the other resistance organizations should accept a single guerrilla army under a single commander-in-chief, but these were both rejected.[106] The agreement was thus purely a military one and failed to settle the political issues. It amounted, as Woodhouse has argued, 'to no more than an indefinite prolongation of the "armistice"'.[107] A 'second round' of civil war was but a few months away.

To conclude: Churchill's and the Foreign Office's stubborn support for the king and their policy of trying to 'sell' George II to a reluctant populace could only have favoured the KKE and EAM who had made the issue of the king their major propaganda theme. Had the British government dissociated itself at an early stage from the royal cause, it would have done much to weaken the psychological hold of the Communists over the entire republican camp.[108] In the event, Churchill's strong preference for monarchical institutions, sometimes verging on obsession, and the continuous feuds between the Foreign Office and SOE, helped EAM/ELAS' efforts, on the basis of its republican and anti-British stance, to become the largest and most powerful resistance organization in Greece.

1944: THE CRITICAL YEAR

The king's rejection of the regency plan provoked a crisis within the government-in-exile. His vague promise that when the moment arose he would decide the timing of his return 'in agreement with his government'[109] did not satisfy the Greek cabinet, which endorsed the Foreign Office's proposal and insisted that the king appoint a regent.[110] Leeper, in a letter to Eden, warned the Foreign Secretary that if the king rejected the proposals, a serious government crisis would follow, allowing EAM to form its own independent government in the 'mountains' which in turn would imply for the British a total loss of control of the Greek resistance.[111] But on March 10, George II, once again, and with Churchill's blessing, rejected the idea of a regency as 'inadmissable'.[112]

These developments, coupled with the failure of the Plaka negotiations, led the Communists to resume their offensive, this time on the diplomatic front. On 10 March 1944, EAM announced the formation of PEEA, the 'Political Committee of National Liberation'. Although the news of PEEA's creation came as a shock to most politicians in Cairo, EAM's action was on the cards for some time. Following the failure of the August 1943 Cairo mission, the EAM's central committee in December 1943 called again on all political parties to form a government of 'national unity in free Greece'.[113] One month later, on 10 January 1944, the Tenth Plenum of the central committee of the KKE endorsed EAM's proposal and a few days later the central committee of EAM decided to begin negotiations with the resistance organizations and various political personalities for the purpose of forming such a government.[114] During the Plaka negotiations EAM, as already noted, demanded the formation of a 'provisional committee' which was to be transformed into a 'government committee' should the government-in-exile reject the plan for the formation of a representative government. But EDES, EKKA, and the BMM rejected EAM's proposal, arguing that the government-in-exile was the only government that the Allies recognized. In these circumstances, EAM, following the example of Tito, who on November 1943 had turned AVNOJ, the 'Antifascist Council of National Liberation', into a 'provisional government', took the bold step of establishing this 'government committee' under a new name and without the participation of EDES or EKKA.

Unlike AVNOJ, however, PEEA was not yet a 'provisional government' but rather an 'administrative body' aiming at the establishment, with Tsouderos' co-operation, of a 'government of national unity'. But its eventual transformation into a government was not ruled out. Therefore, the formation of PEEA conveyed a clear message to the government-in-exile: either it had to accept EAM's calls for the formation of a representative government or take the risk of a rival government emerging in Greece.[115]

The provisional chairman of PEEA was Colonel Bakirtzis (one of the founders of EKKA who had joined EAM early in 1944), who was shortly to be replaced by Professor Svolos, a well-known socialist and the foremost Greek authority on constitutional law. When a host of socialist personalities joined PEEA in April, it looked at first sight as if the KKE represented a minority, with only two members in a 'cabinet' of ten 'secretaries of state', one being George Siandos, the KKE general secretary (deputizing for Zachariadis who was in Dachau). However, as with EAM/ELAS, the real power was in the hands of the KKE. As the Communist Ioannidis has admitted in his recently published memoirs, three of the remaining eight socialists were in reality members of the KKE: 'it appeared that in PEEA we had two Secretaries [of State], but in fact we had five. Kokkalis, Mandakas and Gavriilidis were members of the Party'.[116] Moreover, the Communists held the key 'secretaryships' of Interior (Siandos) and Defence (Mandakas), thus retaining a firm hold on ELAS, on the National Guard (EAM's police), and on OPLA (EAM's secret police).[117]

On 9 April 1944, PEEA organized free elections by secret ballot throughout 'free Greece' (which by that date included over half of the area of the country) for the creation of a 'national council'. The 202 delegates from all parts of Greece, including twenty-two MPs from the Parliament of 1936, were elected to the national council which endorsed the authority of PEEA.[118] The election of the national council in effect represented an additional veiled threat directed against the government-in-exile, since an 'elected' and thus 'legitimate' national council might eventually have decided to declare that PEEA, and not the 'non-elected' government of George II, was the 'true representative' government.[119]

Alarmed by these developments Prime Minister Tsouderos realized that unless he could extract a favourable answer from the king regarding the question of the regency, and unless he could persuade the politicians in Athens to change their attitude about broadening the government and agree to send representatives to Cairo for that purpose, the Communists would set up an independent government in the Greek mountains. The king, however, again stubbornly refused to agree to such a plan.[120] This situation made the position of Tsouderos almost impossible and shortly afterwards led to his fall.

THE MUTINY OF THE GREEK ARMED FORCES IN THE MIDDLE EAST

The announcement of the formation of the PEEA, coupled with the fact that Tsouderos had failed to persuade the king to appoint a regent, sparked off a serious crisis in the 20,000-strong Greek armed forces stationed in the Middle East. On the morning of 31 March, a group of officers representing a 'committee of national unity of the Greek armed forces' submitted to Tsouderos a 'memorandum' in which they demanded from the 'Royal Government in Cairo' the establishment of a truly representative Government of National Unity based on PEEA. Tsouderos rejected the officers' demand but at the same time was forced to resign by republican ministers in his government. Venizelos (the son of the former prime minister) was sworn in but the change proved totally ineffective. Mutinies broke out in several military units with soliders' committees taking over command. The mutineers declared allegiance to PEEA and refused to obey the orders of their superior officers. The revolt soon spread to the First Brigade and the Greek naval units stationed in the port of Alexandria. The Second Brigade also declared its loyalty to PEEA. The only notable exception was the Sacred Battalion which remained loyal to the king and his government throughout the upheaval.[121] With the mutineers aiming for a PEEA-dominated republican government, the British, unwilling to accept this, were left with no alternative but to intervene openly. In a telegram to Leeper, Churchill firmly stated that 'rebellious manifestations in forces which have been constitutionally placed under Allied High Command will not be tolerated'. He then added:

> Our relations are definitely established with the lawfully constituted Greek Government headed by the King, who is an ally of Britain and cannot be discarded to suit a momentary surge of appetite among ambitious emigré nonentities. Neither can Greece find consitutional expression in particular sets of guerrillas, in many cases indistinguishable from banditti, who are masquerading as the saviours of their country[122]

From 16 April on, Admiral Cunningham repeatedly threatened – unless the Greeks themselves quelled the mutiny – to sink all the ships of the Greek fleet 'within five minutes'. Finally on 22 April, Voulgaris, Venizelos' new commander-in-chief, organized boarding parties and took over the Greek ships one by one. The next day the 'Free Greeks' of the First Brigade, who had put on ELAS insignia, surrendered, after being encircled by the British for eighteen days.[123] There is little doubt that had the British not intervened, Venizelos would have formed a new government, under pressure from the mutineers, on the basis of PEEA. In the event, Venizelos was persuaded by Leeper to resign in order to pave the way for the 'man of the hour', George Papandreou, a Liberal of the Centre-Left and a devout anti-Communist.[124] The crisis for the time being had ended. But before the year was out 'the same mentality, the same mistrust, and the same arguments reappeared on both sides when British troops and loyalists and Greek "anti-fascists" clashed again in a much more bloody anomaly'.[125]

Churchill, Leeper, and a number of right-wing Greek historians have claimed that 'the mutiny was planned and instigated by the Communists as part of their overall strategy for monopolizing power'.[126] Little evidence exists, however, to support these contentions. By establishing PEEA the KKE had furnished the occasion but not the cause.[127] The whole mutiny should better be interpreted as the latest phase of the steady rise of republicanism, which had been in progress since the death of Metaxas. It was not merely Communist propaganda but the opportunism of the Greek politicians in Cairo, the king's obstinacy and British intolerance with republican aspirations which contributed to the crisis.[128] In actual fact, three weeks after the mutiny had ended, the KKE, EAM, and PEEA sent a telegram to Churchill, dated 14 May 1944, condemning the whole affair as the 'insane actions of irresponsible persons' and the Communist, Porfyrogennis, in his meeting with the new premier, Papandreou, went as far as saying that 'had Nefeloudis [the alleged chief instigator] been in the mountains, EAM would have hanged him'.[129] Moreover, no evidence was produced at the subsequent trials of the mutineers to show that there had been any communication between them and the 'mountains'.[130] There is little doubt that the mutinies can be attributed to discontented republicans who acted without any authority; a deliberate plot, which had no chance of success under British guns, would have been out of line with the policy of PEEA, whose aim was a peaceful, not a violent, change of the government-in-exile. With the crushing of the mutiny all republican and left-wing army officers were purged and thus the KKE and EAM lost whatever grip they had on the Middle East armed forces. Approximately 10,000 men (almost half of the total strength of the Greek forces) were sent to detention camps in Libya and Eritrea. What remained of the Greek armed forces, grouped into a new unit labelled the 'Third Brigade' (also known as the 'Rimini' or 'Mountain Brigade' after capturing the town of Rimini in the summer of 1944) was royalist and strongly anti-Communist. As will be shown, the arrival of this brigade in Athens in November 1944, was destined to contribute to the outbreak of the 'second round' of the civil war. The British decision to crush the mutiny, was severely criticized by the Soviet ambassador, Novikov,[131] but Churchill's strong reaction forced the Soviets to back down and drop the issue.[132]

THE LEBANON AGREEMENT: IN SEARCH OF NATIONAL UNITY

Papandreou inaugurated his term in officed with a broadcast address to the Greek people. On behalf of the government-in-exile, he propounded a political charter dedicated to liberty and social justice, themes hitherto propagated only by EAM. He declared that his first task was to transform his government into a government of national unity, embracing all parties and resistance organizations. This new government would reconstitute the Greek armed forces in the Middle East, reorganize the guerrilla armies so as to ensure that they served the nation rather than individual parties, and, on liberation, in conditions of tranquillity, would conduct a plebiscite on the future of the monarchy and hold elections for a constituent assembly.[133] Before his arrival in Cairo, the Venizelos government, in the midst of the crisis provoked by the mutiny, had already issued formal invitations to all parties and resistance organizations in Greece to come to a conference in the Middle East. By the time that Papandreou had become premier all factions of the Greek political world, including PEEA, EAM, and the KKE, had already agreed to send representatives.

Despite his call for national unity, Papandreou's efforts were directed primarily to the EAM/KKE challenge, which in his view had to be firmly countered if an eventual Communist takeover was to be averted. As he told Leeper, his inaugural speech was designed to serve as the agenda of the forthcoming conference and 'take the wind out of EAM's sails'.[134] To achieve his ends, Papandreou relied heavily upon, and always sought, substantial British political and military backing.[135] It is not surprising, therefore, that he was 'immediately seized upon by the British authorities as the *deus ex machina*, who would unite political factions at home and abroad' and make sure 'that power would not pass to the militant left'.[136]

At the conference which opened in the Lebanon on 17 May 1944, there were twenty-five individuals representing seventeen political parties and resistance organizations. All the delegates to the conference were republicans. The royalists – a handful of former Populist MPs organized as the Union of Political Co-operation – decided not to attend because they argued that negotiation with EAM would serve only to bestow a 'certain appearance of legality' on a criminal organization whose single aim was the promotion of Communism.[137] Of those attending, many had been literally at each other's throats until summoned to Lebanon. In particular, the delegates of ELAS and EKKA had to be restrained in the opening sessions of the conference: the commander of the latter, Colonel Psarros, had been brutally murdered by the former a few weeks earlier.

Before the departure of the PEEA, EAM/ELAS, and the KKE delegates for the Middle East, the KKE, as we saw, had proceeded to 'legitimize' PEEA's power by forming the national council. This move was probably designed to raise the negotiating power of the delegation since its members could claim to represent most of the Greek people. In addition, the PEEA and EAM delegates were instructed to insist on obtaining the majority of the cabinet seats, in the words of Ioannidis, 'half the ministries, plus one', including the Ministry of Defence, and to secure the transfer of some ministries, especially that of the Ministry of Defence, to the 'mountains'.[138] In the event, however, the PEEA and EAM delegates, faced with a solid front of opposition, did not seek to fulfil either of these written instructions.[139]

Although it had been agreed beforehand that the conference was to be 'purely a Greek affair',[140] every delegate knew who the real master was and on whose authority Papandreou ultimately spoke.[141] With Leeper by his side, Papandreou took the offensive role assigned to him: he opened the conference by accusing EAM/ELAS of 'monopolizing the resistance' and of planning to gain 'the control of the state by force' after liberation; he placed their 'terrorist actions' on an equal footing with those of the Germans and the collaborationist security battalions.[142] Having put 'his opponents on the defensive from the very beginning',[143] Papandreou then warned EAM/ELAS that in the event that civil war broke out, the Greek government would appeal for Allied support and call on the Allies to intervene openly.[144] What was needed in order to prevent the repetition of the 'first round' was the 'elimination of the class army and the formation of a national one'.[145] When even Svolos and the PEEA socialists sided with Papandreou, Rousos, the KKE delegate, completely isolated and outmanoeuvred, made no attempt to defend the policies of his party and of EAM; instead he found himself helplessly adding his voice to the chorus of accusations by disavowing once again the 'deplorable mutiny'.[146]

What is known as the Lebanon Agreement, or the Lebanon Charter, was signed on 20 May 1944 by all the delegates, including the Communists. Its 'eight chapters' provided for the reorganization of the armed forces in the Middle East, the unification of all guerrilla bands in free Greece under the command of the Government of National Unity, the cessation of terrorism in the Greek countryside, the restoration of order and liberty, the dispatch of food and medical supplies to Greece, the punishment of collaborators, and the post-war satisfaction of Greece's economic requirements and territorial claims.[147] On the explosive issue of the king's return Papandreou produced the following carefully worded formula: 'on the question of the monarch', he said, 'all politicians have expressed their views, which they retain when joining the Government of National Unity. Therefore, one of the aims of the National Government is to clarify the issue'.[148] Since the king would be obliged to follow his government's advice, Papandreou regarded it as settled that the king would not return to Greece prior to the holding of a plebiscite.

It is clear that in signing the Lebanon Charter, the PEEA, EAM/ELAS, and KKE representatives failed to comply with the KKE written instructions. More important, as the conference was meant to unite the traditional parties in a common front against EAM, the acceptance of the agreement by the latter's representatives 'was the first step that led to its ultimate defeat and to the success of British policy'.[149] As the Communist Karageorgis later commented, 'the participation of the communists in the conference and their acceptance of the agreement was a terrible tactical mistake, one of the most stupid actions in the history of our Party'.[150] The delegates representing PEEA, EAM/ELAS, and the KKE had come to Lebanon intending to get 'half plus one' portfolios in the key ministries; when Papandreou took the oath of office in the king's presence on 24 May, he offered the 'Left' only a quarter of the posts, five portfolios of secondary importance. The KKE on learning of the agreemen and Papandreou's offer of portfolios, sent a harsh message to the PEEA delegation demanding the reason for their capitulation.[151] In a meeting of the political bureau in the 'mountains' there was even talk of court-martialling and executing the PEEA delegation for 'disobeying Party orders'.[152] After the KKE and EAM/ELAS representatives returned to Greece, the KKE leadership decided to repudiate the agreement, accusing Papandreou of having misled them at the Lebanon Conference. A heated exchange of telegrams took place between the KKE general secretary Siandos and Papandreou. On 4 July, the Communists submitted their 'final terms' for joining the government. Among other things the KKE demanded that all talk of 'dissolving ELAS' should cease; that PEEA should get six ministries and one under-ministry (among which were listed the ministries of Interior and Justice and the under-ministry of Defence) in a cabinet of fifteen seats, instead of five seats out of twenty which Papandreou now offered them; that immediately after the PEEA representatives joined the government, the king should make a statement that he would not seek to return until after a plebiscite; and that a section of the government should be established in 'free Greece', whereupon PEEA would be dissolved.[153] Papandreou emphatically rejected these proposals and appealed to the

British for help. Then suddenly, on 29 July, the KKE dropped their demands for the basic ministries and instead indicated their willingness to enter the government on the single condition that Papandreou should be replaced. When the cabinet and the British refused to accept the latest KKE demand, the Communists announced, on 15 August that they would participate in the Government of National Unity under Papandreou.[154] On 3 September, six representatives of PEEA and EAM entered the government in minor and insignificant posts. This extraordinary and baffling volte-face by the Communists can only be explained in the light of events that were taking place in the international arena.

THE ANGLO–SOVIET PERCENTAGES DEAL AND THE CASERTA AGREEMENT

Alarmed by the Soviet reaction to the British suppression of the mutinies in the Greek armed forces in April 1944, Churchill minuted to Eden on 4 May: 'evidently we are approaching a showdown with the Russians about their Communist intrigues in Italy, Yugoslavia and Greece'.[155] Two weeks later, on 18 May, Eden approached the Soviet ambassador in London, Gusev, and proposed an arrangement concerning Greece and Rumania. According to the British plan, Rumanian affairs would mainly concern the Soviets, while Greek affairs would be left to the British. This arrangement was accepted by the Soviets on condition that the United States approve it.[156] After considerable pressure from Churchill, Roosevelt, bypassing the State Department, personally approved the proposed agreement 'on a three months' trial basis'. In the meantime the British–Soviet understanding had been expanded to include Bulgaria in the area of Soviet responsibility, with Yugoslavia under equal Soviet and British influence. The proposal for a trial period proved unacceptable to Stalin, however. It seems that his aim, much as Churchill suspected, was an exclusive and permanent sphere of influence in eastern Europe, and that he was unwilling, therefore, to enter into any arrangement of a temporary nature which left the post-war alignment of Rumania in doubt. On 15 July, Stalin wrote to Churchill that the whole question of an Anglo–Soviet agreement now required further consideration.[157] Then on 29 July news reached London of the sudden and unexpected arrival of a Soviet military mission in 'free Greece'. The mission, composed of eight Russian officers under Colonel Popov, had parachuted into the country and on the morning of 26 July had reached the ELAS GHQ. Eden was outraged by the development, thinking it 'quite monstrous' of the Soviets to intervene in Greece without prior consultation with London, particularly in view of Britain's expressed willingness to allow them to lead in Rumania.[158] But Eden's fears of a Russian plan to Communize Greece seem to have been wholly unfounded. Far from promising Soviet assistance, Colonel Popov's message to the KKE leaders was that there would be no material help from the Soviet Union and that the KKE must not fight the British. It emerges clearly from Ioannidis' memoirs that the Soviet mission urged the KKE to join Papandreou's cabinet.[159] Similarly, the Soviet embassy in

Cairo had advised Rousos and Svolos, shortly before they left Cairo, that 'the Lebanon Agreement was in line with present political realities and that PEEA should, therefore, join the Papandreou government'.[160] Following these developments the KKE announced, on 15 August, that they would participate in the Cairo Government of National Unity under Papandreou and on 3 September two Communists, Zevgos and Porfyroyennis, as well as three secretaries of PEEA and one member of EAM, took the oath.

Although the political balance seemed to have been modified, the military balance inside Greece had remained unchanged. EAM/ELAS were still the dominant power in mainland Greece. Papandreou, unimpressed by the KKE's conciliatory image, was well aware that since ELAS was the strongest military force in the country, his government needed British armed support to back its claim of legitimacy. Throughout August he desperately attempted to encourage a British intervention.[161] What Papandreou did not know, however, was that the British, despite their noncommittal attitude in August and early September,[162] had on many previous occasions (29 September 1943; 8 May 1944; 19 May 1944; 19 July 1944; 9 August 1944) favourably discussed the possibility of landing forces in Greece in order to ensure that a 'friendly government was installed in Athens' and 'to prevent a communist dictatorship'.[163] On 9 August, the war cabinet agreed to send to Greece an invasion force of 10,000 men and, as Macmillan notes, 'by the end of the first week of September, all arrangements for British troops to go to Greece ... were gradually sorted out'.[164]

Papandreou's next move was to ensure that all guerrilla organizations should come under the command of his government, as agreed in Lebanon. Accordingly, at the end of September, General Wilson summoned the commanders of ELAS and EDES to the Allied GHQ at Caserta, where the Greek government had established itself early in September. By the Caserta Agreement, signed on 26 September, Sarafis and Zervas agreed to place all their forces under the orders of the Greek Government of National Unity, which in turn placed them under General Scobie who was to lead the British expeditionary force. Sarafis at first opposed the agreement, but the Communist, Zevgos, who had accompanied Sarafis and who was now a minister in the government, overruled him, following, one must assume, the line laid down by Moscow.[165] The agreement also defined the guerrilla armies' respective zones of control and contained detailed provisions for the maintenance of law and order. Sarafis' only success was to insist that the clause which defined the tasks of General Scobie as being 'to restore law and order in Greece' be omitted since this was an internal matter for the Greek government to solve. This time the British and Papandreou had to retreat.[166] The agreement was later criticized by Zachariadis as the 'military Lebanon', the KKE having for a second time capitulated to the British.[167] The KKE leader's criticism was, however, unjustifiable: following Popov's intervention the KKE was 'advised' by Moscow to join Papandreou's government. Siandos and Ioannidis realized that the KKE ministers could not have opposed an agreement which Papandreou and the majority of the cabinet strongly supported.

Had they done so, they would have created the worst impression in Greece, if not destroyed altogether the prestige the KKE enjoyed in the country.[168]

Such, then, was the political situation when the Greek government finally arrived in Athens on 18 October 1944, six days after the Germans had evacuated the city. Ten days earlier Churchill had finally concluded in Moscow the (in)famous percentages agreement with Stalin. For Greece, where the coalition government of Papandreou represented on the political level far less than the 90 per cent figure of British 'predominance', the Anglo-Soviet agreement had important results, for it served to define the territorial area in which the arriving British troops might exercise a control to which the USA had explicitly assented, and which the Soviet Union had previously tacitly agreed.[169]

The KKE, who obviously expected some sort of Soviet political support, were completely ignorant of these negotiations. During this time, with the Caserta Agreement concluded, the Communists concentrated their attention on strengthening their political and military position in preparation for a possible post-liberation clash with the British and Papandreou. Ioannidis claims that by December the KKE had secretly armed 6,000 men in Athens and that after Caserta the political bureau decided to bring some forces of ELAS close to the capital 'for any eventuality'.[171] Despite this preparation for conflict, however, the KKE leadership decided to act with moderation and to try to pursue its objectives by political, not military means.

The central issue in the political struggle between Papandreou and the KKE was no longer the 'constitutional question', since by the end of September the king had finally been forced by Papandreou and the British to remain abroad, pending the conduct of a plebiscite.[171] There were, of course, a number of issues, such as the treatment of the security batallions and others accused of collaboration and, more important, the economic problem (wild inflation and massive unemployment) which were most urgent. Greece was again, as in 1941, near the brink of starvation. On these issues, however, there were, at least for the moment, no fundamental differences between Papandreou and the KKE. What was crucial, and could not continue indefinitely, was 'the coexistence of two armed forces, each acknowledging separate political authorities, which were only nominally united in the government'.[172] Inevitably the demobilization issue became the single most important problem that the Greek government had to solve after liberation.

Under the terms of the Caserta Agreement all guerrilla groups were to be disbanded and, together with the Greek armed forces from the Middle East, were to form a new national army. For EAM and the KKE the most crucial issue was to secure an agreement with Papandreou and the British for the demobilization of the Third (Rimini) Brigade which formed the bulk of the reorganized Middle East forces and was fanatically royalist and anti-Communist. On 26 October, Papandreou announced that he and Siandos, the KKE general secretary, had on the previous day agreed that 'all volunteer bodies of ELAS and EDES, and of the Greek armed forces of the Middle East would be disbanded'.[173] However, it soon became clear that Papandreou's interpretation of the term 'volunteer bodies' differed from that of the Communists. Apparently Papandreou did not judge ELAS's chief rival, the Third Brigade, to be a 'volunteer body' and had no plans for its dissolution.[174] On 7 November, Papandreou made it clear that he planned to dissolve ELAS *before* the Third Brigade. He also announced that EAM's civil guard (EP) was to be disbanded and replaced by a 'provisional national guard' on 1 December, and that ELAS and EDES were to be disbanded on 10 December. He then appealed to General Scobie to arrange for the immediate dispatch of the Third Brigade from the Italian front to Athens.[175]

This brought a strong reaction by the KKE, which demanded universal demobilization. According to an American observer, 'in leftist circles it was rumoured that the Brigade had come to put down EAM and bring the King back by force', a suspicion that Siandos repeated in an interview with *The Times* a few days later.[176] But the KKE, although worried by the Third Brigade, which finally arrived in Athens on 8 November, was in no defeatist mood. Aris Velouchiotis, the most famous ELAS *Kapetanios*, urged the KKE leadership to act: 'a hundred per cent of the Army and seventy per cent of the people are eagerly awaiting the signal for action against the forces of darkness'[177] and on 18 November, the political bureau decided that 'if a political solution was not found, ELAS must be prepared for a clash'.[178] The need for war receded temporarily on 20 November. On that day, Papandreou decided to give the officers and soldiers of the Third Brigade 'general leave', under pressure from his PEEA and EAM ministers, which effectively ammounted to the brigade's dissolution. On 27 November it appeared that a compromise solution between Papandreou and EAM had been found. That evening the Greek premier, at a meeting with Svolos and Zevgos, the KKE minister, agreed on a demobilization draft proposal submitted by EAM. The proposal provided for the establishment of a new *unified* national army through the amalgamation of the Third Brigade, a unit of ELAS, and a unit of EDES. The unit of ELAS was to be equal in size and weaponry to that of the other two combined. All remaining bands and units were to demobilize on 10 December.[179]

This arrangement, while seeming to be 'remarkably favourable to EAM',[180] actually would have greatly weakened the position of the KKE, for the proposed unit of ELAS was no match for the well-trained and -equipped unit of the Third Brigade that was to combine with a unit of EDES.[181] In any event, Papandreou went back on the agreement the next day and instead presented Leeper, General Scobie, and non-EAM ministers with a draft decree which omitted any reference to the amalgamation of the Third Brigade with forces of ELAS and EDES. Instead, a unit of ELAS and an equally strong unit of EDES were to be retained, acting *independently* from one another and from the Third Brigade.[186] This arrangement would obviously have provided Papandreou with decisive superiority over the KKE, not least because by keeping the ELAS unit independent, he could have 'transported it to Crete supposingly to fight the Germans, leaving the KKE at the mercy of the Third Brigade'.[182] On 29 November, Papandreou presented the press with *his* draft proposal claiming that it represented the proposals submitted by EAM.[183] The following day EAM published in the KKE daily, *Rizospastis*, the original version of their proposals accusing Papandreou of having altered the text of the agreement.[184] Although at the time Leeper and most observers accused the KKE of duplicity,[185] it is clear that is was Papandreou who had tried to deceive the British, his cabinet and the public[196] in an effort to present EAM with a *fait accompli*: if the KKE refused to accept his demobilization scheme, he could then accuse the Communists of going back on their word.

Following these developments, Zevgos visited Papandreou and submitted to him new proposals which called for the 'simultaneous dissolution of all armed forces', including the Third Brigade.[187] In this way the KKE repudiated its own proposals of 27 November, a fact that has led the orthodox anti-Communist historian Kousoulas to claim that the KKE decided on the night of 29 November 'to seize power through armed action'.[188] According to this account, on the night of 27 November Siandos received a telegram from Tito in which the Yugoslav leader encouraged the KKE to 'take the capital by force', pledging 'moral support'.[189] Although the KKE did indeed receive such a telegram, this was dispatched from Belgrade not on 27 November but three days later.[190] The KKE's volte-face, therefore, was in response to Papandreou's intimidatory tactics and his refusal to dissolve the Third Brigade, not in accordance with some plan of aggression worked out on the basis of promised foreign assistance.

In this atmosphere General Scobie's toughly worded announcement on 1 December, ordering the commanders of ELAS and EDES to make certain that their forces were dissolved by 10 December, and the refusal by the PEEA and EAM ministers to sign the decree on the demobilization of the Civil Guard (the EAM police) provoked the final crisis.[191] Contrary to the conclusions reached by the Greek historian Loulis, that EAM's objective in not signing the decree was to 'provoke a government crisis', it is clear that the responsibility for this crisis rests again with Papandreou.[192] This is clear from a telegram sent by Leeper to the Foreign Office the same day, in which the British ambassador described Papandreou's action in the following way:

> He is this evening drafting a decree which will be sent tonight to all Ministers for signature. *He is sure that Communists will refuse* . . . In any case 6 Ministers of the Left will resign from Government, Papandreou is now forcing the issue on a breach of faith that Communists have refused to let EAM Police hand over their arms. He is therefore not making (the question of demobilization) the issue. *This is very much better.*[193]

In the early morning hours of 2 December, as Leeper had predicted and Papandreou had wished, the ministers of the Left resigned. Papandreou's long effort to drive a wedge through EAM thus met a dismal end: the socialists had decided to back the Communists.[194] The same day the KKE resurrected the ELAS central committee (now composed of Siandos and General Manadakas and Hatzibeis), and EAM declared a general strike for Monday, 4 December. It also called for a mass demonstration in Constitution Square (Syntagma), to take place at 11 a.m. on Sunday, 3 December.[195] Permission for the demonstration was initially granted by Papandreou, but under pressure from Leeper he then decided to forbid it.[196] All the powerful ingredients for a terrible explosion were now present.

THE BATTLE OF ATHENS

On the morning of 3 December 1944, crowds of EAM supporters gathered in the centre of Athens, disregarding the government's prohibition of the demonstration. The police panicked and began firing at the demonstrators as they advanced across Syntagma Square in the direction of the police headquarters. At least ten people were killed and over sixty wounded.[197] Within an hour of the shootings, Dimitrios Partsalidis, the Communist secretary of the central committee of EAM, appeared at the balcony of the KKE offices overlooking the square and declared: 'Henceforth Papandreou is an outlaw. The people will fight for liberty without counting the sacrifices'. Civil war had begun.

On 4 December, with the general strike taking place, fighting broke out in various parts of Athens with ELAS units attacking a number of police stations during their approach towards the centre of the capital. Attacks were extended to government buildings during the following days but care was still taken by ELAS to avoid clashes with British forces and even with Greek troops of the Third Brigade. Papandreou, under pressure from Leeper, offered to resign, but Churchill vetoed his ambassador's initiative telling him that 'this was no time to dabble in Greek politics'.[198] Reactions on the part of General Scobie and his forces were also restrained, despite a strong directive from Churchill on 5 December, charging Scobie with responsibility 'for maintaining order in Athens and for neutralizing or destroying all EAM/ELAS bands approaching the city'. The directive contained the ominous words: 'Do not hesitate to act as if you were in a conquered city where a local rebellion is in progress . . . we have to hold and dominate Athens . . . without bloodshed if possible, but also with bloodshed if necessary'.[199]

If EAM and the KKE counted on some sort of support from the Soviets or the Americans, their hopes were soon frustrated, for the USA and the Soviet Union failed to respond to the pleas which had been addressed to them. The few American soldiers in Athens remained neutral, while the Russian military mission and the Soviet press refrained from criticism, adhering strictly to the October 1944 percentage agreement.[200] Moreover, the KKE had seriously underestimated the British commitment to the Papandreou government. The Communist challenge was for the British, in the words of Churchill, 'a matter of life and death'.[201] Although the British and American public had been shocked by Churchill's 'conquered-city' policy and the British premier had to face a bitter debate in the House of Commons on 8 December,[202] Churchill was determined to destroy the Communists. The same day he cabled Scobie: 'The clear objective is to defeat EAM. The ending of the fighting is subsidiary to this. I am ordering large reinforcements to come to Athens'.[203] Between 13 and 16 December, two British divisions, a tank regiment, two brigades, and other supporting units had landed in Piraeus. On the night of 16 December ELAS launched a three-pronged attack but it failed to drive the British out of Athens. The battle was lost before it really began.[204] Though EAM was weakened by the defection of the Socialists, who protested against the KKE's plan to fight against the British,[205] and although the KKE committed a number of strategic errors (the most serious being the decision to direct a section of ELAS against EDES in Epirus instead of concentrating all their forces in Athens),[206] there is no doubt that the dispatch of British reinforcements was the decisive factor that determined the outcome of the conflict.[207]

By the end of December the British troops had cleared the southern half of Athens and most of Piraeus. Churchill realized, however, that there was no way for his troops to embark on any military operations away from the capital. ELAS could not be destroyed throughout the country. In other words, the problem now became one of securing a political solution. To this unwelcome reality Churchill had to add the hostility of public opinion in Britain and the USA. At the centre of the hostility was the feeling that the trouble could have been averted if Churchill had not been so devoted to the Greek monarch. This view was not only shared by Roosevelt, Stettinius, and MacVeagh, the American ambassador in Athens, but also by Churchill's own advisers, including Eden, Macmillan, and Leeper.[208] They all advised the British premier to persuade the king to establish a regency under Archbishop Damaskinos. On Christmas Eve, with dramatic suddenness, he decided to go to Athens himself, with Eden. They arrived in the afternoon of 25 December, and were joined by Macmillan and Field Marshall Alexander from Italy.

Churchill at once convened a conference attended by all the Greek political parties, including the leaders of KKE and EAM/ELAS, the British authorities, the American and French ambassadors, and Colonel Popov of the Soviet military mission. All parties agreed that there should be a regency at once and that Archbishop Damaskinos should be the regent. But apart from this agreement no other conclusions emerged from the conference. The KKE demanded 40–50 per cent of the seats in the cabinet, including the ministries of the Interior and Justice and the under-secretaryships for War and Foreign Affairs. They also demanded that all collaborators should be punished, that the gendarmerie, the Third Brigade and the National Guard should be dissolved and an immediate plebiscite be held on the constitutional issue; they also called for parliamentary elections in April 1945. These demands were naturally rejected by all the other parties and fighting resumed. Back in London, Churchill, at last convinced of the need for a regency, coerced the king into appointing the Archbishop as regent, which he finally did on 30 December. The following day, again with Churchill's agreement, Damaskinos accepted Papandreou's resignation, and on 3 January, after some hesitation, he appointed General Plastiras, the titular head of EDES and a fierce anti-Communist republican, as head of a new government.[209] The appointment of Plastiras as prime minister, which was accepted by the KKE as a conciliatory sign, coupled with increasing evidence of British military ascendancy, led the ELAS command to decide that further fighting was no longer possible. During 5–6 January, ELAS retreated from Athens and Piraeus but not before it had carried out mass executions in areas under its control and had taken perhaps as many as 35,000 civilian hostages from the Athens district alone. Almost 4,000 of these hostages were executed or died as a result of bad conditions.[210] These atrocities, which did much to fortify the country's lasting hatred for the entire Communist movement, constituted one of the main and most effective propaganda instruments in the hands of future right-wing governments. Moreover, the lingering passions stirred up by such outrages, and the desire for revenge they often inspired, were to serve as powerful contributing forces in the 'third round' of civil war less than two years later.

On 10 January, representatives of EAM/ELAS arrived at General Scobie's headquarters empowered to negotiate and sign a truce. The following day the armistice was signed and on 15 January all hostilities came to an end. British intervention had crushed the strongest and hitherto most popular Greek resistance movement. EAM/ELAS, militarily and psychologically unprepared for battle, had drifted into civil war in an attempt to regain some of the political influence they felt entitled to on the basis of their dominant role in the resistance. Churchill, however, with Soviet and American acquiescence, and with the co-operation of the old Greek political world, succeeded in blocking the rise to power of the Left which, following the war, threatened to replace the pre-1939 Greek royalist world with a socialist republic of some kind. Because Churchill ultimately understood that he could not solve the political impasse in Greece by returning the king in person, he was persuaded to adopt the compromise of establishing a regency which led to the partial reconciliation between the two bourgeois parties (Liberals and Populists). As a consequence of this development Churchill was able to strike in Greece a new political balance, the legacy of which condemned the KKE to thirty years of political isolation.

The formal act which signalled the end of the *Dekemvriana* (December Events), one of the most tragic conflicts in the history of modern Greece, was the political settlement between the new government and EAM signed at Varkiza, a small resort on the outskirts of Athens, on 12 February, the day after the conclusion of the Yalta Conference.[211] Article I of the Varkiza Agreement committed the government to guarantee freedom of speech, of the press, assembly, and association (trade union liberties). Article III granted an amnesty for 'political crimes' committed during the 'second round' of civil war, but not for 'common-law crimes against life and property which were not absolutely necessary to the achievement of the political crime concerned', a clause which in the hands of many Metaxist and collaborationist judges became a weapon against the rank and file of EAM/ELAS. Ten of thousands of resistance fighters were persecuted for crimes committed during the occupation, while their leaders, whose activities were by definition political, were left untouched. (In some cases even the killing of a German or a Bulgarian by a member of EAM/ELAS was considered a crime.) Men of ELAS who had not surrendered their weapons by 15 March 1945, would also not be covered by the amnesty. Article IV called for the release of all civilians still detained by ELAS. Article V provided for the creation of a national army on the basis of regular conscription to which former ELAS members would be admitted. (It made no mention of the Third Brigade, although the Sacred Battalion, a royalist unit, was to be retained and eventually merged with the new army.) Instead, the army was largely filled with royalists, anti-Communists and former members of the security batallions, and the general staff was controlled by IDEA, a secret, extreme right-wing organization. Article VI defined the procedure for the demobilization of ELAS. Articles VII and VIII provided for the purge of the civil service and security services, the gendarmerie and city police. But instead of purging former Fascists and collaborators the government, applying the Metaxist law No. 12036, purged thousands of civil servants who had joined EAM/ELAS, on the grounds that they were members of 'anti-national organizations'.[212] Finally Article IX stipulated that a plebiscite on the constitutional question and elections to a constituent assembly would be conducted in that order 'at the earliest possible time and within the current year'.

Although vague and subject to conflicting interpretations, the Varkiza Agreement seemed to most at the time to conclude satisfactorily the 'second round' of the Greek Civil War. This soon proved not to be the case. The 'bitter truce' was unable to remedy the acute polarization of Greek politics. Mutual suspicion and hatred continued to inflame many minds. In the long run the success of the agreement depended on the ability of the government to establish its authority quickly and firmly across the country, enforce the Varkiza decisions, provide direction and confidence above partisan politics, and procure the means for healing the nation's wounds. A strong and moderate government could have protected the Left from harassment and persecution and put an end to the vicious cycle of violence and counter-violence. But the political forces in Athens, and the British authorities in the background, were incapable or unwilling to produce such a strong government. Instead, political instability continued and the national schism took the form of a vendetta, with the initiative in the hands of the Right. Once again Greece was drifting toward a new period of uncertainty and turmoil. The Varkiza Agreement thus became in the hands of the government an instrument of revenge, the curtain-raiser to a new and more bloody Greek tragedy: the 'third round' of civil war.

EPILOGUE

Three days after the signing of the Varkiza Agreement the KKE leadership defended the decision to sign it by arguing that Varkiza constituted the continuation of the policy of the KKE and EAM for a smooth democratic development in Greece. The KKE's aim was to become a legal party and follow a policy of peaceful integration into the parliamentary system.[213] In his introductory report at the Eleventh Plenum, which met in April 1945, Siandos, the KKE general secretary, made it clear that although the party had committed a number of right- and left-wing errors during the occupation, the policy of its leadership to seek an accommodation with the British and not to seize power by force had been basically correct. The 'December Events' had been the result of political inflexibility: EAM and the KKE had not only underestimated British intersets in Greece and overestimated their own forces but, what is more, had failed to find a compromise solution with Great Britain. Churchill on his part had tried to block the rise to legitimate power of EAM through an armed intervention. After the defeat of the KKE in the *Dekemvriana*, the party had the choice either to conclude an agreement with the British or to continue the guerrilla war. This war, however, would have been a war against the British and the Right and not a national liberation war. 'The Varkiza Agreement', Siandos argued, 'was an agreement born out of necessity; it was not an unconditional surrender. It constituted a minimum freedom of action. It provided an ethical and legal basis for the anti-fascist struggle'.[214]

In a similar fashion the Twelfth Plenum, which met in June 1945 in the presence of Nikos Zachariadis, who had returned to Greece and resumed control of the KKE after he had been found alive by the American troops in the Dachau concentration camp, declared through the mouth of its undisputed leader that the task of the KKE was to organize a 'mass political struggle' to fight against the right-wing terrorism and the threat of a Fascist dictatorship.[215] The aim of the party was to win the majority of the people and not to launch a socialist revolution against their will. 'The immediate transition to socialism', Zachariadis argued, 'was premature for Greece'. The party, in accordance with the resolutions of the Sixth Plenum of 1934, should fight for the establishment of a 'bourgeois democratic republic'. Moreover, in an effort to appease the British Zachariadis, defined Greece's foreign policy as one that must revolve round two poles: the Balkan–European (Soviet) and the Mediterranean (British). In an article published in *Rizospastis*, the KKE daily, a few weeks before the Twelfth Plenum, he declared that the KKE was prepared to recognize Britain's strategic interests in the Mediterranean as long as Greece's independence was not violated.[216] In his speech at the Twelfth Plenum, Zachariadis stated again his belief that Greece should base its foreign policy on developing close and friendly relations with all the Allies and appealed to Prime Minister Voulgaris, who had replaced Plastiras in April 1945, to form a representative government.[217] Only such a government, Zachariadis argued, could enforce the Varkiza and Yalta Agreements and ensure free and democratic elections.

Zachariadis' Anglophile 'revisionist' line, however, bore no fruit. While the KKE and EAM punctually and faithfully carried out their Varkiza obligations (demobilize ELAS and free the hostages) the government in Athens, and the British authorities in the background, did nothing to fulfil their duty. Right across the country 'people suspected of leftist sympathies were being fired from their jobs, refused new employment, harassed, beaten up, arrested, deported, and often killed'.[218] Circulation of the left-wing press was systematically suppressed and in the provinces national guardsmen with the assistance of right-wing bands smashed leftist printing shops, on many occasions killing their editors.[219] Similarly, the restoration of trade union liberties soon proved to be a farce. Although during and immediately after the war, EAM, the KKE, and the socialists represented the majority in the executive of the General Federation of Greek Labour (GSEE), after Varkiza the government intervened and appointed a new right-wing GSEE executive composed of former Metaxists and collaborators.[220] This was also the case with the public services and the security forces. The government purged the army, the police, the gendarmerie, the courts, the universities, etc. of EAM sympathizers instead of purging them of former Fascists and collaborators.[221] To make matters worse, the government provided weapons to right-wing bands, which in close co-operation with the National Guard and the gendarmerie launched a campaign of 'white terror'.

The British did not want to strengthen the right-wing forces, but in their effort to neutralize the Greek Left, hoping that moderate and pro-British elements would gain power, in fact allowed the extreme Right to take control of the whole state apparatus. Their various interventions and experiments in government met with dismal failure. In mid-October Voulgaris resigned, nominally on account of opposition provoked by his announcement of a general election in January 1946. His government, though, had proved unable to control the rising level of right-wing violence and deal with the critical economic situation. A crisis followed, with no politician being able to form a government. Finally, after Damaskinos himself was forced to assume the premiership for a few days, Kanellopoulos formed a cabinet. But three weeks later, under pressure from the British, he gave up in favour of the octagenerian Sofoulis, the leader of the Liberal Party and the last of Venizelos' contemporaries. Sofoulis formed a moderate government and announced the holding of elections, the first since 1936, which it was now decided would precede rather than follow the plebiscite. These were fixed for 31 March 1946.

The character of the new government took the public by surprise. The Populists accused the British of flagrant intervention in Greek internal affairs, and the royalist newspaper *Ellinikon Aima* went so far as to question whether it was fortunate that Britain had won the war. The KKE and EAM on the other hand announced that the Sofoulis government 'will enjoy the tolerance of the Party and EAM' as long as it took all the necessary measures for the conduct of a free and genuine general election.[222] Three weeks later, though, the KKE and EAM published a statement announcing that in view of the fact that Sofoulis had failed to grant a general amnesty, to correct the electoral lists, or to put an end to the monarcho-Fascists' reign of terror they were ending their policy of 'conditional tolerance' and would abstain from the election.[223] There is no doubt that the arguments that the KKE and EAM had put forward in order to justify their decision were correct. The amnesty law declared by the government was never implemented by the 'Metaxist' judiciary, and right-wing violence continued unabated. Moreover, although the electoral lists were known to be false (the right-wing army and gendarmerie had swollen these lists with thousands of names of people who had died during the war and had issued multiple election cards to those of 'proper political persuasion') the government did nothing to correct the situation. Under these conditions there was little hope that the election could be fair. In February Sofoulis informed Bevin that all the parties of the Left would abstain if the election was not postponed and that this would lead to a fresh outbreak of civil war. But the British Foreign Secretary (a Labour government had come to power in July 1945) rejected Sofoulis' appeal. A postponement was simply not under discussion. As the election approached, it increasingly came to be viewed by the British government as an end in itself, with little or no real concern about its actual character, outcome, or consequence. Bevin, who obviously did not cherish the responsibilities his government had inherited in Greece, convinced himself that postponement would not improve conditions, but failed to recognize the absurdity of the situation created by this decision. The whole policy of the British up to this date, and especially the appointment of Sofoulis, was to establish in Greece not a reactionary regime of the Right but a moderate centre which, by offering the Greek people a stable and democratic system of government, would triumph in the election and thus make it possible for the British to withdraw from direct political and military involvement. But if this was the desired policy, Bevin's statements and actions indicate a complete reluctance to prevent the exact opposite from happening. By the end of March the Foreign Office and the Greek government viewed the civil war in Greece as 'inevitable', both preparing when this occurred 'to wash their hands in all innocence'.[224] Rather than resign, Sofoulis chose to cling to his cosmetic role for fear of alienating the British, while Bevin let Greece follow its inevitable course which would at last 'legitimize' Britain's policies in Greece and allow her to bow out gracefully.

The elections were held on 31 March 1946, and were supervised by British, American, and French observers. The Soviet Union declined an invitation to participate in the AMFOGE (Allied Mission For Observing the Greek Elections) obviously wishing to prevent a similar supervision of elections in Bulgaria and Rumania. With 40 per cent of the electorate abstaining, a coalition of monarchist parties won a clear majority.[225] In April 1946, Sofoulis resigned and Constantine Tsaldaris, the leader of the Populist Party and nephew of the pre-war Populist leader Panayis Tsaldaris, formed a cabinet of mostly royalists. Tsaldaris' first act was to announce a plebiscite on the monarchy for 1 September 1946, although the date agreed between the British and Sofoulis had been March 1948. Tsaldaris' harsh measures against the Left and extensive ballot-rigging by the right-wing authorities ensured that the plebiscite resulted in a 68 per cent vote in favour of the monarchy. On 27 September King George II arrived in Athens, only to die six months later and be succeeded by his brother Paul. What Bevin and the Foreign Office had worked to prevent had now happened: constitutional monarchy had been transformed into a 'party monarchy'; the royalists, with British and American backing secured, could now wipe out the entire Left from the political scene.

At the Second Plenum of the central committee of the KKE, in February 1946, Zachariadis took the decision to boycott the elections, in clear defiance of Soviet advice to the contrary and under strong opposition from the political Bureau.[226] Most members of the political bureau and the central committee only learned of the Soviet 'advice' as late as 1948 when the KKE was already in the midst of the civil war.

This decision was subsequently acknowledged by the post-Zachariadis leadership to have been a 'decisive mistake'. Zachariadis had dismissed the notion that peaceful evolution in Greece was possible by the time of the Second Plenum, and now led his party to the disaster that the abstention was supposed to have prevented. After a year of 'white terror', a decision that allowed a right-wing election victory implied not less persecution but more persecution and more terror. If the real problem had been right-wing bands 'slaughtering innocent communists', as Zachariadis put it, then there was even more reason for the KKE to try to block the extreme Right from winning power. But the 'white terror' was not what was at stake. By 1946 the real objective, as far as Zachariadis was concerned, was the creation of a 'revolutionary situation' which would allow the launching of a 'socialist revolution'; the 'white terror', far from being a factor to be eliminated or neutralized, something that participation in the election would have secured, was a factor to be utilized for the purpose in mind. As Zachariadis himself admitted after the defeat of the KKE in the civil war, the decision to boycott the election was also taken on the grounds that the boycott 'would prepare the people better for the new armed confrontation'.[227] It is not difficult to imagine what this 'better' meant. Blinded by his revolutionary illusions and following textbook instructions, Zachariadis became a prisoner of his own ideology. Nevertheless, had the British and Greek governments been successful in enforcing the Varkiza Agreement – in other words, had the KKE and EAM been given the chance to integrate into the parliamentary system – the decision to boycott the election would have become unenforcable as far as the leftist voters were concerned. Although Zachariadis committed a grave error when forcing the KKE to abstain from the election, one should point out that it was not he nor the KKE and EAM who frustrated reconciliation. Zachariadis' statements at the Twelfth Plenum (in June 1945), at the Sixth Conference of the Athens Party Organization (September 1945), and at the Seventh Party Congress (October 1945) indicate clearly that the KKE leader was still advocating the parliamentary alternative throughout 1945, despite his own revolutionary aspirations and the 'white terror'. It was only after the British and Sofoulis rejected the KKE's and EAM's demands for a postponement of the election until conditions improved, that Zachariadis finally abandoned the 'peaceful transition to socialism' line and decided on the abstention in the hope that post-election events would bring about a revolutionary situation in the towns. One year of uncontrolled right-wing terror combined with the certainty of rigged elections provided Zachariadis with the right ground from which to launch his 'socialist revolution'.[228] Perhaps this is something worth remembering when appropriating blame on the Communists, the royalists, and the British.

By the end of 1946 all Communist bands were organized into the centrally commanded 'Democratic Army of Greece' under the leadership of Markos Vafiadis. With limited Yugoslav, Bulgarian, and Albanian assistance, the Democratic Army soon succeeded in taking over the entire north-western sector of the country, near the Greek–Albanian and Yugoslav borders. The 'Free Greece' of the occupation period was again beginning to make its appearance in the countryside; this time, though, the enemies were not the Germans or the Italians but fellow Greeks. In February 1947, the British government informed the state department that because of internal economic difficulties it would have to suspend economic aid to Greece. Truman, who regarded the Greek Communists as 'an instrument of Soviet policy', and believed that the 'fall' of Greece would lead to tumbling dominoes right across the map, lost no time. On 12 March he went before Congress to urge that the United States pick up the burden that the British were dropping of sustaining Greece against internal subversion. In his famous 'two ways of life' speech, which became known as the Truman Doctrine, he appealed for an initial grant of $300 million for Greece and $100 million for Turkey. Greece had now become the first major battlefield of the Cold War. With substantial American assistance and direction, the new Greek government formed under Sofoulis in September 1947 was soon able to reorganize its army and take the offensive. During the same month the Third Plenum of the central committee of the KKE decided to 'transform the Democratic Army into a force that will ensure the establishment of a Free Greece in the shortest possible time, in the North of Greece'.[229] On Christmas Eve 1947, the rebel radio announced the formation of a 'Provisional Democratic Government' headed by Prime Minister and Minister of War, 'General Markos'. Zachariadis, following Stalin's example, assumed no cabinet post but remained the KKE's general secretary. Markos' 'Provisional Government', though, was not recognized even by the Cominform and it soon became clear that Stalin, obviously alarmed by the growing American involvement in an area so close to his satellites, wanted the Greek civil war to be brought to an end.[230] After bitter fighting in 1948, which caused severe losses to both sides and deprived the Communists of most of their popular base, the 'Democratic Army' was cornered and defeated in the summer of 1949. Tito's breach with Stalin, which led to the expulsion of Yugoslavia from the Cominform in July 1948 and Zachariadis' decision to side with Moscow in that controversy, condemned the Communists to an early defeat. In July 1949 Yugoslavia closed its borders to the 'Democratic Army'. The civil war was over.

In 1950, at the Third Party Conference, Zachariadis was casting around for scapegoats for the defeat of the KKE and accused Tito of 'treachery' and of having 'stabbed the KKE in the back'.[231] Although the closing of the frontier contributed to a great extent to the defeat of the 'Democratic Army', it was by no means the decisive factor. The failure of the KKE to develop mass support in the towns in 1946–7 and launch an all-out revolution before the arrival of the American military mission in Greece, the failure of the 'Democratic Army' to solve the problem of reserves, Zachariadis's decision in the summer of 1948 to convert the 'Democratic Army' into a 'regular' force, whose tactics were the very opposite from those advocated by Markos, the massive infusion of American military aid which revitalized the government's 'National Army', and, finally, the failure of the KKE to secure substantial military assistance from the Soviet Union and the countries of the eastern bloc all played their part in the defeat of the guerrillas and the collapse of Zachariadis' revolution.

The civil war of 1946–9, like the occupation and the 'December Events' that preceded it, brought new suffering and destruction to Greece, leaving behind a legacy of repression and foreign intervention (this time American) that culminated in the dictatorship of 1967–74. More than 150,000 Greeks died in the civil war, over 5,000 having been executed for offences against the state and between 70,000 and 100,000 Communists left Greece and became political refugees in the countries of the eastern bloc. In addition, more than 700,000 people became 'displaced' within Greece itself, the great majority having been forced out of their villages by the government in its effort to cut off the guerrillas from their sources of supplies and recruits. To these figures one must also add the children who were forcibly evacuated from the battle zone (both by the government and the 'Democratic Army', for political as well as humanitarian reasons), more than 25,000 of whom settled in the countries of Eastern Europe, some never to see their families again. The Cold War had had its first victim. The post-war antagonism between the United States and the Soviet Union meant that the welfare of small states had to be sacrificed in the interests of 'balance of power' and 'containment'. Greece was not alone among countries that had to pay a price in conforming to the requirements of the ideological schism that divided Europe. But the price she had to pay in the process of discovering her 'proper' political identity was a heavy one. Greece was 'saved' but the Greeks were not.

NOTES

1 For the Founding Charter of SEKE see *KKE Episima Keimena, 1918–1924* (KKE Official Documents), I (Athens, 1964), pp. 5–13. On the history of the Greek socialist movement see Y. Kordatos, *Istoria tou Ellinikou Ergatikou Kinimatos* (Athens, 1972); A. Benaroya, *I Proti Stadiodromia tou Ellinikou Proletariatou* (Athens, 1975); K. Moskof, *I Ethniki kai Koinoniki Synidisi stin Ellada, 1830–1909*, (Athens, 1973). With the notable exception of the book by A. Elefantis, *I Epaggelia tis Adinatis Epanastasis: KKE kai Astismos ston Mesopolomo* (Athens, 1976), there has been no other study of the history of the KKE during the inter-war period.
2 For the text of the decision of the National Council see *KKE Episima Keimena, 1918–1924*, I, p. 31.
3 For the text of the decisions of the Second Congress see *KKE Episima Keimena, 1918–1924*, I, pp. 61–2, 68.
4 For the text of the resolution of the Third Extraordinary Congress see *KKE Episima Keimena, 1918–1924*, p. 499.
5 *KKE Episima Keimena, 1918–1924*, pp. 523–4, 534–42.
6 *KKE Episima Keimena, 1925–1928*, II (Athens, 1974), pp. 99, 101–2, 105.
7 The results of the votes received by SEKE(K)/KKE in the elections held during the period 1923–9 were the following: 1923: 2.25%; 1926: 3.6%; 1928: 1.41%; 1929: 1.70%. By 1931, as a result of the KKE's 'factional struggle without principles' (ie. the conflict between two factions headed by political bureau members Haitas and Siandos), the membership of the party had dropped to 1,500. Tables containing Greece's electoral results in the inter-war period can be found in the Appendix of G. Daphnis, *Ta Ellinika Politika Kommata* (Athens, 1961). For a more detailed analysis of the results (returns for each constituency) see Elefantis, op. cit., pp. 387–401.
8 N. Svoronos, *Analekta Neoellinikis Istorias kai Istoriografias* (Athens, 1987), p. 362. See also Elefantis, op. cit., pp. 104–11.
9 L. S. Stavrianos, *The Balkans since 1453* (New York, 1958), p. 478; Elefantis, op. cit., pp. 82–3, 110–11, 319–24. As Elefantis observes (p. 375), 'the KKE was the party of the

working class and of the proletarian revolution only in a metaphorical sense. The leadership of the KKE wasted its efforts in instilling into the members a "proletarian" ideology, which did not reflect the ideological and social reality of the movement'. See also G. Mavrogordatos, *Stillborn Republic: Social Coalitions and Party Strategies in Greece, 1922–1936* (London, 1983), pp. 147–52.

10 *KKE Episima Keimena, 1929–1933*, III (Athens, 1966), p. 99; Bushkoff, L., 'Marxism, Communism and the revolutionary tradition in the Balkans, 1878–1924: An analysis and an interpretation', *East European Quarterly*, I, 1 (March 1967), p. 380; Elefantis, op. cit., p. 49. On the *Idionymon* see Mavrogordatos, op. cit., p. 336. Mavrogordatos rightly observes that 'the *Idionymon* law was massively and indiscriminately used in 1929–32 for largely partisan purposes, namely, to contain the erosion of Venizelist and particularly LP [Liberal Party] mass support, against radical agitation of any kind. This is also why the perennial debate on whether there was a "real" Communist danger is ultimately beside the point. The actual and present danger was rather that radical (and not just Communist) agitation might irreparably cripple Venizelism as a project for bourgeois hegemony, as an interclass alliance, and, in the last analysis, as a governing coalition'.

11 E. Kofos, *Nationalism and Communism in Macedonia* (Thessaloniki, 1964), pp. 68–89; E. Barker, *Macedonia: Its Place in Balkan Power Politics* (London, 1950), pp. 47–69; Stavrianos, op. cit., p. 670. For KKE decisions on the 'Macedonian Question' see *KKE Episima Keimena, 1918–1924*, pp. 513–18. On the voting behaviour of the refugees see Mavrogordatos, op. cit., pp. 182–225. There is, of course, another reason that explains the failure of the KKE to enlist the support of the refugees. Despite their destitute condition, the majority of them had previously constituted the middle and upper classes of the main towns in Anatolia and as a consequence had never relinquished their bourgeois mentality. Although the KKE viewed them as 'proletarians', they were in fact 'impoverished bourgeois'. As Tsoukalas notes, 'it was only later on, when they had abandoned their dream of reconquering the status they had lost, that they started to act and function as a working class'. See C. Tsoukalas, *The Greek Tragedy* (London, 1969), p. 39.

12 N. Zachariadis, *Theseis ya tin Istoria tou KKE* (Athens, 1939, reprint 1975), p. 30. This is in fact the 'official' history of the KKE during the inter-war period, written by Zachariadis in 1939 in Corfu prison and published for the first time in 1946. The account is oversimplified and reflects the views of the new Stalinist leadership. Despite Zachariadis' dethronement in 1956, the views of the book remained unchallenged for almost two decades. See, for example, *Theseis tis KE tou KKE ya ta Penintachrona tou KKE*, 1968.

13 Nikos Zachariadis was born in 1903 in Asia Minor. In 1923 he came to Greece and became a leading member of the KKE's youth organization. In 1926 he was imprisoned for agitating in favour of a Macedonian state. He escaped in 1929 and went to the Soviet Union where he remained until 1931, studying at the KUTV (Communist University of Eastern Peoples). In that year he was appointed by the Comintern as party leader. In 1935 (Fourth Plenum) he was elected secretary general of the KKE. In 1936, after the establishment of the Metaxas dictatorship, he was imprisoned again and in 1942 he was transferred by the German occupation authorities to the Dachau concentration camp. He was liberated by the Allies at the end of the war and returned to Greece in May 1945, where he resumed again the leadership of the KKE. In 1949 after the defeat of the KKE in the civil war, he fled to the Soviet Union. In March 1956, through the intervention of the Communist parties of the USSR, Rumania, Poland, Hungary, Bulgaria, and Czechoslovakia, he was deposed from the KKE leadership and few months later he was expelled from the party. He died as a 'political refugee' in conditions of inhuman deprivation in a village in north Siberia in 1973.

14 This line remained the party's policy throughout the period of the resistance and the civil war until January 1949 when it reverted for a moment to the slogan of a 'united and independent Macedonia' when the KKE, in desperation, made a last-ditch effort to recruit 'Bulgaro-Macedonians' and 'Slavo-Macedonians' in the 'Democratic Army of

Greece'. (The 'Democratic Army of Greece', the KKE's military organization during the 'third round' of the civil war (1946–9) was established in September 1946 under the command of Markos Vafiadis. For the decisions of the Fifth Plenum (January 1949) see *Voithima ya tin Istoria tou KKE*, (the 'Official History of the KKE' for the period of the resistance and the civil war, henceforth *Voithima*) written by Zachariadis himself (and perhaps by Bartziotas as well) (n.p., 1952), pp. 248–61).

15 See *Deka Chronia Agones, 1935–1945* (a collection of documents published by the Political Bureau of the KKE) (Athens, 1977), pp. 66–7. Emphasis mine.

16 For a more authoritative analysis of the resolutions of the Seventh Congress of the Comintern see E. H. Carr, *The Twilight of the Comintern, 1930–1935* (London, 1982), pp. 403–27; for results of elections see Daphnis, op. cit., Appendix.

17 On the consequences of the world economic crisis on the Greek working classes see *KKE Episima Keimena, 1929–1933*, pp. 145–69, 308–30, 421–33, 457–70; *Voithima*, pp. 62–87. On the question of the radicalism of the refugees see Mavrogordatos, op. cit., pp. 214–25, 335–6.

18 In January 1934, the Sixth Plenum of the central committee of the KKE, one of the most important gatherings in the history of the party, elaborated the 'character of the revolution of Greece'. The central passage of the final resolution reads: 'The imminent revolution of the workers and peasants in Greece will be of a bourgeois-democratic character', *KKE Episima Keimena, 1934–1940*, IV (Athens, 1981), p. 19. Zachariadis, in the *Voithima*, p. 126, notes that with the assistance of the Comintern the KKE, by 'rejecting the dogmatic, unfounded call for an immediate proletarian–socialist revolution', was able to work out a realistic programme and define its immediate strategic objectives and tactics. The aim of the party was to 'win the majority of the working class and fight against fascism'. Nevertheless, the resolution of the Sixth Plenum also spoke of 'the rapid transformation of the bourgeois-democratic revolution into a proletarian socialist one'. What remained to be defined was the word 'rapid'. During the occupation this cryptic passage was to haunt the KKE leaders.

19 This account, of one of the most tragic chapters in the history of modern Greece, is naturally oversimplified, as the events that preceded and followed the Greco-Turkish war of 1922 are outside the scope of the present study. For a scholarly study of Greece's disastrous venture in Asia Minor see Llewellyn Smith, *Ionian Vision, Greece in Asia Minor 1919–1922* (London, 1973); A. A. Pallis, *Greece's Anatolian Venture and After. A survey of the diplomatic and political aspects of the Greek expedition to Asia Minor [1915–1922]* (London, 1937). For the development of the Greek political system during the inter-war period see Mavrogordatos, op. cit.; G. Dafnis, I *Ellas Metaxy dyo Polemon 1923–1940*, 2 vols (Athens, 1974). For the role of the army during this period see T. Veremis, *I Epemvaseis tou Stratou stin Elliniki Politiki 1916–1936* (Athens, 1977).

20 Under the terms of this agreement, known as the 'Sofoulis–Sklavainas Agreement' (Sofoulis was the leader of the Liberals and Sklavainas the representative of the Popular Front), the Popular Front deputies in parliament agreed 'to vote for the Liberal candidate for the office of the Speaker of the House, and support a government formed by the Liberal Party', in exchange for a general amnesty for all political prisoners and exiles, the abolition of the state security agencies, the suppression of all organizations having 'Fascist' objectives, the introduction of the proportional electoral system, and most important, the repeal of the (in)famous 'Idionymon Law'. See the KKE daily *Rizospastis*, 3 April 1936.

21 Dafnis, op. cit., pp. 415–36, and for election results p. 402. It has been suggested, but not yet proven, that the king's choice of Metaxas was favoured by the British, obliged by the death of Venizelos to find a new strong man in Greece. Metaxas, for his part, never lost a chance to assure the British government that his government was determined to work in close co-operation with the British. See Tsoukalas op. cit., p. 51; J. Koliopoulos, *Greece and the British Connection* (Oxford, 1977), pp. 59–60. On the Metaxas dictatorship see

The Greek Communist Party   201

also the book by Dafnis and Metaxas' own diary, I. Metaxas, *To Prosopikon mou Imerologion*, 4 vols (Athens, 1974).

22 A. Pataztis, *Ioannis Sofianopoulos: Enas Epanastatis Choris Epanastasi* (Athens, 1961), pp. 154–6; *KKE Episima Keimena, 1934–1940*, pp. 395–401.

23 L. S. Stavrianos, *Greece: American Dilemma and Opportunity* (Chicago, 1952), p. 30; *Rizospastis*, 10 and 15 May 1936.

24 Something that Zachariadis himself admits in the *Voithima*, pp. 167–8; see also N. Zachariadis, *Ta Provlimata Kathodigisis sto KKE* (Athens, 1978, reprint), pp. 76–8; P. Nefeloudis, *Stis Piges tis Kakodaimonias: Ta Vathitera Aitia tis Diaspasis tou KKE 1918–1968* (Athens, 1974), pp. 117–19; V. Bartziotas, 'I Politiki ton Stelechon mas sto KKE ta Teleftaia Deka Chronia', *Neos Kosmos*, 9 (September 1950), p. 18.

25 According to an estimate of Metaxist propaganda, 50,000 'Communists' were eventually arrested and deported to concentration camps, especially built in some remote islands of the Aegean.

26 Nefeloudis, op. cit., p. 119; A. Solaro, *Istoria tou Koumounistikou Kommatos Ellados* (Athens, 1977), p. 122; J. C. Loulis, 'The Greek Communist Party and the Greek Italian War, 1940–41: An analysis of Zachariadis' Three Letters', *Byzantine and Modern Greek Studies*, 5 (1979), p. 168.

27 Loulis, op. cit., p. 168.

28 Stavrianos, op. cit., p. 76.

29 D. G. Kousoulas, *Revolution and Defeat: The Story of the Greek Communist Party* (London, 1965), p. 130.

30 Tyrimos, a political bureau member and editor in chief of Rizospastis, was arrested in July 1939. According to an officer in the Maniadakis police, Tyrimos decided to collaborate with the Metaxist authorities on learning that his brother, who was studying in Moscow, had been executed as a Trotskyist. See 'To Mystikon Archeion', in the daily *Ethnikos Kiryx*, 11–13 October 1949. Unlike Tyrimos, Michailidis, a member of the political bureau, signed a 'repentance declaration' on the orders of Zachariadis, who instructed him to 'reorganize the party'. He was arrested, however, by Maniadakis' police and became a collaborator. See Nefeloudis, op. cit., p. 119, and *KKE Episima Keimena, 1940–1945*, V (Athens, 1981), pp. 76–7; Solaro, op. cit., pp. 118–20.

31 *KKE Episima Keimena, 1934–1940*, pp. 491–6 and *KKE Episima Keimena, 1940–1945*, pp. 76–7. The Second Panhellenic Conference of the KKE was held in December 1942.

32 *Voithima*, p. 169; Solaro, op. cit., pp. 121–2.

33 Y. Ioannidis, *Anamniseis: Provlimata tis Politikis tou KKE stin Ethniki Antistasi 1940–1945* (Athens, 1979), pp. 68–74 and 503–5. Yannis Ioannidis was born in 1900. In 1931 he became a member of the political bureau and the following year he was elected MP for the Popular Front. Arrested in 1936 by the Metaxist authorities he remained in prison until 1942. After his escape he was appointed organizational secretary of the central committee. With Zachariadis in Dachau, he and George Siandos became the two most powerful individuals in the party's central committee and in EAM/ELAS during the occupation. During the 'third round' of the civil war he became Minister of War in the 'provisional government' set up by the KKE in December 1947. In 1952 he was purged from the political bureau for failing, among other things, to recognize the 'treachery' of Siandos. He was expelled from the central committee in 1961.

34 *KKE Episima Keimena, 1934–1940*, p. 463. Emphasis mine. George Siandos was born in 1890. He worked from a very young age as a tobacco worker. He served in the Greek Army during the Balkan Wars of 1911–12 and the First World War, reaching the rank of a sergeant. He became a member of the KKE in 1920 and member of the political bureau in 1925. He played a leading part in the party's 1929–31 'struggle without principles'. In 1934 he became secretary of the Piraeus Party Organization. In 1936 he was imprisoned

by the Metaxist authorities. He escaped in 1937, but was rearrested in 1939 and imprisoned in Corfu. In September 1941 he escaped while being transferred to Athens to stand trial. In January 1942, at the Eight Plenum, he was elected secretary of the central committee. In 1944 he became Secretary of the Interior of PEEA. He was replaced to the leadership of the KKE by Zachariadis in May 1945. He died in May 1947. In October 1950 he was denounced by Zachariadis as a 'British agent' and a 'class traitor'. During the occupation Siandos was, together with Ioannidis, the most powerful individual in the KKE, EAM, and PEEA. During the 'December events' of 1944 (the 'second round' of civil war) he also took over the control of ELAS's Central Committee, thus assuming the command of all the forces of the Left in the battle of Athens.

35 Loulis, op. cit., p. 171 and fn.
36 Siandos revealed this Comintern directive during his speech at the Second Panhellenic Conference in December 1942. See *Deka Chronia Agones*, op. cit., pp. 141–2.
37 See J. Degras, (ed.), *The Communist International 1919–1943 Documents* (London, 1965), vol. III (1929–43), pp. 450–1.
38 ibid., p. 441.
39 *KKE Episima Keimena, 1940–1945*, p. 9.
40 Ioannidis, op. cit., p. 64 and fn. After the publication of Zachariadis's 'open letter' in the Metaxist press, the Akronafplia Communists sent on 13 November a second letter supporting the position of the KKE's leader: ibid., p. 65. Zachariadis in the *Voithima*, pp. 192–3, claims that the Akronafplia group when sending their first letter knew already of the line he was about to adopt. Ioannidis in his account, op. cit., p. 65, says nothing of the sort.
41 *KKE Episima Keimena, 1940–1945*, pp. 13, 17–22.
42 On this point see Loulis' article already mentioned and O. L. Smith, 'The problem of Zachariadis' first open letter: a reappraisal of the evidence', *Journal of the Hellenic Diaspora*, Winter 1982, pp. 7–20.
43 J. C. Loulis, *The Greek Communist Party, 1940–1944* (London, 1982), pp. 7–8.
44 Nefeloudis, op. cit., pp. 139–42. Contrary to what Elefantis claims in his book, op. cit., p. 286, Zachariadis could not have been informed about the July 1939 directive from Siandos, when the latter was rearrested and imprisoned in Corfu, because by that time he had been transferred to Athens.
45 Smith, op. cit., pp. 17–20.
46 *Voithima*, pp. 192–3.
47 I derived this information in conversation with Vasilis Nefeloudis. This is, of course, confirmed by his brother Pavlos Nefeloudis in his book, op. cit., pp. 139–42.
48 Something that Zachariadis, the Comintern appointee, may have wished to demonstrate.
49 Loulis, *The Greek Communist Party*, p. 8.
50 Ioannidis, op. cit., pp. 65–8.
51 S. Karas, *Politikoi Provlimatismoi* (Athens, 1975), p. 87.
52 Something that even right-wing historians/politicians have to admit. See E. Averoff, *Fotia kai Tsekouri* (Athens, 1974), p. 93; P. Kanellopoulos, *Ta Chronia tou Megalou Polemou 1939–1944* (Athens, 1964), p. 6.
53 Nefeloudis, p. 139.
54 Zachariadis, 'Theseis ya tin Istoria tou KKE', p. 48; Loulis, op. cit., pp. 183–4.
55 *Voithima*, pp. 193–4.
56 ibid., pp. 194–6.
57 ibid., pp. 194–5.
58 ibid., p. 195.
59 Loulis makes the same point in his book *The Greek Communist Party*, p. 9.
60 M. Partsalidis, *Dipli Apokatastasi tis Ethnikis Antistasis* (Athens, 1978), p. 23.
61 The premiers of these cabinets were: General G. Tsolakoglou, 7 April 1941–2 December

1942; G. Logothetopoulos, 2 December 1942–7 April 1943; J. Rallis, 7 April 1943–September 1944.
62 The premiers of the government-in-exile were: E. Tsouderos, 21 April 1941–13 April 1944; S. Venizelos, 13 April 1944–23 April 1944; G. Papandreou, 26 April 1944 –3 January 1945.
63 *KKE Episima Keimena, 1940–1945*, p. 39.
64 These organizations were: the Athens organization, the Piraeus organization, the Thessaly organization and the Macedonian organization. See *KKE Episima Keimena, 1940–1945*, p. 44.
65 For EAM's Founding Charter see *KKE Episima Keimena, 1940–1945*, pp. 54–6.
66 Loulis, *The Greek Communist Party*, p. 42.
67 L. S. Stavrianos, 'The Greek National Liberation Front (EAM): a study in resistance organization and administration', *Journal of Modern History*, 24 (1952), p. 44.
68 J. Campbell, 'The Greek Civil War', in E. Luard (ed.), *International Regulation of Civil War* (New York, 1972), p. 215; J. Petropoulos, 'The traditional parties of Greece during the Axis occupation', in J. O. Iatrides (ed.), *Greece in the 1940s. A Nation in Crisis* (henceforth *Greece in the 1940s*) (Hanover, 1981), pp. 27–36.
69 C. M. Woodhouse, *The Struggle for Greece 1941–1949* (London, 1976), p. 35.
70 C. M. Woodhouse, *Apple of Discord: A Survey of Recent Greek Politics in their International Setting* (London, 1948), pp. 50–1.
71 On this point see also Loulis, *The Greek Communist Party*, pp. 21–5.
72 Ioannidis, op. cit., pp. 75–81.
73 On this point see also K. R. Legg, *Politics in Modern Greece* (Stanford, Stanford University Press, 1969), p. 129.
74 Petropoulos, op. cit., pp. 32–3.
75 The best source for EDES is the work of its deputy chief, K. Pyromaglou, *I Ethniki Antistasis, EAM-ELAS-EDES-EKKA* (Athens, 1975). For EKKA see K. Pyromaglou, *O Georgios Kartalis kai i Epochi tou 1934–1957*, vol. I: 1934–44 (Athens, 1965); G. Kartalis, *Pepragmena* (Athens, 1945).
76 Tsoukalas, op. cit., p. 61.
77 D. Glinos, *Ti Einai kai ti Thelei to Ethniko Apeleftherotiko Metopo* (Athens, 1944).
78 Stavrianos, op. cit., pp. 74–5; Loulis, *The Greek Communist Party*, pp. 50–2; S. Sarafis *ELAS: Greek Resistance Army* (London, 1980), pp. 50, 100, 272, 328. Sarafis was ELAS's commander. The position of the EAM representative was abolished in March 1944 when EAM and the KKE founded a provisional government in the mountains.
79 Woodhouse, *Struggle for Greece*, p. 27.
80 On the question of British foreign policy in Greece during the occupation see the following books: Woodhouse, *Struggle for Greece*, and *Apple of Discord*; E. Barker, *British Foreign Policy in South-East Europe in the Second World War* (London, 1976); L. Woodward, *History of the Second World War: British Foreign Policy in the Second World War*, vol. 3 (London, 1971); E. C. W. Myers, *Greek Entanglement* (London, 1955); G. Chandler, *The Divided Land: An Anglo-Greek Tragedy* (London, 1959); N. Hammonds *Venture Into Greece: With the Guerrillas 1943–44* (London, 1983); R. Leeper, *When Greek Meets Greek* (London, 1950); W. H. McNeill, *The Greek Dilemma, War and Aftermath* (London, 1947); A. E. Eden, *The Reckoning: The Memoirs of Antony Eden*) London, 1965); W. S. Churchill *The Second World War*, vols: V and VI (London, 1952); H. Macmillan, *The Blast of War 1939–1945* (London, 1967); W. Byford-Jones, *The Greek Trilogy: Resistance, Liberation, Revolution* (London, 1945); E. O'Ballance, *The Greek Civil War 1944–1949* (London, 1966); G. M. Alexander, *The Prelude to the Truman Doctrine: British Policy in Greece 1944–1947* (Oxford, 1982); P. Papastratis, *British Policy towards Greece during the Second World War 1941–1944* (London, 1984); J. D. Iatrides, (ed.), *Greece in the 1940s*; M. Sarafis (ed.), *Greece: From*

Resistance to Civil War (Nottingham, 1980); P. Auty and R. Clogg (eds), *British Policy towards Wartime Resistance in Yugoslavia and Greece* (henceforth *British Policy*) (London, 1975). Quotes from Barker, op. cit., p. 148 and Woodhouse, *Struggle for Greece*, p. 36.

81 Leeper, op. cit., p. 11.
82 Barker, op. cit., p. 157; Clogg, 'The Special Operations Executive', in *Greece in the 1940s*, pp. 115–16. Woodhouse (*Struggle for Greece*, p. 26) rejects the popular view that the Gorgopotamos operation contributed to the defeat of the Germans in the battle of El Alamein, noting that it 'came a month late', since the battle began on 23 October 1942.
83 Woodhouse, 'Summer 1943: the critical months', in *British Policy*, p. 137. Emphasis mine.
84 Myers, op. cit., p. 189.
85 ibid., p. 190.
86 Churchill's minute to Eden of June 15, 1943, FO 371/37203 R 5552.
87 Leeper, op. cit., p. 30.
88 Myers, 'The Andarte delegation to Cairo: August 1943', in *British Policy*, pp. 149–50.
89 Woodhouse, 'Summer 1943: the critical months', p. 123.
90 ibid., p. 124.
91 Myers, op. cit., pp. 187–201.
92 ibid., pp. 229–30.
93 E. Tsouderos, *Ellinikes Anomalies sti Mesi Anatoli* (Athens, 1945), pp. 63–5; Ioannidis, op. cit., pp. 187–9; K. Pyromaglou, *O Doureios Ippos. I Ethniki kai Politiki Krisis kata tin Katochi* (Athens, 1978, reprint), pp. 101–29. For the texts of Churchill's and Roosevelt's telgrams see Tsouderos, op. cit., pp. 67–8 and *Foreign Relations of the United States: Diplomatic Papers* (henceforth *FRUS*) (US Government Printing Office, Washington): *The Conferences of Washington and Quebec*, 1943, pp. 915, 933.
94 Clogg, ' "Pearls from Swine": the Foreign Office Papers, SOE and the Greek Resistance', in *British Policy*, p. 192.
95 Woodhouse, *Struggle for Greece*, p. 56; Barker, op. cit., p. 165.
96 Clogg, 'Pearls from Swine', p. 194.
97 Myers, 'The Andarte Delegation to Cairo', p. 166; Woodhouse, too, seems to draw the same conclusion when he notes that 'it can not be disputed that the episode of the resistance delegation made civil war certain'. See his article 'Summer 1943: the critical months', p. 144.
98 Leeper shared Myers' and Woodhouse's views about the monarchy. He reported to the Foreign Office that the king must agree to remaining abroad until the holding of a plebiscite. See Leeper's telegrams to the Foreign Office: FO 371/37198 R 7516 and FO 371/37204 R 7548 and his letter to Sargent FO 371/37204 R 7884 all dated 13 August 1943. Kanellopoulos had estimated that at the outbreak of the war the royalists amounted to no more than 2 per cent of the population as against 60 per cent Liberals and 30 per cent in the Popular Front (Woodhouse, *Struggle for Greece*, p. 22).
99 Woodward, op. cit., p. 354; Leeper to FO, 6 October 1943, FO 371/37205 R 9785; WP (43) 526 'Policy towards Greece', Eden Memorandum, 21 November 1943.
100 Eden to Leeper, 15 August 1943, FO 371/37204 R 7548.
101 P. Papastratis, 'The British and the Greek resistance movements EAM and EDES' in M. Sarafis (ed.), *Greece: From Resistance to Civil War*, p. 36.
102 Leeper's minute to Eden, 7 December 1943, FO 371/37231 R 12837; J. O. Iatrides, *Ambassador MacVeagh Reports: Greece 1923–1947* (Princeton, NJ, 1980), pp. 444–5; FRUS, 1943, vol. IV, p. 160.
103 Eden, op. cit., p. 498.
104 H. Fleischer, 'Contacts between German occupation authorities and the major Greek resistance organizations: sound tactics or collaboration', in *Greece in the 1940s*, pp. 54–6. According to Fleischer the Germans not only signed a truce with Zervas but

The Greek Communist Party 205

also ordered a simultaneous assault on ELAS and the provisioning of EDES with war equipment. Fleisher's evidence seems to contradict Woodhouse's assertion (*Apple of Discord*, p. 168) that 'Greek resistance was diminished by the elimination of all the rivals to ELAS except EDES, which nearly succumbed to combined attacks of Aris Veloukhiotis and the Germans'. On the question of Zervas' collaboration with the Germans see also H. Richter, *1936–1946 Dyo Epanastaseis kai Antepanastaseis stin Ellada*, 2 vols (Athens, 1980), vol. II, pp. 53–5, and Sovetis, op. cit., pp. 315–16. Sovetis claims that during the Plaka negotiations 'Zervas himself repudiated the EDES Central Committee because of its collaboration'.

105 Woodhouse, *Apple of Discord*, Appendix F, pp. 303–4.
106 Sarafis, op. cit., pp. 244–60.
107 Woodhouse, *Apple of Discord*, op. cit., p. 179.
108 J. O. Iatrides, *Revolt in Athens, The Greek Communist 'Second Round' 1944–1945* (Princeton, NJ, 1972), p. 284.
109 Tsouderos, op. cit., p. 78.
110 ibid., p. 85.
111 Y. Andrikopoulos, *1944, Krisimi Chronia, 300 Anekdota Engrafa apo to Prosopiko Archeio Ouinston Tsorstil ya tin Ellada apo 8,3, eos 5,12, 1944* (henceforth cited as *BFOD*), 2 vols (Athens, 1974), vol. I, doc. 5, pp. 20–1.
112 ibid., Doc. 14, p. 38; Tsouderos, op. cit., p. 114.
113 *Keimena tis Ethnikis Antistasis*, 2 vols (Athens, 1981), vol. I, pp. 56–7.
114 *KKE Episima Keimena, 1940–1945* p. 373; V. Bouras, *I Politiki Epitropi Ethnikis Apeleftherosis: PEEA. Eleftheri Ellada 1944* (Athens, 1983), pp. 58–60.
115 Loulis, *The Greek Communist Party*, p. 97.
116 Ioannidis, op. cit., p. 221.
117 P. Rousos, *I Megali Pentaetia. I Ethniki Antistasi kai o Rolos tou KKE*, 2 vols (Athens, 1978), vol. II, p. 62.
118 Bouras, op. cit., p. 113.
119 Loulis, *The Greek Communist Party*, p. 97.
120 Tsouderos, op. cit., p. 121.
121 The best account of the crisis is provided by V. Nefeloudis, in his books *Ellines Polemistes sti Mesi Anatoli* (Athens, 1945) and *I Ethniki Antistasi sti Mesi Anatoli* 2 vols (Athens, 1981). See also H. Fleischer, 'The anomalies in the Greek Middle East forces, 1941–1944', *Journal of the Hellenic Diaspora*, Autumn 1978, pp. 5–36.
122 Churchill, op. cit., vol. V, p. 481. Emphasis mine.
123 Fleischer, op. cit., p. 31; Nefeloudis, *Ellines Polemistes*, pp. 61ff; For details see *BFOD*, vol. I, pp. 36, 65, 70–1, 88–9; 98–9, 108.
124 Leeper, op. cit., p. 47.
125 Fleischer, op. cit., p. 36.
126 Kousoulas, op. cit., p. 187; Churchill, op. cit., vol V, p. 478: 'they [the troops] are very liable to be contaminated by revolutionary and Communist elements there. Satan finds some mischief still for idle hands to do': Leeper, op. cit., p. 41.
127 Woodhouse (*Struggle for Greece*, p. 78) rightly notes that 'the theory that the mutinies in the Army and the Navy in April 1944 were organized by the Communists in order to keep them away from the scene of action at the time of liberation is implausible, not least because PEEA quickly disowned the mutineers'.
128 Iatrides, *Ambassador MacVeagh Reports*, p. 484 and entries dated 3, 4, 10, 15, 18 April 1944.
129 Nefeloudis, op. cit., p. 178; Rousos, op. cit., vol. II, pp. 77–80, 147; Sarafis, op. cit., p. 195.
130 Nefeloudis, *Ellines Polemistes*, pp. 85–114.
131 Iatrides, *Ambassador MacVeagh Reports*, p. 495; *BFOD*, vol. I, doc. 48, p. 83.
132 *BFOD*, vol. I, doc. 50, p. 86 and FO 371/43729 R6133; ibid., doc. 61, p. 102.

133 G. Papandreou, *I Apeleftherosis tis Ellados* (Athens, 1948), pp. 54–6.
134 Leeper to FO 371/43730 R 6763. Papandreou's anti-Communist views are contained in his pamphlet *The Third War*, written during the occupation and published in 1948.
235 Loulis, *The Greek Communist Party*, p. 125.
136 Iatrides, *Revolt in Athens*, pp. 57–8.
137 FO 371/43731 R 7995. PEEA was represented by its President Svolos and two of its secretaries, the socialists Angelopoulos and Askoutsis; EAM by its Communist secretary Porfyrogennis and its socialist central committee member Stratis; the KKE by the political bureau member Rousos and ELAS by its commander, Sarafis, in the role of 'advisory member' to the delegation.
138 Ioannidis, op. cit., pp. 220–1.
139 ibid., pp. 229–30.
140 Leeper, op. cit., p. 49.
141 As the EDES delegate Pyromaglou later caustically recalled (*I Ethniki Antistasis*, p. 122), 'we were assembled to hellenize the decisions of the British regarding Greece. Everyone, instead of formulating their positions according to a correct assessment of the Greek problem, wanted to know "what Leeper wants", before expressing their views'.
142 Papandreou, *I Apeleftherosis*, pp. 67–8.
143 FO 371/43731 R 8013, quoted in Laulis, op. cit., p. 129.
144 Papandreou, op. cit., pp. 69–70.
145 ibid., p. 68. In private, though, Papandreou tried to encourage EDES to attack and dissolve ELAS. When the EDES representative Pyromaglou commented that such an action would provoke a new civil war, Papandreou replied: 'then I will dissolve ELAS with the help of the British'. See Pyromaglou, *I Ethniki Antistasis*, p. 122.
146 Rousos, op. cit., vol. II, p. 128.
147 Papandreou, op. cit., pp. 73–80.
148 ibid., p. 76.
149 Papastratis, 'The Papandreou government and the Lebanon Conference', in *Greece in the 1940s*, p. 130.
150 V. Bartziotas, *I Politiki ton Stelechon*, p. 49.
151 FO 371/43731 R 8161 and FO 371/43732 R 8429. See also Rousos, op. cit., vol. II, p. 150 and 152.
152 Ioannidis, op. cit., pp. 232–3, 260; Rousos, op. cit., pp. 177–8.
153 *KKE Episima Keimena, 1940–1945*, pp. 406–7.
154 ibid., pp. 222–5. The KKE changed its stance probably after the Soviet Embassy in Cairo had advised Rousos that the KKE should join Papandreou's government.
155 Churchill, op. cit., vol. VI, p. 64.
156 ibid., p. 64.
157 ibid., p. 70.
158 FO 371/43772 R 12090; BFOD, vol. VI, p. 15.
159 Ioannidis, op. cit., pp. 250–2, 256–7.
160 *KKE Episima Keimena, 1940–1945*, p. 239; Iatrides, *Revolt in Athens*, p. 75.
161 Papandreou, op. cit., pp. 136–55.
162 Churchill, op. cit., vol. VI, p. 100.
163 *BFOD*, vol. I, doc. 95, pp. 149–50; doc. 106, pp. 184–5; doc. 165, pp. 387–9; vol. II doc. 177, pp. 30–2.
164 Macmillan, *The Blast of War: 1939–1945*, p. 575.
165 Sarafis, op. cit., p. 384. Ioannidis in his memoirs, op. cit., pp. 273–84, recalls that he and Siandos were horrified when they learned of the agreement's terms, especially the fact that a British officer, rather than a Greek one, had been appointed commander-in-chief of the Greek army. However, Ioannidis' account of what exactly happened in Caserta seems rather confused and it is clear that Zevgos, a Communist hard-liner, was

acting in accordance with the line laid down by the KKE leadership after the arrival of the Soviet military mission. See Zevgos's wife's testimony to the historian Papapanayiotou, in Ioannidis, op. cit., pp. 529–30.
166 Sarafis, op. cit., pp. 387–8.
167 The phrase belongs to the Communist Kostas Karageorgis (1906–53) who was a member of the central committee (from 1942) and editor-in-chief of *Rizospastis* (from November 1944). He too was denounced by Zachariadis in 1950 and died in detention.
168 Ioannidis, op. cit., pp. 288–90, 296–305.
169 For the Anglo-Soviet agreement of October 1944 see Churchill, op. cit., Vol. VI, pp. 197–9; S. Xydis, 'The secret Anglo-Soviet agreement on the Balkans of October 9, 1944', *Journal of Central European Affairs*, XV (October 1955), pp. 248–71; S. Xydis, 'Greece and the Yalta Declaration', *The American Slavic and East European Review*, XX (February, 1961), pp. 6–24; Barker, op. cit., pp. 140–7. The KKE even today claims officially that no such agreement was ever signed. The KKE historian, Yorgos Zoidis, told me in an interview that 'such an agreement could only have been signed between two imperialist powers; since the USSR was not an imperialist power, the agreement is Churchill's fabrication'. In other words, what should not have happened never happened. The percentage 'predominance' for the Russians and the 'others' in the other Balkan countries were: 90–10 in Rumania, 50–50 in Yugoslavia, 50–50 in Hungary and 75–25 in Bulgaria. See Churchill, op. cit., vol. VI, p. 198.
170 Ioannidis, op. cit., p. 291.
171 On 9 August 1944, the British Council of Ministers decided that the king should not return before the conduct of a plebescite. See *BFOD*, op. cit., vol. II, doc. 177, p. 32. Although Churchill initially was not in agreement with this decision (ibid., doc. 183, p. 46), by 29 September he had agreed with Eden's views on King George's return and thus the king lost his strongest ally (ibid., doc. 277, p. 122).
172 Woodhouse, *Struggle for Greece*, p. 112.
173 *Kathimerina Nea*, 27 October 1944.
174 ibid., 31 October 1944.
175 *Rizospastis*, 9 November 1944. In summoning the Third Brigade Papandreou evidently hoped to intimidate the Communists, as the (royalist) Brigade was well equipped, trained, and, more importantly, loyal to his government. Probably with the same thoughts in mind, Churchill minuted to Eden on 19 November (FO 371/49735 R 18580), that the Third Brigade 'are the only solid and apparently trustworthy Greek unit, and under no circumstances should they be broken up at the present time'. Woodhouse, however (*Apple of Discord*, p. 215), who knew the political climate far better than most British officials, categorically advised against bringing the Brigade to Greece because such a move, while serving no military purpose, would provoke EAM and contribute to its losing faith in the Papandreou government.
176 McNeill, op. cit., p. 129; *Rizospastis*, 19 November 1944.
177 Quoted in G. M. Alexander, 'The demobilization crisis of November 1944', in *Greece in the 1940s*, p. 158. See also Ioannidis, op. cit., p. 326. On 17 November Aris Velouchiotis summoned all the ELAS *Kapetanioi* to Lamia, where the ELAS HQ had been established, to discuss his proposal for an ELAS attack on Athens. However, since Aris was expressing his own views and not those of the KKE, the other *Kapetanioi*, and especially Vafiadis, rejected his initiative. See M. Vafiadis, *Apomnimonevmata*, vol. III (Athens, 1985), pp. 11–15.
178 Ioannidis, op. cit., p. 332. See also pp. 329–33.
179 Papandreou, op. cit., pp. 209–10.
180 Alexander, *The Demobilization Crisis*, op. cit., p. 164.
181 As McNeill, op. cit., p. 131, correctly observes. Siandos had great reservations about this plan. See Ioannidis, op. cit., pp. 332–3.
182 Ioannidis, op. cit., p. 332.

183 *Rizospastis*, 30 November 1944.
184 ibid.
185 Leeper, op. cit., pp. 97–8; McNeill, op. cit., p. 132; Byford-Jones, op. cit., pp. 130–3; Iatrides too (*Revolt in Athens*, p. 173) reaches the same conclusion. This version of events was also presented by Eden in the House of Commons, *Hansard* 406, cols 603–4.
186 Papandreou himself in his memoirs provides a copy of EAM's text which is identical with the one published in *Rizospastis*, on 30 November but different from the one he later submitted to the British and his non-EAM cabinet. See *Apeleftherosis*, pp. 209–10.
187 ibid., pp. 209–10.
188 Kousoulas, op. cit., p. 200.
189 ibid., pp. 200–1.
190 W. O. 204/8903 quoted in Alexander, 'The demobilization crisis of November 1944', op. cit., p. 165. This telegram fell into British hands.
191 Leeper, op. cit., p. 99. The Communists objected strongly to Scobie's orders because his power derived solely from the authority the Greek government had explicitly vested in him. In the absence of any such authorization from the government (although Papandreou approved of the move), Scobie had no right to act. Thus, Sarafis, op. cit., pp. 489–91 'refused to carry out Scobie's orders'.
192 Loulis' argument (*The Greek Communist Party*, pp. 170–1), that the two demobilization issues (of the Civil Guard and of ELAS) were separate ones, is hardly convincing since EAM and the KKE obviously didn't think so and neither did Papandreou and the British.
193 Leeper to Foreign Office, 1 December 1944, FO 371/43697 R 19802. On 26 November Papandreou was predicting that a resignation of the EAM ministers 'might mean the unleashing of civil war', FO 371/43735 R 19341.
194 At the EAM's central committee meeting of 1 December all its members approved Siandos' proposal for the resignation of the PEEA and the EAM ministers from the Papandreou government.
195 *Rizospastis*, 3 December 1944; Loulis, op. cit., p. 171, considers the resurrection of the central committee of ELAS as constituting a 'direct challenge to the government's authority over its own armed forces', because, 'ELAS was officially under the command of the government and Scobie as stipulated by the Caserta Agreement'. Although it is clear that by resurrecting the ELAS central committee the KKE was preparing for a clash (see Ioannidis, op. cit., pp. 341–4) this act was not in contravention of the Caserta Agreement. Since the PEEA and EAM ministers had resigned, the 'government of national unity' had ceased to exist. ELAS, as the army of EAM, could not therefore obey orders from a government that did not include EAM, or from General Scobie. The Caserta Agreement rested on the existence of a government of national unity.
196 McNeill, op. cit., p. 137; Papandreou's son, Andreas, in his book *Democracy at Gunpoint* (London, 1973), p. 58, maintains that Leeper changed his father's mind on the issue of the demonstration: 'Leeper then stepped in and demanded from the government a ban on the demonstration'.
197 There exists a number of eye-witnesss accounts of the *Dekemvriana*: McNeill, op. cit., pp. 137–42; Byford-Jones, op. cit., pp. 138–40. For a scholarly study of the events see L. Baerentzen, 'The demonstration in Syntagma Square on Sunday the 3rd of December 1944', *Scandinavian Studies in Modern Greek*, 2 (1978), pp. 3–52. See also L. S. Stavrianos, 'The immediate origins of the Battle of Athens', *American Slavic and East European Review*, VII (Dec. 1949), pp. 239–51; W. H. McNeill, 'The outbreak of fighting in Athens, December 1944', *American Slavic and East European Review*, VII (Dec. 1949).
198 Churchill, op. cit., vol. VI, p. 252.
199 ibid., p. 252.
200 ibid., p. 255; *FRUS*, 1944, vol. V, pp. 148–51.
201 ibid., p. 253.

202 *The Times, the Daily Herald, the Manchester Guardian,* all dated 9 December 1944. On 13 December the Trades Union Congress expressed with an outstanding majority – 2,455,000 votes against 137,000 – its regret at the policy of the British government in Greece.
203 Churchill, op. cit., vol. VI, p. 254.
204 Woodhouse, *Struggle for Greece,* p. 131.
205 *Documents Regarding the Situation in Greece,* January 1945, Cmd 6592, London, p. 11.
206 Ioannidis, op. cit., pp. 347–60.
207 Loulis, *The Greek Communist Party,* p. 176.
208 *FRUS,* vol. IV, pp. 150–1; Churchill, op. cit., vol. VI, pp. 261–2; Woodhouse, *Struggle for Greece,* p. 132; Iatrides, *Revolt in Athens,* pp. 210–30.
209 Leeper, op. cit., pp. 120–31.
210 Tsoukalas, op. cit., p. 90; D. Eudes, *The Kapetanios* (London, 1972), p. 222; *What We Saw in Greece: Report of the TUC Delegation* (London, 1945). The actual number of persons executed is of course a matter of controversy. For a different account see H. Richter, *British Intervention in Greece: From Varkiza to Civil War* (London, 1985), pp. 28–9 and fn.
211 For an English text of the Varkiza Agreement see Iatrides, *Revolt in Athesn,* pp. 320–4.
212 On the violation of the Varkiza Agreement see the two White Books published by EAM in 1945: *Lefki Vivlos: Paravaseis tis Varkizas Flevaris-Iounis 1945,* (Athens, June 1945, reprint, 1975); *Lefki Vivlos: 'Dimokratikos' Neofasismos Ioulis-Octovris 1945* (Athens, October 1945). For how Varkiza was applied, or rather not applied, to the civil service, see *Lefki Vivlos Flevaris-Iounis 1945,* p. 33.
213 This is an over-simplified account of one of the most controversial periods in Greek history. For a scholarly study of the strategy of the KKE during the 'third round' of the civil war see my unpublished doctoral thesis, 'The Greek Civil War: the Strategy of the Greek Communist Party 1944–1947' (Oxford, 1988). For quote see *Rizospastis,* 15 February 1945.
214 *KKE Episima Keimena, 1940–1945,* p. 425.
215 *KKE Episima Keimena, 1945–1949,* VI (Athens, 1987), p. 34.
216 *Rizospastis,* 5 June 1945.
217 *KKE Episima Keimena, 1945–1949,* pp. 34–5.
218 D. Yergin, *Shattered Peace,* (London, 1980), p. 291.
219 McNeill, op. cit., p. 199.
220 Something that Woodhouse (*Apple of Discord,* p. 32) himself admits.
221 See n. 216.
222 S. Sarafis, *Meta tin Varkiza* (Athens, 1979), p. 190.
223 ibid., pp. 210–11.
224 Minute by Hatyer, 21 February 1946; minute by McNeil, 1 March 1946; minute by Sargent, 21 February 1946 (FO 371/58676 R 3032). William Hayter was Head of the Southern Department of the British Foreign Office, 1945–1946. Hector McNeil was British Parliamentary Under-Secretary for Foreign Affairs. Sir Orme Sargent was Superintending Under-Secretary of the Southern Department of the British Foreign Office until 1946 and Permanent Under-Secretary of State for Foreign Affairs, 1946.
225 Although 40.3 per cent of the electorate failed to vote the AMFOGE report concluded that only 15 per cent did so for 'party reasons' and that 'had the Leftist parties taken part in the election this would not have altered the general outcome' (*Report of the Allied Mission to Observe the Greek Elections*) (London, HMSO, 1946), Cmd, 6812, pp. 20, 26, 31–2). This estimate as J. Campbell rightly observes ('The Greek Civil War', in E. Luard (ed.), *International Regulation of Civil Wars* (London, 1972), p. 46) was a 'wishful speculation'. The registers were admittedly incomplete, and the observers were unfamiliar with Greek electoral habits and certainly not impartial. This 'abstention' figure was derived from a sample consisting of 1,345 names. The fact, however, that many

people would have been very hesitant to express their real opinion for fear of reprisals was not even considered by AMFOGE. Despite, therefore, the intentions of some of the members of the AMFOGE, it is obvious that the mission could not have contradicted the established policy of their governments. One should not forget that the implicit aim of the mission was to 'legitimize' the policies of their governments in Greece. As Mavrogordatos notes ('The 1946 election and plebiscite: prelude to civil war', in *Greece in the 1940s*, p. 187), 'no matter what their factual findings were, it was inconceivable that they could have challenged the validity of the elections.

226 At the time of the Second Plenum, Dimitrios Partsalidis, leading an EAM delegation, was in Moscow meeting senior Soviet officials. The KKE leadership before taking a final decision on the question of the abstention wanted to know what 'advice' the Soviets had given Partsalidis. The issue of the 'advice' indeed became a crucial one. When Zachariadis during the Plenum put forward the proposal for boycotting the elections he met with strong opposition from a number of political bureau members, which included the Communists Siandos, Hatzis, Vafiadis, Tzimas, Zevgos, and Chrysa Chatzivasileiou. On the face of such an opposition Zachariadis proposed to postpone the decision on the boycott question until Partsalidis was back from Moscow. The 'advice' that Partsalidis in fact brought back from Moscow was that the Soviet authorities were in favour of the KKE and EAM participating in the elections. Zachariadis, however, chose to ignore the Soviet 'advice', and instead imposed his decision on the members of the political bureau. The central committee and the rest of the party were left with the impression that the Soviets too were in favour of abstention. See Partsalidis, *I Dipli Apokatastasi tis Ethnikis Antistasis* (Athens, 1978), p. 196; Vafiadis, *Apomnimonevmata*, pp. 133–4.

227 N. Zachariadis, *Deka Chronia Palis* (Athens, 1978), p. 21.

228 Up until the time of the Seventh Congress (October 1945) Zachariadis, in line with the resolutions of the Sixth Plenum of 1934 (see n. 18), was advocating a policy of peaceful integration into the parliamentary system. In Greece, despite the war, the occupation, the resistance and the 'December Events', the call for the immediate establishment of socialism was premature. At the Seventh Congress, though, the KKE leader questioned whether this policy was after all a realistic alternative, and urged the party 'to prepare the people for the eventuality that the transition to a popular democracy will have to be forced by all the means the people have at their disposal, even by crushing, should this prove necessary, the resistance of the monarchofascist, plutocratic minority'. Although 'popular democracy' was still presented as a 'third parliamentary alternative' (similar to that established in France), by February 1946 this aim had been abandoned and instead Zachariadis decided that the time had come for the KKE to complete the 'bourgeois revolution' achieved by the resistance. Somehow in Zachariadis' mind the bourgeois-democratic stage of development had been completed and the material preconditions had matured to the extent required for the KKE to launch a 'socialist revolution'. See *To Evdomo Synedrio tou KKE*, vol. VI (Athens, 1945), p. 65. Until the middle of 1947, however, the KKE leader did not allow an intensification of guerrilla activity in the mountains and took no measures to move party members from the towns to the mountains. Anxious to retain the comparative freedom provided by legality, Zachariadis refused to recognize Markos' army publicly or endorse his calls for an all-out revolt. Having placed his hopes on an 'urban revolution' and deeply suspicious of guerrilla leaders, which he saw as a threat to the monolithic structure of the party and his authority, Zachariadis throughout 1946 and early 1947 kept up the party's legal pretexts and hindered the development of Markos' forces. The American action in March 1947, however, left him with no choice but to join Markos' 'democratic army' in the mountains. Zachariadis finally left Athens in April 1947.

229 For the resolutions of the Third Plenum of September 1947, see, *KKE Archives*, *Avgi*, 3 January 1980, p. 241. From 2 December 1979 to 23 January 1980, the *KKE Esoterikou* (Eurocommunists) published in its daily newspaper, *Avgi*, a series of documents from its

archives related to the civil war. These documents contain among other things secret telegrams and memoranda which the KKE leadership exchanged with Stalin, Zdhanov, Tito, and Dimitrov. The documents shed a new light on the relationship between the KKE and the leadership of the Soviet, Yugoslav, and Bulgarian Communist parties and the policies the latter followed in Greece.

230 See M. Djilas, *Conversations with Stalin* (London, 1962). According to Djilas (p. 119), 'the Soviet Government took no direct action over the uprising in Greece practically leaving Yugoslavia to face the music alone in the United Nations, nor did it undertake anything decisive to bring about an armistice – not until Stalin found it to his interest'. In February 1948 at a meeting in Moscow between Stalin and the Yugoslav and Bulgarian Communist leaderships, the Soviet leader had this to say about the Greek civil war (p. 164): 'The uprising in Greece will have to fold up'. When Kardjeli demurred at Stalin's advice, arguing that the democratic army of Greece could still win 'if foreign intervention did not grow', Stalin replied: 'if, if! No, they have no prospect of success at all. What do you think, that Great Britain and the United States – the United States, the most powerful state in the world – will permit you to break their line of communication in the Mediterranean? Nonsense. And we have no navy. The uprising in Greece must be stopped, and as quickly as possible'. The documents published in *Avgi* contain powerful evidence to suggest that during the whole period of the civil war Stalin never moved to give more than a minimum of aid to the Greek Communists, despite the fact that in the early part of 1948 they had a real possibility of defeating the Greek government. Thus, at the peak of its strength, in the spring of 1948, the 'democratic army' was less than half the size contemplated at the Third Plenum (26,000 men), while the 'national army', with substantial American assistance, had by 1949 risen to 200,000 men. If one adds to this figure the numbers for the National Guard, the gendarmerie, the civil police, the navy and the airforce, it is obvious that, given the lack of support from Stalin, the KKE's 'revolution' was doomed almost from the very beginning. See *KKE Archives, Avgi* 9, 14, 19, 30 December 1979 and 12 January 1980. On Stalin's foreign policy see also W. O. McCagg *Stalin Embattled, 1943–1948* (Detroit, 1978); G. D. Ra'anan, *International Policy Formation in the USSR* (Hamden, Conn., 1983).

231 N. Zachariadis, *Deka Chronia Palis*, p. 41. Until the Zachariadis–Tito break in 1949, the 'democratic army' relied heavily on Yugoslav support. There is plenty of evidence to show that Tito's involvement in Greece was closely connected with his country's territorial aspirations in Greek Macedonia. Throughout the period of the civil war, the Yugoslavs continued to advertise publicly their interest in Greek Macedonia and Tito's price for his support of the 'democratic army' was the KKE's permission for an influx of military and political organizers from the Yugoslav Macedonian People's Republic, which naturally backed his annexationist plans. After the expulsion of Tito from the Cominform, Zachariadis gradually purged from the ranks of the 'democratic army' anyone who openly supported the Yugoslav leader. In July 1949 Tito closed his country borders to the 'democratic army', declaring once more that all parts of Macedonia should be united in one state, under Yugoslav sponsorship. On the involvement of Yugoslavia in the Greek civil war see E. Barker, *Macedonia: Its Place in Balkan Power Politics* (London, 1950); E. Kofos, *Nationalism and Communism in Macedonia* (Thessaloniki, 1964); E. Barker, 'Yugoslav policy towards Greece' and 'The Yugoslavs and the Greek civil war', in L. Baerentzen, J. O. Iatrides, O. L. Smith, *Studies in the History of the Greek Civil War 1945–49* (Copenhagen, 1987).

ABBREVIATIONS

AKE   Agrotiko Komma Ellados (Agrarian Party of Greece)
AMFOGE   Allied Mission for Observing Greek Elections

AMM	Allied Military Mission
AVNOJ	Antifasisticko Vece Naradnog Oslobodjenja Jugoslavije(Anti-Fascist Council of National Liberation)
BCF	Balkan Communist Federation
BLO	British Liaison Officer
BMM	British Military Mission
CPSU	Communist Party of the Soviet Union
DSE	Dimokratikos Stratos Ellados (Democratic Army of Greece)
EA	Ethniki Allilegyi (National Mutual Aid)
EAM	Ethniko Apeleftherotiko Metopo (National Liberation Front)
EDAM	Ethniko Dimokratiko Apeleftherotiko Metopo (National Democratic Liberation Front)
EDES	Ethnikos Dimokratikos Ellinikos Syndesmos (National Democratic Greek League)
EEAM	Ergatiko Ethniko Apeleftherotiko Metopo (Labour National Liberation Front)
EKKA	Ethniki kai Kinoniki Apeleftherosis (National and Social Liberation)
ELAS	Ethnikos Laikos Apeleftherotikos Stratos (National Popular Liberation Army)
ELD	Enosi Laikis Dimokratias (Union of Popular Democracy)
EP	Ethniki Politikofylaki (National Civil Guard)
EPON	Eniaia Panelladiki Organosi Neon (United Panhellenic Organization of Youth – EAM's youth movement)
ERGAS	Ergatikos Antifasistikos Syndesmos (Labour Anti-Fascist League)
FO	Foreign Office
GHQME	General Headquarters Middle East
GSEE	Geniki Synomospondia Ergaton Ellados (General Confederation of Greek Workers)
IDEA	Ieros Desmos Ellinon Axiomatikon (Sacred Bond of Greek Officers)
KKE	Kommounistikon Komma Ellados (Communist Party of Greece)
KOMEP	Kommounistiki Epitheorisi (Communist Review)
KUTV	Kommunisticheskii Universitet Trudyashcshya Vostoka (Communist University for Easter Workers)
OKNE	Omospondeia Kommounistikon Neolaion Elladas (Federation of Communist Youth of Greece)
PEEA	Politiki Epitropi Ethnikis Antistasis (Political Committee of National Liberation)
SEKE	Sosialistiko Ergatiko Komma Ellados (Socialist Labour Party of Greece)
SKE	Sosialistiko Komma Ellados (Socialist Party of Greece)
SOE	Special Operations Executive
UNRRA	United Nations Relief and Rehabilitation Administration
UNSCOB	United Nations Special Committee on the Balkans
WO	War Office

Appendix: Chronologies

COMINTERN

July 1935	The Comintern adopts the popular front strategy at the Seventh Congress.
March/April 1938	The ministerial crisis in Spain. Under Comintern pressure the Spanish Communist Party reduces its role in government and drops plans for revolutionary change. The popular front becomes a national front.
March 1939	Franco's victory in Spain. The Comintern launches an inquiry into the reasons for defeat. Togliatti criticized.
August 1939	Hitler–Stalin non-aggression pact.
September 1939	German–Soviet Friendship Treaty.
November 1939	Russo–Finnish War. Comintern line on 'imperialist' war. Britain and France held responsible. Catastrophic war would end in new socialist era. Popular fronts to be worked for 'from below'.
May/June 1940	Fall of France.
October 1940	Italian invasion of Greece.
Summer 1940	Baltic states and Bessarabia incorporated into USSR.
April 1941	German invasion of Yugoslavia. Comintern line shifts. Britain and Germany held jointly responsible for the war. New emphasis on the defence of small nations: could a 'national liberation' war lead to revolution?
June 1941	Germany invades USSR. Comintern returns to the popular front strategy. Yugoslav Communist Party launches national liberation war led by popular front 'from below', with socialist revolution the objective. Comintern supports these partisans.
August 1942	Churchill's visit to Moscow. The Comintern launches its anti-sectarian campaign and returns to the policy of national rather than popular fronts. Praise for partisans muted.
March 1943	Comintern praises French Communists for their national front policy.
May 1943	Comintern dissolved as hinderance to national front policy.
Spring 1947	Cold War erupts. Crises in post-war coalition governments. Britain appeals for help in containing Greek civil war.

214 Appendix

September 1947	Founding of the Cominform. The French and Italian Communist Parties criticized for opportunism. The Yugoslavs praised for their popular front 'from below'. No Soviet support for Yugoslav attitude on Greek civil war.
February 1948	USSR vetoes Yugoslav plans for Balkan Federation.
June 1948	Yugoslav Communists expelled from Cominform.

FRANCE

December 1920	Tours Congress. Birth of PCF.
6 February 1934	Attempted coup by right-wing Leagues.
27 July 1935	Pact of unity between PCF/SFIO.
April/May 1936	Popular Front electoral victory.
June 1936	Formation of Popular Front government led by Leon Blum.
March 1937	Fall of Blum's government.
November 1938	Daladier decree laws.
21 August 1939	Molotov–Ribbentrop agreement announced.
26 September 1939	Dissolution by government of the PCF.
20 March 1940	Reynaud replaces Daladier as prime minister.
10 May 1940	German tanks invade France.
16 June 1940	Pétain becomes prime minister.
22 June 1940	Armistice signed.
June/July 1940	PCF attempts unsuccessfully to obtain permission to publish *l'Humanité*.
10 July 1940	Assembly votes full powers to Pétain.
October 1940	Major sweep by Vichy police against Communists.
24 October 1940	Hitler–Pétain meeting at Montoire.
25 May 1941	PCF issues appeal for a National Front of Struggle for French Independence.
May/June 1941	Miners' strike in northern France.
22 June 1941	Germany invades USSR.
February 1942	Creation of the Francs-Tireurs Partisans.
11 November 1942	Germany occupies southern France.
February 1943	Creation of STO (Obligatory Labour Service).
May 1943	Dissolution of Communist International.
27 May 1943	Creation of the Conseil National de la Résistance.
3 June 1943	CFLN (Comité Français de Libération National) formed in Algiers.
April 1944	Communists join the CFLN.
June 1944	CFLN becomes 'Provisional Government of the French Republic'.
26 August 1944	De Gaulle enters Paris.
21 October 1945	PCF obtains 26.1 per cent of the vote in first post-war elections.
21 November 1945	De Gaulle forms government, with five PCF ministers.
10 November 1946	PCF obtains 28.6 per cent of the vote in legislative elections.
18 November 1946	Thorez, in *Times* interview, speaks of a 'French road to socialism'.
April/May 1947	Strikes at Renault over economic conditions.
4/5 May 1947	Prime minister Ramadier expels PCF ministers from the government.

ITALY

21 January 1921	Communist Party of Italy (PCI) formed out of the revolutionary current of Italian Socialist Party at Livorno Congress.
28 October 1922	King appoints Mussolini prime minister. March on Rome.

6 April 1924	General election. Fascists control nearly two-thirds of the seats in the Chamber of Deputies.
20–6 January 1926	Third Congress of PCI (Lyons Congress).
5 November 1926	Mussolini bans all opposition parties and trade unions. Introduction of internal exile (*confino*).
1927	Togliatti in Moscow becomes the general secretary of the PCI.
4 June 1928	Gramsci and other Communist Party leaders sentenced by Fascist courts to twenty years.
11 February 1929	Lateran Pacts signed between Church and Fascist state.
1936	Italian Communist Party's Garibaldi Brigades fight with the Internationals in the defence of the republic in the Spanish Civil War. Togliatti in Spain as political observer for the Comintern.
21 May 1939	Italy signs Pact of Steel with Germany.
10 June 1940	Italy enters the Second World War.
21 June 1940	Italy invades France.
13 September 1940	Italy joins Germany in north African offensive.
28 October 1940	Italy attacks Greece.
December 1940	Italian defeat in Libya.
Feb/April 1941	Italy loses Eritrea, Somalia, and Ethiopia. Germany rescues Italy in Greece.
June 1941	Mussolini decides to participate in the German invasion of the Soviet Union.
5 March 1943	Industrial strikes in Turin and the north.
10 July 1943	Allies invade Sicily.
25 July 1943	King dismisses Mussolini and appoints Marshall Badoglio as prime minister. 45-day government begins.
August 1943	Amnesty for political prisoners frees many Communist Party leaders.
3 September 1943	Allies cross to the mainland of Italy.
8 September 1943	Armistice between Italy and Allies announced. Germany invades and occupies Italy. King and government flee Rome for Allied–occupied south. Army capitulates to German forces.
9 September 1943	Committee of National Liberation (CLN) formed. Communists, Socialists, Christian Democrats, Liberals, members of the Action Party participate. First partisan groups form.
23 September 1943	Mussolini reinstated as head of new Fascist social republic, the Republic of Salò, in the north.
1 October 1943	Allies enter Naples after several days of popular insurrection.
November 1943	Mussolini introduces military conscription under the Republic of Salò. Draft evasion becomes common in the centre and north.
March 1944	Industrial strikes throughout the centre and north in protest against the war. Communist Party plays important organizational role.
13 March 1944	USSR recognizes Badoglio government in southern Italy.
27 March 1944	Togliatti returns to Italy and announces the *svolta* at Salerno.
21 April 1944	Second Badoglio cabinet forms and PCI enters government.
4 June 1944	Rome liberated by the Allies.
9 June 1944	Bonomi government forms; PCI continues in government.
June 1944	Partisans establish first 'free' zones in central and northern Italy.
August 1944	Florence liberated by Allies.
November 1944	Allied advance halts for the winter. Germans prepare Gothic Line defences and carry out reprisals against partisan divisions.
December 1944	Second Bonomi government forms. Togliatti as the PCI representative appointed one of two vice-premiers.

216 *Appendix*

19–25 April 1945	Popular insurrections led by partisans in the north of Italy. Allied liberation follows.
28 April 1945	Mussolini captured and executed by partisans.
19 June 1945	Parri government representing CLN parties forms in Rome. Togliatti is Minister of Justice; PCI Minister of Finance.
10 December 1945	Parri government falls and replaced by coalition led by Christian Democrat De Gasperi.
December 1945	PCI's Fifth Party Congress. Membership at over 1.75 million.
March–April 1946	Local elections in Italy reveal strength of Communist and Socialist Parties in the centre and north.
9 May 1946	King Victor Emmanuel III abdicates in favour of his son, Umberto II.
2 June 1946	Institutional referendum and elections to the constituent assembly. Republic defeats Monarchy 54 per cent to 46 per cent. King leaves Italy for exile.
10 June 1946	Italian Republic declared. Umberto II leaves Italy for exile.
21 June 1946	Togliatti announces amnesty for Fascists.
3–17 January 1947	De Gasperi visits the United States.
20 January–3 February 1947	Crisis in the governing coalition.
26 March 1947	Communist Party supports Article 7 of the Constitution, retaining 1929 Lateran Pacts as the basis for church and state relations in the Republic.
31 May 1947	De Gasperi excludes Communists and Socialists from his fifth government.
1 January 1948	New Constitution enters into effect.
18 April 1948	National Elections. Christian Democrat victory with nearly 48 per cent of the popular vote. Democratic Popular Front (FDP) of Communists and Socialists fails to reach 1946 levels.
14–16 July 1948	Spontaneous general strike in the north follows attempted assassination of Togliatti.

YUGOSLAVIA

1 December 1918	Proclamation of the Kingdom of Serbs, Croats, and Slovenes.
20–23 April 1919	Foundation Congress of Socialist Workers' Party of Yugoslavia (Communist); renamed Communist Party of Yugoslavia (KPJ) June 1920.
28 November 1920	Elections for Yugoslav constituent assembly.
30 December 1920	*Obznana* restricts KPJ operations.
28 June 1921	Enactment of unitary *Vidovdan* constitution.
2 August 1921	KPJ outlawed.
November 1928	Fourth (Dresden) Congress: KPJ adopts programme for destruction of Yugoslav state.
6 January 1929	King Alexander proclaims personal dictatorship; KPJ calls for uprising.
3 October 1929	Kingdom renamed Yugoslavia.
9 October 1934	King Alexander assassinated in Marseilles.
24–5 December 1934	Fourth conference (Ljubljana): KPJ backpedals on separatism.
June 1935	Central Committee Plenum (Split): KPJ embraces popular front and Yugoslav integrity.
August 1937	Tito assumes provisional leadership of KPJ in Paris.
March 1938	Tito repatriates central committee.

Chronologies 217

January 1939	Comintern confirms Tito as KPJ general secretary.
26 August 1939	*Sporazum* establishes autonomous Croatia.
25 June 1940	Establishment of Soviet–Yugoslav diplomatic relations.
19–23 October 1940	Fifth Conference (Zagreb): KPJ celebrates its revival and plots revolutionary strategy.
28 October 1940	Italy invades Greece: war comes to the Balkans.
25 March 1941	Yugoslavia adheres to Tripartite Pact.
27 March 1941	Belgrade *coup d'état* installs King Peter and challenges Hitler.
6 April 1941	Germany invades Yugoslavia and Greece.
10 April 1941	Independent State of Croatia (NDH) proclaimed; KPJ vows to continue struggle.
17 April 1941	Yugoslavia capitulates.
Early May 1941	Central Committee Consultation (Zagreb): revolution through war; Mihailović sets up četnik headquarters on Ravna Gora.
Early June 1941	Spontaneous risings in NDH.
22 June 1941	Germany invades USSR: KPJ summons Yugoslavs to the aid of Soviets.
1 July 1941	Comintern orders KPJ to begin partisan warfare.
13 July 1941	Montenegrin uprising.
August 1941	Serbian uprising.
18 September 1941	Tito takes command of Partisan forces in Serbia; meets Mihailović next day.
26–7 September 1941	Politburo Consultation (Stolice): KPJ resolves to promote nationwide uprising; political struggle to be waged through people's liberation committees.
Early November 1941	Civil war in Serbia: Mihailović seeks Germans' help against Communists.
Late November 1941	Partisans expelled from Serbia.
7 December 1941	KPJ Politburo decides at Drenova to wage class war.
5 March 1942	Comintern queries KPJ tactics and strategy.
4–6 April 1942	KPJ repudiates class war in favour of all-national liberation struggle.
June–August 1942	Partisans' 'long march' westwards across Bosnia.
26–7 November 1942	Inaugural meeting of Anti-Fascist Council of Peoples' Liberation of Yugoslavia (AVNOJ) in Bihać.
January–June 1943	Axis offensives *Weiss* and *Schwarz* fail to destroy partisan movement.
Early March 1943	Tito explores armistice with Germans; partisans defeat četniks in Hercegovina and Montenegro.
April–May 1943	First British missions reach partisans.
September 1943	Partisans reap benefits of Italian surrender.
28–9 November 1943	Second session of AVNOJ (Jajce) proclaims provisional government and prohibits return of King Peter.
January 1944	Churchill begins efforts to unite King Peter and Tito.
May 1944	Last British missions leave Mihailović; German assault on Drvar forces Tito to leave mainland for island of Vis.
16 June 1944	Tito and Šubašić agree on Vis to form united royal–AVNOJ government.
12 August 1944	Tito meets Churchill in Italy.

218 *Appendix*

18 September 1944	Tito flies to Rumanian front and Moscow to arrange entry of Red Army and confer with Stalin.
9 October 1944	Churchill–Stalin 'percentages' agreement.
20 October 1944	Belgrade liberated in Red Army–partisan operation.
7 March 1945	Tito–Šubašić government installed in accord with Yalta decisions.
Early May 1945	Race for Trieste and confrontation in Carinthia between Yugoslavs and Anglo-Americans; Yugoslavia liberated.
11 November 1945	Yugoslav elections return KPJ's People's Front unopposed.
29 November 1945	Yugoslavia becomes a Federative People's Republic.
31 January 1946	Yugoslavia adopts a Soviet-style constitution.
28 June 1948	Yugoslavia expelled from the Cominform.

GREECE

1914	Outbreak of World War I. Britain annexes Cyprus. Bitter quarrel between King Constantine and Premier Venizelos over Greek foreign policy.
1916	Venizelos sets up insurrectionary government in Salonica.
1917	Greece joins the Entente. King Constantine forced into exile.
1918	Armistice. SEKE formed.
1920	King Constantine recalled by popular acclaim.
1921	Greek offensive in Asia Minor.
1922	Turkish national forces led by Kemal defeat the Greek army. Massacre in Smyrna. Constantine abdicates and his elder son George II becomes king.
1923	Treaty of Lausanne. Greece gives up all claims to territory in Asia Minor. Exchange of populations.
1924	Greece becomes a republic. SEKE changes its name to KKE.
1925	General Pangalos establishes a dictatorship.
1926	Pangalos overthrown, and republic restored.
1928	Venizelos becomes premier again. He stays in power until 1933.
1931	Nikos Zachariadis appointed by Comintern secretary of KKE.
1933	Popular Party (royalists) win elections. Plastiras' republican *coup* fails.
1935	Second republican *coup* put down after some days of fighting in Athens and Macedonia. Extensive purge of Greek army favouring royalists. King George called back by extensively rigged plebiscite.
1936	New elections result in parliamentary deadlock between republicans and royalists. The king appoints General John Metaxas, leader of a small Fascist party, premier. Metaxas dissolves Parliament and establishes dictatorship. Zachariadis and most members of political bureau arrested.
1939	Outbreak of Second World War.
1940	Italy declares war on Greece, but after initial successes Italian troops driven back inside Albanian territory.
1941	British troops land in Greece but too weak to oppose German invasion. Greek army of Epirus surrenders. General Tsolakoglou becomes quisling prime minister while King George and cabinet headed by Premier Tsouderos flee to Cairo. Famine in Greece, winter 1941–2. KKE forms EAM and its army ELAS. Zervas with the help of the British forms EDES. Kartalis forms EKKA.
1942	Destruction of Gorgopotamos Bridge marks the arrival of British military mission in Greece. First important act of resistance.

Chronologies 219

1943 Rapid growth of EAM/ELAS. British work to unite all guerrilla armies under one command. 'Military Agreement' signed. Italian surrender strengthens ELAS. Failure of Cairo Mission and outbreak of large-scale civil war between ELAS and EDES. British cut all their links with EAM/ELAS.

1944 'Plaka Agreement' ends 'first round' of civil war between EAM/ELAS and EDES (February). EAM forms PEEA (March). Provisional government of Mountains challenges legality of Cairo government-in-exile. Mutiny in the Greek armed forces in the Middle East (April). Lebanon Conference (May). Papandreou forms a government of national unity. EAM after initial hesitation agrees to join the government (August). Government transferred to Italy (September). 'Casserta Agreement' signed. The government returns to liberated Athens (October). EAM ministers resign over the issue of demobilization of guerrilla armies (2 December). Demonstration at Syntagma Square leads to bloodshed (3 December). Outbreak of civil war, with British supporting the Right. Churchill flies to Athens (25 December).

1945 Archbishop Damaskinos appointed regent and Plastiras becomes premier. ELAS signs armistice (10 January). 'Varkiza Agreement' ends 'second round' of civil war (February). ELAS dissolved. 'White terror'. Plastiras resigns (April), succeeded by Voulgaris, who resigns in October. Impasse. Regent premier for a few days, succeeded by Kanellopoulos (October) and Sofoulis (November). McNeil's intervention. Preparation for elections. KKE's Eleventh Plenum (April), Twelfth Plenum (June), and Seventh Congress (October). Zachariadis found alive in Dachau resumes leadership of KKE (May).

1946 Elections 31 March return royalist majority. KKE, EAM, and parties of the Left abstain. Tsaldaris becomes premier. 'White terror' intensifies. Plebiscite results in return of King George (September). KKE forms the Democratic Army of Greece. 'Third round' of civil war.

1947 'Truman Doctrine' (March). King George dies (April), succeeded by his brother Paul. Under American pressure a new government formed under Sofoulis (September). A joint Greek–American General Staff formed (November). KKE announces the formation of a 'provisional government' in the mountains (December).

1948 General Van Fleet arrives in Athens as commander of the Joint US Military Advisory and Planning Group (February). Stalin orders leaderships of Bulgarian and Yugoslav Communists parties to stop assisting Greek Communists (February). Tito–Stalin break and expulsion of Yugoslavia from Cominform (June). Bitter fighting between democratic army and Greek national army. Greece becomes a key battleground in the Cold War.

1949 KKE sides with Moscow in Tito's quarrel with Stalin. Yugoslavia closes its frontiers to the democratic army (July). The democratic army cornered and defeated (August). Guerrillas flee to eastern Europe and Soviet Union.

1956 Zachariadis deposed.

Notes on contributors

TONY R JUDT is Professor of History at New York University. He studied at Cambridge University and has taught at the University of California, Berkeley, and at St Anne's College, Oxford. His books include *La Reconstruction du Parti Socialiste 1921–1926, Socialism in Provence 1871–1914* and *Marxism and the French Left*, and he has also published articles on the history of East-Central Europe in the twentieth century. He is presently preparing a study of the East European political trials of the Stalinist years.

GEOFFREY SWAIN studied at Sussex University and at the London School of Economics, and he is presently Lecturer in European History at Bristol Polytechnic. His doctoral research into the pre-1917 Bolshevik Party has been published in a number of articles and in the monograph, *Russian Social Democracy and the Legal Labour Movement, 1906–1914*. His article in this collection forms part of a series of studies on various aspects of the history of the Communist International.

LYNNE TAYLOR has studied at the London School of Economics and is at the University of Michigan, where she is currently completing a doctoral thesis on northern France under the German occupation.

DAVID TRAVIS studied at Trinity Hall, Cambridge, where he did doctoral research on Communism in Modena during and after the resistance. He has been a Junior Research Fellow at St Anne's College, Oxford, and an Assistant Professor of History at the University of Washington. His current research is on political movements in contemporary Italy.

HARIS VLAVIANOS obtained his B.Sc. (Economics) from the University of Bristol and M.Phil and D.Phil (International Relations) from the University of Oxford. His doctoral thesis is a study of the strategy of the Greek Communist Party during the period of resistance and the civil war. He is currently preparing an article on the causes of the defeat of the democratic army of Greece and a biography of Nikos Zachariadis, the leader of the KKE 1931–56. He has also published four books of poetry and two books with translations of the works of Walt Whitman, Geoffrey Hill,

Philip Larkin, Robert Graves, and Ezra Pound. His poetry has been translated into English and has appeared in various magazines and anthologies.

MARK WHEELER was educated at the Universities of Michigan and Cambridge and now teaches Balkan history at the School of Slavonic and East European Studies in the University of London. He is the author of *Britain and the War for Yugoslavia, 1940–1943* and a contributor to *Diplomacy and Intelligence during the Second World War: Essays in Honour of F. H. Hinsley* (edited by Richard Langhorne). He is currently at work on the history of the British Special Operations Executive in Yugoslavia.

Index

Abwehr 136
Action Party (Italy) 87, 89, 93, 99, 101
Adereth, M. 55, 60
AKE (Agrarian Party of Greece) 169
Akronafplia (prison) 164–5, 167, 169
Albania 1, 12–13, 47–8, 86, 112
  (Communist Party of), 114, 122, 124,
  133, 151
Alexander, General 94, 190
Alexander, King of Yugoslavia 113, 115
Alexandria 180
Algiers 73
Allies 5 (landing in N. Africa), 89 (Italian
  campaign), 91 (policy in Italy), 94
  (liberation of Rome by), 97 (post-war
  presence in Italy), 106 (occupation of
  Italy)
Alsace-Lorraine 56, 68
AMFOGE 195
Amouroux, H. 57, 59, 63, 67
Anarchists, in Spanish Civil War 10
Anglo-Soviet percentages agreement 184
Aniche mining strike, 1941 70
Anschluss 120
Appenine mountains 89 (Resistance in),
  95
Aragon, L. 57
Athens 14, 20, 165–6, 168 (German entry
  into, 1941), 181, 186–7, 189–92 (Battle
  of, December 1944), 195
Austria 8, 29 (German occupation of), 34,
  43, 95, 116 (Communist Party of), 128
Austro-Hungarian Empire 12
l'Avant-Garde 63
AVNOJ 43, 46, 146, 148 (meeting at Jajce,
  November 1943), 149 178

Bačka, Hungarian occupation of 126
Badoglio, Marshall P. 6, 86–9, 92–4
Bakintzis, Colonel 178
Balkan Federation 14, 19, 48, 116
Balkan Question 4
Balkans 1, 4, 6, 9, 10, 12–14, 36–7, 42, 43,
  65, 120, 124, 127–8, 161–2, 173
Ballanger, R. 66
Baltic states 9, 24, 35–6
Banat 124
Barbarossa *see* USSR, Nazi invasion of
Bastille Day 1944, demonstration on 75
Bauer, O. 8
BCF 157
Bédarieux 70
Belgium 5, 17 (Communist Party of), 23,
  54, 56, 59
Belgrade 112, 122–4, 126, 129–31,
  149–50, 188
Beneš, E. 24
Bessarabia 36, 120 (Soviet seizure of)
Bevin, E. 195
Bihać 145–6
Billoux, F. 63, 73
Blum, L. 5, 11, 22, 63
Bologna 90, 94
Bolshevik Revolution *see* October
  Revolution
Bonomi, I. 94
Bordeaux 66
Bosnia 2, 110–51
Bouches du Rhône 63
Bread and Wine 83
Britain 12, 14 (support for Greek
  monarchy), 19–20, 29–30, 33–5, 44, 122
  (interests in Greece), 123 (policy in

Britain—*continued*
  Yugoslavia), 134–8 (contacts with Mihailović), 141 (intelligence mission to Yugoslavia), 143 (help to cetniks), 147 (mission to Tito), 149, 170 (military mission to Greece), 172–7 (policy in Greece), 195
Brittany 66–7
Bukovina 36, 120 (Soviet seizure of)
Bulgaria 1, 11–14, 19, 24, 35, 39, 43, 47–8, 122, 124, 151, 161, 184
Buxières-les-Mines 70

Cahiers du bolchévisme 63–4
Cairo *see* Egypt
Calabria 82
Casado, General 31–3
Caserta Agreement 185–6
Catalonia 32–3
Catelas, J. 60
Ceretti, G. 46
Ce Soir 54
cetniks 43, 111, 128–9, 133, 136–7, 139–43, 145, 147, 149–50
CFLN 73
CFTC 74–5
CGIL 94, 98, 105
CGT 54–5, 74–5
Chevigne, P. de 59
China 23
Christ Stopped at Eboli 83
Churchill, W. S. 4, 14 (meeting with Stalin, 1944), 41 (meeting with Stalin, 1942), 47, 148–9, 150 (meeting with Stalin, 1944), 172–8, 180–1, 184, 186, 189–91, 193
Claudin, F. 29, 32
CLN 89, 94, 99, 101–2, 104
Clogg, R. 176
Clissold, S. 121
CNF 72
CNR 74
Cold War 22–3 (historiography), 30, 103–4, 197–8
COMAC 74
Combat 73
Cominform 4, 17–18, 23, 29–30, 46, 48, 104, 111, 197
Comintern 1, 2 (dissolution of), 3, 7–8, 10, 13, 15 (dissolution of), 16, 17 (7th Congress), 18, 20, 29–48, 81, 84–6, 93, 110–11, 113–14, 115 (6th Congress), 116, 117 (7th Congress), 118–22, 126, 130–1, 133, 137–8, 140–1, 143, 145–7 (dissolution of), 157–9, 160 (7th Congress), 165–8
comités populaires 58
concentration camps 34; *see also* Dachau
Connor, W. 114, 127
Constantine I, King 161
Constantinople *see* Istanbul
Corfu 151 (channel), 164, 166
Cortes 31, 33
Cot, P. 57
Courrières 70 (mining strike, 1941)
Courtois, S. 61, 69
CPSU 33 (politburo), 46, 104, 120, 141
Crete 168 (German capture of), 187
Croatia 12–13, 19, 43 (Peasant Party), 111–51
Cunningham, Admiral 180
Cvetković, D. 119, 121–2
Czechoslovakia 4, 6, 7, 9, 11, 18 (1948 coup), 23 (1948 coup), 24, 32, 34, 43, 44 (resistance in), 110, 119

Dachau 170, 179, 193
Daix, P. 65
Daladier, E. 53–6, 59, 63
Dalmatia 143
Dangon, M. 59
Darlan, Admiral F. 73
DC (Christian Democrat Party of Italy) 87, 93, 99–101, 103–4, 106
Debarge, C. 66
Dedijer, V. 141
Delgado, C. 35
Damaskinos, Archbishop 176, 190, 194
democratic centralism 4
Denmark 5, 35–6
Diaz, P. 31–3, 41, 46
Diermitor (mount) 110
Dimitrov, G. 1, 20, 29–30, 34–6, 38–46, 48, 111, 118–19, 123, 150, 165
Djilas, M. 120, 126, 130–2, 136, 139–42, 146–7
'Dolomite declaration' 144
Dourges 70 (mining strike, 1941)
Drossier, M. 61
Duclos, J. 15, 54, 57–8, 62–3

EA 169
EAM 161–94, 196
EDAM 171
Eden, A. 149, 174, 176–8, 184, 190
EDES 171–5, 177–8, 186–8, 190
EEAM 169
Egypt 168, 170, 173–5, 176 (Cairo Conference, 1943), 178–81, 185
Ehrlich, B. 59, 67
EKKA 171–2, 174–5, 177–8, 182
ELAS 169, 171–7, 179–80, 182–93
ELD 169
Emilia-Romagna 90, 101, 105
Epirus 190
Eritrea 181
Eurocommunism 48

Finland 35, 65
Finno-Soviet war 35
First International 45
First World War 2, 7–8, 12, 35, 37, 80, 161
Fischer, E. 30, 35, 45
Florence 90, 94
FN 71. 73
Foča 110, 140–1
Fourcaud, Captain 68
Frachon, B. 55, 57
La France au travail 60
Franco, F. 32
Franco-Soviet alliance (1935) 29
Francs-Tireurs 73
Frenay, H. 68
Fried, E. 54
Fronte democratico popolare 103
Frunze military academy 36
FTP 71, 74–5

Gard 70
Gasperi, A. de 100, 103
Gaulle, Charles de 5, 15, 36, 42, 64–5, 72–5
Gaullists 5; *see also* Gaulle, Charles de
Genoa 90
George II, King of Greece 162, 168, 172–3, 178–9, 195
German–Soviet Friendship Treaty (29 September 1939) 34
Gillolin, D. 59
Giraud, General G. 73
Glezos, M. 169
Glinos, D. 169

Gorkić, M. 117–18
'Gothic line' 94
Gramsci, A. 20–1, 82
Grand Alliance 45
Greco-Turkish war 7, 158–9
Grenier, F. 42, 72–3
Gross, J. T. 24
GSEE 194
Guingouin, G. 66–7
Gypsies (persecution of, in Croatia) 124

Havez, A. 66–7
Henaff, E. 71
Hérault 70
Héring, General 57
Hitler, A. 1, 3, 8, 22, 30, 32, 34, 36, 44, 61, 63–4, 86, 110, 112, 118, 122–3, 124 (Yugoslav policy), 125, 127, 129, 134, 138–9
Homolje massif 130
HSS (Croat Peasant Party) 119, 122, 132, 138, 143
l'Humanité 54, 59–60, 63, 65, 67, 70–1
Hungary 4, 6, 8–9, 11–12, 18, 23, 104

IDEA 192
IMRO 114, 117
'Institutional Question' (in Italy) 100–1
Ioannides, Y. 164–5, 184–6
Istanbul 120, 158, 161
Istria 126

Jews 5, 124 (persecution of, in Croatia)
Jovanović, D. 128

Kalodikis, S. 165
Kanakis, C. 164
Karas, S. 167
Kardelj, E. 110, 130, 135–6, 138–9
Kanellopoulos, P. 194
KEE 173
Kemal, Mustafa 161
KIM 45
KKE 157–98
Koestler, A. 10
Kolarov, V. 39
Kondylis, General 162
Kopinić, J. 129, 131, 137, 140
Koryzis, A. 168
Kosovo 120, 124, 126 (Albanian seizure of), 150
KPJ 13, 19, 38, 40, 43–4, 110–51

Kragujevac 134
Kraljevo 134
Kremlin 2, 17
Kruschev, N. 104
Ktistakis, V. 164

Langevin, P. 65
Lateran Pacts 102–3
Laval, P. 5, 61, 71, 72
Lebanon Agreement (1944) 182–3, 185
Leclerc, General P. 75
Lecoeur, A. 66, 70–1
Leeper, R. 173, 175–8, 180–2, 187–90
Lenin 7, 35, 37–8, 61, 81, 142
leninism 7, 18, 159
Leonhard, W. 44–5
Lescure, F. de 65
Levi, C. 83
Liberal Party (Italy) 99
Libération 73
Libya 181
Lidice 5
Liguria 90
Limousin 66
Ljubljana 116, 125
Lombardy 90, 101, 105
Longo, L. 21
Loulis, J. C. 188
Lux Hotel (Moscow) 46
Luxemburg, R. 7, 37
Lyon 84 (Third Congress of PCI)

Maclean, F. 148
MacVeagh, Ambassador 190
Macedonia 13–14, 35, 39, 114–51, 159–61, 166
Maček, V. 119, 121–2, 132
Macmillan 185, 190
Madrid 32
Malenkov, G. 47
Malraux, A. 10
Maniadakis, C. 164–8, 188
Mansion, J. 68
Manuilsky, D. 30, 36
Marchais, G. 22
Marshall Aid 23, 30, 47, 103
Marty, A. 10–11, 54
Marx, K. 45
Marxism 13, 20, 97, 102
Metaxas, General J. 159–60, 162–72, 180, 192, 194

Michailidis, Y. 164, 166, 168
Michel, H. 61
Michelet, E. 68
Mihailović, D. 111, 128, 130, 132–8, 140, 144–5, 147–50
Milan 86, 90
Miletić, P. 118
Moch, J. 24
Modena 91
Molotov, V. 65, 111, 149
Molotov–Ribbentrop Pact, August 1939 *see* Nazi–Soviet Pact
Montefiorino, Republic of 91
Montenegro 13, 110–51
Mortimer, E. 57, 60
Monzie, A. de 57
Moscow 8, 10, 16, 18, 33, 35, 43–4, 46, 48, 53, 55, 59, 63, 81, 83, 110–11, 114, 118–19, 123, 129–32, 137–8, 141–3, 145, 147, 149–51, 185–6
Munich 32, 53–4, 119
Mussolini, B. 6, 16, 38, 54, 63, 80–2, 84–90, 93, 95, 97, 99–101, 122, 165
Myers, Brigadier 170, 173–6

Naples 88 (liberation of, 1943), 89, 148
NATO 23
Nazi–Soviet Pact 2, 10, 18, 30, 33–6, 47, 53–4, 61–2, 64–5, 71, 85, 119, 165
NDH 123–5, 129, 132, 134, 137
Nedić, General M. 125, 136
Nelefoudis, V. 163, 166, 181
Negrin, J. 31, 33
Neretva, battle of 147
Netherlands 5
NKVD 30, 118, 120, 129
Noguères, H. 61
Nord 56, 66–7, 70
North Africa (Allied landings, 1942) 73
Norway 5, 36, 65
Nova Varoš 138–9
November decrees 54
Novikov, N. V. 181

October Revolution 42, 136, 147
Osvobodilna Fronta 135, 138–9, 144
Official History of the KKE 154, 166
OKNE 166–7
OPLA 179
Orwell, G. 10
Ottoman Empire *see* Turkey

Ouzoulias, A. 71

Pannequin, R. 67
Papagos, General A. 162
Papandreou, G. 169, 180–9
Papayannis, D. 163–4
Paris 16, 56–9, 61, 67–8, 74–5, 83, 118–19, 161 (Peace Conference, 1919)
Parri, F. 99, 101–2
Partsaldis, D. 163, 189
Pas de Calais 56, 66, 70
Paul, M. 66, 67
Paul, Prince Regent 122
Pavelić, A. 123–4, 137, 144
PCF 5, 11, 15, 22, 39, 47, 53–76, 119
PCI 17, 21, 39, 42–3, 80–107, 116
PEEA 178–85, 187–8
People's democracies 30
Péri, G. 64
Pétain, P. 5, 56, 61, 63, 71, 73
Peter II, King 122–3, 128, 145, 147–9
Petranović, B. 142
Pieck, W. 34, 36, 118
Piedmont 90, 101, 105
Pijade, M. 110, 140–1
Piraeus 169, 190–1
Pius XII *see* Vatican
PKE/OCC 164–5
Plaka Bridge (February 1944 agreement) 177–8
Plastiras, General N. 161–2, 190, 193
Pleterski, J. 115
Ploumbidis, N. 163
Poland 1–6, 8–9, 11, 13, 18 (Communist Party of), 19, 21 (martial law, 1981), 23–4, 34, 46, 151
Politzer, G. 56–7
Popov, Colonel 184–5, 190
Popović, V. 130
Popular Front 8, 11, 15, 29–32, 34–5, 40–1, 45, 54, 115–19, 160
POUM 10
Proleter 120, 142, 146
Psarros, Colonel 171, 182
PSI 81–2 (Livorno Congress, 1921), 99, 101, 103

Radio Free Milan 44, 46
Radio Free Yugoslavia 137, 145
Rajk, L. 11
Ravna Gora 134

Red Army 2, 7, 35, 40, 111–12, 121, 127–8, 130–1, 138–9, 144, 149–50
Reggio-Emilia 91
Reynaud, P. 56–7, 63
Ribar, I.-L. 110
Ribbentrop, J. von 36, 37 (meeting with Molotov, November 1940)
Rimini (capture of, 1944) 181
Riom trial 22, 63
Rizospastis 164, 167, 188, 193
Roche, P. 67
la Rochelle 67
Rogatica 140
Rol-Tanguy, H. 67, 75
Romagon, M. 67
Rome 88–9, 94 (liberation of)
Roosevelt, F. D. R. 175–6, 190
Rossi, A. 57, 60, 63
Rouen 68
Rousos, P. 182, 185
Royan 61
Rumania 7, 9, 11–12, 19, 24, 35–6, 122, 130, 184
Russia 7, 12; *see also* USSR

St Etienne 70
Saló, Republic of 5, 6, 88–90
Salonica 161, 163, 169
Salerno, *svolta* of 16, 92–4
Sandžak 137–8, 148
Sarraut, A. 54
Šatarov-Šarlo, M. 121, 126
Sauckel, F. 71–2
Schrocht, J. 59
Scobie, General 185, 187–9, 191
Second International 41, 157
SEKE 157
Serbia 12–13, 113–51
Sèvres, Treaty of 161
SFIO 63, 74
Shoup, P. 121, 144
show trials 11 (France), 117 (Moscow)
Siandos, G. 163–5, 179, 183, 185–8, 192–3
Siberia 44
Sikorski, General 149
Silone, I. 83
Simović, General D. 122–3
Skafidas, G. 163–4
SKE 169
Sklavenas 163

SKOJ 117, 134, 138
Slánsky, R. 11
Slovakia 7, 13, 34–5, 40 (Communist Party of), 42
Slovenia 12, 35, 113–51
Smyrna 161
Snow, E. 126
SOE 169, 172–4, 177
Sofoulis, T. 194–7
Sofranopoulos, J. 163
Somme 57
Soviet Union *see* USSR
Spain 1, 9, 11–12, 24, 29, 30–1, 39, 42, 47
Spanish Civil War 3, 9 (importance of), 10, 29, 31–4, 46–7, 84, 85 (Garibaldi Brigades), 90–5 (Garibaldi Brigades), 118 (Yugoslav volunteers)
Spanish revolution 11, 29; *see also* Spanish Civil War
Split 117
Spriano, P. 29
Srebrenjak-Antonov, I. 129
Srem 124
Stalin, J. 1–3, 7, 13, 14 (meeting with Churchill, 1944), 15, 18–20, 23–4, 29–34, 36–7, 41 (August 1942 meeting with Churchill), 42, 44–8, 61, 84–5, 111, 114, 116–18, 126–7, 138, 148–51, 184, 186, 197
Stalingrad, battle of 10, 21, 72
Stavrianos, L. 158
Stepanov 33
Stettinius, E. 190
STO 72
Šubašić, I. 43, 149, 150
Sutjeska, battle of 147
Svolos, A. 178, 182, 185, 187
Svoronos, N. 158
Sweden 65
Szklarska Poreba 23

Teheran, Conference 149, 176
Theotokis, J. 163
Theses on the History of the KKE 159
Thessaly 14 (Greek acquisition of)
Third International *see* Comintern
'Third period' 8
Thorez, M. 15, 18, 22, 24, 34, 39, 42, 47, 54, 58, 62–3
Tillon, C. 11, 55, 67, 71, 75

Tito, J. B. 3, 4, 11, 13–14, 18, 19, 31, 38–44, 48, 80, 110–51, 178, 188, 197
Togliatti, P. 3, 6, 9–11, 16–17, 20–2, 29, 31–4, 36–8, 41, 44–8, 83–5, 92–6, 98–9, 102, 105 (attempted assassination of, July 1948)
Tréand, M. 59–60, 64
Trieste 44, 126, 150 (May 1945 crisis)
Tripartite Pact 37, 122
'trotskyist' 43, 118
Troyes 67
Truman, President H. *see* USA
Tsaldaris, C. 195
Tsaldaris, P. 161–2, 171, 195
Tsouderos, E. 168, 179
Turin 90
Turkey 12, 14, 103, 161, 197
Tuscany 90, 94, 101, 105
Tyrimos, M. 164

Ufa (Siberia) 45–6
UNEF 65
l'Unita 83
'united front' 17, 34, 37, 41, 84–5, 93, 115, 119, 128
USA 4, 14 (support for Greek monarchy), 19–20, 44, 45 (Communist party of), 47 (intervention in Greece), 103 (presence in Italy, 1947), 147 (support for Tito), 186 (assent to British role in Greece), 189–90 (neutrality in battle of Athens), 197 (Truman Doctrine)
USSR 4, 8, 9, 11, 14–15, 19, 22–4, 29, 33–7, 40–2, 48, 53–5, 57, 61–5, 72, 75–6, 85, 92, 98, 103–4, 111, 119–20, 122–3, 129–32, 138–40, 147, 151, 166–7, 186, 189, 197, 30 (Nazi invasion of), 64, 66, 69–71, 75–6, 127–8
Ustase 114, 116–17, 123–7, 129, 131, 134, 137
'Užice Republic' 134, 136–7

Vafiadis, M. 196–7
Vallet, R. 71
Varkiza Agreement 191–4, 196
Vatican 102–3
Velouchiotis, A. 187
Venezia Giulia 126
Venizelos, E. (snr) 158–63, 170–1, 194
Venizelos, S. (jnr) 179–81
Versailles, Treaty of 115

Vichy 2, 5, 22, 56, 58–9, 61–3, 65, 67, 70–2, 74
Victor Emmanuel III, King 86, 100
la Vie Ouvrière 68, 70
Vienna 117
Vis, Island of 149
Vlahović, V. 45
Vojvodina 131
Voulgaris, P. 180, 193–4
Vukmanović-Tempo, S. 130

Wall, I. 66
Wallace, D. 176
'Walter' *see* Tito
Warsaw 7

Wilson, General 185
Woodhouse, C. M. 170, 172, 175, 177
Workers' and Peasants' Group 54

Yalta 1, 23, 75, 149, 191, 193

Zachariadis, N. 20, 158–60, 163–8, 179, 193, 195–7
Zagreb 38, 43, 110, 117, 120, 122, 126, 129, 131
Zervas, Colonel N. 171, 177, 185
Zevgos, I. 185, 187–8
Zhdanov, A. 30, 46–7
Zujović, S. 130

For Product Safety Concerns and Information please contact our EU
representative GPSR@taylorandfrancis.com
Taylor & Francis Verlag GmbH, Kaufingerstraße 24, 80331 München, Germany

www.ingramcontent.com/pod-product-compliance
Lightning Source LLC
Chambersburg PA
CBHW070603300426
44113CB00010B/1387